P9-CRS-503

FOUNDATIONS OF EDUCATION

HISTORY AND THEORY OF TEACHING CHILDREN AND YOUTHS WITH VISUAL IMPAIRMENTS

Volume I
Second Edition

M. Cay Holbrook
and
Alan J. Koenig,
Editors

WAGGONER LIBRARY
DISCARD

WAGGONER LIBRARY
TREVECCA NAZARENE UNIVERSITY

AFB PRESS

American Foundation for the Blind

Foundations of Education: History and Theory of Teaching Children and Youths with Visual Impairments is copyright © 2000 by AFB Press, American Foundation for the Blind, 11 Penn Plaza, Suite 300, New York, NY 10001.

All rights reserved. No part of this work may be reproduced or transmitted in any form or by any means, electronic or mechanical, including photocopying and recording, or by any information storage or retrieval system, except as may be expressly permitted by the 1976 Copyright Act, or in writing from the publisher. Requests for permission should be addressed in writing to AFB Press, American Foundation for the Blind, 11 Penn Plaza, Suite 300, New York, NY 10001.

Printed in the United States of America
2007 reprinting

Library of Congress Cataloging-in-Publication Data

Foundations of education / M. Cay Holbrook and Alan J. Koenig, editors.
    p. cm.
    Vol. 2: Alan J. Koenig and M. Cay Holbrook, editors.
    Vol. 2: 2nd ed.
    Includes bibliographical references and index.
    Contents: v. 1. History and theory of teaching children and youths with visual impairments—v. 2. Instructional strategies for teaching children and youths with visual impairments.
    ISBN 0-89128-340-4 (v. 1 : alk. paper)—ISBN 0-89128-339-0 (v. 2 : alk. paper)
    1. Visually handicapped—Education.   2. Visually handicapped children—Education.   I. Holbrook, M. Cay, 1955–   II. Koenig, Alan J., 1954–

HV1626 .F65 2000
371.91′1—dc21

00-040575

The American Foundation for the Blind—the organization to which Helen Keller devoted more than 40 years of her life—is a national nonprofit whose mission is to eliminate the inequities faced by the ten million Americans who are blind or visually impaired. Headquartered in New York City, AFB maintains offices in Atlanta, Chicago, Dallas, and San Francisco, and a governmental relations office in Washington, DC.

This book is dedicated to Dr. Geraldine T. Scholl. The publication in 1986 of Foundations of Education, *which was edited by Dr. Scholl, was a turning point in the professionalization of the field of visual impairment. We thank Dr. Scholl for her graciousness and generosity as a colleague who has committed her life to preparing exemplary teachers of students with visual impairments.*

C O N T E N T S

PROJECT ADVISORY BOARD

Lou Alonso, M.A.
Professor Emeritus, Department of
    Counseling, Educational Psychology,
    and Special Education
Michigan State University
East Lansing, Michigan

Michael Bina, Ed.D.
Superintendent
Indiana School for the Blind
Indianapolis, Indiana

Anne L. Corn, Ed.D.
Professor of Special Education,
    Ophthalmology, and Visual Sciences
Vanderbilt University
Nashville, Tennessee

Jane N. Erin, Ph.D.
Associate Professor
College of Education
University of Arizona
Tucson, Arizona

Kay Alicyn Ferrell, Ph.D.
Professor, Division of Special Education and
    Director of the Division of Special Education
University of Northern Colorado
Greeley, Colorado

Kathleen M. Huebner, Ph.D.
Associate Dean and Associate Professor,
Department of Graduate Studies
    in Vision Impairment and
Director of Community Rehabilitation Services
Institute for the Visually Impaired
Pennsylvania College of Optometry
Elkins Park, Pennsylvania

Jean D. Martin
Education Specialist for the Blind
    and Visually Impaired and Director,
    Minnesota Resource Center for the Blind
    and Visually Impaired
Minnesota Department of Children,
    Families, and Learning
Faribault, Minnesota

Donna McNear, M.A.
Teacher of the Blind and Visually
    Impaired
Rum River Special Education Cooperative
Cambridge, Minnesota

Madeline Milian, Ed.D.
Associate Professor, College of Education
University of Northern Colorado
Greeley, Colorado

Evelyn J. Rex, Ph.D.
Professor Emeritus
Illinois State University
Normal, Illinois

Geraldine T. Scholl, Ph.D.
Professor Emeritus, Department
    of Education
University of Michigan
Ann Arbor, Michigan

Susan J. Spungin, Ed.D.
Vice President, Education and
    International Programs
American Foundation for the Blind
New York, New York

CHAPTER REVIEWERS

Lou Alonso
Michigan State University, East Lansing

Michael Bina
Indiana School for the Blind

Jane N. Erin
University of Arizona

Moniqueka Gold
Department of Defense Schools,
Clarksville, Texas

Jean D. Martin
Minnesota Department of Children,
    Families, and Learning

Mary Nelle McLennan
American Printing House for the Blind

Evelyn Rex
Illinois State University

Alfred A. Rosenbloom
The Chicago Lighthouse

Jeanne L. Rosenthal
M.D., Private Practice, New York

Sharon Zell Sacks
California School for the Blind

Geraldine T. Scholl
University of Michigan, Ann Arbor

Susan J. Spungin
American Foundation for the Blind

Dean O. Stenehjem
Washington State School for the Blind

David Warren
University of California at Riverside

Stuart H. Wittenstein
California School for the Blind

FOREWORD

Since 1943, teachers of students who are blind or visually impaired have looked to the literature of the field for information and guidance. Dating from that year there has been a total of four seminal texts on the subject of educating visually impaired children: *Education and Health of the Partially Sighted,* by Winifred Hathaway, published in 1943, and revised in 1947 and 1954; *The Visually Handicapped Child in School,* edited by Berthold Lowenfeld and published by the American Foundation for the Blind (AFB) and John Day in 1973; *Foundations of Education for Blind and Visually Handicapped Children and Youth: Theory and Practice,* edited by Geraldine T. Scholl and published by AFB in 1986; and now, in the year 2000,the second edition of *Foundations of Education,* published by AFB in two volumes: *History and Theory of Teaching Children and Youths with Visual Impairments* and *Instructional Strategies for Teaching Children and Youths with Visual Impairments.* If judged by size alone, this two-volume work contains at least ten times the amount of material found in the earlier texts, all information teachers of students with visual impairments need to know.

The different titles of these texts and the changing terminology they employ reflect a change in attitude within the field. Earlier nomenclature used, such as the blind and partially sighted, was replaced by visually handicapped in the Lowenfeld and Scholl texts. And this new edition of *Foundations of Education* uses yet another description in place of handicapped—impaired. The concept of impairment represents a shift away from the patronizing attitudes of the charity model, prevalent in the 1960s, 1970s, and 1980s, when use of the value-loaded word "handicapped" was common. This change in terminology from "handicapped" to "impaired" reflects, I believe, the most significant movement in the field of blindness and visual impairment over the past 30 years—that of the consumers' movement, or the demands on the part of visually impaired persons and their families and friends for improved services, recognition, and quality of life. In the new millennium, the student who is visually impaired is no longer viewed as a passive recipient of instruction, but rather as an active partner in the educational process, leading to a sense of self-worth and empowerment for individual students.

Over the last 30 years the educational field working with blind children has moved away from placements in residential schools to what is perceived as a more integrated setting in public schools, and educational placements have moved toward mainstreaming and inclusion. Now teachers are challenged to meet all needs of their students in a one-size-fits-all placement model—the itinerant program, representing placement of approximately 80 percent of the student population. This model, developed in the 1940s, was never intended as an appropriate placement for all students with visual impairments. Nevertheless, its use has become the norm, owing to increasing caseload size. The results have created major academic and social deficits for the student who is visually impaired. In addition, competition for scarce resources has increased as all children with disabilities fight for the right to equal access to education. Because of low prevalence rates of visual impairments, compared to rates of other disabilities, visually impaired students' unique needs are often ignored. An effort to homogenize differences in the name of cost-cutting efficiency continues to be a major issue as we enter the 21st century. The promotion of generic as opposed to disability-specific programs and services that are designed to meet students' special needs serves as the umbrella under which many of the issues involving the education of children who are visually impaired fall.

The issues that we bring to the 21st century reflect, for the most part, a lack of needed resources. The foremost issues in the field of educating students with visual impairments are the following:

1. A lack of sufficient specialized training at both the preservice and in-service level for all teachers of visually impaired students;

2. The need for an assured educational placement continuum, including residential, resource room, special class, and itinerant programs, which allows for the changing needs of visually impaired students throughout their academic careers;

3. The need for appropriate teacher-student ratios in caseloads, which are required for the implementation of the expanded core curriculum in order to assure successful inclusion of students;

4. A need for respect for braille as the literacy tool for students who are blind, as opposed to its relegation as a second-class communication system;

5. The need for equal access to computer technology, ensuring equal access to both academic and vocational opportunity for most students who are visually impaired;

6. The need for accurate demographic tracking and child counts;

7. The growing shortage of teachers and orientation and mobility instructors;

8. The lack of access to textbooks in the appropriate media in a timely fashion for students, and no agreement on standards for mark-up language for electronic books;

9. The need to provide services to the ever-increasing population of children who are visually and multiply impaired, which will require a change of role of the teacher of students with visual impairments to that of a teacher of students with sensory impairments; and

10. The need to honor and provide time for compensatory skill development with respect to the unique learning needs of all children who are blind or have low vision, from birth on.

This new edition of *Foundations of Education* sets out information based on history as well as theory and principles, reflecting a belief that if we do not fully understand and learn from where we have been, we will be at a great disadvantage determining where we need to go. The educational field working with children who are visually impaired has come a long way since the Hathaway text in 1943. It has moved from a teaching profession that depended on word of mouth or the oral tradition for its own skill development to one that has over the years developed a body of knowledge and has become professionalized. This two-volume work represents over 50 years of accumulated knowledge shared with the reader by some of the great leaders in the educational field. Drs. Cay Holbrook and Alan Koenig, editors of this volume, deserve our profound thanks for coordinating the contributions of so many authors and giving the field a major textbook that allows educators working with children with visual impairments to welcome in the 21st century with confidence.

Susan J. Spungin
*Vice President, Education
and International Programs
American Foundation for the Blind*

ACKNOWLEDGMENTS

In the late 1600s Sir Isaac Newton wrote a letter to Robert Hooke, which contained the following famous line: "If I have seen further than you and Descartes, it is by standing upon the shoulders of giants." These words have been used in many situations to describe the important contribution of people whose work serves as a foundation for future endeavors. Such is the case with this textbook. The information contained in these pages is based on the work of individuals of great stature in the education of students with visual impairments.

We have been fortunate to work on this project with many dedicated individuals. The ongoing contributions of these people have been instrumental in the completion of this textbook. At the beginning of this project the American Foundation for the Blind (AFB) established a Project Advisory Board for the purpose of obtaining input in the planning and development of the text. Members of this group gave of their time and expertise in many ways and through many channels, from formal meetings to teleconferences to informal support. The members of the Project Advisory Board were Lou Alonso, Michael Bina, Anne L. Corn, Jane N. Erin, Kay Alicyn Ferrell, Kathleen M. Huebner, Jean D. Martin, Donna McNear, Madeline Milian, Evelyn Rex, Geraldine T. Scholl, and Susan J. Spungin. We greatly appreciate the assistance provided by this group.

We were also fortunate to have had the chapters in this volume written by dedicated, knowl-edgeable educators. The authors of this textbook are all individuals who are deeply involved in professional activities and who have many pressing demands on their time. Their efforts and commitment to this project were impressive and exciting. It is impossible to express our gratitude fully to these talented individuals: Carol B. Allman, Kay Alicyn Ferrell, Phil Hatlen, Kathleen M. Huebner, Sandra Lewis, Madeline Milian, Rosanne K. Silberman, Dean W. Tuttle, Naomi R. Tuttle, Marjorie E. Ward, and Karen E. Wolffe.

In addition, we would like to thank others who provided information for the text through sidebars or other assistance: Michael Bina, Joan B. Chase, Denise Rozell, Susan J. Spungin, and Stuart Wittenstein.

We would also like to extend special thanks to Dr. Geraldine T. Scholl, for the kindness and support she extended to us as we worked throughout this project. Her approval and assistance were extremely important to us.

Dr. Lou Alonso provided valuable and thoughtful feedback throughout the development of this project. She worked tirelessly on very tight timelines to give us her assessment of chapters in this text as well as in its companion volume on instructional strategies. Her involvement provided us with encouragement and confidence.

We would also like to express our appreciation to the editors and staff at AFB Press. Natalie Hilzen worked tirelessly to make this project a reality. She is a gifted editor who met the challenges of this large project with grace and sensitivity. Others at AFB—Ellen Bilofsky, Carol Boston, and Beatrice Jacinto—and their colleague Barbara Chernow were also crucial to the completion of a manuscript of high quality.

Finally, we would like to acknowledge the individuals on whose shoulders we stand. Many have already been mentioned in these pages as contributors to this text and its companion volume. Others are mentioned within the chapters of this book. We realize that we are a fleeting part of the rich history of this field, which includes such names as Natalie Barraga, Louis Braille, Berthold Lowenfeld, Anne Sullivan Macy, and Sally Mangold. The best we can do to stand on the shoulders of these giants is to follow their example of reaching for excellence in services to students who are visually impaired.

M. Cay Holbrook
University of British Columbia
Vancouver

Alan J. Koenig
Texas Tech University
Lubbock

INTRODUCTION

Students who are blind or visually impaired have received educational services for over 200 years. The first of these services were provided by men and women who, despite the prevailing attitudes and practices of their day, believed that children who were blind were capable of success in education and in life. These early pioneers and the countless others who have come after them have provided us with a rich, solid foundation for our profession. Through documented accounts of observation, instruction, and formal research, we have grown into a profession with a clear understanding of the theories that underlie what and how we teach students with visual impairments.

Teachers of students who are visually impaired work with a wide variety of students every day. They provide educational services to students of all ages and ability levels who are learning academic skills, as well as skills needed for success outside of the classroom. There are no absolute rules for providing these services. Teachers must carefully examine the needs of their students in light of the information available on the way in which students with visual impairments learn and then make decisions about the best way to provide instruction. In order to accomplish this complex task, it is important that teachers have an understanding of the foundations that help us plan effective instruction.

Experienced teachers of students who are visually impaired add their own dimension of expertise to these foundations as they work with students and get a more complete understanding of the way students learn. Most beginning teachers, however, have no experience on which to draw when making decisions about appropriate instructional strategies. It is important for inexperienced teachers of visually impaired students to develop a clear understanding of the complex issues facing these students and their parents. These complex issues have an impact on students' development as well as on educational programming.

Foundations of Education: History and Theory of Teaching Children and Youths with Visual Impairments, as well as its companion volume, *Foundations of Education: Instructional Strategies for Teaching Children and Youths with Visual Impairments,* are designed to provide information on both theory and practice for beginning teachers. Although the volume on educational strategies provides more direct and focused information about instructional practices, the volume you are reading provides information about the underlying theory that guides our practice. This textbook is intended to be a text for teachers who are starting their professional lives. It provides basic information that will be helpful to university students in graduate or undergraduate teacher training programs. Experienced teachers and other professionals already in the field, as well as parents, may also find the information absorbing and useful.

Foundations of Education: History and Theory of Teaching Children and Youths with Visual Impairments contains 10 chapters. The first chapter presents a historical perspective on the field of visual impairments. This chapter focuses specifically on events that have influenced the way in which we provide educational services to students today. Our history is rich and complex. It is a formidable task for one chapter to address the entire history of our field. For this reason, Chapter One emphasizes the events of the past 50 years, especially those events that relate to the provision of educational services in a range of service delivery settings.

Chapter Two contains general information about blindness and visual impairment, giving readers a perspective on the population we serve. Next, Chapter Three addresses the structure of the eye and medical and clinical issues related to visual impairment. Although we expect that university students will receive a more comprehensive discussion of the causes of visual impairment within their coursework, this chapter is designed to provide basic information that will help give an overview preceding the remainder of this book and its companion volume.

The next three chapters address developmental issues. Chapter Four provides information about early childhood development. Chapter Five addresses the development of students in middle childhood and adolescence. Chapter Six addresses the psychosocial needs of students with visual impairments.

Unique populations are addressed in the next two chapters of this book. Chapter Seven provides information about students who are blind or visually impaired and have additional disabilities, whereas Chapter Eight addresses the complex issues related to students who are visually impaired and who are from diverse cultural backgrounds.

The last two chapters in this text address educational programming (Chapter Nine) and professional concerns (Chapter Ten). These chapters present information for the beginning teacher about the issues related to the unique job of providing educational services to students who are blind or visually impaired.

Foundations of Education: History and Theory of Teaching Children and Youths with Visual Impairments joins the other literature in our field to provide a comprehensive perspective on the students with whom we work and the issues related to our profession. It is intended to prompt readers to engage in ongoing efforts to learn more about the students they teach and to pursue unfolding knowledge about the best practices of our profession.

THE CONTRIBUTORS

M. Cay Holbrook, Ph.D., is Associate Professor in the Faculty of Education at the University of British Columbia in Vancouver, BC, Canada. She received her doctoral degree from Florida State University in 1986 and has prepared teachers of students with visual impairments at Johns Hopkins University and the University of Arkansas at Little Rock. Dr. Holbrook has taught children with visual impairments in public school programs in South Carolina, Georgia, and Florida and has been actively involved in the Association for Education and Rehabilitation of the Blind and Visually Impaired and the Council for Exceptional Children. She has presented numerous workshops to teachers and parents relating to the education of children with visual impairments.

Alan J. Koenig, Ed.D., is Professor and Associate Dean of Graduate Education in the College of Education at Texas Tech University in Lubbock. He received his doctoral degree from Vanderbilt University in 1987 and has been preparing teachers of students with visual impairments since that time. Previously, he taught children with visual impairments and served as a state consultant in visual impairment for the state of Iowa. Dr. Koenig is actively involved in professional organizations and has served as the president of the Division on Visual Impairments of the Council for Exceptional Children. He is a leading researcher in the area of the development of literacy skills for students who are visually impaired.

Carol B. Allman, Ph.D., is Program Director of Exceptional Student Education in the Bureau of Instructional Support and Community Services at the Florida Department of Education.

Joan B. Chase, Ed.D., is a psychologist and private consultant in Dunedin, Florida.

Kay Alicyn Ferrell, Ph.D., is Professor of Education and Director of the Division of Special Education at the University of Northern Colorado in Greeley.

Phil Hatlen, Ed.D., is Superintendent of the Texas School for the Blind and Visually Impaired in Austin, Texas.

Kathleen M. Huebner, Ph.D., is Associate Dean and Associate Professor in the Department of Graduate Studies in Vision Impairment and Director of Community Rehabilitation Services, Institute for the Visually Impaired, at the Pennsylvania College of Optometry in Elkins Park.

Sandra Lewis, Ed.D., is Associate Professor and Coordinator, Program in Visual Impairment, at the Florida State University in Tallahassee.

Madeline Milian, Ed.D., is Associate Professor in the College of Education at the University of Northern Colorado in Greeley.

Geraldine T. Scholl, Ph.D., is Professor Emeritus in the Department of Education at the University of Michigan in Ann Arbor.

Rosanne K. Silberman, Ed.D., is Professor of Special Education and Coordinator, Graduate Teacher Preparation Programs in Blindness and Visual Impairment and Severe Disabilities Including Deafblindness, at Hunter College of the City University of New York.

Susan J. Spungin, Ed.D., is Vice President of Education and International Programs at the American Foundation for the Blind.

Dean W. Tuttle, Ph.D., is Professor Emeritus at the University of Northern Colorado in Greeley.

Naomi R. Tuttle is an instructor at the Hadley School for the Blind in Winnetka, Illinois.

Marjorie E. Ward, Ph.D., is Associate Professor in the School of Teaching and Learning at Ohio State University in Columbus.

Stuart H. Wittenstein, Ed.D., is Superintendent of the California School for the Blind in Fremont and President of the Division on Visual Impairments of the Council for Exceptional Children.

Karen E. Wolffe is a career counselor and private consultant in Austin, Texas, and National Program Associate, American Foundation for the Blind.

CHAPTER 1

Historical Perspectives

Phil Hatlen

KEY POINTS

◆ Formal efforts to provide educational services to students with visual impairments began in France more than 200 years ago.

◆ Early efforts to include students with disabilities in general education classrooms involved students with visual impairments.

◆ The development of an effective, workable system of reading and writing was critical to the establishment of educational programs for students who were blind.

◆ Key legislation provided support for educational services but did not ensure appropriate programming.

◆ The most powerful efforts to change educational systems and programming have involved professionals, parents, and consumers working together.

Special thanks are extended to Geraldine T. Scholl, Professor Emeritus, School of Education, The University of Michigan, Ann Arbor, for her contributions to an earlier version of this chapter.

The discussion on the early history of educational services in this chapter is based largely on Ferne K. Roberts, "Education for the Visually Handicapped: A Social and Educational History," in Foundations of Education for Blind and Visually Handicapped Children and Youth: Theory and Practice, *Geraldine T. Scholl, ed. (New York: American Foundation for the Blind, 1986).*

The task of recording events of historical significance is daunting. For an understanding of events that occurred before the 20th century and during the first few decades of the 21st century, professionals must rely on written documentation, but more recent historical accounts can also be obtained from those who lived and participated in the events. For this reason, this chapter is divided into two distinct parts. The first part discusses important events and people who influenced the development of educational services to students with visual impairments before the 20th century. The second part focuses on more recent historical events that molded the way in which educational services are provided to students with visual impairments today. In addition, tables presenting a chronology of important historical events and a summary of legislative milestones appear at the end of the chapter.

EARLY HISTORY

Many important events occurred in the education of students with visual impairments prior to 1900. Dedicated individuals with a strong commitment to these students fought against prevailing societal attitudes to establish a starting point from which all educational services have grown. Knowledge and understanding of these key events and influential people help professionals today understand the roots of efforts to educate students with visual impairments. (See Sidebar 1.1.)

Throughout history, stories have been told about remarkable and talented people who were blind and managed, often with insightful assistance from others, to educate themselves and make significant contributions to their societies. Homer, for example, is a legendary figure whose epic poems, the *Iliad* and the *Odyssey,* were known before 700 B.C. Other, later illustrious blind persons were Nicholas Saunderson (1682–1739), a noted professor of mathematics at Cambridge University, whose sponsor was Isaac Newton; François Huber (1750–1831), a Swiss naturalist who studied the life of bees; and Maria Theresia von Paradis (1759–1824), a Viennese pianist and music teacher for whom Mozart wrote the Concerto for Piano and Orchestra in B-flat. However, until the mid-18th century, none of the scattered attempts to educate children who were blind resulted in the development of systematic programs.

During the 18th century, France became the cradle of new attitudes toward blindness and the location of the first school for children who were blind. The philosophical groundwork was laid by Denis Diderot, physician to King Louis XV and a great philosopher of the Enlightenment. In 1749, Diderot published *Letter on the Blind for the Use of Those Who See,* much of which was based on his contacts with Saunderson and von Paradis. The competence of Saunderson and von Paradis convinced Diderot that people who were blind could be intellectually competent and could lead regular lives.

Diderot and his contemporaries, including Thomas Paine, Thomas Jefferson, and Benjamin Franklin in the United States, espoused the needs, rights, values, and obligations of the individual. However, a significant step in the education of blind persons was taken in Paris in 1784 by Valentin Haüy, who established L'Institution Nationale des Jeunes Aveugles (Institute for Blind Youths). Haüy attributed his interest in educating children who were blind to the following two experiences. One night in a café he saw a troupe of men who were blind dressed in grotesque cos-

tumes and performing a skit that elicited pity and ridicule from the audience; his revulsion made him resolve to teach people who were blind to read so they could earn their living in more dignified ways. Several years later, after attending a concert by von Paradis, Haüy was intrigued to learn about her ability to read and write using pin-pricked letters (Koestler, 1976; Lowenfeld, 1975).

Haüy set about pursuing his interest in educating children who were blind. His first student, François Lesueur, was an intelligent adolescent who was blind and had been supporting his widowed mother and siblings by begging. François agreed to study half the day and to continue begging the other half; eventually Haüy subsidized his education so that he could give up begging.

The enrollment at the Institute for Blind Youths grew rapidly, partially as a result of demonstrations of students' ability to read and write, to perform music, and to carry out everyday activities—accomplishments that Haüy believed all blind students could acquire. With these demonstrations, Haüy hoped to elicit admiration for the students' competence, not pity for their blindness. In 1786, King Louis XVI asked Haüy to take about 30 of the institute's students to Versailles for six days so he could see the effects of their education. Although Haüy hoped that the king would take the institute under his protection, this did not occur (Illingworth, 1910).

Haüy's contribution to the education of students who were blind was nevertheless a lasting one. Haüy founded the first school for students who were blind that became a model for many of the schools that followed it. He emphasized reading and fostered the development of embossed print, and he believed in the vocational potential of his students and instituted vocational training at his school.

Despite the many blind persons who succeeded in educational or vocational activities during this early period, public expectations for people with disabilities were low. Furthermore, there was little support for and encouragement of people who were blind.

Early educational programs in the United States for students who were visually impaired fol-

Important Historical Figures

SIDEBAR 1·1

Many people have contributed to the development of quality services for children and youths who are visually impaired. The list of professionals who have had an impact on individual lives is unending. However, some people have played a critical role in the history of the field of visual impairments. The following list represents individuals who have provided historically significant contributions.

DENIS DIDEROT

French encyclopedist, philosopher. Diderot was enormously influential in shaping the rationalistic spirit of the 18th century. As the physician for King Louis XV, his philosophical essay, *Lettre sur les aveugles* (Letter on the Blind) in 1749 laid the philosophical foundation for educating students who were blind. The essay recounted his personal contacts with two accomplished persons who were blind: Nicholas Saunderson, a mathematics professor at Cambridge; and Marie Theresia von Paradis, a Viennese pianist and music teacher. These experiences convinced Diderot that people who were blind could live productive lives if they were properly educated.

VALENTINE HAÜY

Pioneer in the education of children who were blind. Valentine Haüy, born in France, was the founder of the first residential school for the blind, the Institute for Blind Youths in Paris.

JOHANN WILHELM KLEIN

Pioneer educator, one of the founding fathers for the education of children who are blind. Klein's book, *Lehrbuch zum Unterrichte der Blinden* (Textbook on the Education of the Blind), published in 1819, described a harness for a guide dog and outlined the method of training dog and traveler that resembles those methods used today. He wrote extensively on his theories of education of students who are blind, including the belief in placing children in local school programs.

LOUIS BRAILLE

Teacher, innovator. Louis Braille became blind at an early age as the result of an injury. He entered the Institute for Blind Youths in Paris at age 10 and at age 15 developed the six-dot code known today as braille. He also developed separate codes for mathematics and music and published the first braille book in 1827. Braille later became a teacher at the Institute for Blind Youths.

SAMUEL GRIDLEY HOWE

Pioneer educator, administrator, founder of the Perkins School for the Blind. Samuel Gridley Howe was a pioneer in the education of children who were blind in the United States. He supported the education of Laura Bridgman at Perkins. His notes on the methods he used were intrumental in helping Anne Sullivan teach Helen Keller.

LAURA BRIDGMAN

Student. Laura Bridgman was the first student with deaf-blindness to be educated in the United States. She was taught by Samuel Gridley Howe at the Perkins Institute, where she acquired a basic education and some manual skills.

MICHAEL ANAGNOS

Pioneer. Michael Anagnos was the director of the Perkins Institution and founded the Kindergarten for Little Blind Children, which marked the first school to begin the education of children who were blind at age five. He recommended that Anne Sullivan, who had recently graduated from Perkins, become Helen Keller's tutor and provided Anne with support from Perkins.

FRANK HALL

Superintendent, inventor. Frank Hall was appointed superintendent of the Illinois Institution for the Education of the Blind in 1890. In 1892 he exhibited his version of the braille typewriter at the convention of the American Association

(continued on next page)

Important Historical Figures (Continued)

of Instructors of the Blind. His machine was a significant factor in establishing the dominance of the braille code during the time when there were several competing embossed codes.

ANNE SULLIVAN MACY

Teacher. Anne Sullivan Macy was educated at Perkins Institution. Following graduation she was sent by Perkins to Tuscumbia, Alabama, to educate Helen Keller. She used the manual alphabet to give Helen the key to language. Anne remained Helen's life-long teacher, companion, and guide until she died in 1936.

HELEN KELLER

Advocate, counselor, fund-raiser, and suffragete. Helen Keller became deaf-blind at the age of 18 months. She was the first deaf-blind person to receive a degree from Radcliffe College. She began working for AFB in 1924 as a fund-raiser and remained a member of the AFB staff until her death. She had a distinguished 50-year career, providing lectures and contributing to magazines on the topics of blindness, deafness, socialism, social issues, and women's rights.

THOMAS CUTSFORTH

Psychologist. Thomas Cutsforth attended the Oregon School for the Blind from 1905 to 1912. He attended the University of Oregon, earning his baccalaureate and masters degrees. An advocate of public school education for children with visual impairments, he published a book, *The Blind in School and Society*, based on his doctoral research.

JOHN CURTIS

Pioneer educator. John Curtis was an advocate of day school programs for the education of children who were blind. In September 1900, he established the nation's first classes in public schools for children who were blind.

ROBERT IRWIN

Research director, AFB. Robert Irwin was the first blind graduate of the University of Washington. He received a graduate degree at Harvard Graduate School, specializing in the education for students who were blind. His book *The War of the Dots* documents the struggle to standardize an embossed code for people who were blind.

WINNIFRED HATHAWAY

Pioneer educator. Winnifred Hathaway was associate director of the National Society of the Prevention of Blindness. Winnifred Hathaway described the special provisions that enabled children with low vision to be educated in America.

BERTHOLD LOWENFELD

Author, researcher. Berthold Lowenfeld was a director of the Talking Book Project and enlisted the cooperation of the 14 leading schools for the blind in testing the ways in which children gathered information through their fingers and ears. The results of his studies were so persuasive that a permanent place was assured for recorded books in the education of students who are blind.

GEORGIE LEE ABEL

Education specialist and consultant. Georgie Lee Abel taught at a residential school for the blind for nearly 20 years. She joined AFB in 1954 as an educational consultant. She conducted studies of programs for preschool children who were blind, which revealed uneven quality of services.

KENNETH JERNIGAN

Teacher, advocate, lobbyist. Kenneth Jernigan was the president of the National Federation of the Blind from 1968 to 1986. He created the Newsline for the Blind Network and the International Braille and Technology Center in Baltimore.

(continued on next page)

Important Historical Figures (Continued)

EMERSON FOULKE

Psychologist. Emerson Foulke conducted tests with children who were blind, focusing on speech comprehension and "speed hearing." His research demonstrated that these children could comprehend material at a faster rate and had an influence on the way that children are taught to use their listening skills.

JOSEPHINE TAYLOR

Educator, advocate. Josephine Taylor served as project officer and branch chief with the special education section of the U.S. Department of Education and helped develop university training programs in visual impairment.

Compiled by Susan J. Spungin, Vice President, Education and International Programs, American Foundation for the Blind.

lowed the residential school model developed by Haüy. The first three U.S. residential schools were the New England Asylum for the Blind (later the Perkins School for the Blind), established by Samuel Gridley Howe in Boston in 1829; the New York Institution for the Education of the Blind (later the New York Institute for Special Education), established in New York in 1831; and the Pennsylvania Institution for the Instruction of the Blind (now the Overbrook School for the Blind), established in Philadelphia in 1832. These three schools, which were privately funded and supported, were the forerunners of subsequent educational programs because they demonstrated the success of educating students who were blind. The first school established with state funds was in Ohio in 1837; the subsequent residential schools were typically established by states when they gained statehood. According to Bledsoe (1971), the following states never had residential schools: Alaska, Delaware, Maine, Nevada, New Hampshire, Rhode Island, Vermont, and Wyoming. These states have traditionally paid tuition to send children who were blind or who required residential school placement to schools in neighboring states. Sidebar 1.2 lists the dates of establishment of residential schools for students who are blind in the United States and Canada.

The existence of the European residential school model and the fact that in the early 19th century it was fashionable for the well-to-do to send their children to boarding schools made it seem logical and desirable to establish residential schools for children who were blind in the United States (Irwin, 1955). Howe, director of the Perkins School for the Blind, came home from visiting schools in Europe with three convictions that helped him shape the educational program of his school: each child who was blind must be considered an individual and be educated according to his or her interests and abilities; the curriculum of the residential schools should conform as closely as possible to that of public day schools, with added emphasis on music and crafts; and students who were blind must be prepared to take their places in the social and economic lives of their communities (Lowenfeld, 1973).

Residential school education of African American children who were blind tended to follow the segregation or integration patterns of their various geographic areas. Before the Civil War and the Emancipation Proclamation, it is doubtful whether any African American children who were blind were educated in the South, since education was largely denied to their sighted siblings. Slowly, southern residential schools began to open separate facilities for these children. In 1931, there were 10 separate departments in residential schools and 5 independently administered schools for African American children (Koestler, 1976). Generally, the programs for these children were inferior. One of the reasons for the inferiority of these

SIDEBAR 1.2

Residential Schools in the United States and Canada

School	Date of Founding
Perkins School for the Blind (MA)	1829
New York Institute for Special Education	1831
Overbrook School for the Blind (PA)	1832
Ohio State School for the Blind	1837
Virginia School for the Deaf and the Blind (Staunton)	1839
Kentucky School for the Blind	1842
Tennessee School for the Blind	1844
Governor Morehead School (NC)	1845
Indiana School for the Blind	1847
Michigan School for the Deaf and Blind	1848
Mississippi School for the Blind	1848
South Carolina School for the Deaf and Blind	1849
Illinois School for the Visually Impaired	1849
Wisconsin School for the Visually Handicapped	1849
Missouri School for the Blind	1851
Georgia Academy for the Blind	1852
Iowa Braille and Sight Saving School	1853
Maryland School for the Blind	1853
Texas School for the Blind and Visually Impaired	1856
Alabama Institute for the Deaf and the Blind	1858
Arkansas School for the Blind	1859
California School for the Blind	1860
Minnesota State Academy for the Blind	1866
Kansas State School for the Blind	1867
New York State School for the Blind	1868
Sir Frederick Fraser School (Nova Scotia)	1870
West Virginia Schools for the Deaf and the Blind	1870
W. Ross Macdonald School (Ontario)	1872
Oregon School for the Blind	1873
Colorado School for the Deaf and the Blind	1874
Nebraska School for the Visually Handicapped	1875
Florida School for the Deaf and the Blind	1885
Washington State School for the Blind	1886
Western Pennsylvania School for Blind Children	1887
St. Joseph's School for the Blind (NJ)	1891
Connecticut Institute for the Blind (Oak Hill School)	1893
Montana School for the Deaf and the Blind	1893
Utah Schools for the Deaf and the Blind	1896
Louisiana School for the Visually Impaired	1897

(continued on next page)

Residential Schools in the United States and Canada (Continued)	
School	**Date of Founding**
Oklahoma School for the Blind (Parkview School)	1897
South Dakota School for the Blind and Visually Impaired	1900
New Mexico School for the Visually Handicapped	1903
Lavelle School for the Blind (NY)	1904
Idaho School for the Deaf and the Blind	1906
Virginia School for the Deaf and the Blind (Hampton)	1906
North Dakota School for the Blind	1908
Arizona State Schools for the Deaf and the Blind	1912
Hawaii Center for the Deaf and the Blind	1914
Instituto Loaiza Cordero Para Niños Ciegos (Puerto Rico)	1919
Royer-Greaves School for the Blind (PA)	1921
The Hope School (IL)	1957

Compiled by Stuart H. Wittenstein, Superintendent, California School for the Blind.
Note: The current names of schools are shown. All schools listed are residential schools; no day schools are included.

programs was the poor quality of equipment and educational materials that were often hand-me-downs, with the frequently disastrous results that the dots in braille books were so worn down that they were impossible to read. Another reason was that African American teachers were often unable to attend the limited number of segregated training facilities or to afford the cost of travel to nonsegregated facilities in other parts of the country (Koestler, 1976).

Throughout the 19th century, residential schools were usually the sole resources for the education of children with visual impairments. However, the concept of separate residential schools for the blind came under attack when the first residential schools were founded. Howe, although helping to found or dedicate several residential schools, was an outspoken advocate of public day school education.

In 1871, at the convention of the American Association of Instructors of the Blind (AAIB)—later the Association for the Education of the Visually Handicapped (AEVH)—Howe deplored the social sequestration of residential schools and advocated public day school education in all subjects not requiring visible illustration (Howe, 1871). He also described a cottage system that he had recently implemented at Perkins as an alternative to large dormitories. There were strong objections to this idea from several residential school superintendents, who thought that children must be educated for society, not for family life, and that the cottage plan would foster an unhealthy attachment to family-style living in adulthood (Frampton & Kearney, 1953)—an argument difficult to understand in the light of 20th-century beliefs about child development.

The cottage system was nevertheless adopted in 1911 by John Bledsoe, superintendent of the Maryland School for the Blind. Bledsoe was committed to the notion that children who were blind could be perfectly normal and that cottage-style living units would foster normalcy. His was the first residential school using a cottage-family plan (Bledsoe, 1971). A later section of this chapter elaborates on the development of schools and public school classes for students who are blind and other service delivery options.

Education of Students Who Were Deaf-Blind

During the mid-19th century, Howe supported the education of a girl who was deaf-blind at the Perkins School for the Blind. This effort, the admission of Laura Bridgman to Perkins in 1837, was greeted with national and international praise and astonishment. Laura became deaf and blind after she contracted scarlet fever at the age of 18 months. Howe heard about her, found her family, convinced her parents that she could be educated at Perkins, and provided much of Laura's instruction. As it turned out, Laura lived the rest of her life at the school.

Laura learned to read raised letters, at first associating words with objects by rote. Howe was with her when her breakthrough in understanding the meaning of language occurred: "At once the countenance lighted . . . it was an immortal spirit, eagerly seizing upon a new link of union with other spirits" (Howe, 1840, p. 26). Laura was the chief attraction at Perkins on visitors' days, and many famous people, including Charles Dickens (Dickens, 1907), went to see her. In 1841, Oliver Caswell, who also became deaf and blind from scarlet fever, was admitted to Perkins, and he and Laura were educated together (Schwartz, 1956).

Helen Keller was the most well-known student who was deaf-blind to be educated at Perkins. When Howe died in 1876, his son-in-law, Michael Anagnos, succeeded him as director of Perkins. Anne Sullivan had just graduated from Perkins when, in 1887, Anagnos heard from Helen Keller's parents. Helen's mother had read *American Notes,* in which Dickens mentioned Howe's education of Laura Bridgman. Anagnos recommended Sullivan, gave her access to Howe's extensive notes on his methods of instructing Laura and Oliver, and lent his moral support to her efforts to teach Helen (Koestler, 1976).

Reading and Writing

One of the great challenges that early educators of students who were blind faced was to find a suitable system for reading and writing. Early efforts included various methods—writing on wax tablets, letters carved in wood, forming letters with wire, and using knots of a variety of thicknesses and at different distances on a thread. A momentus contribution to the advancement of education for children who are blind was made by Louis Braille in the 1800s. The genesis of the embossed dot code and Braille's adaptation of it are discussed in Sidebar 1.3. Braille's contribution was significant and long lasting, for without a system of effective communication through reading and writing, it is doubtful that the education of students who were blind would have progressed to the extent that it did (Lowenfeld, 1975).

Haüy used Roman letters printed in relief. Prior to Braille's contribution, Howe developed Boston Line Type, an angular modification of Roman letters. The most successful of these early codes was that of William Moon, who used Roman capital letters in bare outline. In 1884, Moon was the official type in many institutions in England; it was used in the United States until the 1940s because adults who were newly blinded and were not able to master braille found it easy to learn (Rodenberg, 1955). Rodenberg (1955, p. 4) summarized the problem with these efforts with a quote from Pierre Villey's *The World of the Blind:* "The fact is . . . they were talking to the fingers the language of the eyes."

Although it was known that Roman letters outlined in pin points were more easily identified than the line type letters, it remained for Charles Barbier, a French engineer and cavalry officer, to develop the first point system, in an attempt to create a signal code that could be read and written in the dark (Rex, Koenig, Wormsley & Baker, 1994). Barbier used cells of 12 points—six high and two wide—and developed a writing board with grooves and window-like openings. He exhibited his system at the institute for the blind in Paris where the young Louis Braille was in attendance. Braille was impressed and adopted the system, but he used cells three dots high and two dots wide, which made 63 possible combinations of dots. By 1834, at the age of 25, he had carefully worked out his system for a braille code, of which Koestler (1976, p. 92) wrote: The "genius of Louis Braille's system was its simplicity." Braille worked

Tactile Reading and Writing

The education of students with visual impairments did not truly begin until a workable method of reading and writing was devised. Early efforts to resolve this problem included a system of knots on a length of twine, writing on wax tablets, and the use of carved-wood Roman letters (Illingworth, 1910; Lowenfeld, 1971). None of these systems gave rise to an enduring, workable method.

Valentin Haüy and his first student noticed that the reverse sides of printed pages had tactilely legible characters. At that time, printers routinely used wet paper for printing, so the paper itself took on the forms of the letters to some extent. Haüy had letters cast in reverse that, when printed on wet paper, left tactile impressions in the correct position and order. Subsequently, he modified the letters somewhat to make them easier to read. For writing, his students used a metal pen with a rounded tip to produce raised letters in reverse on the back of heavy paper (Illingworth, 1910; Lowenfeld, 1973). This system for reading and writing was used at the residential school in Paris until 1854 and in all the other early schools in Europe and the United States.

Louis Braille, born in 1809 in Coupvray near Paris, was blinded at age 3 while playing with one of his father's harness-making tools. At first, he attended the local village school, but at age 10 he was admitted to the Institute for Blind Youths in Paris. That school emphasized music as a vocational goal for many of its students, and Braille later became a church organist. At age 19, he was asked to join the teaching staff at the school, and it was there in 1829, at age 20, that he published an explanation of his embossed dot code, which, he believed, would be superior to the embossed letters that Haüy had used. Braille's point system was based on the work of an army artillary officer, Charles Barbier, who in the early eighteen hundreds devised a raised dot code that could be read by touch during night maneuvers. "Ecriture Nocturne" (night writing) had a 12-dot cell, with 6 vertical dots in two rows. By 1834, Braille had perfected the code for literary braille and was working on a code for music notation. The officials at the institute were not easily convinced that Braille's dot system was more effective than Haüy's embossed letter system and resisted using it because the teachers would have had to learn a new code and because they believed that it would set people who were blind apart from people who were sighted. However, the students to whom Braille had taught his system preferred it. Finally, in 1844, Guadet, the vice-principal of the institute, described the raised-dot system and paid tribute to Braille (Roblin, 1960).

Braille died of pulmonary consumption in 1852 and was buried in his hometown, Coupvray, France (Roblin, 1960). On the centennial of his death, his body was to be removed to the Pantheon in Paris. This proposed removal so incensed the citizens of Coupvray that the governmental authorities finally made one concession: The bones from Braille's hands still lie in an urn at his original grave site.

out the code for reading and writing as well as for music, but his system was not officially accepted in his own school until two years after his death (Koestler, 1976; Rodenberg, 1955).

Meanwhile, the British had taken Braille's system and in 1905 worked out three levels of braille that they called Revised Braille: Grade 1, which was spelled out letter by letter; Grade 2, which used some contractions; and Grade 3, which was highly contracted (Rodenberg, 1955). The Missouri School for the Blind in St. Louis was the first American school to adopt braille around 1860

(Lowenfeld, 1976). In the United States, two other point systems emerged: New York Point and American Braille. William Wait, of the New York Institute for the Education of the Blind, developed New York Point, which used a cell two points high and one to four points in width with the smaller number of points assigned to frequently occurring letters. By 1890 New York Point was known everywhere in the United States. American Braille, developed by Joel Smith at Perkins, was announced at the AAIB convention in 1878. Smith kept the braille cell, but assigned letters on the basis of frequency of occurrence (Rodenberg, 1955). These two systems, in addition to British Revised Braille, stimulated what came to be called the "War of the Dots" (Lowenfeld, 1975), which encited professional arguments over the use of various dot systems.

People who were blind who lived in the last decade of the 19th century and the first decade of the 20th faced the dilemma of having to learn at least two point systems and several line systems for reading. In addition, the relatively new American Printing House for the Blind (APH) had to publish books in two or more systems to satisfy the needs of customers. It is little wonder, then, that a group of people who were blind held a charter meeting in St. Louis in 1895 to address the situation. This meeting led to the organization in 1905, of the American Association of Workers for the Blind. At their first meeting, they appointed a Uniform Type Committee. By 1912, the committee had tested 1,200 blind American and British readers. Although the British system was preferred by the majority, the American committee accepted only part of the Grade 2 contractions and called it Grade 1½. Thus began what Lowenfeld (1975) named the "Battle of Contractions." When a large number of books in the British system was ordered from England to supplement the libraries in the United States, more people who were blind learned and preferred the British system. Rodenberg (1955, p. 11) wrote that the system was "ushered to its universal triumph by the intimate experience of the blind themselves."

The American Foundation for the Blind (AFB) was founded by the combined efforts of the Amer-ican Association of Workers for the Blind (AAWB) and the AAIB, and so its fundamental purpose was to provide national leadership in education and rehabilitation. Robert B. Irwin, the first executive director of AFB, was an ardent supporter of braille, and he wanted an end to the controversy surrounding adoption of a single code. These two factors contributed to AFB's leadership in settling some of the diverse issues surrounding braille. In addition, M. C. Migel, philanthropist and AFB president, was willing to invest money in efforts that would result in the adoption of braille. Thus, for many reasons, the time was ripe to settle the controversy of the War of the Dots and the Battle of Contractions. In July 1932, a conference of representatives from both countries was convened in London, resulting in a compromise that led to the publication of a handbook setting forth Standard English Braille. The September 1932 issue of the *Outlook for the Blind,* published by AFB, announced the results in an article entitled "Uniform Braille for the English-Speaking World Achieved" (Irwin, 1932).

To ensure consistency of treatment by braille printing houses and ongoing surveillance and periodic updating of the braille code, the American Braille Commission was organized. The commission was superseded by the Joint Uniform Braille Commission of AAIB and AAWB in 1950, which became the Braille Authority of North America (BANA) in 1958. In 1968, the National Advisory Council to BANA was formed to ensure a closer working relationship between producers and users of braille. Today BANA remains the official standard-setting body for braille producers and users in the United States and Canada.

EDUCATIONAL PROGRAMMING IN THE 20TH CENTURY

Early historical events set the stage for the rapid progress that occurred during the 20th century. Although it is difficult to divide historical events into periods with an arbitrary time frame, the following discussion concentrates on the significant events that had an impact on the education of students with visual impairments after 1900. Progress in providing an appropriate education for students with visual impairments is presented according to the following dominant themes: legislation, educational options, educational content, technology, and personnel preparation.

Legislation

Federal Legislation

Legislation had a profound impact throughout the 19th and 20th centuries on the shape of educational services for students with visual impairments. Most legislation addressed the larger population of individuals with disabilities and also applied to individuals who are visually impaired.

An early example of legislation that specifically addressed blindness was Chapter 186—"An Act to Promote the Education of the Blind"— passed by Congress in 1879 to establish the American Printing House for the Blind (APH). APH was founded with federal money to produce textbooks in braille, large type, and recorded form and to develop or adapt instructional materials for use by students who were blind. Congress divided the appropriation for APH into two funds: one to produce instructional materials and the other to provide a means by which schools could obtain APH products. The second appropriation, called the federal quota system, provided a "line of credit," an amount of money determined by the number of students served, that schools serving students who are blind could use to purchase APH books and instructional materials. For example, if a school has 100 students and the amount available in its line of credit is $100 per student, the school could obtain $10,000 worth of APH products. In 1956, an amendment to the act extended eligibility to all children who are blind enrolled in public day school programs, and the APH charter was amended to include as ex-officio trustees all "chief state school officers" or their designees. In 1970, eligibility was again extended to include children in nonprofit private institutions, such as multiservice agencies for the blind that offer educational

programs for blind children with additional disabilities (Nolan, 1983). Chapter 186 continues to be a vital source of funds for all programs that provide education to people who are blind (see also the later discussion of APH in the section on Technology).

Most of the national legislation related to blindness that Congress passed between 1872 and 1935 was concerned with adults and was related to such matters as dog guides, rates for mailing books and periodicals, and the payment of a single fare on public transportation by a person who is blind and an accompanying sighted guide.

The Social Security Act (P.L. 74-271), passed in 1935, included a definition of blindness that the American Medical Association adopted in 1934. That definition became the definition of legal blindness, or economic blindness, because it was the criterion for eligibility for many government-financed benefits and services (Koestler, 1976). This definition is as follows:

> Central visual acuity of 20/200 or less in the better eye with corrective glasses or central visual acuity of more than 20/200 if there is a visual field defect in which the peripheral field is contracted to such an extent that the widest diameter of the visual field subtends an angular distance no greater than 20 degrees in the better eye. (Koestler, 1976, p. 45)

As is discussed later in this chapter, this definition was used by educators for a number of years in the placement of students with visual impairments. It was modified for educational purposes following the publication of Barraga's (1964) study on students with low vision, which showed that children who were classified as legally blind could successfully use their remaining vision in many instances. Today, most educators use a functional definition that is concerned with the impact of visual impairment on the performance of daily activities to identify children who are eligible for educational services because of a visual impairment.

The next significant piece of legislation related specifically to education of children with visual impairments was passed by Congress in 1965, when the Elementary and Secondary Education Act was amended to provide support for the education of children with disabilities in state-operated and -supported schools, including residential schools for children who were blind. This amendment (P.L. 89-313) was the first step in mandating educational programs for all children with disabilities.

Education for All Handicapped Children Act. Although some previous legislation influenced the education of students with visual impairments, the passage of the Education for All Handicapped Children Act (P.L. 94-142), in 1975 dramatically changed educational thinking and services throughout the United States. The impetus for this legislation was the growing awareness that thousands of students with severe multiple disabilities, many of whom were placed in large state institutions, had been denied an education. The power of P.L. 94-142 is that it stated in clear, unequivocal language that all children with disabilities are entitled to a free and appropriate education. Other landmark aspects of the law (renamed the Individuals with Disabilities Education Act, or IDEA, in 1990) included the following:

◆ An emphasis on comprehensive and appropriate assessment,

◆ The requirement of an Individualized Education Program (IEP) for every child with a disability,

◆ A four-step process of services: identification, assessment, development of an IEP, and placement,

◆ The requirement to treat parents as equal partners with teachers in educational planning and programming, and

◆ A due-process procedure to mediate differences between schools and parents.

Lowenfeld (1980) stated that the decade of the 1970s would be remembered as the "time of legislation" and that the 1980s would be the "decade of

implementation." Although it is true that P.L. 94-142 is the most significant legislation affecting the education of children and youths with disabilities, the implementation of IDEA has been problematic, and many would say that universal fulfillment of the mandates of IDEA is still an elusive goal. (A full discussion of the requirements of IDEA appears in Chapter 9 of this volume.)

Despite the profound impact of P.L. 94-142 on educational services for students who are visually impaired, it should be noted that parents and professionals who worked on behalf of these students attempted to address some serious issues in educational practices even before the federal law required some of these changes. Examples of P.L. 94-142 mandates that were already in practice in services to students with visual impairments include the following:

◆ *Students with multiple disabilities.* Many schools for students who were blind and some local day schools began serving students with visual impairments and additional disabilities long before P.L. 94-142 mandated a "free and appropriate education for all children with disabilities" (Best & Winn, 1968).

◆ *Inclusive education.* Since the 1900s, students who were visually impaired had, in many cases, been placed in general education classes. The mandate of P.L. 94-142, requiring that children with disabilities spend as much time as appropriate with age-mates without disabilities, was already a reality for many students who were visually impaired.

◆ *Parents as partners.* Educators had discovered years before the passage of P.L. 94-142 that it was essential to include instructional planning and that the practice of discouraging parents' involvement is detrimental to students' education.

Although many of the practices outlined in the provision of P.L. 94-142 were therefore not new to educators of students with visual impairments, several aspects of this legislation proved challenging.

As was already indicated, the legislation required that each student with a disability have an IEP and that a four-step process should be followed for implementing services for a child with a disability: (1) identification and referral, (2) assessment, (3) IEP development, and (4) placement. Shortly after the passage of P.L. 94-142, formal and informal conferences were held throughout the United States to help special educators learn to write IEPs. During these conferences, many teachers discovered that they did not know how to properly assess students, since they had never been required to do so. Thus, it was necessary for many teachers to learn concurrently how to assess students, develop IEPs, and determine placements on the basis of children's educational needs. For many, perhaps most, teachers of students with visual impairments, the legislation required a higher level of accountability than had existed before its passage.

The passage of P.L. 94-142 also touched on a number of issues related to the amount of time a student might spend in a classroom with classmates without disabilities. This concept was eventually referred to as the least-restrictive environment, a commonly used term that did not appear in the law. The concept of placement options began to be delineated in terms of the number of minutes a child spent in a general education classroom, a practice referred to as *integration*. Integration could mean anything from attending a segregated class (that is, a class for students with visual impairments) in a general education school building to being placed for most, or all, of the day in a general education classroom. Eventually, such placements became known as *mainstreaming*, a term that narrowed the definition of least-restrictive environment to definite placement in a general education classroom for at least part of the day. Finally, in the later decades of the 20th century, as described later in this chapter, many began using the term *inclusion* or *full inclusion*

to refer to an environment in which students with visual impairments attend general education classes full time with their classmates without disabilities.

As an addition to the continuum of placement options available to all students with disabilities, inclusion is a potential option for those who have the competence and skills to be successful in such a setting or for those for whom this setting would be an appropriate learning environment. However, placement needs to be determined by educational needs, and the same student may require different environments at different times during his or her education. (A more complete discussion of placement decisions can be found in Chapter 9 of this volume.)

Further Legislation. Several additional federal legislative efforts have had a dramatic impact on educational services for students who are visually impaired. First, in 1986, Congress passed P.L. 99-457, the amendments to P.L. 94-142. This law provided funds to states for the enactment or expansion of developmental services for infants and toddlers with disabilities. P.L. 99-457 was the first federal legislation that recognized the need for intense intervention services for infants and toddlers with disabilities and their families. Each state that implemented this legislation needed to identify a lead agency to oversee this program, and services to families and children expanded greatly as a result. Some states with laws that had limited educational services to students aged 3–21 or 5–21 lowered the age at which mandated special education services were provided to birth, on the basis of the successes of programs enacted because of P.L. 99-457.

Second, in 1990, Congress reauthorized (renewed) P.L. 94-142 as IDEA. In addition, amendments strengthening IDEA were passed in 1997. Two new significant provisions were the listing of orientation and mobility as a related service and the support of braille as equal to print for instruction in reading and writing. (See Sidebar 1.4 for a review of the significant legislation in this area.)

The Right to a Free Appropriate Public Education

SIDEBAR 1.4

A series of legislative initiatives in the last quarter of the 20th century truly created a revolution in the education of children with disabilities. A number of strands, including pressure from parents of disabled children and other advocates, the influence of the civil rights movement, and a commitment to prevention and early intervention, came together to mold governmental policy and make public education a right of *all* children, regardless of their disabilities.

The foundation of this change was Section 504 of the Vocational Rehabilitation Act Amendments of 1973 (P.L. 93-112), which first granted basic civil rights protection to people with disabilities. Section 504 stated that no individual can be discriminated against or denied benefits "solely by reason of his handicap" by any organization that received federal funds.

The landmark legislation for education of children with disabilities was the 1975 Education for All Handicapped Children Act (P.L. 94-142). This act established the right to a "free appropriate public education"—that is, an education appropriate to the needs of the individual child—for all children aged 6–21, regardless of their disabilities. It mandated a nonbiased assessment and the development of an Individualized Education Program (IEP) for each child by a multidisciplinary team. It also required the involvement of parents in planning and implementing services for their children and parents' and children's right to confidentiality and to due process. Financial incentives were offered to states to provide services to children with disabilities aged 3–5, but services for this age group were not mandated.

When the Education for All Handicapped Children Act was reauthorized in 1986 (P.L. 99-457), the legislation was considerably strengthened. The act now mandated preschool services under the same requirements as for older children, lowering the age for mandated education

from age 6 to age 3. It also created a category of free early childhood services for children from birth to age 2 who had disabilities or were at risk of developmental delay. Each child and family was entitled to a written Individualized Family Service Plan (IFSP) developed by a multidisciplinary team, together with the family, that would be reviewed every six months and evaluated annually. A case manager would be identified, and transitional steps to the special education services offered to older children would be specified. Although early intervention services were not mandated, the law created a strong incentive to provide them by making grants available to each state. Each state was to establish a Child Find system to identify eligible infants and toddlers and a lead agency to carry out the early intervention program.

The 1990 amendments to the Education for All Handicapped Children Act (P.L. 101-476) renamed it the Individuals with Disabilities Education Act (IDEA). Changes in the law emphasized the needs of families with disabilities and the importance of parents in evaluating and setting goals for their children.

Subsequent amendments to IDEA in 1997 (P.L. 105-17) instituted a number of significant changes, including the following:

- ◆ Added orientation and mobility as a "related service" under the law for students with visual impairments;
- ◆ Made the presumption that children with visual impairments will receive instruction in braille unless an IEP team specifically decides otherwise;
- ◆ Mandated consideration of assistive technology devices and services in developing an IEP;
- ◆ Strengthened the requirement for placement in the least-restrictive

(continued on next page)

The Right to a Free Appropriate Public Education (Continued)

environment and emphasized the "continuum of placement options," ranging from inclusion in general education classes, special classes, special schools, home instruction, to instruction in hospitals and institutions;

◆ Emphasized the participation of parents in eligibility and placement decisions and strengthened the requirement for parents' informed consent for any evaluations;

◆ Mandated the participation of students

with disabilities in state- and district-wide assessments;

◆ Increased emphasis on the participation of children with disabilities in the general education curriculum;

◆ Required general education teachers to participate in the IEP team process if the students are in general education programs;

◆ Created mediation services to resolve parent-school difficulties; and

◆ Established disciplinary procedures for students with disabilities.

State Legislation

Most states had legislation regarding the delivery of services to students with disabilities long before the passage of P.L. 94-142, often focusing on the "right" to an education and funding available from the states. Since the 1980s, many states have passed laws to ensure that students who are blind are taught braille. Beginning with Louisiana in 1985 and Minnesota in 1988, states passed legislation that was intended to counteract the perceived decline in students' literacy and use of braille. Landmark "braille legislation," passed by the Texas legislature in 1991, has served as a model for braille legislation passed by many other states. Several features of the Texas legislation that were unique at the time have since been incorporated into other state laws. One such feature is the use of the term *functional blindness* instead of *legal blindness*. This new term refers to children and youths who use tactual and auditory senses as their primary avenues for gathering information. The Texas law includes the following provisions:

◆ The administration of a learning media assessment designed to help the educational team determine a student's appropriate literacy media,

◆ Teachers' demonstration of proficiency in braille,

◆ The requirement that braille must always be given equal consideration to print as a reading medium, and

◆ The mandate that textbook publishers must furnish electronic files of textbooks with literary content in a timely manner that assures the braille reader access to textbooks at the same time as sighted classmates.

As a result of efforts by educators, national organizations such as the National Federation of the Blind (NFB) and AFB, many states have introduced similar requirements.

Policy Guidance Paper

In 1995, the U.S. Department of Education issued a policy guidance statement on educating students with visual impairmetns (see Appendix A), which presented written guidelines on what constitutes appropriate educational services for students who are visually impaired. The introduction to the paper stated that "services for some blind and visually impaired students are not appropriately addressing their unique educational and learning needs." With these words, the department made a powerful statement in support of specialized education and learning of students who are visually impaired. Of particular importance is that the document stressed the need for a continuum of placement options and for an expanded core curriculum (required areas of learning that extend beyond what is expected of sighted children, e.g., independent living skills, career education, and adaptive technology) for students who are visually impaired.

Personnel Preparation

In the 1950s, Congress began to take a serious interest in the preparation of teachers for students with disabilities. In 1958, it passed P.L. 85-926, which provided funding to colleges and universities for personnel preparation for teachers of students with mental retardation. Congress supported the preparation of teachers for students who are deaf in 1961, with the passage of P.L. 87-276, and teachers for all categories of students with disabilities, with the passage of P.L. 88-164 in 1963. The impact of P.L. 88-164 was enormous; many universities added preparation for teachers of students with disabilities to their curricular offerings. Federal support for personnel preparation, in the form of stipends for students and funds to universities to employ instructors, has resulted in countless students with visual impairments receiving a high-quality education from qualified specialized teachers. More information on personnel preparation programs is presented later in this chapter.

Educational Options

As was already indicated, early educational programs for students with visual impairments followed a residential school model. Schools for the blind in the United States were founded not because of a philosophical commitment to separate education, but because of geographic necessity caused by the low prevalence of blindness in children. Thus, it was logical that the first programs that were established in general education were in large cities with populations of children with visual impairments that were sizeable enough to justify the provision of specialized services in local schools.

In the United States, the first classes in public schools for students with visual impairments were established in Chicago in 1900 under the auspices of the Illinois School for the Blind (Lowenfeld, 1975). Soon programs were established in the larger cities in Michigan, Minnesota, New Jersey, New York, and Ohio. In most of these programs, children participated in some regular classes and returned to special classes for instruction in braille, typing, and other special subjects. Early residential schools for the blind and local school programs used the legal definition of blindness in order to qualify students for services. This meant that any child who was identified as legally blind was taught as though he or she was totally blind and primarily used the tactile or auditory senses for learning. Students who needed services based on vision loss, but were not legally blind, were labeled "partially seeing" and were provided instruction in typing and used large-print books (Hathaway, 1959).

In the 1930s, some schools for the blind began to send selected high school students to secondary schools in the community for two reasons. First, even the largest schools for the blind could offer only a limited academic curriculum for their students because they did not have the number of students to justify offering, for example, an array of foreign languages. Second, some superintendents began to believe that the students whom they had so carefully educated at their residential schools for as many as eight years were ready to learn and compete in an environment with sighted students. Thus, the "integration" or "inclusion" of students who were visually impaired with sighted students was advocated by some residential school administrators long before it became a common practice.

In 1909, while attending a conference in London, Edward E. Allen, then director of the Perkins School for the Blind, visited a newly established school for children with low vision, called the Myope School. He saw this type of program as a solution to the challenge of enrolling students who were blind who would read braille in the same school or class with those with sufficient vision to read and write in print. In 1913, he worked with school officials to initiate such a program in Roxbury, Massachusetts. Soon similar programs were begun in Chicago, Cleveland, Detroit, Milwaukee, and New York (Hathaway, 1959). The success of these classes changed the practice of keeping children with all degrees of vision together. Hence, children who had sufficient vision to read print were labeled "partially seeing," and the classes they attended were called sight-saving or sight-conservation classes. The instruction in these classes was planned based on the prevailing theory that sight could be "used up" and that children with visual impairments were at risk for further deterioration of their vision unless special care was taken. Most of those who read print used large-type books and materials, and their school activities were planned to alternate "eye use" and "eye rest" periods (Hathaway, 1959).

Because of the overreliance on acuity measurements from ophthalmologists, some children were assigned to read braille with blindfolds to prevent them from reading by using whatever remaining vision they might have. Supervisors of programs were often reluctant to move children from braille classes to sight-saving classes if the ophthalmologists recommended braille. Perhaps the most pervasive factor in preventing consideration of the most appropriate reading media for students who were labeled partially seeing was the continued use, well into the second half of the 20th century, of the legal definition of blindness in determining reading media.

In these early classes, some students spent most of the school day in a general education class alongside their sighted peers, while others attended special classes full time. This was often influenced by the relationship of the special class teacher with general education teachers. Thus, it would be difficult to describe a "typical" class because of the great variations in practices. The practice of students in special classes spending some time in general education classes was often termed "integration" by educators of students

with visual impairments. Pioneers of educational "integration" for students with visual impairments recognized that without appropriate support, students likely would not succeed.

In the early 1920s, some residential schools had their own printing facilities for braille books. Only two of these facilities were large enough to do more than local work for their residential schools: the Howe Memorial Press at Perkins School for the Blind and the Clovernook Center in Cincinnati (Koestler, 1976). As was noted earlier, however, teachers usually had to rely heavily on volunteer readers and transcribers to have appropriate materials for the instruction of their pupils.

As the large population of children with retrolental fibroplasia (RLF) (now called retinopathy of prematurity [ROP]) began to near school age (see Sidebar 1.5), educators and parents were faced with the fact that educational services, both residential schools and the few local day school programs in existance, would not be able to meet these children's needs. The residential schools could serve only a limited number of students, and the local day schools were already stretched to the maximum.

In 1954, AFB published *The Pine Brook Report,* a monograph that presented the proceedings of one of the first professional meetings that addressed the urgent problem of educating the literally thousands of children who were blinded by RLF. The *Pine Brook Report* (AFB, p. 16) contained clear definitions of several approaches to the education of children with visual impairments in local day school programs:

The Cooperative Plan. This plan is one in which the blind child is enrolled with a teacher of blind children in a special room from which he goes to the regular classrooms for a portion of his school day. In this plan the special room becomes his home room from which his program planning stems, in cooperation with the regular classroom teachers.

The Integrated Plan. This plan is one in which the blind child is enrolled in the regular classroom. Available to him and to his regular

The Drama of Retrolental Fibroplasia, Now Known as Retinopathy of Prematurity

When Dr. Edward E. Allen, director emeritus of the Perkins School for the Blind, welcomed the new group of 12 students in the Harvard Course on Education of the Blind (operated in conjunction with the Perkins School), in September 1941, he told them they were entering a dying profession. Ophthalmia neonatorum (sores in babies' eyes) had been wiped out with the insertion of silver nitrate into the eyes of newborns; and inoculations for viral conditions, such as measles and scarlet fever, which often caused visual impairments in young children, had drastically reduced the incidence of visual impairments. He did not know that at that time, pediatricians and ophthalmologists at the Massachusetts Eye and Ear Infirmary were puzzling over a strange eye condition that had recently been identified in premature infants.

Two infants who were born prematurely at the Boston Lying-In Hospital, one in July and the other in November 1940, "were the forerunners of an epidemic of blindness which rose to unsurpassed heights through the world in the next twelve years" (Silverman, 1980, p. 3), affecting approximately 10,000 prematurely born infants throughout the world. In 1942, ophthalmologists and pediatricians in the Boston area puzzled over this strange condition. Retrolental fibroplasia (RLF), as the condition later came to be known (which literally means "scar tissue behind the lens of the eye"), was so-named by one of the physicians, a scholar of Latin and Greek. (Today this condition is referred to as retinopathy of prematurity [ROP].)

With no clues to the cause of RLF, physicians first treated the condition by trial and error, using vitamin E, adrenocorticotropic hormone (a pituitary hormone that stimulates the cortex of the adrenal glands), and controlled light in incubators. Although some success was obtained with each form of treatment, there was not sufficient evidence to make firm recommendations. Meanwhile, all along there was a suspicion that oxygen might be the contributing cause.

At the 1952 meeting of the American Academy of Ophthalmology and Otolaryngology, it was decided to conduct a national study. After considerable debate, "it was agreed that a joint effort should be undertaken to determine whether the frequency of occurrence of RLF is dependent upon the amount of oxygen used in the management of premature infants" (Silverman, 1980, p. 38). Eighteen hospitals agreed to participate in the National Cooperative Study, as it was called. The Kresge Eye Institute in Detroit, under the direction of Dr. V. Everett Kinsey, was designated the coordination center. The center was to be notified of the births of all premature infants who had survived 48 hours. Infants were assigned to treatment categories in sets of three for each hospital: One was allotted to the routine oxygen group for every two assigned to the curtailed oxygen treatment group. The study began July 1, 1953; September 1954 was considered the earliest possible date for a responsible report. Oxygen for the curtailed group would not exceed 50 percent unless the clinical condition of an infant required greater amounts. On September 19,1954, Kinsey presented the preliminary results, which dispelled "all doubt concerning the causal role of oxygen in RLF" (Silverman, 1980, p. 41). Thus the epidemic of RLF came to a dramatic halt.

Although the epidemic of RLF was curtailed, a flood of malpractice legal suits began, as well as ethical questions about assigning infants randomly to treatment conditions. The National

(continued on next page)

The Drama of Retrolental Fibroplasia (Continued)

Cooperative Study is considered a milestone in medical research, but it left unanswered many questions that were raised during the experiment about the administration of oxygen. Silverman (1980, p. 143) summarized these issues: "To this day, when oxygen is administered to premature infants, they are exposed to the in-tertwined risks of brain damage, death and RLF with nothing more than authoritative guessing in protection."

Source: Adapted from William A. Silverman, *Retrolental Fibroplasia: A Modern Parable* (New York: Grune & Stratton, 1980).

---

teachers is a full-time qualified teacher of blind children and also a resource room. The regular teachers turn to the teacher of blind children for assistance in planning the child's program, for guidance in adapting the classroom procedures, and for providing, as necessary, specialized instruction appropriate to the blind child's needs.

The Itinerant Teacher Plan. This plan is one in which the blind child is enrolled in the regular class in his home school where his needs are met through the cooperative efforts of the regular teacher and those of the itinerant teacher qualified to offer this special service.

This publication, together with AFB's employment of several national education consultants in the early 1950s, provided the best direction to states and local districts for developing educational services.

The RLF population dramatically changed education for children with visual impairments in the United States. Three factors influenced this change. The first factor was the sheer number of children who needed educational services and the realization that the existing services would fall far short of the demand. Although in the past, a child who was the only blind child in a 50-mile radius had to attend a residential school for the blind, now many communities had a sufficient number of children with visual impairments and could justify employing a teacher and providing instruc-

tional resources. The low prevalence of children with visual impairments was no longer a valid reason for sending children to residential schools. The second factor was that many children with RLF were from middle- to upper-class families. The incubators that saved the lives of premature infants but often caused blindness were "high tech" for their time and were available only in hospitals with modern neonatal care (Koestler, 1976). Many of the children's parents were influential in their communities, and did not want to send their children several hundred miles away to attend residential schools. They asserted their considerable influence on local school boards and other decision makers, and local districts often rapidly geared up to serve children blinded by RLF. The third factor was that both communities and professionals were ready for a new approach to educating students who were blind. Some basic adaptations of the general education curriculum to make it accessible to students who were blind had already been made. However, a critical element in the ability of early resource rooms in local schools to provide an education approaching equality with that provided to sighted children was the rapid growth of volunteer braille-transcribing groups throughout the country.

Thus, the success of the few local day school programs that began and thrived in the first half of the 20th century was a strong impetus for the rapid expansion of educational services in local school districts. With solid support from parents, cautious support from administrators, and the enthusiastic backing of many professionals, children with RLF were welcomed into local elementary schools in increasing numbers in the mid-1950s. Most of these programs adopted an "inclusive" philosophy. Children who were blind were, for the most part, placed solely in general education classrooms, where they spent the entire school day. Instead of only one child who was blind in a local school, there might be 5 to 20 children with visual impairments. Usually, somewhere in the elementary school, there was a classroom that was designated as the resource room for the students who were blind. This room housed a resource teacher whose responsibility was to facilitate inclusive education. The resource teacher might spend part of the day working with the general classroom teachers to ensure that each child had appropriate instructional materials and that the classroom teachers knew how to engage the children in classroom activities and part of the day providing direct services to children in the resource room. A child would be pulled out of the general education classroom and be given individual, specialized instruction by the resource teacher in braille reading and writing and in typing. In addition to the traditional core curriculum, there was instruction in orientation and mobility (O&M) by a mobility specialist, beginning around 1965.

Literally thousands of children with RLF received their entire education in this type of setting during the 1950s and 1960s. Although the profession has since discovered some flaws in this system, such as the assumption that the only needs of these children were academic and that support for social skills and socialization in general was not to be provided, it was at the time an exciting, revolutionary approach to the education of students who were visually impaired.

The speed with which this revolution occurred was surprising. The large numbers of children with RLF created pressures for rapid systemic change and development. In little more than a decade, the entire thrust of education for children who were blind had moved from residential schools to local day schools. As services for children with visual impairments evolved, there soon became two types of educational programs: one for children who were classified as "partially sighted" and were learning through their visual sense and one for children who were blind and were learning through tactile and auditory senses (see the section on the Use and Stimulation of Low Vision later in this chapter). The resource room model was sometimes used for both groups, although children who were partially sighted were often served in neighborhood schools by itinerant teachers, teachers of students with visual impairments who moved from school to school in order to work with those students and their classroom teachers. (As was mentioned previously, in the early years of this rapid change in educational services, the legal definition of blindness was used to determine whether a child would be classified as blind or partially sighted. Therefore, the resource rooms that served students who were blind usually included children with visual acuities of 20/200 or less.)

Some children did not attend their neighborhood schools, since even with the rise in the prevalence of blindness caused by RLF, there were often not enough children who were blind within a school's boundaries to justify a resource room and resource teacher. In these situations, children were transported to centrally located schools that others from the community also attended.

This rapid growth of day school programs had an effect on the role of residential schools. Most of these schools continued to thrive as educational centers for academic students until well into the 1950s. But as early as the mid-1950s, the educational climate began to change. Parents were advocating for local school services; local districts were amenable to, if not enthusiastic about, educating students who were visually impaired in their school districts of residence; and a slow, steady stream of teachers was becoming available to support students in inclusive educational settings.

Of particular importance during this period was recognition of the need for a strong support system for teachers in general education classrooms. A common theme of the day was that the success of students with visual impairments in resource room and itinerant programs was directly related to the amount of support that classroom teachers and the students received from specialized teachers who were trained to instruct students with visual impairments. In fact, local school districts were discouraged from beginning educational services for students with visual impairments until they had employed qualified, certified "vision specialists." Many early efforts at inclusion would probably have failed were it not for the recognition that the classroom teacher, the parent, and the teacher of students with visual impairments were equally important partners on an educational team.

Lines of responsibility were carefully drawn between the classroom teacher and the teacher of students with visual impairments. The classroom teacher was not expected to develop expertise in adapting or presenting curricula if that task fell within the responsibility of the teacher of students with visual impairments. For a child who was visually impaired to be effectively served in a general education classroom, the classroom teacher should not have had to spend more time working with that child than with any other child in the classroom.

It is interesting to note that educators of children with other disabilities followed a similar sequence to that taken by educators of children with visual impairments. Early efforts to "integrate" children with severe and profound disabilities consisted of moving these children from separate facilities into general education schools but keeping the children in separate classrooms. Then, these educators, as educators of students with visual impairments had done, moved from using the term *integration* to *mainstreaming* to *least-restrictive environment* to *inclusion*.

Shortly after the passage of P.L. 94-142 in 1975, the term *integration*, used by educators of students with visual impairments to describe the placement of children in regular classrooms since the early 1950s, became the commonly used term for implementing the notion of least-restrictive environment. In practice, early efforts toward integration of students with disabilities took the form of abandoning segregated residential schools and placing classrooms of these children in general education schools. The extent of integration

with students without disabilities varied greatly, but often consisted of children with disabilities being on playgrounds and in cafeterias at the same time as nondisabled students. Education, for the most part, was still provided in separate, segregated classrooms.

By 1980, the term *integration* had given way to *mainstreaming*. Mainstreaming was defined as the placement of a child with disabilities for some portion of the school day in a regular classroom with nondisabled classmates, often, for nonacademic subjects.

Late in the 1980s, *mainstreaming* gave way to *inclusion,* a term that has been interpreted in many ways. In practice, inclusion typically meant that a child with a disability was assigned to a regular classroom as her or his homeroom and spent the majority, if not all, of the day in that setting. The term has had many by-products, including *full inclusion, inclusive education, community-based instruction, education in natural environments,* and *inclusive living.* Some proponents of inclusion believe that persons with disabilities have the right to live in settings with nondisabled persons and that any setting that segregates them is inherently bad. The most adamant proponents of inclusion believe that full inclusion is appropriate for all students with disabilities and that even pull-out services (the practice of removing a child from a regular classroom for a period of time to address a specific need) is not acceptable (see Chapter 9 of this volume for more detailed information on the continuum of placement alternatives for students with visual impairments).

Today, teachers in general education classrooms are assisted, in many cases, by paraeducators, and they and children with visual impairments frequently receive less than one hour per week of support services from teachers of students with visual impairments, though this does not conform to best practices. Yet the population of children in today's schools is increasingly diverse and includes students with multiple disabilities; of great cultural, ethnic, and racial variation; and from homes in which one parent is the head of the household, both parents work, or a foreign language is spoken. Given the multiplicity of the circumstances and needs of today's children, cooperative efforts among general classroom teachers, teachers of students with visual impairments, and families are more important than ever.

By the early 1960s, schools for the blind were experiencing a significant drop in referrals of students with academic potential, often because these students were placed in integrated settings. These schools began receiving an ever-increasing number of referrals of students with additional disabilities. While local districts increasingly provided services to students who were visually impaired with academic potential, they were frequently unprepared and lacked personnel who were trained to educate children with dual sensory disabilities or mental retardation, severe learning disabilities, or emotional disturbance.

At this time, most teachers at schools for the blind knew little about how to instruct students with visual impairments and additional disabilities. However, they quickly undertook educational efforts on behalf of children with complex disabilities. This transition required extensive changes and adjustments in the curriculum and goals of all schools, especially residential schools. Many teachers who were well versed in academic subject matter found themselves teaching basic functional and developmental skills to students whose chronological ages were often far different from their developmental ages.

During this period, it was not unusual for a school for the blind to make the transition from a school that was mainly for academically proficient students to a school that primarily served students whose educational needs were functional and developmental. Their adjustment to the students' needs and recognition of their role as part of a continuum of educational placements is a noteworthy chapter in the history of schools for the blind. The faculty of effective residential schools are now on the cutting edge of effective instructional programs for students with visual impairments with additional disabilities.

From 1955 until 1985, almost all residential schools maintained a population of academically capable students. Given that the success of students with visual impairments in local schools required a strong support system for general education teachers, these students in rural areas often found it difficult to obtain adequate services at the local level. Many children from rural areas continued to attend schools for the blind and, in most instances, constituted a small but important portion of the student body.

As the profession continues to define the role of both residential schools and general education programs in the education of students with visual impairments, many issues remain to be be explored. Educators who are involved in delivering services are considering the best ways to take advantage of the full continuum of service and placement options. Some traditional residential schools have already changed their role and function, adding to their role as residential schools a myriad of responsibilities that have an impact on all students who are visually impaired in their states. Some residential schools have added statewide assessment services, technical assistance to local school districts, and professional development for teachers of students with visual impairments to their missions. Some of these schools for the blind are poised to play the role of the hub of services for all students in their states and to coordinate outreach and other functions.

At the same time, local schools are examining the most effective ways to provide services to students in public school settings. These programs are looking for solutions to issues, including the following:

◆ Providing instruction to all students in the areas of the expanded core curriculum (see also the section on National Initiatives later in this chapter),

◆ Ensuring that all instructional materials are accessible to students with visual impairments,

◆ Serving students effectively in rural and sparsely populated regions, and

◆ Obtaining an adequate supply of appropriately trained teachers.

Educational Content

Throughout the history of education for students with visual impairments, there have been changes in the focus of educational content. Professionals continually evaluate the emphasis of academic instruction and other curricular issues.

Early residential schools and day school classes for children with visual impairments followed the same, generally strongly academic curriculum as did general education programs. Residential schools frequently also offered technical courses, such as piano tuning, broom making, and chair caning. More capable students usually attended college and prepared for careers in teaching, social work, law, and other professions. Students who did not attend college sometimes moved from a residential school setting to a sheltered workshop that had residential facilities. Sheltered workshops typically provide employment almost exclusively to people with disabilities, and the work environment is carefully controlled to minimize the impact of the disability on the employees' success. Participation in competitive employment was unusual.

Several factors are important in describing the curriculum of early schools for the blind. First, these schools were highly selective about admitting students. They could be selective because they were the only source of educational services for most children who were blind, and their limited resources made it most feasible (at that time) to choose students with the most academic potential. Second, because of the limited availability of teacher preparation programs in the education of students with visual impairments, most teachers were grounded in subject matter, not in special education.

However, limitations in the curriculum related to vocational education were primarily the result of not exploring the extent to which children with visual impairments could be prepared to work in competitive employment alongside sighted workers. Thus, specialized areas of employment, such as piano tuning, chair caning, and basket weaving, emerged. Most educational programs for students who were blind focused on preparing non-college-bound students in one of these vocations. By the end of the 1950s most of these programs had disappeared because of the emerging educational philosophy that stressed a liberal arts education with no emphasis on career education until well after high school graduation.

Continual advancement in technology, research, and curriculum development had a dramatic impact on instructional services to students who were visually impaired. Adaptation of the curriculum for sighted students (traditional core curriculum); recognition of the need for a specialized curriculum; development of a functional, useful curriculum for students with multiple disabilities; and recognition of curricular needs that go beyond the traditional core curriculum all contributed to the beginning of an era in which the individual needs of students were emphasized.

Use and Stimulation of Low Vision

As is true of many of the changes and advances since the 1950s, the arrival of the population of children who were blinded by RLF required the profession to distinguish between "blind students" and "partially sighted students." With no educational guidelines to determine appropriate placements based on educational needs, educators turned to the medical profession and adopted the definition of legal blindness as the method for determining placements in educational programs. Children who were considered legally blind were expected to become braille readers and to learn primarily through tactile and auditory input. The unofficial definition of "partial sight" was a visual acuity of 20/70 to 20/200. Children in this category were expected to learn visually and were assumed to need minimum support, other than large-print books and instruction in typing.

Because students with visual acuities of less than 20/200 were considered blind, they were instructed in braille reading and writing even though they had sufficient vision to read print. Consequently, many students attempted to read braille by sight, rather than touch. Often, their teachers attempted to teach them braille by blind-folding them. Teachers and many persons in the medical profession believed that students would damage their eyes by using them. This situation changed quickly following the publication of Barraga's (1964) landmark study. This study was responsible for changing the practices of educating children who were legally blind and had remaining vision. It found that a program of visual stimulation could improve the utilization of remaining vision.

Soon after Barraga's study, educators replaced reliance on the legal definition of blindness with a functional definition that used information about how a student uses his or her vision in daily activities and was more appropriate for education. The unofficial definition of *partially sighted* became broader, changing the primary reading medium from braille to print for approximately two-thirds of the children who were labeled "legally blind," so that vision became their primary avenue for learning. Thus, those who had been taught primarily through their auditory and tactile senses now also learned through their visual sense. Because of Barraga's pioneering study and those who built on it, children today are given the opportunity to learn to use the senses that are most educationally appropriate for them.

Over the years, the terminology describing children with visual impairments has continued to change. The term *partially sighted* is no longer in general use. Children (and adults) whose primary source for information is visual, are now referred to as individuals with *low vision*.

An additional influence on work with children with low vision has been the development of useful optical devices (e.g., magnifiers, telescopes). In the early 1950s, students with low vision seldom received optical devices, even prescription eyeglasses. Often eye care professionals were reluctant to prescribe expensive magnifiers while the children's eyes were still growing and changing. Thus, it was rare to find a child below age 14 with an optical device. Today preschool children are fitted with eyeglasses and optical devices that enable them to use their vision effectively in a variety of ways.

There was also a dramatic shift in the role of ophthalmologists and optometrists during the 1960s and 1970s. In the 1950s, optometrists were considered somewhat less than professionals. Some believe that this allegiance to the medical profession significantly delayed the development of the use of optical devices for children. Although this belief has not been documented by research, the information that follows is commonly accepted as fact among professionals in education of students who are visually impaired.

During the first half of the 20th century, the belief prevailed that in practically all cases of visual impairments in children, the medical cause of the impairment was not stable and hence that a child should be followed closely by a physician, an ophthalmologist. Therefore, teachers routinely referred children with visual impairments to ophthalmologists. At that time, it was thought that it was acceptable to be examined by an optometrist for such conditions as astigmatism, myopia (nearsightedness), and hyperopia (farsightedness) because only the measurement of visual acuity and the prescription of lenses were involved. For children with significant visual impairments, however, it was believed that ophthalmologists were needed, in case the medical conditions required attention.

After the publication of Barraga's (1964) findings on the use and benefits of stimulating vision, ophthalmologists as a group often remained slow to prescribe optical devices for children and were frequently regarded as being primarily interested in medical interventions. Many educators began to recognize that optometrists were interested in dealing with low vision and related issues. Thus, a shift in the role of optometrists and their involvement with students with low vision occurred during the 1960s and 1970s.

In the 1970s, as students who were blinded from RLF began to graduate from high school, educators in general turned their attention to students with low vision. This greater attention resulted in teachers and parents availing themselves more frequently of the skills and interests of optometrists, who were willing to work with and prescribe optical devices and lenses for young children. Today, low vision services, encompassing assessment, prescription of devices, and training in the use of devices, are delivered by teams that are often headed by optometrists, who, along with other eye care specialists, are an important source of clinical evaluations. In addition, the role of teachers and O&M instructors in conducting functional low vision evaluations has become an essential and routine part of the process of determining the educational needs of students with low vision. Generally, a clinical low vision evaluation is conducted in the office of a licensed eye care specialist, whereas a functional low vision evaluation is conducted by professionals in education who collect data as students live their daily educational and personal lives. A detailed explanation of functional vision assessments can be found in Chapter 4 of *Foundations of Education: Instructional Strategies for Teaching Children and Youths with Visual Impairments.*

Orientation and Mobility

In the late 1920s, people who were blind were being trained to use dog guides as a means of facilitating independent travel. The day after Pearl Harbor, the Seeing Eye dog guide school announced that it would supply dog guides to any war-blinded veteran without charge to either the veteran or the U.S. government (Koestler, 1976). Although dog guides have been used by a relatively small part of the population of individuals who are blind, formal training in the use of dog guides exerted a major influence on future training programs by demonstrating the necessity for a formalized program of O&M training. The importance of this concept was recognized by Richard Hoover at the Valley Forge General Hospital and by Russell Williams at the Hines Hospital rehabilitation centers for veterans who were blinded during World War II (Miyagawa, 1999). However, both these programs used the long cane as the mobility device, rather than the dog guide. A further impetus for using canes was provided by the state white cane laws, which required drivers to yield the right of way to people who were blind and used canes.

In the area of education, in recognition of the importance of independent travel before the teaching of travel techniques became a formalized profession, schools for the blind offered "foot travel instruction" to students until the 1960s. The instructors were usually teachers who were blind and were considered proficient independent travelers. Often, this instruction was provided without any device, such as a long cane.

Beginning in the early 1950s, some teachers became aware of a new approach to teaching independent travel to people who were blind: mobility training. Mobility training had its origins at the Veterans Administration hospitals that served veterans who had been blinded during World War II. A longer version of the white cane, called the Hoover cane, had been developed, and systematic instruction in its use was being provided, on the assumption that the cane was a tool for travel, not a badge of blindness.

By the late 1950s, many teachers concluded that they could teach these approaches to independent travel effectively to students in school. Educators, such as Kay Gruber and Georgie Lee Abel, both consultants with AFB, worked with some early "mobility therapists" who were trained as instructors (notably Pete Wurzburger and Stan Saturko) to offer summer institutes at various universities for teachers of children with visual impairments. These teachers gained some skills in teaching independent travel techniques that they knew would be important for youngsters, but they were not prepared to offer comprehensive O&M training.

In 1960, Boston College established the first university-based preparation program for O&M instructors, and in 1961, Western Michigan University opened the second. Soon other university programs were begun: California State College at Los Angeles, Florida State University, San Francisco State College, University of Northern Colorado, and the University of Pittsburgh. Graduates of these first formal training programs for O&M instructors at first provided services only to adults. But soon they were employed by schools. By 1974, almost half the mobility specialists were involved in delivering services to the school-age population (Welsh & Blasch, 1974; Mills, 1987). By 1970, instruction in O&M was firmly ensconced as a required course for students who were blind in high school. In addition to braille, this subject became the first disability-specific educational need that was formally identified as being necessary for students who were blind.

Focus on Literacy

In the early 1970s, the beginning of a significant drop in the percentage of children who were legally blind and were being taught to read and write in braille was evident in APH annual reports. Many educators explained this decline by pointing out that Barraga's (1964) research had dramatically changed the number of children being taught braille. If vision was determined to be the most efficient sense for reading and writing, then children were taught to read using their remaining vision. The dividing line between whether braille or print was the best medium for a particular child remained elusive until the early 1990s.

In the meantime, a number of theories about what many educators, consumers, and parents were describing as a literacy crisis were proposed. Many consumers believed that the decline was related to teachers' and others' lack of knowledge or appreciation of braille. However, other consumers, educators, and parents stressed that the shortage of qualified teachers was a major problem in providing literacy instruction. Still others believed that the trend toward inclusion, and the frequent, concomitant decrease in the amount of time that teachers of students with visual impairments were able to spend with students was the most serious issue. A teacher of students with visual impairments with a large caseload and a sizable geographic area to serve would not be successful in teaching braille reading and writing if instruction was provided for only one or two hours per week.

Another factor that was suspected in the decline of braille literacy was the interpretation in some quarters of Barraga's (1964) research results. Although this research did not suggest that children with any degree of remaining vision should learn print reading and writing, regardless

of peed, efficiency, and fatigue, in the 1970s and 1980s many students were graduating from high school with very slow print reading rates. Spungin (1990) listed eight areas that are most frequently cited as explanations for the lack of use of braille: (1) medical advances that have saved many more infants who would not have survived but who have other disabilities, particularly mental retardation and learning disabilities, in addition to visual loss; (2) the work of Barraga, which demonstrated that training in visual efficiency could enable many children to move from tactile reading to visual reading; (3) diminished positive attitudes toward braille users; (4) university preparation programs that have given only lip service to teaching braille so that teachers are not proficient in this medium; (5) the complexity of the braille code; (6) the dependence on audiotapes and speech-output devices; (7) reduced time in the school day because of the focus on inclusion, which leaves little time to spend on teaching necessary skills, such as braille; and (8) the IEP process, which favors what is available in a school district, rather than what a child needs to function adequately in a competitive world.

Although unanimous agreement about the reasons put forth for the decline in the literacy of students who were visually impaired was not reached, parents, consumers, and professionals did unite in a resolve to correct this problem. Consumer groups, such as NFB, and many parents and educators became advocates of improved literacy. AFB assumed a leadership role in improving the literacy of students, through both advocacy and direct action.

It should be noted that the literacy movement began primarily as a braille literacy movement. Indeed, the legislation on literacy that the majority of states have passed has been directed specifically toward promoting braille reading and writing. The 1997 changes in IDEA also focused on braille by requiring that braille be taught to a student who is legally blind unless the educational team decides otherwise. Overall, an awareness of the importance of braille as a reading and writing medium and of determining appropriate options and learning media for students who are visually impaired has been greatly enhanced by efforts to improve students' literacy.

Transition

In 1986, Haring and McCormick stated: "The achievement of full integration implies appropriate educational programming for successful transition from schools to community. . . . Transition is a new field," (p. 481). This quote implied, correctly, that the concept of transition grew from concerted efforts to integrate students with disabilities following the passage of P.L. 94-142. Although children experience many transitions during their educational careers (from preschool to kindergarten and from elementary school to middle school, for example), the early references to transition in the literature of special education described it as moving from school to the world of work.

Wolffe (1998, p. 343) described transition for students with visual impairments this way: "To successfully move from school environments to community environments, students who have visual impairments with other disabilities must receive instruction in activities of daily living skills, social skills, and career exploration and employability skills before they leave school." Thus, the ingredients of successful transition parallel the expanded core curriculum for students who are visually impaired, which includes the unique skills that students with visual impairments need to live independently and productively. (For a discussion of the core curriculum and the expanded core curriculum, see Chapter 10 in this volume.)

In the early 1980s, a major event occurred that has strengthened efforts to achieve successful transitions of young people who are visually impaired. The professional association comprised of rehabilitation workers with blind adults (American Association of Workers for the Blind) and the organization representing educators of students with visual impairments (Association for the Education of the Visually Handicapped) merged into a single professional association, the Association for Education and Rehabilitation of the Blind and Visually Impaired (AER). A strong rationale for this merger was that the transition from school and home to work and community should be as seamless as possible. If rehabilitation personnel who work primarily with adults, and teachers had opportunities to share ideas, meet together, and better understand each other's job responsibilities, then students would benefit by moving from school to the community much more easily.

Perhaps the most profound impact of the transition movement has been the increased realization by professionals and parents that students who are visually impaired need more than an academic education if they are to move easily into the community. To live independently and work in the community and to be socially assimilated into community groups requires knowledge that is not necessarily learned by casual exposure to the behavior of others or observing the environment. In fact, many of the social and independent living skills that are needed to transition must be taught before the transition is attempted. Both the education and rehabilitation professions have taken on some responsibility in providing instruction in the nonacademic areas of learning that are essential to transition.

As a result of the heightened awareness of the need to prepare students for life after school, the term *transition* is now firmly embedded in the special education culture. Its meaning is clear: a smooth process for youths in moving from school and home to work and community. Responsibility for the development of transition lies with both educators and rehabilitation professionals. IDEA mandates Individual Transition Plans for students with disabilities, beginning at age 14. Thus, transition is a part of educational planning and services for every high school student with a visual impairment. Also, in a growing number of rehabilitation centers for persons who are visually impaired, "transition skills," such as independent living skills, social skills, organization skills, and vocational skills, are becoming a part of the curriculum. Although the concept of transition is relatively recent in the context of the history of educational efforts, its impact on the curriculum of future high school students is likely to be significant.

Multiple Disabilities

When the history of special education in the 20th century is written, prominent among the topics will be the inclusion of all students with disabilities into educational services. As late as the 1960s, it was a common practice for local school districts to refuse educational placement to students with disabilities (Smith, Polloway, Patton, & Dowdy, 1998). In the 1940s and 1950s, this practice was applied to many of the children who were blinded from RLF when they were referred for placement at local schools or residential schools for the blind. Yet, educational services for children with visual impairments and additional disabilities have been reported in the literature many times since before the early 1950s. Therefore, even though many children were denied an education because of their multiple disabilities, others were accepted by schools. Huffman (1957) wrote one of the first curriculum guides for teaching students who were blind and had additional disabilities.

By the late 1950s, local school programs for students who were visually impaired were growing rapidly throughout the country. The majority of these programs placed children in general education classrooms, and provided resource room support from the teachers of students with visual impairments. In fact, resource room programs were often highly selective in the children they admitted, hoping to ensure academic success that would prove that the integration of children with visual impairments into general education classrooms was successful.

Because children who were blind and had no additional disabilities were typically accepted into local school programs but those children with additional disabilities were not, students in local school programs tended to be academically capable. Students with additional disabilities often had great difficulty obtaining access to educational services. The result was a dramatic change in the role of residential schools for the blind. Beginning in the early 1960s, the number of referrals for admission to schools for the blind from academically capable children began to diminish and those for students with additional disabilities soared (Sacks,

1998). Within a few years, the population of many schools for the blind changed from almost all academic students to almost all students with developmental delays. After a period of adjustment, over a number of years, many teachers at schools for the blind became expert in serving students with multiple disabilities. The second half of the 20th century will be remembered as a time when schools for the blind developed new programs and new expertise. Thus, it was some time after educators had accepted their responsibility to provide educational opportunities for children with visual impairments and additional disabilities that the provisions of PL 94-142 mandated educational services for all children with disabilities.

A significant subgroup of students with multiple disabilities is comprised of students who are deaf-blind. Helen Keller is the best-known deaf-blind person in the country and perhaps the world. Her educational and other accomplishments were very inspiring. As a result, other families requested attendance in school programs for their deaf-blind children. Because of the success of the Perkins School for the Blind, and also because schools for deaf children were not quick to attempt educational efforts with deaf-blind students, educational services for these children with multiple disabilities became more widely available at schools for the blind. In the 1950s, four such schools in the United States provided educational services for deaf-blind children: the Alabama Institute for the Deaf and Blind, the California School for the Blind, Perkins School for the Blind, and Washington State School for the Blind.

Rubella and Usher syndrome were common causes of deaf-blindness. In 1964–1965, a major epidemic of rubella occurred in the United States. If a woman contracted rubella in the first trimester of pregnancy, there was a high probability that her baby would be born carrying the live rubella virus. Approximately 30,000 infants who were born with the rubella virus in these years had severe disabilities (Cooper, 1969). Most of these infants had multiple disabilities, including cataracts, glaucoma, heart disease, hearing defects, and brain injury.

The United States responded quickly to what was viewed as a national emergency. In 1968, Congress passed legislation that established the Helen Keller National Center for Deaf-Blind Youths and Adults in New York and additional legislation that established regional offices of the center for the education of children with deaf-blindness. Since the passage of this legislation, educational funding is now allocated to each state. But before this change, it should be noted that the federal legislation that established regional centers for the education of children with deaf-blindness was the first time that education for students with disabilities was offered across state boundaries. Universities geared up to serve the rubella deaf-blind population, and soon several personnel preparation centers were established, also with the assistance of federal funds. Even before an adequate supply of teachers became available, dozens of new programs for educating children with deaf-blindness were established throughout the country.

Children who were deaf-blind as a result of rubella frequently had severe to moderate hearing losses and cataracts that were often removed in early childhood. These children had more severe deafness than vision loss. Many of them could see to retrieve a small object from distances of up to 20 feet, but still seemed to have visual problems that had an impact on their learning. Many also presented behavioral challenges that were often attributed to the isolation and resulting communication barriers experienced when two major sources of sensory input are impaired.

Preventive medicine has substantially reduced deaf-blindness from the rubella virus. However, many programs that began in response to the epidemic continue to offer educational programming for children who are deaf-blind regardless of the course.

Technology

Braille Writing Machines

Teaching aids during the first half of the 20th century were relatively simple, compared with those available during the second half. The first braillewriter, developed by Frank H. Hall, superintendent of the Illinois School for the Blind, was exhibited at the convention of the AAIB in 1892. A limited number of Hall braillewriters were manufactured and they were still in use well into the second half of the 20th century. AFB developed a quieter and more efficient braillewriter in 1932 but this machine was heavy to carry (16 pounds), so it did not become popular.

Until the middle of the 20th century, writing braille sometimes presented a challenge. Various designs of braillewriters were available, as indicated above, but they were not dependable, were poorly designed, and were sometimes quite expensive. Thus, most braille users depended on a slate and stylus. The slate is a frame comprised of recessed holes that correspond to the dots of a braille cell. The stylus is a sharp, handheld rod, that pushes paper that is laid over the slate and forms braille. Although considered slow and laborious by some, the great majority of blind people who use slates and styli believe the device is an invaluable writing tool.

In the early 1950s, the House Memorial Press at the Perkins School for the Blind began marketing a new braillewriter called the Perkins Brailler. The Perkins Brailler was a wonderfully designed, almost indestructable machine, and it revolutionized the writing of braille. It was lighter and more efficient than older braille writers. Although technology has taken the production of braille, both commercial and personal, to an even higher level, the Perkins Brailler is still considered the faithful standby and the most dependable method for producing small quantities of braille. It is still in use today.

Production of Books in Accessible Media

The early books in braille were embossed on one side, which facilitated the reading of braille by sight. However, the storage of books consumed a great deal of space. In addition, Grade 1½ braille (a code that is between the complete writing out letter by letter of Grade 1 and the 189 contractions of Grade 2) was used. Embossing on both sides was not developed until the mid-1920s amid much controversy, but it reduced the bulk and weight of the braille books. The introduction of Grade 2 braille and embossing books on both sides (called interpoint) during the late 1940s helped alleviate the problem of book storage. The use of Grade 2 braille was not widespread until the 1950s.

Technology had a direct impact on educational content for students who are visually impaired by dramatically changing the quality and quantity of adapted instructional materials for students. Prior to 1950, there was no way of producing braille other than by using a laborious printing-press method at APH, Clovernook, and other braille suppliers or through the use of volunteer braille transcribers. The enrollment of braille readers in general education classrooms caused significant problems in the production of braille textbooks. APH could produce only a limited supply, and those were most often the ones requested by schools for the blind. However, local school districts had the latitude of adopting any one of literally dozens of textbooks on every school subject except when their states adopted specific ones. The chance that a local district would select a textbook in reading, for example, that had already been produced in braille was minimal.

Residential schools for students with visual impairments continued to use what was available from APH. Local school districts depended on volunteer transcribers, and in many locations, each local district program had its own transcribing group. The rapid and efficient growth of braille transcribing groups was instrumental in supplying materials to students with visual impairments. Transcribing groups flourished primarily because there was something exciting about supporting children who read braille in regular classrooms. Placing children with disabilities in regular classrooms was rare in the 1950s and 1960s, except for a growing number of students who were blind or visually impaired. Without large numbers of braille transcribers, these students would not have succeeded in regular classrooms where having the same learning materials as their sighted peers was essential. At this time in history, women

were not typically employed, and many were looking for new hobbies and interests as their children began to leave home. Like sign language, braille has a certain appeal to the general public. So, when teachers of students with visual impairments began advertising classes in braille transcribing, there was no shortage of interested people. These volunteers became the foundation of support services for braille readers in inclusive education settings.

Concurrent with volunteers who produced braille came the increase in large-print books. The experience of the National Association for the Visually Handicapped (NAVH) may serve as an example of the importance of volunteer transcribing groups. Founded in the 1950s by Lorraine Marchi, the parent of two sons with albinism who were enrolled in the San Francisco Unified School District, NAVH recruited many volunteers who would use modified typewriters to produce large-print textbooks. Marchi expanded this service nationwide, and NAVH continued to produce large-print textbooks in this manner for many years. Today, photocopying and computers and commercial printers produce high-quality large-print materials quickly and efficiently and greatly supplement the efforts of volunteer groups.

Talking Books and Recorded Media

The evolution of auditory materials also expanded the access of students with visual impairments to educational materials. While people who were blind frequently lagged behind people who were sighted in reaping the benefits of technological progress (Koestler, 1976), there was a notable exception. Talking Book machines, developed in 1932 by AFB, were the forerunner of other methods of recording and retrieving auditory information. These devices were black boxes, about 15 inches square and 11 inches deep, that were designed to play recorded books and some educational materials on long-playing records, which were also developed by AFB in 1934, long before they were available to the general public. It is interesting to note that Thomas Edison, in his application for a patent for his recording machine, listed as a potential use "phonograph books, which will speak to blind people without effort on their part" (Koestler, 1976, p. 130). (Other early technological inventions that have greatly enhanced the lives of persons who are blind are the telephone and the typewriter.)

For many years, students and adults who were blind depended on live readers for access to materials that are not easily available in braille. Shortly after World War II, the wire recorder, the predecessor to the tape recorder, was produced. In addition, companies began manufacturing dictating machines that students and adults who were blind came to use. A major advantage of these new machines over Talking Books was that they allowed students to record as well as listen. But it was the open-reel tape recorder that revolutionized the production of auditory books and materials for students with visual impairments. In the 1960s, high school students would often carry a brailler and a tape recorder with them from class to class.

Modern recording now provides high-quality audiocassette tapes that can be indexed and read using compressed speech. The ability to find one's place on an audiocassette tape quickly and to listen to material at a speed more rapid than it was recorded are tremendous advances for listeners with visual impairments.

Microcomputer Technology

Toward the end of the 20th century came the most dramatic technological advance for students with visual impairments. This advance began with the development of the personal computer. Many adults with visual impairments immediately observed that computers would allow them to do something they had never been able to do before: store and retrieve information easily.

Until the early 1980s it was not uncommon for students with visual impairments to produce an assignment in braille and bring it to the resource room. The teacher of students with visual impairments would write the print word above each braille word on the assignment (interline) and give it back to the student, who would take it back to the general classroom teacher. Now the student can write a paper in braille, proofread it, and then reproduce it in print to be turned in to the classroom teacher. Some of the advances that technology has provided are as follows:

- Through the use of scanners, specially prepared software, and adapted computers, it is possible to produce literary braille from print copy almost instantaneously. This ability has resulted in a revolution in how braille is produced and how volunteer transcribers are used.

- Students now have note-taking devices that they can carry comfortably from class to class and then download through a computer into braille, print, large-print, or an auditory form.

- Computers and the peripherals developed specifically for persons with visual impairments to gain access to what is on computers through synthetic speech software have become a primary tool that students use to unlock a wealth of subjects.

- Electronic files of books used by book publishers are now being used to produce literary-style braille. This process will soon be possible for Nemeth code (scientific and mathematical) braille. As technological advances continue, the benefits for students with visual impairments will continue to increase at a rapid rate. For more detailed information on technology, see Chapter 14 in *Foundations of Education: Instructional Strategies for Teaching Children and Youths with Visual Impairments.*

Personnel Preparation

During the first 85 years of the history of residential schools for children with visual impairments, teachers and houseparents acquired their specialized skills through apprenticeship, the system that was developed in Europe. Most of the teachers in the early residential schools had no previous teaching experience. Many had only high school degrees, and many were graduates of the schools in which they were employed (Koestler, 1976). As late as 1949–50, Irwin (1955) wrote:

> The great majority of teachers in the schools for the blind have not been especially trained for their work. During the first twenty-five years of the century superintendents seemed to feel that almost anyone could teach blind children. (p. 135)

Since many children with low vision were enrolled in residential schools, their teachers faced the same situation. When Edward E. Allen in Boston and Robert Irwin in Cleveland pioneered day school classes for the "partially sighted" and the idea began to spread, the acuteness of the teacher preparation problem was evident: The teachers in day school programs did not even have the advantage of apprenticeship under experienced teachers because there were none. As Hathaway (1959) noted:

> For some years after the first educational facilities were made available to partially sighted children in 1913, there was no established precedent for teachers to follow, and no opportunity for them to prepare for this very specialized work. Each teacher had, therefore, to try to solve through the trial and error method the problems that were constantly arising, thus experimenting to a certain extent, with children who had difficulties enough of their own to meet. (p. 64)

University-Based Preparation

The first university-based teacher preparation course was offered at the University of California in 1918 (Best, 1934). However, the first enduring sequences of training courses were established in Boston and Nashville in the early 1920s. In 1921, Allen, superintendent of the Perkins Institution, took a giant step toward the professionalization of residential school faculties when he approached the Harvard Graduate School of Education with a proposal to initiate a six-month training program to be operated in cooperation with Perkins. The program was established as the Harvard Course on Education of the Blind. By 1925, the need for supervised practice was recognized, and a second six-month sequence was developed. This portion of the program, called the Special Methods Course, was given under the direction of a Perkins faculty member and included a residential apprenticeship of lectures, observations, and student teaching. The total sequence offered graduate credits toward a master's degree. Thus, the standard was set for teachers of children with visual impairments—advanced training at the graduate level (Koestler, 1976). The program was subsequently moved to Boston University and then to Boston College.

Also in 1925, I. S. Wampler, superintendent of the Tennessee School for the Blind, initiated a six-week summer course in cooperation with George Peabody College for Teachers. The trainees lived at the Tennessee school and attended classes at Peabody, which were taught by Wampler and visiting faculty. This course was discontinued in 1928 for financial reasons, but it was revived in 1931 at a nominal cost to students. However, even the nominal cost was prohibitive during the Great Depression, and the program lapsed again until 1935 when AFB gave Peabody College a one-year grant that enabled it to start up again (Koestler, 1976).

Beginning in the late 1940s, there was a surge of interest in special education, and several universities established teacher preparation sequences in various areas of exceptionality. Four factors appear to have influenced the renewal of interest in preparing teachers of children with visual impairments. They were (1) the rapid expansion of day and residential school programs to meet the demand for placements for children with RLF; (2) the differentiation of teaching roles for various types of schools and programs owing to the philosophical shift toward educating children in their home communities; (3) new teaching skills required by the shift from the conservation of sight to the use of vision; and (4) the belief that techniques for teaching daily living skills and independent mobility, systematized and demonstrated by the Veterans Administration program for blinded veterans of World War II, were adaptable for use with children (Roberts, 1973). One of the first of this new wave of training centers was the Department of Special Education at San Francisco State College, a graduate-level department that opened in 1948 with a full-time faculty position in each of eight major areas of special education, including visual impairment.

The two new sequences attracted different populations: the Perkins-Harvard program was designed for teachers who had just graduated from colleges or normal schools. The Tennessee School-Peabody summer sessions were best suited to teachers who were already teaching but who wanted to upgrade their knowledge and skills or who wished to enter the field of visual impairment. These two patterns persisted during the 1950s, when the sudden rise in the number of children with visual impairments due to the postwar baby boom and the advent of RLF created an unprecedented need for teachers.

In 1957, Dr. Samuel Ashcroft, at that time the only educator in the country with a doctorate in education of students with visual impairments, was employed by George Peabody College to develop and direct a year-round graduate teacher preparation program. In the 1960s and 1970s, full-time graduate preparation became the predominant pattern as a result of federal funding and the rising concern about teachers' competencies.

Professional Qualifications of Teachers

Within a decade after the first university-based teacher preparation courses were instituted, the field was actively working on delineating the qualifications of teachers of children with visual impairments. At that time, state departments of education did not have criteria or procedures for certifying teachers of children with disabilities.

In 1932, AAIB appointed a committee to formulate recommendations regarding qualifications for teachers of children who were blind. Certification was to be granted on the completion of university-based preservice or in-service courses and a demonstrated ability to read and write braille. There was a grandfather clause that al-

lowed the substitution of successful teaching experience for some of the formal course work. The certification system was adopted at AAIB's 1938 convention, and the first awards were made in 1940. As late as 1985, some schools still relied on this certification system (at that time through AER) because their states had inadequate or no procedures for teachers of children with visual impairments.

In 1954, the U.S. Office of Education published a status report (Mackie & Dunn, 1954), and in the next few years it issued consensus reports on studies of the competencies of teachers in various areas of exceptionality (Mackie & Cohoe, 1956; Mackie & Dunn, 1955). In each study, 100 teachers identified and evaluated the competencies that were important in their work. Subsequently, special education supervisors, specialists in state departments of education, and nationally recognized leaders grouped and evaluated the competencies. The consensus of the two studies in the area of visual impairment was that the optimum teacher preparation model should include an undergraduate major in elementary education, two or more years of successful teaching in a general education classroom, and graduate training in the education of children with visual impairments, including 50–250 hours of practice teaching.

In response to the field's concern about professional preparation, AFB published *Training Facilities for the Preparation of Teachers of Blind Children in the United States* in 1953. In 1957, AFB appointed a Teacher Education Advisory Committee to work with its staff to formulate standards for the preparation of teachers of children who were blind. Two national work sessions were convened by that committee in 1958 and 1959 to develop program objectives for a teacher education sequence. The resulting document, *A Teacher Education Program for Those Who Serve Blind Children and Youth* (AFB, 1961) proposed a broader view of the range of competencies required for the adequate education of children with visual impairments than that of earlier publications. It included the enlistment of assistance from specialists within and outside schools to meet the personal, social, and learning needs of these children and youths.

Concurrently, the National Society for the Prevention of Blindness (NSPB; now Prevent Blindness America) was developing guidelines for a basic teacher preparation program for teachers of "partially sighted" children. A minimum schedule of courses had been presented in 1925, but a review was needed, and in 1957 an advisory committee was appointed to assist in the fourth revision of Hathaway's (1959) book, *Education and Health of the Partially Seeing Child*. At that time, it was estimated that 70,000 children who were partially sighted were in school but that only 8,000 were being served by qualified teachers. It was recommended that a basic 120-clock-hour sequence that would prepare teachers to work in cooperative, resource room, or itinerant programs should include at least 30 clock hours in each of the following areas: organization and administration of facilities for educating partially sighted children; procedures for conducting work in elementary, junior high, and senior high schools; observation and practice teaching with children in all three program models; and anatomy, physiology, and hygiene of the eye (Hathaway, 1959; NSPB, 1956).

Another step in the specification of qualifications for teachers of children with disabilities was taken by the Council for Exceptional Children (CEC) in the 1960s. The Professional Standards Committee, with funding from many agencies including AFB and NSPB, organized a massive project on professional standards. Over two years, approximately 700 special educators participated in the formulation of standards for preparing personnel for special education administration and supervision and for preparing teachers in seven areas of exceptionality, including visual impairment. The standards for preparing personnel to teach children with visual impairments included basic preparation in general education, an overview of all areas of exceptionality, and specific preparation in the area of visual impairment (CEC, 1966). In the early 1990s, CEC initiated an ambitious project to establish and validate knowledge and skills for special educators. This project first validated a "Common Core" of knowledge

SIDEBAR 1.6

Major Award Winners

AER MARY K. BAUMAN AWARD

This award was established to honor an individual who has made a significant contribution to the education of children who are blind or visually impaired. It is presented during each bi-annual AER conference. The recipients of the AER Mary K. Bauman Award have been:

1982	Mary K. Bauman
1984	Josephine Taylor
1986	Elinor Long
1988	Georgie Lee Abel
1990	J. Max Woolly
1992	John Ed Chiles
1994	William H. English
1996	Jane N. Erin
1998	Mary Nelle McLennan
2000	Philip Hatlen

CEC-DVI DISTINGUISHED SERVICE AWARD

This award is given yearly during the annual conference of the Council for Exceptional Children at the business meeting of the Division on Visual Impairments. It is presented to a member of CEC-DVI who exhibits exemplary leadership and commitment to the field of visual impairments. The recipients of the CEC-DIV Distinguished Service Award have been:

1984	Natalie Barraga
1985	Charles Woodcock
1986	Marjorie Ward
1987	Anne Corn
1988	Ralph Peabody
1989	Berthold Lowenfeld
1990	Sam Ashcroft
1991	Dean Tuttle
1992	Evelyn Rex
1993	Virginia Sowell
1994	Randall Harley
1995	Kay Alicyn Ferrell
1996	Herb Miller
1997	Alan Koenig
1998	Rosanne K. Silberman
1999	Bob Brasher
2000	Mary Jean Sanspree

and skills, which was common across all areas of special education. Then exceptionality-specific sets of knowledge and skills were validated. The then Division of Visual Impairment of CEC initiated the process of drafting the knowledge and skills in visual impairments, which were subsequently validated by a sample of the DVI membership. In the mid-1990s, the Professional Standards and Practices Standing Committee of CEC formally adopted the Knowledge and Skills for All Beginning Special Education Teachers of Students with Visual Impairments. This document, along with the Common Core, are presented in Appendices F and G of this volume.

With the widespread development of competence-based education in teacher preparation programs in the United States, educators of teachers of children with visual impairments worked to define the specialized competencies that were necessary to teach children with visual impairments over and above those necessary to teach sighted children. Between 1973 and 1975, AFB coordinated six meetings of 28 professional teacher-educators of children with visual impairments from 22 colleges and universities. At these meetings, the document, *Competency-Based Curriculum for Teachers of the Visually Handicapped: A National Study* (Spungin, 1977) was compiled. To make the material more realistic, a national study was conducted to learn the reactions of teachers from both public and residential school settings.

The competencies involved seven teaching activities: assessment and evaluation, educational instructional strategies, guidance and counseling, administration and supervision, media and technology, school-community relations, and research. Each goal area listed prerequisite entry-level behaviors in which teachers had to demonstrate proficiency before they could acquire new competencies for that area.

As efforts to define teachers' competencies and educational standards continued, university programs grew rapidly, largely because of the presence of Josephine L. Taylor, branch chief of the Personnel Preparation Division at the U.S. Department of Education. After years of experience as a teacher of children with visual impairments and an administrator of local day school programs for children who were visually impaired, Taylor brought her expertise to the federal government, and at once recognized the potential for meeting the desperate need for teachers by infusing federal funds into university preparation programs. The pattern of funding universities that began in the early 1960s involved the submission of grant proposals to the U.S. Department of Education by universities that were interested in preparing teachers of students with visual impairments. If approved, the funding provided stipends for students, as well as money for faculty salaries and other costs.

Beginning in the 1970s, two events had a profound impact on the preparation of teachers of students with visual impairments. First, federal funds became scarce, largely because the total amount of funds available remained constant while the number of universities that applied for these funds increased. This increased competition resulted in significantly lower grant awards, and some universities with a history of many years of federal funds suddenly found themselves denied grants. The second event was a sudden and dramatic reduction of applicants for teacher preparation programs.

Although federal funds resulted in many programs that would not have existed otherwise, the universities that were, and remained, totally dependent on federal funds were severely threatened when funds became scarce. The decline in applicants for teacher preparation programs may have been related to the reduction in federal funds, but may also have been part of a larger trend that was taking place among young people away from the profession of education. There has been a good deal of speculation about the reason for the decline in persons interested in teaching students who are blind or visually impaired. Often, the decrease of federal grants is blamed. While this may be some part of the reason, there are other cultural and social factors that also had an impact on enrollment.

Whatever the reasons for these trends, they have had a severe impact on the preparation of teachers in the United States. The decline of stipend money had at least some impact on applicants for programs. It also meant less financial support for universities, which caused administrators to look seriously at the number of students who were enrolled. As these numbers decreased, both faculty and entire programs became vulnerable. A teacher preparation program with 30 students and 3 full-time faculty, with 2 supported on federal funds, in 1967, might have had 8 students and 1 university-hired faculty member (with no support from federal funds) in 1992. This was not an unusual scenario, and a number of highly respected university teacher preparation programs were closed.

Beginning in 1960, personnel preparation for O&M instructors was offered for the first time at Boston College. Other universities soon developed programs. Originally, these graduate-level programs concentrated on training O&M instructors for adults who were blind in rehabilitation programs, but they soon recognized that O&M must also be taught to school-age students.

Today, because O&M is acknowledged to be essential for persons with visual impairments of all ages, beginning at birth, and regardless of additional disabilities, the demand for these specialists continues to grow. However, O&M programs also suffer because of a required low student–professor ratio during the preparation process that makes it difficult for universities, mindful of typical ratios, to justify employing professors in O&M.

In both the education of students with visual impairments and O&M there continues to be a chronic shortage of qualified teachers. Because of this shortage, there have been some efforts in recent years to attempt some innovative approaches to teacher preparation. Various forms of distance education are being implemented, as are summer-only programs. Programs such as these attempt to accommodate experienced classroom teachers and others who are exploring new and different professional challenges. Often, employed workers and practicing teachers are not willing or financially able to leave their jobs for a year and/or enroll at a distant university. Therefore, universities are considering ways in which practicing classroom teachers and other employed adults can receive high-quality preparation without leaving home and without quitting their jobs (such as interactive television and Web-based courses).

NATIONAL INITIATIVES

At the beginning of a new century and into a new millennium, the profession is attempting to address, among other questions, the best methods of educating students who are visually impaired, the roles of residential and general education programs in doing so, the competencies and supports that teachers need to provide the best general and special education for these students, the range of options and resources to provide for students with a diversity of needs, and ways to remedy severe shortages of trained personnel. A number of national initiatives have attempted to bring the expertise of the entire profession to bear on finding solutions to these problematic issues.

The National Agenda

In 1993, a small group of professional educators and parents began to meet out of a concern for the quality of educational services for students with visual impairments. At the time, U.S. President George Bush had announced general Education Goals for the Year 2000 (1991). Goals for the Year 2000 for educating students with visual impairments were established as a necessary and desirable objective by the movement that was begun by the small group.

A determined grassroots effort was subsequently undertaken, in which surveys were conducted to establish a set of goals agreed upon by the majority of educators and parents responding. Many teachers and parents returned survey forms, and from hundreds of returns came a set of eight goals (Corn, Hatlen, Huebner, Ryan, & Siller, 1995). To be accepted as a part of the National Agenda, a goal needed to be considered attainable and measurable. Sidebar 1.7 lists the eight goals of the National Agenda. From the outset, the National Agenda was established as a joint project among

Goals of the National Agenda

1: REFERRAL

Students and their families will be referred to an appropriate education program within 30 days of identification of a suspected visual impairment.

2: PARENTAL PARTICIPATION

Policies and procedures will be implemented to ensure the right of all parents to full participation and equal partnership in the educational process.

3: PERSONNEL PREPARATION

Universities, with a minimum of one full-time faculty member in the area of visual impairment, will prepare a sufficient number of educators of students with visual impairments to meet the need for personnel throughout the country.

4: PROVISION OF EDUCATIONAL SERVICES

Service providers will determine caseloads on the basis of the needs of students and will require ongoing professional development for all teachers and orientation and mobility instructors.

5: ARRAY OF SERVICES

Local educational programs will ensure that all students have access to a full array of placement options.

6: ASSESSMENT

Assessments of students will be conducted, in collaboration with parents, by personnel with expertise in the education of students with visual impairments.

7: ACCESS TO INSTRUCTIONAL MATERIALS

Access to developmental and educational services will include the assurance that instructional materials are available to students in the appropriate media and at the same time as they are to sighted students.

8: CORE CURRICULUM

Educational and developmental goals, including instruction, will reflect the assessed needs of each student in all areas of the academic and disability-specific core curricula.

---

parents, educators, and consumers and captured the excitement and dedication of educators and parents throughout the country. Although the goals were not met throughout the United States by the year 2000, work toward meeting them is proceeding in most states in the country.

There have been many productive outcomes from the National Agenda movement, including the development of the concept of the expanded core curriculum, which clearly defines educational areas of need unique to students who are visually impaired, formulated to help meet Goal 8. Just as the National Agenda has been endorsed and accepted by every major organization for professionals and parents, so has the expanded core curriculum. The acknowledgment that children and youths with visual impairments have educa-

tional needs that are nonacademic and disability specific has resulted in a better understanding of what these children need to learn and the skills that teachers need to have.

The National Plan to Train Personnel

Students with visual impairments have unique needs, and the personnel who teach them require specialized training to meet those needs. As federal funding has become more competitive and less available, many university programs that train teachers of students with visual impairments have been dismantled, and it has become more difficult to attract students into the remaining programs. As a result, there is a shortage of trained personnel in the field.

To address the crucial need for more trained personnel, the Office of Special Education Programs of the U.S. Department of Education funded a two-year project in 1997 to develop a national plan for training capable and qualified personnel to educate children with visual impairments. A consortium of organizations in the field, including the Division on Visual Impairments of CEC, Division 17 on Personnel Preparation of AER, and AFB, worked together to develop this national strategic plan (*National Plan*, 2000). The five goals of the plan, which was intended to enhance the quality of education and literacy of students and to respond to the overall needs of children and youths of all ages, were as follows:

♦ To conduct a systemic and systematic needs assessment of the shortage of personnel in the United States,

♦ To identify activities for developing a comprehensive approach to serving students with blindness, deaf-blindness, or low vision,

♦ To improve the quality of personnel preparation programs that recruit and prepare teachers and related personnel to instruct students who are blind, are deaf-blind, or have low vision,

♦ To identify successful models of preparing personnel who teach students with visual impairments, and

♦ To develop a national plan based on a consensus of the major groups in the field of blindness.

Efforts related to the plan continue to explore the feasibility of establishing a national technical assistance network and other possibilities, such as the creation of national research and training centers in the field.

NASDE Guidelines

In 1999, the National Association of State Directors of Special Education (NASDE) and the Hilton/Perkins Program of the Perkins School for the Blind disseminated educational service guidelines for students who are visually impaired. The intent of the guidelines was to provide assistance to state and local education agencies, service providers, and parents and to describe the essential elements and features of programs that must be considered when designing appropriate services for students who are visually impaired, including those with multiple disabilities. A full continuum of educational options is included. The document was the collaborative effort of 13 national consumer, advocacy, and educational organizations that have a special interest in the provision of services to persons with visual impairments and their families. Representatives of these organizations formulated the guidelines, and a larger panel of content experts reviewed them. *Blind and Visually Impaired Students: Educational Service Guidelines* (Pugh & Erin, 1999) discusses the unique educational needs of students with visual impairments, public policy and legislation that affect these students and their right to full participation in the general school curriculum, and the role of parents as equal partners in the educational process. In addition, it describes the processes of identifying and assessing the needs of individual students; program options and placements; and the specialized knowledge, skills, and attributes needed to provide educational and O&M services to students.

SUMMARY

The rich history of progress in educating children with visual impairments is one in which teachers of these students can take pride. At the beginning of the 20th century, only a select few children who were blind received an education, and nearly all of them were enrolled in schools for the blind. Today, all students with visual impairments receive an education, and most of them are enrolled in their neighborhood schools, in general education classes, with ongoing support systems. Today's profession has a strong commitment to a continuum of placement options in which the individual needs of students are respected. At the beginning of the 20th century, there was no effective legislation to protect and advocate for the rights of students with disabilities. Today, IDEA, as well as other federal and state initiatives like the Americans with Disabilities Act, have guaranteed and solidified educational rights for students with visual impairments. The role of technology in daily activities has dramatically increased educational, recreational, and vocational opportunities for persons with visual impairments. Teacher preparation has come of age and has progressed from an era in which education for students with visual impairments was a "folk art," passed on from generation to generation, usually by word of mouth, to an era of increasing professionalism and commitment to high standards of excellence.

STUDY QUESTIONS

1. Why is it important for professionals today to understand the historical perspectives of the past?

2. Many have played important roles in shaping the professional landscape of education for students with visual impairments. What do you think are characteristics of leaders who have made an historical contribution?

3. Pick one of the many names of influential professionals mentioned in this chapter. Examine other sources to find out additional information about the person and report your findings to your classmates.

4. What was the "War of the Dots"? What was its significance?

5. Residential schools for the blind are often under attack as segregated settings for students with visual impairments. Describe the history of residential schools, their importance in the past, and their role in the future.

6. What impact has technology had on the history of education for students who are visually impaired? What new technologies may change the future for these students?

REFERENCES

American Foundation for the Blind. (1954). *The Pine Brook Report.* New York: Author.

American Foundation for the Blind. (1953). *Training facilities for the preparation of teachers of blind children in the United States.* New York: Author.

American Foundation for the Blind. (1961). *A teacher education program for those who serve blind children and youth.* New York: Author.

America 2000: An education strategy (1991). Washington, D.C.: U.S. Department of Education.

Barraga, N. C. (1964). *Increased visual behavior in low vision children.* New York: American Foundation for the Blind.

Best, H. (1934). *Blindness and the blind in the United States.* New York: Macmillan.

Best, J. P., & Winn, R. J. (1968). A place to go in Texas. *International Journal for the Education of the Blind, 18,* 2–10.

Bledsoe, C. W. (1971). The family of residential schools. *Blindness,* pp. 25–26.

Cooper, L. (1969). The child with rubella syndrome. *New Outlook for the Blind, 63,* 290–298.

Corn, A. L., Hatlen, P., Huebner, K. M., Ryan, F., & Siller, M. A. (1995). *The national agenda for the education of children and youths with visual impairments, including those with multiple disabilities.* New York: AFB Press.

Council for Exceptional Children. (1966). *Professional standards for personnel in the education of exceptional children.* Reston, VA: Author.

Dickens, C. (1907). *American notes and pictures from Italy.* New York: E. P. Dutton.

Diderot, D. (1749). *Lettre sur les aveugles a l'usage de ceux qui voient* [Letter on the blind for the use of those who see]. London.

Frampton, M. E., & Kearney, E. (1953). *The residential school.* New York: Edwin Gould Printery.

Haring, N. G., & McCormick, L. (1986). *Exceptional children and youth.* Columbus, OH: Charles E. Merrill.

Hathaway, W. (1959). *Education and health of the partially seeing child* (4th ed.). New York: Columbia University Press.

Howe, S. G. (1840). Appendix A in *Eighth annual report of the trustees of the Perkins Institution and Massachusetts Asylum for the Blind.* Boston: John H. Eastburn.

Huffman, M. B. (1957). *Fun comes first for blind slow learners*. Springfield, IL: Charles C Thomas.

Illingworth, W. H. (1910). *History of the education of the blind*. London: Sampson, Low, Marston, & Co.

Irwin, R. B. (1955). *As I saw it*. New York: American Foundation for the Blind.

Irwin, R. B. (1932). Uniform braille for the English-speaking world achieved. *Outlook for the Blind, 26, 3*, 137–138.

Koestler, F. (1976). *The unseen minority: A social history of blindness in the United States*. New York: David McKay Co.

Lowenfeld, B. (1971). *Our blind children* (3rd ed.). Springfield, IL: Charles C Thomas.

Lowenfeld, B. (ed.) (1973). *The visually handicapped child in school*. New York: John Day.

Lowenfeld, B. (1975). *The changing status of the blind*. Springfield, IL: Charles C Thomas.

Lowenfeld, B. (1980). Psychological problems of children with severely impaired vision. In W. M. Cruickshank (Ed.), *Psychology of Exceptional Children and Youth*. (4th ed.). Englewood Cliffs, NJ: Prentice Hall.

Mackie, R. P., & Cohoe, E. (1956). *Teachers of children who are partially seeing*. Washington, DC: U.S. Government Printing Office.

Mackie, R. P., & Dunn, L. M. (1954). *College and university programs for the preparation of teachers of exceptional children*. Washington, DC: U.S. Government Printing Office.

Mackie, R. P., & Dunn, L. M. (1955). *Teachers of children who are blind*. Washington, DC: U.S. Government Printing Office.

Mills, R. J. (1982). *Foundations of orientation and mobility*. New York: AFB Press.

Miyagawa, S. (1999). *Journey to excellence*. Lakeville, MN: Galde Press.

National plan for training personnel to serve children with blindness and low vision. (2000). Reston, VA: Council for Exceptional Children.

National Society to Prevent Blindness. (1956), *Recommended basic course for preparation of teachers of partially seeing children*. New York: Author.

Nolan, C. Y. (1983). *Providing educational materials under the act to promote the education of the blind*. Lexington, KY: American Printing House for the Blind.

Pugh, G. S., & Erin, J. (Eds.). (1999). *Blind and visually impaired students: Educational service guidelines*. Watertown, MA: Perkins School for the Blind.

Rex, E. J., Koenig, A. J., Wormsley, D. P. & Baker, R. L. (1994). *Foundations of braille literacy*. New York: AFB.

Roberts, F. K. (1986). Education for the visually handicapped: A social and educational history. In G. T. Scholl (Ed.), *Foundations of education for blind and visually handicapped children and youth: Theory and practice* (pp. 1–18). New York: American Foundation for the Blind.

Roblin, J. (1960). *Louis Braille*. London: Royal National Institute for the Blind.

Rodenberg, L. W. (1955). *The story of embossed books for the blind*. New York: American Foundation for the Blind.

Sacks, S. Z. (1998). Educating students who have visual impairments with other disabilities: An overview. In S. Z. Sacks and R. K. Silberman (Eds.), *Educating students who have visual impairments with other disabilities*. New York: American Foundation for the Blind.

Schwartz, H. (1956). *Samuel Gridley Howe*. Cambridge, MA: Harvard University Press.

Silverman, W. A. (1980). *Retrolental fibroplasia: A modern parable*. New York: Grune & Stratton.

Smith, T. E. C., Polloway, E. A., Patton, J. R., & Dowdy, C. A. (1998). *Teaching students with special needs in inclusive settings* (2nd ed.). Boston: Allyn and Bacon.

Spungin, S. J. (1977). *Competency-based curriculum for teachers of the visually handicapped: A national study*. New York: American Foundation for the Blind.

Spungin, S. J. (1990). *Braille literacy: Issues for blind persons, families, professionals and producers of braille*. New York: American Foundation for the Blind.

Welsh, R. L., & Blasch, B. B. (1974). Manpower need in orientation and mobility. *New Outlook for the Blind, 68*, 433–443.

Chronology of Events in the History of Education of People Who Are Visually Impaired

1749	In his "Letter on the Blind for the Use of Those Who See," Denis Diderot states that learning through touch involves different mental processes than those involved with sight.
1774	*Letter on the Education of the Blind* is published by Demodocus, who is thought to be a blind man.
1776	Abbé de l'Epée publishes a book on instructing people who are deaf-mutes, which may have influenced Haüy to teach blind children.
1779	Thomas Jefferson's education bill calls for state-sponsored education of girls as well as boys.
1780	Proponents of humanism and the Enlightenment form the Société Philantropique in France, which is interested in aiding people who are blind.
1784	Valentine Haüy establishes L'Institution Nationale des Jeunes Aveugles (Institute for Blind Youths), the first school for children who are blind in Paris. He experiments with various sizes and forms of raised Roman letters to teach students who are blind to read.
1791	The first school for the blind in England opens in Liverpool.
1808	Charles Barbier invents Écriture Nocturne (night writing) for use by French soldiers at night.
1809	Louis Braille is born in Coupvray, France.
1817	The American Asylum for the Education and Instruction of the Deaf (now the American School for the Deaf) in Hartford, Connecticut, the first educational program for exceptional children and youths, is formally established in the United States with Rev. Thomas H. Gallaudet as the principal.
1823	The first state school for the deaf is established in Kentucky.
1825–50	Teachers of blind students, often blind graduates of residential schools, are prepared through apprenticeship programs during this period.
1827	James Gall publishes *First Book for Teaching the Art of Reading to the Blind,* the first English-language work in raised type.
1829	The first U.S. patent for a typewriter is issued.
1829	Louis Braille publishes an explanation of his embossed dot code, which was inspired by Barbier.
1829	The New England Asylum for the Blind (later the Perkins School for the Blind) is incorporated in Watertown, Massachusetts.
1831	The New York Institution for the Education of the Blind (now the New York Institute for Special Education) is incorporated.

(continued on next page)

Chronology of Events (Continued)

1831	Samuel Gridley Howe becomes the director of the New England Asylum for the Blind (now the Perkins School for the Blind).
1832	The first students are accepted at the Perkins School for the Blind and the New York Institution for the Blind.
1832	The Scottish Art Society offers a prize for the best and most practical system of embossing for people who are blind. A medal is awarded to Dr. Edmund Fry for his modified Roman form.
1832	The Pennsylvania Institution for the Instruction of the Blind (later the Overbrook School for the Blind) is founded.
1833	*Gospel of St. Mark,* the first book in raised print in the United States, is printed in Philadelphia.
1834	Louis Braille perfects the literary braille code.
1835	*Acts of the Apostles* is the first book embossed in Boston Line Type, a tactile code developed by Samuel Gridley Howe.
1836	Henry Martyn Taylor devises a tangible mathematics apparatus for computations.
1837	The Perkins School for the Blind establishes a printing plant, later named the Howe Memorial Press.
1837	Ohio establishes the first state-supported residential school for the blind.
1837	Laura Bridgman, the first child who is deaf-blind to be educated, is admitted to Perkins School for the Blind.
1839	A state-supported normal school for training general education teachers is started in Lexington, Massachusetts.
1842	Charles Dickens describes his visit to the Perkins School for the Blind in *American Notes.*
1847	Dr. Robert Moon develops his raised-line type, referred to as Moon Type.
1851	Herman von Helmholtz invents the ophthalmoscope.
1852	Boston Line Type becomes the predominant reading medium for people who are blind in the United States until braille, a point system, is later adopted.
1852	Louis Braille dies of pulmonary consumption.
1854	France officially adopts braille as a reading mode for people who are blind.
1855	Dr. William Moon and the Moon Society volunteers begin touring Britain and instructing people who are blind in reading in their homes.
1858	The Kentucky legislature establishes the American Printing House for the Blind (APH) as an offshoot of the Kentucky School for the Blind.

(continued on next page)

Chronology of Events (Continued)

1859–1952	John Dewey, the American educator and philosopher, advocates individualized learning and direct experience as the tenets for educational programs.
1860	The Missouri School for the Blind becomes the first institute in the United States to use braille.
1866	Samuel Gridley Howe, the first director of the Perkins School for the Blind, expresses concern about segregated education for students who are blind in residential schools.
1868	The first conference of Executives of American Schools for the Deaf is held.
1868	William B. Wait develops the New York Point raised-dot system at the New York Institution for the Blind.
1868	Braille is accepted in Great Britain.
1871	The first pamphlet on braille music notation is published.
1871	Stereotype plates are created for braille production.
1871	The American Association of Instructors of the Blind (AAIB) is founded and endorses New York Point.
1872	The Scottish Education Act calls for educating children who are blind with sighted children.
1873	The first Congress of Teachers of the Blind is held in Vienna.
1876	Alexander Graham Bell invents the telephone.
1877	Thomas Edison invents the tin foil phonograph and lists "Books for Blind People" on his patent application.
1878	Joel W. Smith at the Perkins School for the Blind develops the American raised-point system, modeled closely on braille, which becomes the foundation for American braille.
1880	Helen Keller is born in Tuscumbia, Alabama, on June 27.
1880	Anne Sullivan enters the Perkins School for the Blind.
1882	The Pennsylvania Institution starts an organized kindergarten for students who are blind.
1887	Anne Sullivan gives Helen Keller, age 7, an understanding of language.
1887	The Perkins School for the Blind founds a kindergarten for babies who are blind.
1888	The International Congress for Standardization of Braille Music Notation is held in Cologne, Germany.
1891	Thomas H. Gallaudet begins the first teacher training program for students who are deaf.

(continued on next page)

Chronology of Events (Continued)

1892	Frank Hall and Gustav A. Sieber develop the braillewriter, the first mechanical device for writing braille.
1893	The first nursery for neglected babies who are blind is started in Hartford, Connecticut.
1893	The Blind and Deaf Children Act in England provides compulsory elementary education for children aged 5–16.
1895	The American Blind People's Higher Education and General Improvement Association (later the American Association of Workers for the Blind) is founded.
1895	The Royal Normal College in England starts a college to train persons who are blind as teachers.
1898	Alexander Graham Bell states: "Handicapped children have a right to an education in the public school."
1898	The first day school for the blind is established in England.
1899	The braille shorthand system is developed.
1899	Chicago establishes the first day school classes for "crippled children."
1900	Wisconsin and Michigan authorize subsidies for the excess cost of classes for students who are deaf in public schools, the first financial support for any children with disabilities.
1900	The Tactile Print Investigating Committee is appointed to resolve the problem of numerous tactile reading systems.
1900	Day school classes for students with visual impairments are established in Chicago.
1902	A library and reading room for people who are blind opens in San Francisco.
1903	*The Story of My Life,* by Helen Keller, is published.
1904	Helen Keller, the first deaf-blind person to earn a college degree, graduates from Radcliffe College in Cambridge, Massachusetts.
1905	The American Blind People's Higher Education and General Improvement Association becomes the American Association of Workers for the Blind (AAWB).
1905	Britain adopts the uniform braille code.
1905	The New York Association for the Blind (now Lighthouse International) is founded.
1905	The Uniform Type Committee is formed.
1907	Helen Keller, who had learned four embossed codes, pleads for a single code.
1907	The first issue of *Outlook for the Blind* is published in April by Charles Campbell (and later by the American Foundation for the Blind); it becomes *The New Outlook for the Blind* in January 1952 and then the *Journal of Visual Impairment & Blindness* in January 1976.

(continued on next page)

Chronology of Events (Continued)

1908	The first class for "high myopes" begins in London.
1909	The First White House Conference on Children and Youth is held.
1909	Robert B. Irwin organizes braille reading classes in Cleveland public schools.
1909	Ohio appoints the first state supervisor of education for children who are visually impaired.
1910	The Arthur Sunshine Home and Kindergarten for Blind Babies opens in Summit, New Jersey.
1911	New York State makes education compulsory for students who are blind.
1912	Students who are blind in public day-school classes become eligible to receive APH materials.
1913	Robert B. Irwin uses 36-point type in books for "partially seeing" students.
1913	The first classes for "partially seeing" students are started in Roxbury, Massachusetts, and Cleveland, Ohio.
1913	The Uniform Type Committee recommends a system based on British braille.
1914	Robert B. Irwin and H.H. Goddard adapt the Binet Test for Blind Pupils.
1915	The National Society for the Prevention of Blindness (NSPB) is founded.
1916	Samuel P. Hayes establishes departments of psychological research at Overbrook and Perkins.
1918	The University of California offers the first university preparation course for teachers of students who are blind.
1918	APH adopts Revised Standard English Braille for textbooks.
1919	*The Blind, Their Condition, and the Work Done for Them in the United States,* by Harry Best, is published.
1920	Barr, Stroud, and Fournier d'Albe patent the optophone, the first reading machine for people who are blind, which translates printed letters into musical tones.
1921	Edward E. Allen establishes a formal teacher training program at Perkins School for the Blind.
1921	The American Foundation for the Blind (AFB) is founded.
1921	Teachers College at Columbia University offers the first summer program for teachers of students who are partially sighted.
1921	The American Red Cross adopts braille transcribing as part of its volunteer service.
1922	The Council for Exceptional Children (CEC) is founded.
1923	APH expands its tangible apparatus facilities.

(continued on next page)

Chronology of Events (Continued)

1925	Peabody College for Teachers establishes the first summer preparation program for teachers of students who are blind.
1925	The Perkins-Harvard course for teachers gives graduate college credits.
1925	The Carnegie Corporation funds an APH study of braille interpoint equipment.
1927	Frank Dyer patents his process for producing long-playing records.
1928	The first issue of *Teacher's Forum* is published by AFB.
1928	The crusade begins to eliminate ophthalmia neonatorum by putting silver nitrate in newborn babies' eyes.
1928	AFB supervises the distribution of radios to citizens who are blind, the foundation's first direct service for these individuals.
1929	The Seeing Eye, the first dog guide school in the United States, is incorporated.
1930	The White House Conference on Child Health and Protection assigns a committee to study the needs of exceptional children. Recommendations include the establishment of braille day-school classes throughout the country and special attention directed toward vocational adjustments, social training, and kindergarten training.
1930	The National Institute for the Blind introduces a high-speed rotary press for embossed type.
1930	NSPB and AFB cooperate on a standard eye examination report.
1930	The Hayes-Binet test for pupils who are blind is developed by Samuel P. Hayes.
1931	The Library of Congress establishes the National Library Service for the Blind and Physically Handicapped and begins to distribute braille materials and phonograph records to readers who are blind in accordance with the Pratt-Smoot Act of 1930.
1931	The first World Conference on Work for the Blind is held in New York.
1931	Three states issue certificates to special education teachers of children who are blind.
1932	AFB develops Talking Books, long-playing records and playback machines.
1932	AAIB establishes a committee to develop a teacher certification program.
1932	Standard English Braille is adopted as uniform type by the American and British Uniform Type Committees.
1933	APH adopts Standard English Braille Grade 2 for junior and senior high school textbooks.
1933	*The Blind in School and Society,* by Thomas Cutsforth, a doctoral candidate who is blind, is published by AFB.
1934	The first Talking Books on long-playing records are produced.
1934	The American Medical Association (AMA) defines legal blindness.

(continued on next page)

Chronology of Events (Continued)

1934	AAIB establishes teacher certification guidelines.
1934	Dog guides are permitted on the day coaches of three major railroads.
1935	Columbia University starts a year-round program for teachers of students who are blind at Teachers College.
1935	The Social Security Act is passed. It adopts the AMA's definition of legal blindness.
1935	President Franklin Delano Roosevelt signs an executive order allotting funds to the Library of Congress to develop a Talking Book machine.
1936	APH produces recorded material.
1937	Ralph G. Hurlin develops a formula to estimate the population of people who are blind.
1938	AAIB sets up its teacher certification program.
1938	Father Thomas Carroll begins work at the Catholic Guild for the Blind.
1939	The dictaphone is used as an instructional aid in sight-saving classes.
1939	Visagraph, a device that produces raised print or diagrams, is demonstrated at the World's Fair by Robert E. Naumburg.
1939–45	Berthold Lowenfeld explores the educational role of recorded books and demonstrates the value of Talking Books in the teaching process.
1940	The National Federation of the Blind (NFB) is founded.
1941	The growing incidence of visual impairments in premature infants, later identified as retrolental fibroplasia (RLF), is noted in infants.
1942	Alfred Kestenbaum, a physician, develops the microlense, a simple reading device.
1942	Interim Hayes-Binet Tests for the Blind are developed.
1942	The first textbook on children with low vision, *Education and Health of the Partially Sighted Child* by Winifred Hathaway, is published.
1944	Richard E. Hoover at the Valley Forge Hospital and Russell Williams at Hines Hospital and others develop long-cane mobility techniques.
1944	Retrolental fibroplasia (now known as retinopathy of prematurity) is identified by Dr. Theodore Terry and others at Massachusetts Eye and Ear Infirmary.
1945	The National Braille Association is established.
1947	APH begins the regular publication of large-type books.
1947	The Perkins Brailler, an improvement over older methods, is designed and developed by David Abraham of Howe Press.
1948	The Council for Education of the Partially Seeing is established as a division of the Council for Exceptional Children.
1948	Recording for the Blind (now Recording for the Blind and Dyslexic) is established.

(continued on next page)

Chronology of Events (Continued)

1950	*Blindness: Modern Approaches to the Unseen Environment,* by Paul Zahl is published.
1950	*Vision: Its Development in Infant and Child,* by Arnold Gesell, is published.
1951	First issue of the *International Journal for the Education of the Blind* (now *Education of the Visually Handicapped*) is published by AAIB.
1953	The Nemeth Braille Mathematics Code is established.
1953	Father Thomas Carroll holds the Gloucester Conference to define the role and training of mobility instructors.
1953	The first low vision clinics open at the New York Lighthouse and the Industrial Home for the Blind.
1953	National Aid to the Visually Handicapped, a private organization dedicated solely to producing large-type textbooks for school-age children, is founded in San Francisco.
1954	A study links RLF to high oxygen treatment in premature babies.
1954	The National Association for Visually Handicapped (NAVH) is founded.
1954	The U.S. Office of Education holds a conference on the qualifications and preparation of teachers of exceptional children.
1954	The *Pine Brook Report* (from AFB) identifies different educational options for students who are blind or visually impaired and the type of teacher preparation required.
1955	The Perkins School for the Blind starts the first training program for teachers of deaf-blind students in association with Boston University.
1956	The Subnormal Vision Clinic (later called the Low Vision Center) is established at the Maryland Workshop for the Blind.
1956	Educational materials from APH are made available to day-school pupils.
1957	The thermoform machine is developed to reproduce raised-line diagrams or graphics.
1957	The Visotoner, a reading device that produces sounds for letters, and Visotactor, a reading machine that produces vibrations to the fingers, are developed.
1957	Peabody College for Teachers of Vanderbilt University in Nashville sets up a year-round program for teachers of students who are blind.
1957	The Industrial Home for the Blind reports on its optical aids service and defines the basic model for what has become the standard low vision service.
1957	Richard Hoover, an ophthalmologist, presents the functional definitions of blindness.
1957	The *Maxfield-Buccholz Social Maturity Scale for Blind Preschool Children* is published.
1958	*A Psychiatrist Works with Blindness,* by Louis Cholden, is published by AFB.

(continued on next page)

Chronology of Events (Continued)

1959	The American Optometric Association establishes the Committee on Aid to the Partially Sighted.
1960	Boston College starts the first university program for O&M instructors.
1961	Gerald Fonda evaluates telescopic spectacles for mobility.
1961	Father Thomas Carroll publishes *Blindness: What It Is, What It Does and How to Live With It.*
1961	The American Council of the Blind (ACB) is founded.
1962	The concept of the instructional materials centers is formulated through the recommendations of a presidential task force.
1962	The Model Reporting Area for Blindness Statistics begins to publish data on the incidence (new cases) and prevalence (existing cases) of blindness.
1963	Computers are adapted to produce braille outputs.
1963	Dr. Ruth Kaarlela coordinates the first graduate Home Teacher of the Adult Blind training program (later Department of Blind Rehabilitation) at Western Michigan University, Kalamazoo.
1963	Natalie Barraga studies the increased visual behavior of children and develops a visual efficiency scale and sequential learning activities and materials for training children with low vision.
1964–65	The rubella (German measles) epidemic in pregnant women causes handicapping conditions, including deafness and blindness in babies.
1965	The prototype of the Sonicguide (the Kay binaural sensory aid) is invented.
1965	Samuel C. Ashcroft, Carol Halliday, and Natalie Barraga replicate Barraga's original study on visual efficiency.
1966	The CEC Project on Professional Standards defines *visually handicapped* to include both blind and partially sighted.
1966	The report of the Commission on Standards and Accreditation of Services for the Blind attempts to set standards for services to people who are visually impaired.
1967	Ruth Holmes replicates Barraga's 1963 study (published in 1964) and reports on the visual efficiency training of adolescents with low vision.
1967	San Francisco State University and Florida State University establish the first programs to train mobility instructors of children.
1967	The National Accreditation Council for Agencies Serving the Blind and Visually Handicapped (NAC) is founded.
1968	Helen Keller dies.
1968	AAIB becomes the Association for Education of the Visually Handicapped (AEVH).

(continued on next page)

Chronology of Events (Continued)

1968	Certification of mobility instructors by AAWB begins.
1968	Federally funded deaf-blind programs are established.
1969	*The Making of Blind Men, A Study of Adult Socialization,* by Robert Scott, is published by the Russell Sage Foundation.
1969	Samuel Genensky, a mathematician with low vision, and his colleagues at the Rand Corporation in Santa Monica, California, report on their development of closed-circuit television (CCTV).
1970	Natalie Barraga's *Teachers Guide for the Development of Visual Learning Abilities and Utilization of Low Vision,* including the Visual Efficiency Scale, is published by APH.
1970	The U.S. Office of Education sponsors Low Vision Conferences around the United States.
1970	Eleanor E. Faye's book, *The Low Vision Patient: Clinical Experience with Adults and Children,* is published.
1970	CCTVs become commercially available.
1970	The Mowat sensor is developed.
1971	The Optacon tactile reading machine is developed by John Linvill and James C. Bliss.
1971	"Blindness and Services to the Blind in the United States: A Report of the Subcommittee on Rehabilitation, National Institution on Neurological Diseases and Blindness" is published by the Organization for Social and Technical Innovation.
1971	Virginia Bishop's textbook, *Teaching the Visually Limited Child,* is published.
1972	Western Michigan University institutes the first required course on low vision as part of its program for preparing O&M personnel.
1972	The Banks pocket brailler is developed by Alfred Banks in San Diego, California, and produced by International Business Machines.
1972	Head Start programs are mandated to take children with disabilities.
1973	Berthold Lowenfeld's book, *The Visually Handicapped Child in School,* is published.
1974	CEC revises Professional Standards and Guidelines in Special Education.
1975	The talking calculator with audio and visual output is developed.
1975	The first microcomputer is developed.
1975	Eleanor E. Faye and Clare Hood's book, *Low Vision,* is published.
1976	Large-print calculators become available.
1976	Four states require by law that all general classroom teachers must be prepared to include exceptional pupils in their classes.

(continued on next page)

Chronology of Events (Continued)

1976	Raymond C. Kurzweil develops the Kurzweil Reader, a prototype translator of printed material into synthesized speech.
1976	*The Unseen Minority: A Social History of Blindness in the United States,* by Frances Koestler, is published.
1976	*New Outlook for the Blind* is renamed the *Journal of Visual Impairment & Blindness.*
1977	The White House Conference on Handicapped Individuals is held.
1977	Susan Jay Spungin publishes her teachers' competence study.
1977	The Association of Instructional Resource Centers for the Visually Handicapped is founded.
1977	The first mass-market personal computers are launched.
1978	The Rehabilitation Services Administration of the U.S. Department of Education (RSA) funds university O&M programs for all disabilities ("Generic O&M") at the University of Wisconsin, Madison (funding discontinued in 1983).
1979	The American Council of Blind Parents is formed by ACB.
1979	The Department of Health, Education & Welfare becomes two separate departments—Education and Health and Human Services; RSA is transferred to the Department of Education.
1979	The first Special Study Institute for State Education Consultants for the Visually Handicapped is sponsored by the University of Michigan with federal funds.
1980	The National Association of Parents of the Visually Impaired (NAPVI) is established.
1980	*Foundations of Orientation and Mobility,* edited by Richard L. Welsh and Bruce B. Blasch, is published by AFB.
1981	Autoimmunodeficiency syndrome (AIDS) is identified.
1981	Viewscan, a reading aid, and the Viewscan Text System (VTS) are developed.
1982	The North American Conference on Visually Handicapped Infants and Preschool Children is held.
1983	The *Rehabilitation Optometry Journal* (later renamed the *Journal of Vision Rehabilitation*) is founded by Randall Jose.
1983	*Understanding Low Vision,* edited by Randall Jose, is published by AFB.
1983	*Vision Research: A National Plan: 1983–87,* is published by the National Eye Institute and includes a panel on low vision.
1983	The Pennsylvania College of Optometry offers a master's degree in low vision rehabilitation.
1983	The first braille embosser attachment to a microcomputer is developed.

(continued on next page)

Chronology of Events (Continued)

1983	Project C.A.B.L.E. (Computer Access for Blind Employment) is established at the Carroll Center.
1983	AFB assumes the sponsorship of the Special Study Institutes for Educational Leadership personnel, which is renamed the Josephine L. Taylor Leadership Institute.
1984	AAWB and AEVH merge as the Association for Education and Rehabilitation of Blind and Visually Impaired (AERBVI).
1984	The Peabody Preschool O&M Project (HCEEP Model Demonstration Project) is funded.
1984	Microcomputers become widely used by people with visual impairments.
1984	NFB creates the Division of Parents of Blind Children.
1985	The World Council for the Welfare of the Blind and the International Federation of the Blind merge as the World Blind Union.
1986	AFB opens the National Technology Center.
1989	*The Profession of Orientation and Mobility in the 1980s,* by William Jacobson, is published by AFB.
1989	The World Wide Web revolutionizes communication through the Internet.
1990	*Preschool Orientation and Mobility Screening,* by B. Dodson-Burk and E. Hill, is published by Division 9 of AER.
1993	First bienniel "Getting in Touch with Literacy" conference is held in Little Rock, Arkansas.
1995	The National Agenda for the Education of Children and Youths with Visual Impairments, Including Those With Multiple Disabilities, is endorsed by organizations nationwide.
1996	*Foundations of Low Vision,* edited by Anne L. Corn and Alan J. Koenig, is published by AFB.
1997	The second edition of *Foundations of Orientation and Mobility,* edited by Bruce B. Blasch, William R. Wiener, and Richard L. Welsh, is published by AFB.
1998	The Virginia Murray Sowell Center for Research and Education in Visual Impairment is established at Texas Tech University.
2000	Academy for certification of Vision Rehabilitation and Education Professionals is established.
2000	American Foundation for the Blind National Literacy Center established.

Compiled by Geraldine T. Scholl, Professor Emeritus, School of Education, The University of Michigan, Ann Arbor.

A Summary of Legislation

1827   P.L. 19-8, the first federal legislation concerning persons who are blind, provides land in Florida and Kentucky for facilities for people with disabilities.

1857   P.L. 34-46 establishes the Columbia Institution for the Deaf and Dumb in the District of Columbia.

1879   P.L. 45-186, the Congressional Act of 1879, An Act to Promote the Education of the Blind, authorizes funds for the American Printing House for the Blind (APH).

1894   The Columbia Institution for the Deaf and Dumb, Collegiate Division, is renamed Gallaudet College.

1906   P.L. 59-288 modifies the requirements of P.L. 45-186.

1911   The National Library for the Blind is incorporated in the District of Columbia.

1919   P.L. 66-24 provides additional funds to APH.

1931   The Pratt-Smoot Act (P.L. 71-787) provides funding for literature for adults who are blind.

1941   P.L. 77-270 amends P.L. 45-186, an act promoting the circulation of reading matter for persons who are blind, to include braillewriters and other appliances when mailed for repair.

1949   P.L. 81-290 provides for the sending of braillewriters to or from persons who are blind at the same rates as provided, regardless of the purpose for which they are mailed.

1958   P.L. 85-926 provides funding for personnel preparation in mental retardation.

1961   P.L. 87-276 provides funds for preparing teachers of persons who are hearing-impaired and speech-impaired.

1963   P.L. 88-164 extends funding for personnel preparation for all categories of children with disabilities.

1964   P.L. 88-164, Title II, supports universities in creating departments for teachers of exceptional children.

1965   P.L. 89-313, Title I, amends the Elementary and Secondary Education Act to provide support for education of children with disabilities in state-operated and state-supported schools and in hospitals.

1968   P.L. 90-489 amends the Public Health Service Act to provide for the establishment of the National Eye Institute in the National Institutes of Health.

1968   P.L. 90-538, the Handicapped Children's Early Education Assistance Act, authorizes preschool and early education programs for children with disabilities.

1968   P.L. 91-61 provides for a National Center on Educational Media and Materials for the Handicapped.

1969   P.L. 89-750, Title VI, is amended to establish programs for students with learning disabilities.

1972   P.L. 92-318, the Education Amendments of 1972, prohibits discrimination against people who are blind.

(continued on next page)

A Summary of Legislation (Continued)

1973 Section 504 of the Vocational Rehabilitation Act Amendments of 1973 prohibits discrimination on the basis of disability in organizations that receive federal funds.

1975 P.L. 94-142, the Education for All Handicapped Children Act, guarantees a free appropriate public education, with special education, related services, and Individualized Education Programs (IEPs), for each child with a disability.

1976 *Taylor vs. Maryland School for the Blind* affirms the right of educators to make educational decisions as long as the decisions are not arbitrary or capricious.

1976 P.L. 94-553 provides for the Register of Copyrights to establish, by regulation, standardized forms and procedures by which copyright owners may voluntarily grant to the Library of Congress a license to reproduce the copyrighted material by means of braille or similar tactile symbols or phonorecords or both and to distribute them solely for the use of people who are blind or physically disabled.

1976 Vocational education legislation is expanded to include children with disabilities.

1978 P.L. 95-602, the Rehabilitation Act of 1978, authorizes funds to integrate children with disabilities into recreational programs and to provide rehabilitation for persons with severe disabilities for whom employment may not be the primary goal.

1984 P.L. 98-221, the Rehabilitation Acts Amendment of 1984, provides for the operation of the Helen Keller National Center for Deaf-Blind Youths and Adults.

1986 P.L. 99-457, the Education for All Handicapped Children Act Amendments, extends mandated special education programs of P.L. 94-142 to children aged 3–5 and initiates early intervention programs for infants and toddlers from birth to age 2.

1988 P.L. 100-630 makes certain technical and conforming amendments to the Education for All Handicapped Children Act and the Rehabilitation Act of 1973.

1990 The Americans with Disabilities Act (P.L. 101-336) prohibits discrimination on the basis of disability.

1990 P.L. 101-476 strengthens the Education for All Handicapped Children Act, and renames it the Individuals with Disabilities Education Act (IDEA).

1997 P.L. 105-17 strengthens IDEA, affirms that children with visual impairments will receive instruction in braille unless the IEP team decides otherwise, and adds orientation and mobility as a related service under the act.

Compiled by Geraldine T. Scholl, Professor Emeritus, School of Education, The University of Michigan, Ann Arbor.

CHAPTER 2

Visual Impairment

Kathleen M. Huebner

KEY POINTS

◆ The population of students with visual impairments is diverse.

◆ Visual impairment among children is considered a low-prevalence disability.

◆ Perceptions and misunderstandings about visual impairments have a great impact on the way in which people who are visually impaired are treated by others.

◆ It is important for teachers of students with visual impairments to have a clear understanding of correct and appropriate terminology.

◆ Professionals who are concerned with the education of students who are visually impaired must work to ensure that accurate child count data is available regarding students who are blind or visually impaired.

Students who are blind or visually impaired are a heterogeneous group. Just like those without visual impairments, they have unique, individual characteristics; they differ in intellectual ability, developmental rate, social competence, and other factors. Their one common characteristic is that they are all visually impaired, that is, they have less-than-fully functional visual systems that can interfere with expected progress in general education programs unless they receive specialized

instruction. However, even within this common characteristic, there are differences. Students differ in the nature of their visual impairments, the extent of their visual capability, and their ability to use whatever vision they have. Some students have clear vision with significant field losses, as if they are looking through the tube of a paper towel or a straw. Others may have significantly diminished acuities, or blurry vision, as if they are looking through waxed paper, and have full fields of vision. (See Chapter 3 in this volume for more detailed information on visual impairments.) No two children with visual impairments see in the same way. In fact, the nature of visual impairment is such that children can have identical acuities and fields of vision but may not see in the same way. Furthermore, their personalities, motivation, cognitive abilities, and degree to which they have learned to use their vision vary and affect their visual performance. Some students naturally take full advantage of their existing vision, whereas others do not and may benefit from learning to do so; modifications and interventions may be required for them to be able to take full advantage of educational experiences.

Most students with visual impairments attend school and receive specialized educational services in their home communities through a variety of service models, such as in resource rooms or self-contained classrooms or from itinerant teachers or teacher consultants, whereas others attend special schools for children who are visually impaired. (See Chapter 9 in this volume.)

This chapter presents definitions of common terms related to visual impairment. Although there may be some minor differences in terminology from one geographic area to another, the terms and definitions given here are widely accepted. Individuals, various professionals, departments of education, the medical community, and parent and consumer organizations, as well as policy makers, often define terms used in special education differently. Since teachers of students with visual impairments provide services in many different educational settings, it is important for them to learn the meaning of the terms used in each setting. In short, to communicate effectively and to plan and implement educational programs, members of educational teams and others need to understand specific terms and to note and clarify subtle differences in definitions and descriptions among settings and from one school district or state to another. Furthermore, to meet each student's unique individual needs, teachers of students who are visually impaired usually work with one student at a time. To do so, they need to know all the factors that influence each student's learning. Knowledge of the terms and definitions included in this chapter will help teachers understand these individual factors.

It is also important to understand the nature of this population as a whole as it relates to how instruction is provided, to how students learn, and to issues of teachers' caseloads and service delivery options. (See Chapter 9 in this volume, for a fuller discussion of these issues.) Thus this chapter presents information on the demographics (statistics about the population as a whole) of students who are visually impaired, including those whose visual impairments are accompanied by additional disabilities. It includes basic information on child counts, or how the number of children who are visually impaired are identified and counted, particularly for government funding of specialized educational services.

In addition, the opinions and attitudes of the general public toward people who are blind or visually impaired can have a significant effect on an individual's education, socialization, opportunities, and employment, and misconceptions perpetuate inappropriate stereotypes and stigmas. Therefore, the chapter gives examples of how the mass media (television, radio, movies, newspapers, and magazines) continue to present misconceptions of and myths about individuals with visual impairments and presents factual explanations that can be used to counteract these myths. Teachers of students with visual impairments have a responsibility to educate the public not only about the needs of students, but also about the students' abilities, potential, talents, complexity, and individuality.

UNDERSTANDING VISUAL IMPAIRMENT

An understanding of visual impairment is rooted in individual life experiences. Some people have interacted with family members, friends, or neighbors who are blind. Others have only seen or read about fictional characters and real people who were visually impaired in films, books, and other media. Most people have played childhood games, such as pin the tail on the donkey or blind man's bluff, that they thought simulated blindness because they had to close their eyes or wear blindfolds. Such limited and nondirect experiences, however, provide little basis for a true understanding of the nature and effects of blindness.

During their university course work, teachers and other professionals in the field may wear blindfolds or goggles with various lenses to simulate visual impairments. This is intended to provide a better understanding of how people function with limited or no vision. These simulations provide only temporary situations in which vision cannot be used and do not give people who are sighted a true indication of what it is like to be permanently visually impaired. People who are sighted have a visual memory of what things, places, and people look like even during these simulations.

Nevertheless, simulations help professionals gain some understanding of the impact of visual impairment on learning in general, and in specific skill areas, such as social, communication, independent travel (orientation and mobility [O&M]), daily living, personal, home and financial management, recreation and leisure, and employment. They help professionals understand how different environmental factors influence visual effectiveness and efficiency and the emotional impact of visual impairments. Such experiences help teachers and other professionals anticipate what students need to learn and to better understand students' potential strengths and frustrations.

Those who have some knowledge of visual impairment would generally describe blindness as the inability to see. Some use the terms *total blindness, blindness,* and *legal blindness* interchangeably (Rosenblum & Erin 1998), yet these terms do not mean exactly the same things and the differences are important. The differences among these terms are discussed later in this chapter.

COMMON TERMS AND IMPLICATIONS

Social acceptance and rejection of terminology changes over time. For example, many years ago, individuals with mental retardation were classified as and referred to by such terms as *idiot, moron,* or *feebleminded.* These and other terms were later determined to be demeaning, and the terminology was changed to *mentally retarded.* Over time, *retarded* was used in derogatory ways by people in the general public to refer to someone whom they considered to be "stupid" or incompetent. Although the term *mental retardation* is still officially accepted by the Council for Exceptional Children and the American Association on Mental Retardation, the term *developmentally delayed* is widely used in an attempt to avoid the perceived negative connotation of *retardation,* and the term *cognitively impaired* is used to distinguish those who have learning disabilities (disabilities related to thinking or processing information) but are

not developmentally delayed. Similarly, *deaf and dumb* was recognized as being inaccurate because the inability to speak is not always associated with the inability to hear, and *dumb* had popularly come to mean unintelligent; thus, the terms for this population that are most widely used today are *deaf* or *hard of hearing.*

In the field of visual impairment, the terminology has also changed because of the desire to refine and specify characteristics. Terms of the past included *medically blind, economically blind, braille blind, partially seeing, partially blind, residual vision, visually limited, visually defective,* and *vocationally blind.* Each of these terms had specific definitions and applications, and many were used to categorize and demonstrate eligibility for government-funded services. Today, most descriptors do not provide specific information about what a person can or cannot see or the quality of a person's sight and do not indicate how functional vision may change because of physical or environmental circumstances. For teachers and others who provide services to children with visual impairments, it is essential to understand the functional implications of each student's visual impairment (the impact of the visual impairment on an individual's daily life), as well as the medical diagnosis and clinical characteristics of the student's vision.

Today some professionals and parents believe that it is important to use "person-first" language. The thought behind person-first language is that when writing or speaking, the important words should be written or said first, and that the person is more important than his or her disability. Thus "a child who is blind" is used rather than "a blind child." A term such as "the blind" is unacceptable to those who support person-first language since this term essentially defines a person by his or her disability alone. While there is no universal agreement among professionals, parents, and individuals with disabilities regarding the use of person-first language, it is important for professionals to be sensitive in their written and spoken expression when referring to persons who are visually impaired. Studies of individuals with disabilities have been conducted to determine their preferences regarding how they wish to be described. One survey of 15 year olds who were visually impaired found no significant differences in language preference. However, a common factor that was found was the desire "to be treated as normal and not to emphasize real or perceived limitations" (Abagio & Downing, 1990, p. 220). Nevertheless, students or their family members often prefer a particular term and may be offended by others that they believe are not appropriate; for example, some people who are severely visually impaired are offended when they are referred to as being blind. Thus, professionals need to respect students' and families' preferences and should not impose their own preferred terms. Furthermore, throughout the educational careers of students who are visually impaired, the terminology is bound to change for a variety of reasons (such as consideration for students and their parents and use of new terminology in legislation). It is the responsibility of professionals to stay up to date, recognize when changes are needed, and influence and support positive changes.

Adventitious and Congenital Loss of Vision

Partly because all people learn from the experiences of seeing, it is critical for teachers and orientation and mobility (O&M) specialists to know whether individual students ever had useful vision. (O&M specialists are professionals who teach children with visual impairments to travel safely and confidently.) Two terms are generally used to describe when a person first lost his or her vision: *adventitious* and *congenital.*

Adventitious means that the impairment or condition was acquired after birth, generally as a result of an accident or disease. The term is used to refer to the loss of vision after *visual memory* (the ability to remember what objects, places, and people look like) is established, generally by age 5 (Lowenfeld, 1971; Sardegna & Otis, 1991). Students who had some vision until they were 5 years old are likely to have some visual memory and will use it to learn. Thus, teaching new concepts,

strategies, skills, and information can be built on their visual memory, as well as their senses other than sight (including hearing, touch, and smell). Therefore, it is important to know when a child became visually impaired and if he or she has visual memory, since this information will affect the child's learning style and the teaching styles that are used.

Congenital means before or at birth. In the case of children who are visually impaired, the term refers to a loss of vision that occurred before visual memory was established. Students who never experienced vision or do not have visual memory learn differently from those who lost it adventitiously. They rely totally on senses other than vision to learn, and have nonvisual learning styles that require different teaching strategies. To help them learn, teachers need to emphasize the use of all their sensory potential. Students who have had poor visual acuity or restricted fields of vision since birth see the world differently from those who are adventitiously visually impaired or sighted and may miss some visual learning opportunities. Thus, they may require more direct instruction that involves tactile and other sensory input, since they do not have or may have limited visual observation skills and may miss or misunderstand some concepts and behaviors.

Many different terms convey information about the way a person sees. Although most have precise definitions, some have many different definitions and are sometimes carelessly or unknowingly misused.

Blindness

One term that is often misused is *blind.* Technically, the word *blind* is used to refer to individuals with *no* vision or only light perception (the ability to determine the presence or absence of light). A person with light perception will notice when he or she moves from a bright, sunlit entryway into a dark family room but will not be able to identify objects in the room visually. Some individuals are born blind (are congenitally blind), and others acquire blindness (are adventitiously blind). The term *blind* is sometimes misapplied to individuals who have some vision. It is not uncommon for members of the medical community to jot down "blind" when a person has substantial low vision, that is, a severe visual impairment that, even with the best correction, interferes with the performance of daily tasks. In some cases this error occurs because a person has multiple disabilities that severely impede his or her motor and communication skills or an eye care specialist does not have experience or training in assessing the visual ability and potential visual ability of this population.

The general public does not fully understand what constitutes blindness. Some people believe that if someone has a significant uncorrectable visual acuity, he or she is blind, although this is not necessarily the case. Everyone uses existing vision differently, but most people with visual impairments learn to take advantage of the vision they have, whereas blindness is equivalent to the *total* lack of vision. A person who is visually impaired can be blind under certain environmental conditions and have significant functional vision under other conditions, as occurs with night blindness. It is important, therefore, for teachers to observe each student's visual ability and potential even if the student's eye report simply says "blind."

Since *blind* has a harsh or negative connotation to some people, some prefer to use a less severe term, such as visually impaired, to describe all people who are visually impaired, even those for whom *blind* is appropriate. Professionals who work with individuals who are visually impaired must carefully examine their own attitudes about blindness and use terminology appropriately. *Blind* is an accurate and appropriate term to use when referring to total blindness. The word *blind* is only a physical description of a person's vision; it does not indicate the person's abilities, intelligence, personality, or interests.

Legal blindness is an arbitrary term that has limited value for educational or rehabilitation efforts, except that it is used to determine eligibility for some government-funded services (National Eye Institute, 1999). Legal blindness is defined as central visual acuity of 20/200 or less in the better eye with best correction or a central visual acuity

of more than 20/200 if there is a visual field defect in which the peripheral field is contracted to such an extent that the widest diameter of the visual field subtends an angular distance of no greater than 20 degrees. This clinical definition was developed by a committee of the Ophthalmology section of the American Medical Association (AMA), which was appointed to develop a scientific definition of blindness suitable for the development of government statutes. It was incorporated into the Social Security Act of 1935 (Schloss, 1963) and continues to be used to determine classifications of blindness and eligibility for services. The definition was later adopted by most industrialized nations. In countries that use the metric system, the visual acuity measure of 20/200 is written as 6/60.

To be legally blind one does not need to be totally blind. To be classified as legally blind, a person must have significantly reduced visual acuity or a significantly reduced visual field. The expression 20/200 refers to acuity, or the measurement of the sharpness of vision in relation to the ability to discriminate details (Canadian National Institute for the Blind, CNIB, 1999; Levack, 1994). It means that a person who is legally blind can see what a person with normal visual acuity sees at 200 feet only if the distance is reduced to no greater than 20 feet, even with the best possible correction through spectacles, contact lenses, or surgical intervention. If a person has a visual acuity of 20/20, or less but a visual field that is reduced to only 20 degrees, he or she can also be classified as legally blind. The typical person has a visual field of approximately 160 to 180 degrees.

Some of the government or other benefits determined by the classification of legal blindness include some special education and rehabilitation services, Internal Revenue Service income tax exemptions, free telephone directory assistance, transportation benefits, free mailing of materials related to visual impairment, and free library services (books and magazines on audiotape). The Canadian National Institute for the Blind (CNIB) (1999) uses the AMA definition of legal blindness but uses the term *registered blind* to determine eligibility for government-sponsored benefits. Most states in the United States no longer require that students meet the clinical definition of legal blindness to receive special education services; rather, they generally use the terms *educationally blind* or *low vision* to determine if students should be receiving specialized services. The term *functionally blind* is used by some state departments of education and special schools to describe children with or without usable vision who could benefit from instruction in braille reading and writing (Corn & Koenig, 1996). Definitions of legal blindness do not consider an individual's visual functioning (ability to use vision). Such factors as tolerance of light and contrast sensitivity, along with motivation, age of onset of the visual impairment, and cognitive ability, also need to be considered.

All states use specific terminology to determine if students are eligible for services from teachers who are certified in teaching students who are visually impaired and O&M specialists. Most states and special schools define a student as educationally blind when the student does not use vision as a primary sensory channel to obtain information for learning. Teachers of students with visual impairments should become familiar with the services, definitions, and regulations specific to the states or schools in which they are employed. They can obtain copies of federal and state laws and regulations from their state departments of education and program supervisors, and, in many states, can obtain special education and disability-specific handbooks of guidelines for services that have been developed for parents and teachers.

Low Vision

Low vision is defined as central visual acuity of 20/70 to 20/200 in the better eye with correction or a visual field of 20 to 40 degrees or less in the better eye with correction (Brilliant & Graboyes, 1999). According to the World Health Organization (WHO, 1999a), low vision is a visual acuity worse than 20/60 with the best correction or a significant field loss. Because of the emphasis on reading and

driving in modern societies, some researchers classify low vision as a visual acuity of less than 20/40 (National Eye Institute, 1999). Although no country has adopted a legal definition of low vision, WHO (quoted in Best & Corn, 1992, p. 309) uses the following clinical description of a person with low vision: "A person with low vision is one who has impairment of visual function, even after treatment and/or standard refractive correction, and has a visual acuity of less than 6/18 [the metric equivalent of 10/60] to light perception or a visual field of less than 10 degrees from the point of fixation, but who uses, or is potentially able to use, vision for the planning and/or execution of a task."

Clinical definitions—that is, definitions based on clinical measurements alone—do not consider an individual's efficiency and effectiveness in using existing vision or what the individual may actually see. They do not explain the visual functioning abilities or the deficits that can cause difficulties in communicating, traveling, cooking, using a computer, performing a job, or engaging in other daily living activities. Corn (1980, p. 3) stated that a person who has low vision is "still severely visually impaired after correction, but . . . may increase visual functioning through the use of optical [devices], nonoptical [devices], environmental modifications and/or techniques."

Some state departments of education and special schools define students with low vision as those with reduced visual acuities or limited visual fields that inhibit the optimal processing of information through the visual modality and generally requires modifications or specialized materials to enable them to benefit from the educational process. Teachers are compelled to consider students' level of visual functioning and potential visual functioning, as well as existing acuities or visual fields when planning educational programs.

Visual Impairment, Disability, and Handicap

Three frequently used terms in the fields of special education and rehabilitation whose definitions are not universally agreed upon are *impairment, disability,* and *handicap.* These terms are often used indiscriminately without regard to the differences in their meaning. *Impairment* generally refers to a recognizable defect, injury, deficiency, malfunctioning, or lessening of function of an organ or any part of the body, such as an eye (Sardegna & Otis, 1991). Impairments can be thought of as "disturbances at the level of origin" (WHO, 1999a). A study of professionals, university students in special education courses, and other university students concluded that there is a consistent positive perception of the term *visually impaired* (Rosenblum & Erin, 1998).

There are many definitions of *visual impairment.* However, most definitions are similar and include a statement regarding the impact of a student's decrease in visual functioning on the educational process or need for rehabilitation services. In most cases, the term *visual impairment* is used as an overall term that encompasses all people with decreased vision, regardless of the severity of their vision loss, as can be seen in the following example: "A pupil has a visual impairment which, even with correction, adversely affects a pupil's educational performance" (California State Department of Education, 1997, p. 82).

For the purposes of a national survey of middle-aged and older Americans (The Lighthouse, 1995), the respondents with impaired vision were classified as either severely visually impaired—"A person cannot recognize a friend at arm's length even when wearing glasses or contact lenses, or cannot read ordinary newspaper print even when wearing glasses or contact lenses, or reports poor or very poor vision even when wearing glasses or contact lenses, or is blind in both eyes" (p. 5) or moderately visually impaired—"A person cannot recognize a friend across a room (but can recognize them at arm's length), or has any other trouble seeing even when wearing glasses or contact lenses and is not otherwise severely impaired, or is blind in one eye" (p. 5). Levack (1994, p. 234) defined visual impairment as "identified organic differences in the visual system which are so severe that even after medical and conventional optical intervention, the student is unable to receive an appropriate education within the regular educational setting without special education services."

In some states, the term *visually impaired for educational purposes* is used to describe children whose visual condition is such that special provisions are necessary for their successful education. This definition or some variation of it is what state departments of education most often use to classify students for special education services from certified teachers of students with visual impairments and O&M specialists.

Disability is a physical, sensory, psychological, or neurological deviation that results in reduced function or loss of a particular body part or organ that makes a person unable to perform certain tasks (such as walking, reading, or shopping) in the same manner as most persons without disabilities. Disabilities are descriptions of the functional levels of the individuals experiencing the impairments (WHO, 1999a). One or more of five general areas may be affected: health, social-attitudinal, mobility, cognitive-intellectual, and communication (Kelly & Vergason, 1985; Sardegna & Otis, 1991). Rosenblum and Erin (1998) concluded from their study of perceptions of terms that *visually disabled* had negative connotations. At present, the term adopted by the federal government and used in the Individuals with Disabilities Education Act (IDEA) is *disability,* although states, schools, agencies, and individuals often use other terms.

Generally, *handicapped* is used to describe the result of any condition or deviation (mental, sensory, physical, or emotional) that inhibits or prevents achievement or acceptance (Kelly & Vergason, 1985; Sardegna & Otis, 1991). WHO (1999a) described a handicap as a disadvantage that results from an impairment or disability that limits or prevents the fulfillment of a chosen activity or role. Handicapped is a concept that is influenced by the society and culture in which a person lives.

Other Terms

Two additional terms that are commonly used in special education of students with visual impairments are *braille reader* and *print reader.* Literacy continues to be a valued competence in most societies—"the very key to prosperity, since [it] opens the way to information by tearing down barriers of myth and ignorance" (Schroeder, 1989, p. 290). Both braille and print facilitate equal opportunity for mastery of basic literacy skills (Caton, 1991). Some students use a variety of modes for reading, such as braille, print, optical devices, computers, and closed-circuit televisions.

A *print reader* (or visual reader) is someone who primarily uses large print or regular print with or without optical devices for reading, whereas a *braille reader* mainly uses braille for reading and writing. Some students benefit most from using print only, braille only, or large print and optical devices, while others need to use a variety of combinations of print and braille, depending on the visual and learning tasks.

A key element of the educational process for students with visual impairments is ongoing learning media assessments (an objective and systematic process determining learning and literacy media, Koenig & Holbrook, 1995) and subsequent decision making that influence educational programs and students' learning. Students need instruction in their preferred reading and writing modes and academic books and other materials in the media determined to be most appropriate. Goal 7 of the *National Agenda for the Education of Children and Youths with Visual Impairments, Including Those with Multiple Disabilities*, a document authored by a coalition of educators and parents to ensure effective educational services, states: "Access to developmental and educational services will include an assurance that instructional materials are available to students in the appropriate media and at the same time as their sighted peers" (Corn, Hatlen, Huebner, Ryan, & Siller, 1995, p. 21).

The terms defined here are only some of the many terms related to providing services to children who are visually impaired, including those with additional disabilities. What is important to remember is that since terms change over time, teachers of students with visual impairments need to know the specific terms used by states and special schools at a given time and use them appropriately. They must also learn and be sensitive to the terms that students and their families prefer, be sure that all members of students' educational teams are using the same definitions, and use the terms accurately in spoken and written communications.

BELIEFS AND MISCONCEPTIONS

In the United States and Canada, the word blind is used metaphorically in phrases, such as *blind faith, blind fate, blind destiny,* or *blind belief,* to refer to what is intangible, unobservable, and beyond human control. Metaphors frequently pair *blind* with negative concepts unrelated to the inability to see, as in such phrases as *blind greed, blind drunk, blind stupor,* and *robbing a person blind* (Rosenblum & Erin, 1998). Other phrases, such as *betting on the blind, blind date, blind alley,* and *blind chance,* imply a lack of information or excessive risk taking. The use of these phrases perpetuates negative preconceptions about individuals who are visually impaired because the phrases express limitations without regard for ability and do not reflect socially positive concepts.

Most people have little knowledge of the abilities of and challenges faced by people who are visually impaired. This fact is exemplified in a study of the attitudes of people who are sighted toward blindness (The Lighthouse, 1995). Of the 1,219 sighted participants, aged 45 and older, the majority feared blindness more than other physical impairment. (Mental or emotional illness was feared more than blindness.) Some participants expressed positive attitudes toward people with visual impairments and their capabilities, but when asked how they felt when they met people with visual impairments, 84 percent said they felt admiration; 26 percent, fear; and 23 percent, awkwardness or embarrassment. Even today, most people have misconceptions about what visual impairment is and how it affects learning, socialization, emotions, travel, finances, personal and household management, daily living skills, employment opportunities and employability, and family responsibilities. People who are visually impaired use numerous learning strategies, skills, and techniques to achieve daily and lifelong goals safely, independently, and confidently. These strategies, coupled with motivation, intelligence, perseverance, talent, experiences, and other qualities, should culminate in the realization of success as determined by individuals. (See Sidebar 2.1 for some of the more common misconceptions—myths and facts about people who are visually impaired.)

Influence of the Mass Media

Television and other mass media are major sources of information and influence and have the potential to shape the public's perception of individuals who are visually impaired. When media messages produce or confirm stereotypes and emphasize people's limitations, rather than abilities and alternative methods of accomplishing routine tasks, they reinforce misconceptions about visual impairments. These misconceptions have a negative impact on the ways in which the general public views and interacts with individuals of all ages who are visually impaired. As Jernigan (1999, p. 6) stated: "the real problem of blindness is not the loss of eyesight but the misconceptions and misunderstandings which exist. The public (whether it be the general public, the agencies, or the blind themselves) has created the problem and must accept the responsibility for solving it."

Several scholars have analyzed the mass media's characterizations of individuals who are visually impaired (Bina, 1993; Kent, 1989, 1990, 1996, 1997; Kirtley, 1975; Monbeck, 1973; Norden, 1994; Twersky, 1955; Wilkins, 1996). Monbeck (1973) identified the following traits that are typically assigned to fictional characters who are blind in literature: miserable, helpless, useless, maladjusted, mysterious, evil, pitiful, living in darkness, punished for past sins, to be feared and avoided, possessing superhuman powers and in-

sights, or morally superior. This is quite a range of characteristics, few of which most people would choose to emulate.

Norden (1994) and Wilkins (1996) examined the historical roots of stereotypes about people who are blind presented in visual images and films. They both found that people who are blind are depicted in similar ways in movies—as helpless, spiritually gifted, foolish, despairing, evil, saintly, exceptionally wise, easily tricked, vengeful, superstars, and heroes who overcome obstacles and have special sensory abilities. Clearly, these characterizations represent the extremes found in the general population; persons with visual impairments are rarely depicted as ordinary members of society. Norden concluded that the common concept of disability in 20th-century films is the isolation of sweet innocents, obsessive avengers, noble warriors, or superstars, all of whom are outsiders, set apart from general society. Similarly, Klobas (1988) concluded that television programs and films still tend to rely on mundane story lines and stereotypes of the past.

A review of headlines of newspaper articles provides a snapshot of how individuals who are blind are portrayed in daily newspapers throughout the United States. Examples include these: "Blind Golfer Has Feel for Game" (Ulman, 1997); "Though Blind, This Determined Boy Has His Sights on Success" (Brewer, 1998); "Blind Friend Makes Good Hiking Companion" (Brewer, 1997); "Margaret Smith Led Rich, Full Life Despite Blindness" (Cardenas, 1997); "Blindness Doesn't Hinder Expert Piano Mover" (Walton, 1998); "A Lesson in Perseverance. Dream Realized: Woman Reaches Goal of Teaching Despite Blindness" (Frankston, 1998); and "OSU Professor Hasn't Let Blindness Hinder Him" (Hernandez, 1997); "Blind Man is Struck and Killed by Van" (Orlando & Golson, 1998). These and similar headlines emphasize the individual's disability and, in most instances, place blindness before the person. Placing the disability first attracts readers, but it often carries an unspoken message of surprise or disbelief that the individual has succeeded or prospered in spite of his or her blindness.

SIDEBAR 2.1

Myths and Facts about Visual Impairment

MYTH	FACT
People who are blind have a sixth sense.	People who are blind do not have any additional senses. Some develop their ability to use and trust their other senses (such as hearing and touch) beyond that of persons who are sighted. Some individuals who are blind develop their hearing and tactile/kinesthetic senses to the point where they have "object perception" or "facial vision," that is, the ability to recognize the presence or absence of a wall in front of or beside them or of an overhead object, such as a marquee. People who are blind learn to hear the change in the quality of sounds between an open and a closed-in area. Some also feel changes in temperature and air pressure that people who are sighted do not generally notice. This ability is often misconstrued as a sixth sense.
People who are blind only see blackness or grayness.	The minority of people with visual impairments are totally blind (Brilliant & Graboyes, 1999). Those who are totally blind often report seeing a neutral gray, rather than blackness or light or dark. Some people who are blind report seeing flashes of colored light. In *The World I Live In,* Helen Keller (1908) reported seeing a white-darkness. Some people who are blind are able to distinguish the absence and presence of light, which is called light perception.
People who are blind do not dream.	People who are blind do dream. In *The Story of My Life,* (1976, p. 269), Helen Keller stated "I rarely sleep without dreaming. . . . After Miss Sullivan came to me, the more I learned, the oftener I dreamed." Keller described her dreams in several books. In *The World I Live In* (1908, pp. 161–162), she described her dreams as "sensations, odors, tastes, and ideas which I did not remember to have had in reality. . . . Once in a dream I held in my hand a pearl. I have no memory vision of a real pearl. It was a smooth, exquisitely molded crystal."

(continued on next page)

Myths and Facts *(Continued)*

MYTH	FACT
People who are blind need to be spoken for.	People who are blind should be addressed directly. The vast majority are competent and able to form their own ideas and philosophies and are able to express them. If you are in a situation in which it may be difficult for a person who is visually impaired to know that you have approached him or her, let the person know that you are there by greeting him or her and identifying yourself.
People who are blind are easily able to recognize who a person is just by hearing the person's voice.	Although some people who are visually impaired have excellent auditory memories, all do not find it easy to identify a person by his or her voice. It is impolite to ask a visually impaired person to "guess" one's identity just by hearing one's voice. The more appropriate social behavior is to greet the person and identify oneself.
People who are blind have better-than-average musical abilities.	Although there are many well-known and accomplished musicians who are visually impaired, the percentage of those who are musically inclined is no greater than among people who are not disabled.
People who are blind should not travel alone unless they use dog guides.	People who are visually impaired achieve independent mobility through different systems, only one of which is the use of dog guides. They also use sighted guides, long canes, and some also use electronic travel devices (ETAs) and/or optical devices. Sighted guides are people who have sufficient vision to guide a person who is severely visually impaired and are always in the forward position. With long canes, the length of the cane is individually determined so as to provide the user with sufficient warning about dropoffs (stairs and curbs) and obstacles in a path. ETAs and optical devices may be used by themselves or in combination with other travel devices. Independent travel for individuals who are visually impaired requires learning safety skills; the use of some type of travel and/or low vision de-

(continued on next page)

Myths and Facts *(Continued)*

MYTH	FACT
	vice: environmental concepts; O&M skills; and auditory, tactile, kinesthetic, and olfactory cues. Many people who are visually impaired are safe, confident, and independent travelers, and many travel independently whenever and wherever they choose. Some individuals who have low vision can and do drive automobiles (Corn & Rosenblum, 2000).
All people who are blind are sad, depressed, and angry. All people who are blind are jolly and fun loving.	Every person who is visually impaired is an individual with a unique and complex personality and experiences a variety of emotions.
When speaking with people who are visually impaired, never use such terms as *see* or *look* or refer to specific colors.	People who are visually impaired use the same everyday language as is used in the cultures in which they live. Sighted persons should *not* avoid using "visual terms" when conversing with people who are visually impaired. For example, it is acceptable to ask a student, "Did you see the president's address on television last night?" However, be cautious about using terms like *over there* and pointing. For example, in a classroom situation, read the mathematics problems presented; do not just point to the problems. When giving directions to a person who cannot determine which way you are pointing, give specific and usable directions, such as these: "Continue in the direction you are facing and cross the next two streets, Maple and Cherry. Cross Cherry and turn right. The library is the third building on your left."
When you talk to a person who is severely visually impaired, you must speak loudly.	The majority of people who are visually impaired do not have hearing losses and do not require people to speak to them loudly. Do not assume that a person who is visually impaired is also deaf or hard of hearing.
People who are blind cannot hold self-supporting jobs and are on welfare.	People who are visually impaired successfully hold a wide variety of jobs and enjoy fulfilling careers and occupations. For example, some are

(continued on next page)

Myths and Facts *(Continued)*

MYTH	FACT
People who are blind cannot hold self-supporting jobs and are on welfare.	teachers, professors, carpenters, physicians, computer programmers, beekeepers, judges, store owners, accountants, budget analysts, customer service representatives, insurance professionals, managers, real estate agents, salespersons, mechanics, stockbrokers, tax specialists, interpreters, secretaries, librarians, counselors, social workers, nurses, massage therapists, and scientists. AFB maintains a Careers and Technology Information Bank (1999) that lists nearly 2,000 employed individuals who are visually impaired in more than 100 types of jobs. AFB helps young students connect with employed adults who can serve as mentors. In addition, both the National Federation of the Blind (NFB) and the American Council of the Blind (ACB) have many professional divisions and interest groups that are career oriented.

Effects of Public Perceptions

According to Mauer (1989), how people speak about blindness is at least as important to the future of individuals who are blind as the buildings in which they receive services, the funds that are appropriated for services, and devices and technology designed specifically for their use. Mauer further stated: "If the words used to describe the condition of the blind are dismal . . . chances for equality are . . . bleak."

An underlying belief of the National Federation of the Blind (NFB), a leading consumer and advocacy organization with 50,000 members, speaks to the need for people who are blind to "achieve self-confidence and self-respect" and to the role that public perception plays in the lives of individuals who are blind. In 1992, Kenneth Jernigan (quoted in Severo, 1998), past-president of the NFB and blind himself, stated that "the real

problem of blindness is not the loss of eyesight. The real problem is the misunderstanding and lack of information that exist. If a blind person has proper training and opportunity, blindness can be reduced to the level of a physical nuisance." Carl Augusto, president of the American Foundation for the Blind (AFB), one of the leading national organizations in the field of blindness and visual impairment, and himself visually impaired since an early age, stated (personal communication, October 14, 1998): "Blindness and severe visual impairment are serious disabilities that can have a profound effect on a person and family members. However, with the right attitude, the right skills, and if given an opportunity, blind and visually impaired people can, and do, live and work alongside their sighted peers with dignity and success."

These leaders' words further support the fact that the public's understanding of persons who are visually impaired is not accurate and that the realization of an individual's potential is not diminished by the fact that the person is visually impaired. All professionals in the field of visual impairment have a responsibility to work to eliminate stereotypes by educating the public about the potential and capabilities of individuals who are visually impaired.

DEMOGRAPHICS

Teachers of students with visual impairments have the opportunity to work with children of all ages; races; and degrees and types of visual, social-emotional, physical, neurological, and cognitive abilities; as well as of various ethnic backgrounds and cultures (with different social values, beliefs, and traditions); and economic levels. Each student has a unique personality. To gain a better understanding of the diversity of students who are visually impaired, some prevailing demographic information is presented in this section. This information may help teachers anticipate the variety of students with whom they are likely to work.

Prevalence and Incidence

Demographics is a descriptive term that is applied to statistical studies of physical conditions; vital statistics, such as birth and health; and socioeconomic status. Much demographic information is reported as prevalence and incidence data, according to the National Society for the Prevention of Blindness, now Prevent Blindness America (1980). *Prevalence* is the number of new and existing cases of a condition in a defined population at a specific point in time, such as five years; in other words, how common is a condition in the population. *Incidence* is the number of new cases of a condition that occurred within both a defined population and period of time, usually a year. Both prevalence and incidence may be reported as absolute numbers or rates, although incidence

is most often reported in ratios (such as 1 in 1,000 live births) and prevalence is usually reported in percentages (for instance, 5 percent of the population). Except for conditions that are of short durations, like a cold or flu, or that are rapidly terminal, prevalence is larger than incidence (C. Kirchner, personal communication, January 12, 1999).

Reliable data on the incidence and prevalence of blindness and visual impairment are difficult to obtain (Kirchner, 1999) for many reasons:

◆ The United States, Canada, and most other countries do not have mandatory national registries of individuals who are blind or visually impaired;

◆ There is disagreement about the definitions for blindness and visual impairment; and

◆ Some studies do not report definitions, thus making it difficult to apply their findings to demographic data.

Child Counts

Special education services in the United States are based on federal requirements that were first established in 1975 by P.L. 94-142, the Education for All Handicapped Children Act. The federal government, through the Individuals with Disabilities Education Act (IDEA), the reauthorization of P.L. 94-142, and the 1997 amendments to IDEA (P.L. 105-17), requires states to collect data on the numbers of children they serve in special education programs. Briefly, the purposes of the reauthorization and amendments were to ensure free, appropriate public education and prepare children with disabilities for employment and independent living, protect the rights of these children and their parents, assist agencies in providing education for all children with disabilities, improve educational results for children with disabilities, and assess and ensure the effectiveness of special education (OSERS, 1999). The states are allowed to count each child receiving services only once. Many students who are visually impaired have additional difficulties that require special attention, such as learning disabilities, speech or language impairments, hearing impairments or deafness, cognitive delay, autism, or traumatic brain injury. These students are often identified in a category other than visual impairment and are not included in the count of the number of students who require special education intervention because of their visual impairments.

Project PRISM, a federally funded study of the sequence and rate of development of 202 children from birth to age 5 who were visually impaired, stated in its executive summary report (Ferrell, 1998) that 59.9 percent of those who registered with the project were diagnosed with an additional medical condition or disability. Because children receiving special education services are reported in only one classification, those who have additional disabilities are most often reported as having multiple disabilities and are not identified as having a visual impairment. This practice may help to explain the consistently low number of children with visual impairments who are reported to the federal government compared to the higher number of students who are reported by the American Printing House for the Blind (APH) (see Tables 2.1, 2.2, and 2.3). APH is an organization designated under the 1879 Act to Promote the Education of the Blind as the official United States supplier of educational materials for students with visual impairments under a federal funding quota system (APH, 1999).

The unduplicated federal count results in significant undercounts that are used to appropriate funding. Local education agencies (LEAs), usually local school districts or collaboratives, are responsible for submitting the data to the states. (Neighboring school districts often form collaborative partnerships that enroll students who are visually impaired in order to hire qualified teachers and provide disability specific services.) Each child receiving special education services is counted in one special education category even if the child receives additional special education services for other disabilities. Teachers need to realize that states and districts typically use these child counts to make decisions about funding and programs. It is often necessary for state consultants or teachers to remind decision makers that these unduplicated child counts do not include all students who are visually impaired and who need to be receiving services.

Sources of data on children with visual impairments in the United States presented here include the U.S. Department of Education, the department's Office of Special Education and Rehabilitative Services and Office of Special Education Programs. An additional source of data is the National Center for Health Statistics: Health Interview Survey (NCHS-HIS). The National Health Interview Survey of 1992 (Benson & Murano, 1994) reported that 1 percent of persons under age 18 (approximately 694,000 children and

Table 2.1. Number of Children with Visual Impairments Aged 6–21 Served by the Individuals with Disabilities Education Act (IDEA), Part B, and the Number Registered by the American Printing House for the Blind (APH): 1990–1997

Year	Served by IDEA	Served by APH
1990–91	26,570	50,080
1991–92	25,093	51,813
1992–93	23,691	52,791
1993–94	24,826	53,576
1994–95	25,104	54,763
1995–96	25,443	56,275
1996–97	25,739	56,690
1997–98	26,070	57,425

Source: Based on U.S. Department of Education, *Twenty-First Annual Report to Congress on the Implementation of the Individuals with Disabilities Education Act* (Washington, DC: Author, 1999), p. A-159 and on American Printing House for the Blind, *Annual Report* (Louisville, KY, 1995, 1996, 1997, 1998, 1999).

Table 2.2   Students Registered with the American Printing House for the Blind, by Type of Program: 1995–1998

Type of Program	1995	1996	1997	1998
Schools for students with visual impairments	4,489	4,575	4,588	4,558
State departments of education	45,756	47,188	47,787	48,399
Programs for children with multiple handicaps	1,917	1,891	1,938	1,894
Rehabilitation programs	2,601	2,621	2,377	2,574
Totals	54,763	56,275	56,690	57,425

Source: Adapted from American Printing House for the Blind, *Annual Report* (Louisville, KY, 1995, 1996, 1997, 1988).

youths) are visually impaired (defined as blindness in one or both eyes or any other trouble seeing even when wearing glasses).

Chaing, Bassie, and Javitt (1992) found that in the United States, 2,561 children under age 5 (.01 percent) and 50,699 aged 5–19 (0.9 percent) were legally blind. Nelson and Dimitrova (1993) estimated that 95,410 children and youths under 18 (0.2 percent of the population) were severely visually impaired, defined as the inability to see to read ordinary newspaper print even with best possible corrective lenses.

Table 2.3   Students Registered with the American Printing House for the Blind, by Type of Reader: 1995–1998

Type of Reader	1995	1996	1997	1998
Visual readers	14,104	14,341	14,388	14,461
Braille readers	5,271	5,449	5,439	5,461
Auditory readers	4,658	4,428	4,133	4,051
Prereaders	13,104	14,010	14,632	14,924
Nonreaders	17,626	18,047	18,098	18,528
Totals	54,763	56,275	56,690	57,425

Source: Adapted from American Printing House for the Blind, *Annual Report* (Louisville, KY: 1995, 1996, 1997, 1998).

Race and Ethnicity

Little data have been reported on visual impairment among various racial and ethnic groups. Of the total population of all children in the United States aged 5–15, the vast majority attend school. However, school-enrollment rates differ among younger and older children. Hispanic children aged 3–4 are less likely to be enrolled in school than are white or African American children of the same age. White youths aged 16–21 are more likely to be in school than are Hispanic youths of the same age, and white youths aged 18–21 are more likely to be in school than African American youths of the same age ("School Enrollment Rates," 1997). However, "legal blindness is . . . more prevalent among non-Whites than it is among Whites. Twenty percent of legally blind persons are estimated to be non-White, but only 16 percent of Americans are non-White. Among non-Whites, approximately 5.7 out of 1,000 are estimated to be legally blind. There is no significant difference in the prevalence rates of legal blindness for men and women" ("Legal Blindness in the United States," 1997, p. 413).

The U.S. Bureau of the Census's Survey of Income and Program Participation reported that over 19 percent of Americans had one or more disabilities (Bradsher, 1996). In this self-reported disability study, *disability* was defined as a limitation in one or more functional activities, including socially defined roles or tasks like reading a newspaper or driving a car. The following groups had the highest to lowest rates of disability: Native Americans, 21.9 percent; African-Americans, 20 percent; whites, 19.7 percent; Hispanics, 15.3 percent; Asians and Pacific Islanders, 9.9 percent. Differences among racial and ethnic groups were reported to be more pronounced among people between the ages of 15–64. (See Chapter 8 for more information on cultural diversity.)

Households

In the National Longitudinal Transition Study of Special Education Students (U.S. Department of Education, 1988), researchers interviewed parents of students aged 13–21 who were visually impaired and receiving specialized services and found that of the students, 37 percent lived with single parents, 12 percent lived with heads of households who were disabled, and 17 percent lived with other children with disabilities. Furthermore, 37 percent of the students lived with heads of households with no high school diploma, 33 percent lived with those with high school diplomas, and 30 percent lived with those with some college or college degrees. In the United States, of the 3,141 counties, 77 percent are in rural areas, and about a quarter of these rural counties (mainly in the Southeast, West, and Appalachia) have populations with low incomes. Visual impairment is more likely to occur among those with incomes no higher that 150 percent of the poverty level (34 percent) than among those with higher incomes (27 percent). Twenty percent or more of the U.S. population were consistently found to have incomes below the poverty level from 1960 to 1990 (Economic Research Service, 1995). Visual impairment is more prevalent among people who have fewer social and economic resources (The Lighthouse, 1995).

Infant Mortality

Of the world's large industrialized nations, the United States has one of the highest rates of infant mortality (the number of infants per thousand who die before their first birthdays) and one of the lowest rates of life expectancy. Of the infant mortality rates of 20 countries (both industrialized and developing) with populations of 5 million or more, the U.S. infant mortality rate was surpassed only by the rates of Algeria, Turkey, Mexico, Portugal, and Greece. Furthermore, although the overall infant mortality rate in 1995 in this country was 7.9 per thousand, the rate for African American infants was twice the rate for white infants ("Life Expectancy and Infant Mortality in International Perspective," 1997).

Career Exploration

Students who are visually impaired are more likely than other students with disabilities to meet or exceed the requirements in English, mathematics, foreign languages, and computer science. They also rate themselves as being above average or high on measures of academic and writing ability, ambition, intellectual self-confidence, and emotional health (Henderson, 1995). However, fewer teenagers who are visually impaired have any work experience outside the home before they graduate from high school. Hence, many of them are not learning job-related skills and behaviors and leave school less prepared for employment than their sighted counterparts (Wolffe, 1999). Studies of adolescents and young adults (aged 15–21), with and without visual impairments, have found that "many students who are visually impaired, particularly those with low vision, require extensive support to succeed academically in integrated school environments" (Sacks, Wolffe, & Tierney, 1998, p. 476).

INTERNATIONAL PERSPECTIVE

Approximately 180 million people throughout the world are visually impaired, and this figure is expected to double in the next 25 years unless significant public health actions are taken (more than two-thirds of the instances of blindness in the world could be avoided through preventive measures and treatment; see WHO, 1997). Of these 180 million, 40 to 45 million are blind.

Ninety percent of the world's people who are blind live in developing countries (in Asia, Africa, and South America), and nearly 60 percent of them reside in sub-Saharan Africa, China, and India (WHO, 1999a, b). Africa and Asia have the highest prevalence rates, accounting for 53 percent of the people who are blind in the world (World Blind Union, 1999; WHO, 1992).

Worldwide, the distribution of blindness by age group is 3.9 percent for those aged 0–14, 6.5 percent for those aged 15–44, 31.7 percent for those aged 45–59, and 58 percent for those aged 60 and older (Thylefors, Negrel, Pararajasgaram, & Dadzie, 1995). Furthermore, about 1.5 million children worldwide under age 16 have a corrected visual acuity in the best eye of less than 3/60, count fingers at 3m, or have central visual fields of less than 10 degrees (WHO, 1992). The number of blind persons worldwide is increasing by up to 2 million per year. By 2020, the number of elderly persons (aged 60 and over) will almost double and reach 1.2 billion, of whom more than three-quarters will be living in developing countries (WHO, 1997). Furthermore, of the approximately 370 million people who live in the 15 countries that are member states of the European Union, 2 percent (7.4 million) have significant visual impairments (Royal National Institute for the Blind, 1999).

Approximately 1.1 million Americans (or about 44 persons per 10,000) are legally blind. Of that number, about .02 percent are under age 5, 4 percent are aged 5–19, 15 percent are aged 20–44, 16 percent are aged 45–64, 12 percent are aged 65–74, 19 percent are aged 75–84, and 34 percent are aged 85 or older (Chaing et al., 1992). According to The Lighthouse study (1995), 120,000 Americans are blind (are totally blind or have light perception only) and 3 million are unable to read regular newsprint. Of adults aged 45 and older, 13.5 million reported some form of visual impairment. The proportion of adults who report some form of visual impairment increases dramatically with age. In other words, the older people get, the more likely they are to have visual impairments.

Data on individuals with visual impairments are limited. Because of the application of different criteria, the lack of national registries, and the absence of definitions of terms, it is difficult to sort and compare data from which to generalize. Clearly, additional studies are needed to understand the larger picture of visual impairment in the United States and to plan for the future. Nevertheless, it is known that the number of people with visual impairments has been increasing and that this trend may continue within the general population, including children. However, federal data released in 1997 raise doubts about a clear upward trend (Kirchner, 1999; Kirchner & Schmeidler, 1997; McNeil, 1997; U.S. Bureau of the Census, 1997). Kirchner (1999a), suggests that societal trends such as medical advances and improved fitness may point to an eventual decrease in prevalence.

CAUSES OF VISUAL IMPAIRMENT

Globally, the major causes of bilateral blindness are cataracts (42 percent), degenerative and metabolic diseases (23 percent), trachoma (16 percent), glaucoma (14 percent), and onchocerciasis (river blindness) and xerophthalmia (vitamin A deficiency) (5 percent) (Thylefors et al., 1995). The major age-related causes of blindness and visual disability worldwide include cataracts (approximately 16 million people), glaucoma (5.2 million people), diabetic retinopathy (2 million people), and age-related macular degeneration (ARMD) (3 million people).

For children from birth to age 19, the leading causes of legal blindness, from greater to lesser frequency, in the United States, are congenital cataracts, optic atrophy, albinism, retinopathy of prematurity (ROP), and rod-cone dystrophy (Brilliant & Graboyes, 1999). Ferrell's (1998) longitudinal study of 202 infants and toddlers found that the leading diagnoses for the children in this study were cortical visual impairment (20.6 percent), retinopathy of prematurity (19.1 percent), and optic nerve hypoplasia (16.6 percent). The frequency of visual disorders differed according to the severity of additional disabilities. For children without additional disabilities, optic nerve hypoplasia and albinism were the most frequent visual disorders. For children with mild additional impairments, ROP and optic nerve hypoplasia were the most frequent, and for those with severe additional impairments, cortical visual impairment and ROP were the most frequent. The frequency of visual disorders also differed by ethnic groups. Among African American children, colobomas and other structural anomalies were the most frequent; among Hispanic children, ROP was the most frequent; and among children of mixed ethnicity optic nerve hypoplasia was the most frequent (Ferrell, 1998).

According to Brilliant and Graboyes (1999), for those aged 20 to 44, the leading causes of legal blindness are the same as those from birth through age 19, with the exception of congenital cataract and ROP and the addition of myopia, retinitis pigmentosa, diabetic retinopathy, and macular degeneration. The most common causes of visual impairments, from greater to lesser frequency, for adults are diabetic retinopathy, glaucoma, retinitis pigmentosa, macular degeneration, and cataracts for those 45–65; macular degeneration, diabetic retinopathy, glaucoma, cataracts, and retinitis pigmentosa for those aged 65–74; ARMD, glaucoma, cataract, and diabetic retinopathy for those aged 75 and older. The majority of people with visual impairments who have some remaining vision, and "of the 11.5 million people [in the United States] who are visually impaired (i.e., cannot read standard-size newsprint with conventional lenses), approximately half a million (4 percent) are considered legally blind" (Brilliant & Graboyes, 1999, p. 7).

SUMMARY

This chapter has presented a perspective on the diversity of the population and the public's perception of individuals who are visually impaired. It has defined some terms that are used by professionals who provide services to people who are visually impaired. In time, definitions will become more precise and more accurate counts and de-

mographic information about the characteristics of the children who are visually impaired will be available. Vigilance is required not only to maintain professional responsibilities, but to expand them and effect positive change. The population of students with visual impairments is diverse. Teachers need to adjust their educational strategies for each student and consider all the student's strengths and difficulties.

Furthermore, many background factors need to be considered when planning and implementing educational and O&M programs for students who have visual impairments. The population of students any teacher works with is becoming more diverse. In some urban schools, students have been known to represent nearly 100 different countries of origin within the walls of one high school. For many of these students, English is not their primary language. Thus, teachers need to learn about and be responsive to the values, attitudes, behaviors, belief systems, customs, expectations, socioeconomic status, educational levels, and other characteristics of the cultures within which their students live. Factors specific to a student's impairment are also critical to include in overall planning. Such factors include cognitive ability, severity and type of visual impairment, date of onset of visual impairment, cause of visual impairment, and presence of additional disabilities. Finally, it is important that every member of a student's educational team uses the same terms and has the same understanding of the terms being used.

STUDY QUESTIONS

1. There is some controversy about the use of terminology when referring to people with disabilities. Why does this controversy exist? Why is it important for teachers to be sensitive about the use of terminology?

2. This chapter states: "Public opinion and attitudes toward individuals who are visually impaired can have a significant effect on

an individual's education, socialization, opportunities, and employment." Do you agree with this statement? Why or why not?

3. Rent and view three films in which a major character is blind. Provide a brief summary of the films, along with an analysis of how the films support or refute the myths discussed in this chapter.

4. Why is it important for professionals to know whether a student is congenitally or adventitiously visually impaired?

5. Why is it difficult to determine accurate demographic data for the population of students who are visually impaired? Why is it important to have accurate demographic data?

6. Initiate a discussion about blindness among friends or family members who are not in your classes. Ask general questions about their knowledge and perception of blindness. Note their knowledge about blindness and their comfort in participating in this discussion.

REFERENCES

Abagio, P., & Downing, J. (1990). Using labels: Study of client preferences. *Journal of Visual Impairment & Blindness, 76*, 218–220.

American Foundation for the Blind. (1999). *Facts about the American Foundation for the blind* [On-line]. Available: http://www.afb.org/facts.html

American Printing House for the Blind. (1995). *Annual report.* Louisville, KY: Author.

American Printing House for the Blind. (1996). *Annual report.* Louisville, KY: Author.

American Printing House for the Blind. (1997). *Annual report.* Louisville, KY: Author.

American Printing House for the Blind. (1998). *Annual report.* Louisville, KY: Author.

American Printing House for the Blind. (1999). *What is the American Printing House for the Blind?* [On-line]. Availble: http://www.APH.org/hist.htm

Benson, V., & Murano, M. A. (1994). Current estimates from the National Health Interview Survey, 1992. National Center for Health Statistics. *Vital health Statistics, 10.*

Best, A. B., & Corn, A. L. (1992). The management of low vision is children: Report of the 1992 World Health Organization consultation. *Journal of Visual Impairment & Blindness, 87*, 307–309.

Bina, M. J. (1993). [Review of the book *Images of disability on television*]. *Journal of Visual Impairment & Blindness, 87*, 287–288.

Bradsher, J. E. (1996). Disability among racial and ethnic groups, *Disability Statistics Abstract, 10.* San Francisco: Disability Statistics Rehabilitation Research and Training Center, University of California.

Brewer, C. (1997, April 22). Blind friend makes good hiking companion. *Knoxville News–Sentinal* [On-line]. Available: http://www.knoxnews.com

Brewer, C. (1998, February 2). Though blind, this determined boy has his sights on success. *Bergen Record Corp.* [On-line]. Available: http://www.bergen-record.com

Brilliant, R. L., & Graboyes, M. (1999). Historical overview of low vision: Classifications and perceptions. In R. L. Brilliant (Ed.), *Essentials of low vision practice* (pp. 2–9). Boston: Butterworth Heinemann.

California State Department of Education. (1997). California Code of Regulations, Title 5, Education, Section 3030. In J. Hazekamp & J. Lundin (Eds.), *Program guidelines for students who are visually impaired.* Sacramento, CA: Author.

Canadian National Institute for the Blind (CNIB). (1999). Myths and misconceptions about blindness. In *Living with vision loss* (Chap. 1) [On-Line]. Available: http://www.cnib.ca/pandp/lwvl/wvlch1.htm

Cardenas, E. L. (1997, January 28). Obituaries: Margaret Smith led rich full life despite blindness. *Detroit News.* [On-line]. Available: http://www.detnews.com

Careers and technology information bank (CTIB). (1999). *Journal of Visual Impairment & Blindness, 93*, 51.

Caton, H. (1991). *Print and braille literacy: Selecting appropriate learning media.* Louisville, KY: Author.

Chaing, Y., Bassi, L. J., & Javitt, J. C. (1992). Federal budgetary costs of blindness. *Milbank Quarterly, 70*, 319–340.

Corn, A. L. (1980). *Development and assessment of an in-service training program for teachers of the visually handicapped: Optical aids in the classroom.* Unpublished doctoral dissertation, Teachers College, Columbia University.

Corn, A. L., Hatlen, P., Huebner, K. M., Ryan, F., & Siller, M. A. (1995). *The national agenda for the education of children and youths with visual impairments, including those with multiple disabilities.* New York: AFB Press.

Corn, A. L., & Koenig, A. J. (1996). Perspectives on low vision. In A. L. Corn & A.J. Koenig (Eds.), *Foundations of low vision: Clinical and functional perspectives* (pp. 3–25). New York: AFB Press.

Corn, A. L., & Rosenblum, L. P. (2000). *Finding wheels.* Austin, TX: Pro-Ed.

Economic Research Service. (1995), *Understanding rural America.* Washington, DC: U.S. Department of Agriculture, Economic Research Service.

Ferrell, K. A. (1998). *Project PRISM: A longitudinal study of developmental patterns of children who are visually impaired. Executive summary.* Greeley: University of Northern Colorado.

Frankston, J. (1998, February 4). Dream realized: Woman reaches goal of teaching despite blindness. Students see only teacher they love—and her dog. *Akron Beacon Journal.* [On-line]. Available: http://www. newslibrary.com

Henderson, C. (1995). *College freshman with disabilities: A triennial statistical profile.* Washington, D.C.: American Council on Education.

Hernandez, R. (1997, November 24). OSU professor hasn't let blindness hinder him. *The Oregonian.* [On-line]. Available: http://www.Oregonlive.com

Jernigan, K. (1999). *Blindness—Concepts and misconceptions.* Baltimore, MD: National Federation of the Blind. [On-line]. Available: http://www.nfb.org/ blindnesc.htm

Keller, H. (1908). *The world I live in.* New York: Century.

Keller, H. (1976). *The story of my life.* New York: Andor.

Kelly, L. J., & Vergason, G. A. (1985). *Dictionary of special education and rehabilitation* (2nd ed.). Denver, CO: Love.

Kent, D. (1989). Shackled imagination: Literary illusions about blindness. *Journal of Vision Impairment & Blindness, 83,* 145–150.

Kent, D. (1990). [Review of the book *Disability drama in television and film*]. *Journal of Vision Impairment & Blindness, 84,* 82–84.

Kent, D. (1996). [Review of the book *The cinema of isolation: A history of physical disability in movies*]. JVIB News Service, 90, 1–5.

Kent, D. (1997). [Review of the book *Images that injure: Pictorial stereotypes in the media*]. JVIB News Service, 91, 7–10.

Kirchner, C. (1999). Trends affecting prevalence of visual impairment and demand for services. *Journal of Vision Impairment & Blindness, 93,* 53–57.

Kirchner, C., & Schmeidler, E. (1997). Prevalence and employment of people in the United States who are blind or visually impaired. *Journal of Vision Impairment & Blindness, 91,* 508–511.

Kirtley, D. (1975). *The psychology of blindness.* Chicago: Nelson Hall.

Klobas, L. E. (1988). *Disability drama in television & film.* Jefferson, NC: McFarland.

Koenig, A. J., & Holbrook, M. C. (1995). Learning media assessment of students with visual impairments (2nd ed.). Austin: Texas School for the Blind and Visually Impaired.

Legal blindness in the United States (Demographics Update). (1997b). *Journal of Visual Impairment & Blindness, 91,* 413.

Levack, N. (1994). *Low vision: A resource guide with adaptations for students with visual impairments* (2nd ed.). Austin: Texas School for the Blind and Visually Impaired.

Life Expectancy and infant mortality in international perspective (Demographics Update). (1997). *Journal of Visual Impairment & Blindness, 91,* 318.

The Lighthouse. (1995). *The Lighthouse national survey on vision loss: The experience, attitudes and knowledge of middle-aged and older Americans: Executive summary.* New York: Author.

Lowenfeld, B. (1971). *Our blind children* (3rd ed.). Springfield, IL: Charles C Thomas.

Mauer, M. (1989, July). *Language and the future of the blind.* Paper presented at the annual convention of the National Federation of the Blind, Denver, CO. [On-line]. Available: http:/www.nfb.org/convens/ speeches/banque89.txt

McNeil, J. M. (1997). Americans with disabilities: 1994–95. *Current Population Reports* (Series 70, No. 61), Washington, DC: U.S. Bureau of the Census.

Monbeck, M. (1973). *The meaning of blindness: Attitudes toward blindness and blind people.* Bloomington: Indiana University Press.

National Eye Institute (1999). *Report of the visual impairment and its rehabilitation panel.* [On-line]. Available: http://www.nei.nih.gov/textsite/publications/plan/neiplan/impairment.htm

National Federation of the Blind. (1999). *About the National Federation of the Blind.* [On-line]. Available: http://www.nfb.org/aboutnfb.htm

National Society for the Prevention of Blindness. (1980). *Vision problems in the U.S.: Data analysis.* New York: Author.

Nelson, K. A., & Dimitrova, G. (1993). Severe visual impairment in the United States and in each state, 1990. *Journal of Visual Impairment & Blindness, 87,* 80–85.

Norden, M. F. (1994). *The cinema of isolation: A history of physical disability in the movies.* New Brunswick, NJ: Rutgers University Press.

Orlando, A., & Golson, J. (1998, March 4). Blind man is struck and killed by van. *Star-Ledger.* [On-line]. Available: http://www.nj.com/starledger

OSERS. (1999). *IDEA '97: General information* [On-line].

Available: http://www.ed.gov/offices/OSERS/overview.html

Rosenblum, L. P., & Erin, J. N. (1998), Perceptions of terms used to describe individuals with visual impairments. *RE:view, 30*, 15–26.

Royal National Institute for the Blind. (1999). *Visual impairment and the Euro: Easing the transition to the Euro for visually impaired people* [On-line]. Available: http://www.rnib.org.uk/wedo/campaign/euro.htm

Sacks, S. Z., Wolffe, K., & Tierney, D. (1998). Lifestyles of students with visual impairments: Preliminary studies of social networks. *Exceptional children, 64*, 463–478.

Sardegna, J., & Otis, T. P. (1991). *The encyclopedia of blindness and visual impairment*. New York: Facts on File.

Schloss, I. P. (1963). Implications of altering the definition of blindness. *Research Bulletin No. 3* (pp. 111–116). New York: American Foundation for the Blind.

School enrollment rates in the United States (Demographics Update). (1997). *Journal of Visual Impairment & Blindness, 91*, 94.

Schroeder, F. (1989). Literacy: The key to opportunity. *Journal of Visual Impairment & Blindness, 83*, 290–293.

Severo, R. (1998). *Kenneth Jernigan, 71, Advocate for the blind. The New York Times, Wednesday, October 14* [On-line]. Available: http://www.nfb.org

Thylefors, B., Negrel, A., Pararajasgaram, R., & Dadzie K. Y. (1995). Global data on blindness. *Bulletin of the World Health Organization, 73*, 115–121.

Twersky, J. (1955). *Blindness in literature: Examples of depictions and attitudes*. New York: Alfred A. Knopf.

Ulman, H. (1997). Blind golfer has feel for game. *Myrtle Beach Sun News*. [On-line]. Available: http://www.myrtlebeachaccess.com

U.S. Bureau of the Census. (1997). *Statistical abstracts of the United States: 1997* (117th ed.). Washington, DC: U.S. Government Printing Office.

U.S. Department of Education. (1988). The National Longitudinal Transition Study of Special Education Students. *Statistical Almanac. Volume 6: Youth categorized as visually impaired.* Washington, DC: Author.

U.S. Department of Education. (1997). *Nineteenth annual report to congress on the implementation of the Individuals with Disabilities Education Act.* Washington, DC: Author.

Walton, R. D. (1998, February 21). Blindness doesn't hinder expert piano mover. *Indianapolis Star News.* [On-line]. Available: http://www.StarNews.com

Wilkins, L. (1996). The blind in the media: A vision of stereotypes in action. In P. M. Lester (Ed.), *Images that injure: Pictorial stereotypes in the media* (pp. 127–134). Westport, CT: Praeger.

Wolffe, K. E. (1999). *Skills for success: A career education handbook for children and adolescents with visual impairments.* New York: AFB Press.

World Blind Union. (1999). *Factsheet 10: The world picture* [On-line]. Available: http://194.224.11.75:8080/umc/facts/facts10.htm

World Health Organization. (1992). *Prevention of childhood blindness.* Geneva, Switzerland: Author.

World Health Organization. (1997). Blindness and visual disability: Part V of VII: Seeing ahead—Projections into the next century. *Fact Sheet N 146* [On-line]. http://www.who.int/inf-fs/en/fact146.html

World Health Organization. (1999a). *The international classification of impairments, disabilities, and handicaps.* [On-line]. Available: http://www.who.int/whosis/icidh/icidh.html

World Health Organization. (1999b). *Prevention of blindness and deafness.* [On-line]. Available: http://www.who.int/pbd

World Health Organization. (1999c). *Vision 2020.* [On-line]. Available: http://www.who.int/pbd/Vision 2020/vision-e.html

CHAPTER 3

The Visual System

Marjorie E. Ward

KEY POINTS

- For most people, the visual sense acts to integrate information obtained by the other senses.
- Each part of the eye performs an important function in the transmission of information from light rays to the brain.
- There are numerous causes of visual impairments. The extent and impact of the visual impairments may differ, depending on the causes.
- Some visual impairments are hereditary; others are not. Some visual impairments are associated with other disabilities; others are closely related to environmental factors.
- The proper and appropriate diagnosis of a visual impairment is critical and provides important information to parents of visually impaired students and to professionals.

Sensory receptor cells initiate the process of transporting the world to the mind. They send information across increasingly complex and intricate systems that most people take for granted. Some 10,000 taste buds housed in the tongue detect

The author wishes to acknowledge with appreciation the review of this chapter by Robert J. Derek, M.D., Associate Professor of Ophthalmology, Department of Ophthalmology, The Ohio State University.

sweet, sour, salty, and bitter flavors. With each inhalation of air, the cilia of the olfactory nerve cells in the membranes lining the upper passages of the nose trigger impulses that carry scents to the brain. Millions of nerve cells lodged in the skin react to pain, heat and cold, pressure, and texture and can feel vibrations, motion, and position. The delicate hair cells of the inner ear signal changes in air pressure in ways that the brain interprets as sound. When light rays activate some of the 126 million receptor cells of the retina at the back of the inside of the eye and those cells send their impulses to the brain, the brain processes the impulses, integrates them with any other sensory information just received, and informs a person of what he or she has seen.

For most people, the sense of sight plays the mediator role for the other senses to help organize and negotiate the environment and put tastes, sounds, aromas, tactile impressions, objects, and people in perspective. This sense of sight and the vision of the world gained from it incorporate electromagnetic, chemical, and electrical energy and require precise muscle coordination to control the movements of the exquisitely sensitive structures of the visual system, of which the eyes are a part.

This chapter presents information about the eyes and their key role in the process of seeing and in the visual system overall. The first section focuses on anatomy and physiology—the structures of the healthy eye and how they function. Following sections address the causes of visual impairments and factors that can damage structures and interrupt function. In addition, the chapter describes the clinical information that eye specialists contribute to the analysis and understanding of visual function and illustrates how clinical information obtained from eye specialists can be interpreted by teachers of students with visual impairments and used for educational and instructional purposes.

THE EYE AND ITS FUNCTION

An examination of the anatomy, that is, the structures of the eye, provides a better understanding of

how the structures of the eye can function alone and in relation to each other to contribute to the efficiency of the visual system (see Figure 3.1). A basic understanding of structure and function of the eye lays the foundation for studying the growth and development of children with visual impairments in later chapters. This examination of the anatomy of the eye starts with the point that light rays first encounter on their route into the eye and works back to their destination in the occipital lobe of the brain, where sensory data are given meaning.

Eyelids and Orbit

Each eyeball lies in a pear-shaped bony orbital cavity (also called the orbit or eye socket), the front of which can be closed off by the upper and lower eyelids. The eyelids play a vital role in pro-

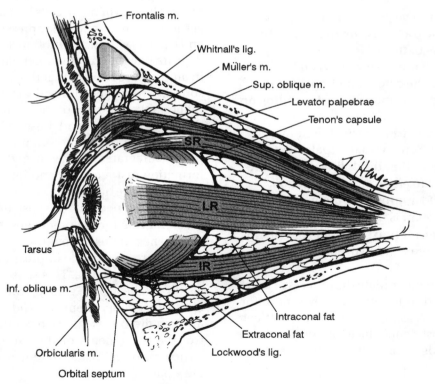

Figure 3.1. Sagittal Section of the Eyebrow, Upper and Lower Eyelids, Globe, and Extraocular (Exterior) Muscles of Left Eye. The medial rectus muscle is not shown in this illustration.

Source: Reprinted, by permission, from K. W. Wright, Ed., *Textbook of Ophthalmology* (Baltimore, MD: Williams & Wilkins, 1997), p. 9.

tecting the entire visual system. They can shut to prevent light, dirt, and wind from entering the eye and open to allow light rays to pass through and travel to the receptor cells inside the back of the healthy eyeball. The eyelids contain additional glands that secrete oils and substances to help lubricate the front of the eye and prevent the evaporation of tears. Opening and closing the eyelids aids the flow of tears across the eyeball. The eyebrows, eyelashes, and eyelids, together with the bony tissue of the orbit, provide a cushion against bumps and strikes and a shield against dirt, perspiration, and bright lights.

The orbital cavity is made up of seven bony, triangle-shaped plates that form a pear shape or pyramid with the apex positioned posterior to (toward the rear of) the face and the wider open end anterior (toward the front), so when the eyelids are open, light rays can enter the eye (Wright, 1997). The eyeball fills about one-fifth of the orbit. The nose separates the two orbital cavities. The nasal or medial plates of the two orbits are approximately parallel to each other, and the two lateral walls of the orbits are about 90 degrees from each other.

The fat and connective tissues that surround each eyeball inside the orbit provide more protection for the eyeball, also called the globe, as well as for the optic nerve that exits from the back of the eyeball and the six extrinsic muscles (also called the extraocular muscles) that are attached to the eyeball and to the walls of the orbit. The extrinsic muscles of each eye work together to move the eyeball in the directions of gaze. The four rectus muscles are primarily responsible for turning the eye toward the nose or toward the temple and up or down. The two oblique muscles act to turn and rotate the eye up and out or down and in, depending on the position from which the eye is moving. Table 3.1 lists the primary and secondary actions for which each muscle is responsible.

The six muscles of one eye are yoked with the six extrinsic muscles of the other eye so both eyes can move together to focus on a distant visual target. Table 3.2 illustrates how the six pairs of muscles are coordinated in normally functioning eyes to move the eyes together in the cardinal directions of gaze. Which muscles contract and relax to

Table 3.1 Functions of the Ocular Muscles

Muscle	Primary Action	Secondary Actions
Lateral rectus	Abduction	None
Medial rectus	Adduction	None
Superior rectus	Elevation	Adduction, intorsion
Inferior rectus	Depression	Adduction, extorsion
Superior oblique	Intorsion	Depression, abduction
Inferior oblique	Extorsion	Elevation, abduction

Source: Adapted from D. G. Vaughan, T. Ashbury, and P. Riordan-Eva, *General Ophthalmology*, 15th ed. (New York: The McGraw-Hill Companies, 1999), p. 218.

direct the eyes in the desired direction to the desired target depends on their current position and status. For example, for looking away from a page of text to an object to the right while holding one's head in the straight ahead position, the primary muscle action would come from the right lateral rectus muscle and the left medial rectus muscle, as shown in Figure 3.2. To allow these muscles to move the eyes to the right evenly and smoothly, the right medial rectus and the left lateral rectus must relax. The muscles also work together so they can converge to focus on a visual target at close range.

The extrinsic muscles are innervated by cranial nerves in the central nervous system. Clear binocular vision (the ability of the two eyes to focus on one object and the ability of the brain to fuse the two images into one single image) depends on the ability of the eyes to move together in a finely and smoothly coordinated fashion so that the messages that reach the brain from the eyes are clean and sharp. When an individual has a condition, such as cerebral palsy, that affects the central nervous system, problems are often found with eye muscle coordination.

Besides the eyeball, muscles, protective fat, and connective tissue, the orbit contains blood vessels, nerves, and the lacrimal gland. The lacrimal gland is situated in the forward upper

Table 3.2. Yoke Muscles in Cardinal Positions of Gaze

Eyes up and right	RSR and LIO
Eyes up and left	LSR and RIO
Eyes right	RLR and LMR
Eyes left	LLR and RMR
Eyes down and right	RIR and LSO
Eyes down and left	LIR and RSO

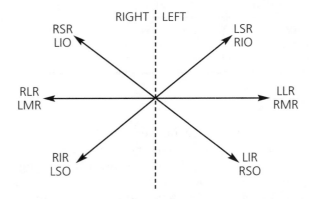

Source: Reprinted, by permission, from D. G. Vaughan, T. Ashbury, and P. Riordan-Eva, *General Ophthalmology,* 15th ed. (New York: The McGraw-Hill Companies, 1999), p. 218.

the specialized cells in the conjunctiva contribute mucous to the tear layer that lubricates the front of the eyeball, especially the cornea. In addition, other cells in the conjunctiva fight off germs and attack foreign matter and microorganisms that enter when the eyelids are open. One of the most common eye disease in Western countries is conjunctivitis, an inflammation of this thin protective covering.

Eyeball

The eyeball is a slightly elongated and flattened sphere, approximately 24 mm front to back, 23 mm vertically, and 23.5 mm on the horizontal axis (Wright, 1997). One can think of the eyeball as having three layers: the outer protective layer; the middle vascular layer; and the inner nerve layer, where light rays should come to a point of focus. Information from the nerve layer is transmitted as electrical impulses to the occipital (rear) lobe of the brain, where it is interpreted and processed for storage and retrieval.

outer portion of the orbit, as shown in Figure 3.3. It secretes tears that flow down over the surface of the globe into the fold below the margin of the lower eyelid and finally drain out through the lacrimal sac that empties into the nose and nasopharynx. Ordinarily, one is not aware of the flow of tears, but if the supply is insufficient to lubricate the front parts of the eye, the eye can feel gritty and irritated or burning. The oversupply or overproduction of tears can result from allergens, environmental irritants, foreign bodies, upper respiratory infections, bright lights, or emotional upset, to name a few of the causes (Vaughan, Asbury, & Riordan-Eva, 1999).

The conjunctiva, a transparent mucous membrane, covers the posterior surface of the eyelids and the white front portion of the eyeball. Some of

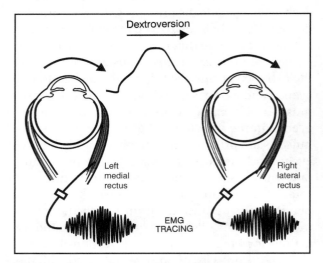

Figure 3.2. Yoke Muscles Move the Eyes to the Right. The left medial rectus and right lateral rectus are innervated. The left lateral rectus and right medial rectus relax.

Source: Adapted from K. W. Wright, Ed., *Textbook of Ophthalmology* (Baltimore, MD: Williams & Wilkins, 1997), p. 238.

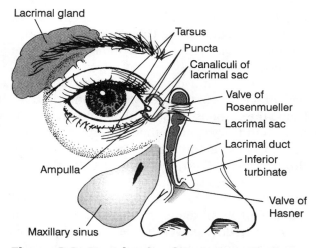

Figure 3.3. Nasolacrimal Excretory System.
Source: Reprinted, by permission, from K. W. Wright, Ed., *Textbook of Ophthalmology* (Baltimore, MD: Williams & Wilkins, 1997), p. 7.

Outer Layer

The outer layer consists of the tough, fibrous white part of the eye called the sclera and the transparent, avascular cornea. Although the cornea is only about 1 mm thick at the periphery in the mature eye and about 0.5–0.6 mm thick at the center, it has five clearly defined layers of cells, membranes, and fibers (see Figure 3.4). The cornea must remain avascular (without blood supply) and in a state of relative dehydration to retain its transparency. Injury or infection can upset the delicate balance and introduce germs that can lead to corneal scarring. As was previously mentioned, the tears help wash away irritants and ward off germs that enter the front of the orbital cavity through the open lids and can cause inflammation and infection. The cornea gets oxygen from the environment and

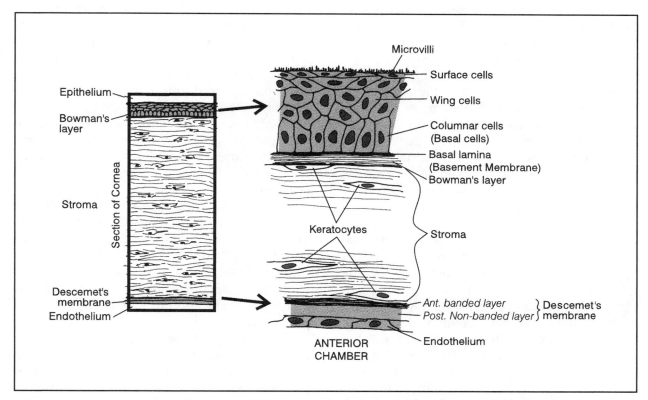

Figure 3.4. Diagrammatic Representation of the Corneal Ultrastructure Through All Five Layers.
Source: Reprinted, by permission, from K. W. Wright, Ed., *Textbook of Ophthalmology* (Baltimore, MD: Williams & Wilkins, 1997), p. 20.

from the aqueous humor, a fluid that circulates inside the eye in the anterior chamber behind the cornea.

Middle Layer

The middle layer of the eyeball, referred to as the uveal tract, consists of the choroid, iris, and ciliary body. The choroid is rich in blood supply and lies between the sclera and the inner nerve layer. The function of the choroid is to provide nutrients to the retinal nerve layer.

The iris is a "musculovascular diaphragm with a central opening" (Wright, 1997, p. 28), that is, a ring with an inner hole that can vary in diameter to let more or less light into the back of the eye. The dilator muscle contracts to increase the size of the pupil while the sphincter muscle contracts to draw the edges of the iris together to decrease the size of the pupil. These muscles are antagonistic; they must work together, one relaxing and one contracting, to control the pupil. The iris vascular system provides nutrition for the front of the eye. The color of the iris depends on the amount of pigmentation in the front portion of the iris.

The ciliary body serves two major functions carried out by the ciliary process and the ciliary muscle. The ciliary process secretes a liquid, called the aqueous humor, that circulates through the pupil from the posterior chamber into the anterior chamber right behind the cornea. The aqueous flows out of the eye through the trabecular meshwork into the canal of Schlemm. The aqueous provides nutrition as well as some oxygen for the cornea. The intraocular pressure depends upon the production; outflow; and, to a lesser extent, the absorption of the aqueous (Wright, 1997). If the aqueous builds up in the anterior and posterior chambers, the pressure within the eye can rise to dangerous levels associated with the various types of glaucoma. Until recently, increased intraocular pressure beyond the range considered to be normal was considered the hallmark of glaucoma. Recent research has suggested, however, that although increased pressure in the eye is a common and important risk factor for glaucoma, the significant feature of glaucoma of all types is a specific pattern of optic nerve damage (Wright, 1997). The glaucomas account for approximately 10 percent of blindness in the United States today.

The ciliary muscle helps control the thickness of the lens of the eye by contracting and relaxing the suspensory fibers that hold the lens in place and that regulate the tension on the lens. The lens lies behind the iris and pupil, the hole through which light rays pass to enter the lens and continue to the back of the eye. Changes in the tension of these fibers or ligaments, called zonules of Zinn, allow the transparent lens to vary its refractive power (power to bend light rays and to accommodate to preserve clear focus for near as well as distant objects). The lens is not really a part of the middle layer of the eye, but its work is affected by the action of the suspensory ligaments that enable the lens to alter its curvature. The lens is the only refractive medium or light-bending structure in the eye that can adjust its curvature and thus its refractive power. Most of the refraction of light that enters the eye is accomplished one by the cornea. The lens, however, is responsible for the fine-tuning of light rays so they can come to a point of focus on the inner retinal layer. This ability to adjust the curvature is essential for accommodation to near and distant objects. As an individual grows older, the elasticity of the lens decreases as the fiberlike cells continue to develop and compress within the lens capsule. The ability of the lens to alter its curvature also decreases. Reading glasses are usually necessary around age 45, when the loss of the accommodative power of the lens is significantly great enough to make it difficult to see detail at close range. This loss of accommodation that is due to the natural aging process is called presbyopia.

For a variety of reasons, the lens may lose its transparency, which results in the formation of a cataract. A cataract, an opacity, or clouding, of part of or the entire lens, prevents light from traveling to the retinal layer. A cataract cannot be "cured," but the cloudy lens can be removed when a person experiences blurred vision. Once the natural lens of the eye has been removed, the optical system of the eye is out of balance. Without some compensation for the loss of the refractive power of the natural lens, light rays cannot come to a point of focus on the retina. Until recently, contact lenses were typically worn to make up for the absence of the natural lens, but today most adults and some children over age 2 are candidates for intraocular lens implants. At the time of surgery to remove the opaque lens, an artificial lens, often made of silicone, is positioned where the natural lens had been. After surgery with implants, some individuals have good vision, but most need spectacles for normal or near-normal vision.

The aging process accounts for the majority of cataracts. Since it often brings with it other changes in the structures of the eye, especially in the cells of the retina, not all people have good vision after cataract surgery. In addition to aging, certain metabolic disorders, injuries, inflammations, reactions to medications, and some systemic diseases may lead to the formation of cataracts. Some children are born with cataracts, and their early treatment, even in the first month of life, is critical to the development of good, functional vision.

Inner Layer

The inner layer of the eye is the nerve layer called the retina. The retina is made up of nine distinct cell layers and approximately 126 million rod and cone cells (Wright, 1997). Its thinnest point, the macula, is also the point of clearest vision. The macula is located on the temporal side of the optic disk near where the many ganglion cells of the retina exit the back of the eye as the optic nerve. The fovea centralis, the central portion of the macula, contains only tightly packed cone cells that are sensitive to color, form, low spatial frequency, contrast sensitivity, and fine detail. Some cone cells are dispersed among the 120 million rods that are dominant in the peripheral regions of the retina. Rods are sensitive to motion and the presence of light and thus are essential for night vision or vision in areas of reduced light. A healthy retinal layer is critical to the efficient transmission of impulses back to the brain. In a premature in-

fant, the retinal layer may not be completely developed and may be vulnerable to the oxygen that frequently must be administered to maintain life. In a full-term infant, the macula and fovea are typically not fully developed until several months after birth (Vaughan et al., 1999; Wright, 1997).

Degenerative diseases of the retina that damage the cone cells in the macular region can cause losses in central vision, a common occurrence in older adults who, simply because of age, are at risk for age-related macular degeneration. Color vision becomes vulnerable if the cone cells are compromised for any reason. Other conditions, like retinitis pigmentosa, can affect the rod cells and lead to decreased night vision.

Other structures of the internal eye are the anterior and posterior chambers and the vitreous cavity. The anterior chamber lies behind the posterior surface of the cornea and the anterior surface of the iris. The posterior chamber lies behind the iris and pupil and in front of the anterior surface of the lens. Both chambers are filled with aqueous humor, the clear watery liquid secreted by the ciliary process already described.

The vitreous cavity, a large chamber, is filled with a transparent, avascular, physiological gel. The vitreous is 99 percent water and makes up about two-thirds of the volume of the eyeball and three-fourths of the weight. The vitreous gel may become stained by blood if there are hemorrhages in the back of the eye, as may occur in some types of diabetic retinopathy, which is discussed later in this chapter.

Of the retina's nine layers, the internal limiting membrane is the layer that is adjacent to the vitreous. The retinal pigment epithelium, the outer layer, rests on the inner layer of the choroid, which provides nutrition for the retina. The rods and cones lie under the retinal pigment epithelium. In the course of time and use, discs in the outer portion of the rods and cones are removed and replaced by new ones. The new ones at the bottom of the stack move up in the rods and cones as the old discs are pushed out to where they can be digested by the retinal pigment epithelium in a process called phagocytosis, an efficient waste management system.

Optic Pathways

When the rods and cones of the retina are stimulated by light rays, they send their messages to the brain via the 1 million fibers in back of the optic nerve. The optic nerve is the second cranial nerve (CN 2) and, like other central nerves, cannot regenerate or be repaired if it is damaged. The fibers of the optic nerve divide after leaving each eyeball and orbital cavity. Fibers that carry impulses from the nasal retina of the left eye decussate (separate) and cross over at the optic chiasm, the place where they join fibers from the temporal retina of the right eye. Together, they form the right optic tract and travel to the lateral geniculate nucleus, where they synapse with cells that continue and fan out as radiations that relay information to the visual areas of the occipital cortex of the occipital lobe of the brain. Right nasal retinal fibers cross at the optic chiasm to join left temporal retinal fibers to form the left optic tract, which carries information to the lateral geniculate nucleus and from there along the optic radiations to the left side of the occipital cortex (see Figure 3.5). Information is then transferred to other areas of the cortex for interpretation and processing (Newell, 1996; Wright, 1997). Information from each eye in the normal visual system arrives on each side of the brain.

Damage to various parts of the optic pathways can sometimes be localized by determining what portions of an individual's visual field are restricted. For example, if damage occurred to the right optic nerve at a point in front of the optic chiasm, vision in the right eye would be affected. If damage occurred at the optic chiasm, impulses from the nasal portions of each retina would be interrupted, resulting in losses in the left and right temporal fields. When the eyes are directed straight ahead to a distant visual target, light rays entering the eyes from the left strike the nasal retina in the left eye and the temporal retina in the right eye and light rays entering from the right strike the nasal retina in the right eye and the temporal retina of the left eye. Therefore, if impulses from the left and right nasal retinas are not transmitted past the damaged point, the result is the loss of both temporal fields in both the left and right eyes. Figure 3.5 suggests how injuries at specific sites along the optic nerves and pathways would affect the receipt of stimuli from regions of the visual field.

In some instances, an individual is said to be cortically blind or to have cortical visual impairment. Cortical visual impairment can result from lesions that occur along the visual pathway from the lateral geniculate nucleus back to the visual cortex. Problems along the optic nerve between the retina and the lateral geniculate body are grouped with conditions affecting the eyeball, all of which are considered ocular visual impairments (Jan & Groenveld, 1993). The visual behavioral characteristics of those with ocular impairments and children with cortical impairments are typically different, unless the impairments involve sites on both sides of the lateral geniculate body. The eyes and eye movements of children with cortical visual impairments appear normal, as do the children's pupillary reactions to light. But these children often have variable visual function even within a few minutes, a short visual attention span, attraction to light and light gazing, and limited field of vision, among other characteristics (Jan & Groenveld, 1993).

Many children with cortical visual impairments have other neurological problems as well. Although sophisticated electrophysiological and other diagnostic tests can aid the diagnosis of cortical visual impairment, careful observations of general and visual behaviors can provide valuable information for both diagnosis and instruction.

STRUCTURAL PROBLEMS THAT AFFECT FUNCTION

In the normal and healthy eye, rays of light travel through the transparent cornea, the major refractive surface of the eye; through the aqueous to the lens, where fine adjustments are made; on through the vitreous; and, finally, to the retina. Refractive errors and muscle imbalance can, however, introduce difficulties that lead to degradation in the image that is transmitted to the brain from the retina via the optic nerve fibers.

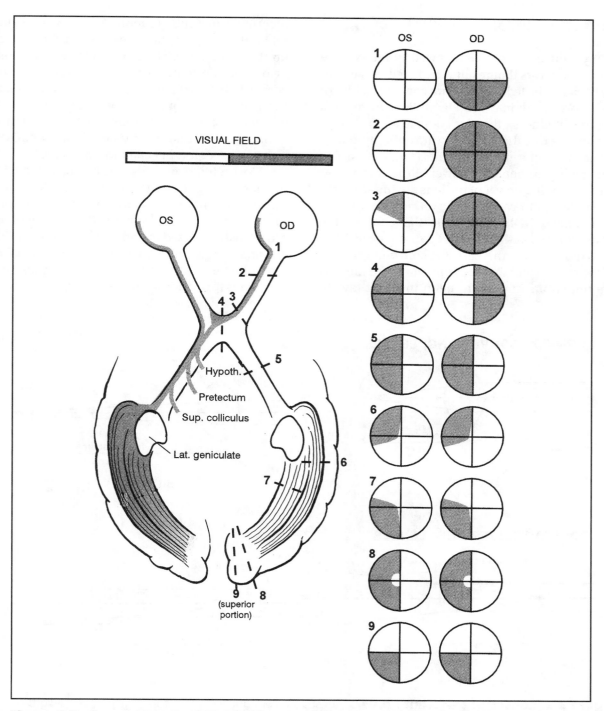

Figure 3.5. Arrangement of Nerve Fibers as They Travel from the Optic Nerves to the Occipital Lobe of the Brain.

Source: Adapted from K. W. Wright, Ed., *Textbook of Ophthalmology* (Baltimore, MD: Williams & Wilkins, 1997), p. 138.

Refractive Errors

Many individuals, children as well as adults, have refractive errors that result in reduced visual acuity because the light rays do not come to a point of focus on the retina (see Figure 3.6). In myopia (nearsightedness), the rays come to a point of focus in front of the retina because the eyeball is longer than normal on the horizontal axis. The converging, or bending, power of the cornea and the fine-tuning power of the lens are too strong to make the light rays reach the retina to produce a clear image. In hyperopia (farsightedness), the point of focus is slightly (and hypothetically) behind the retina. In this case, the converging power of the cornea and the fine adjustments of the lens are not strong enough to bend the light rays to

meet at the focal point (point of clear focus) on the retina. In astigmatism, some rays may converge on the retina while others may converge in front or behind the retina because the surface of the cornea is uneven or oblong, rather than spherical. In the case of myopia, near vision is better than distance vision. In hyperopia, distance vision is typically better than near vision. In astigmatism, vision can be blurry at all points of focus.

Most refractive errors can be corrected with eyeglasses or contact lenses. Concave spherical (divergent or minus) lenses are used to correct for myopia, and convex spherical (convergent or plus) lenses are used to correct for hyperopia. For astigmatism, cylindrical lenses are prescribed that have different refractive powers along specific meridians to provide what the eye requires in con-

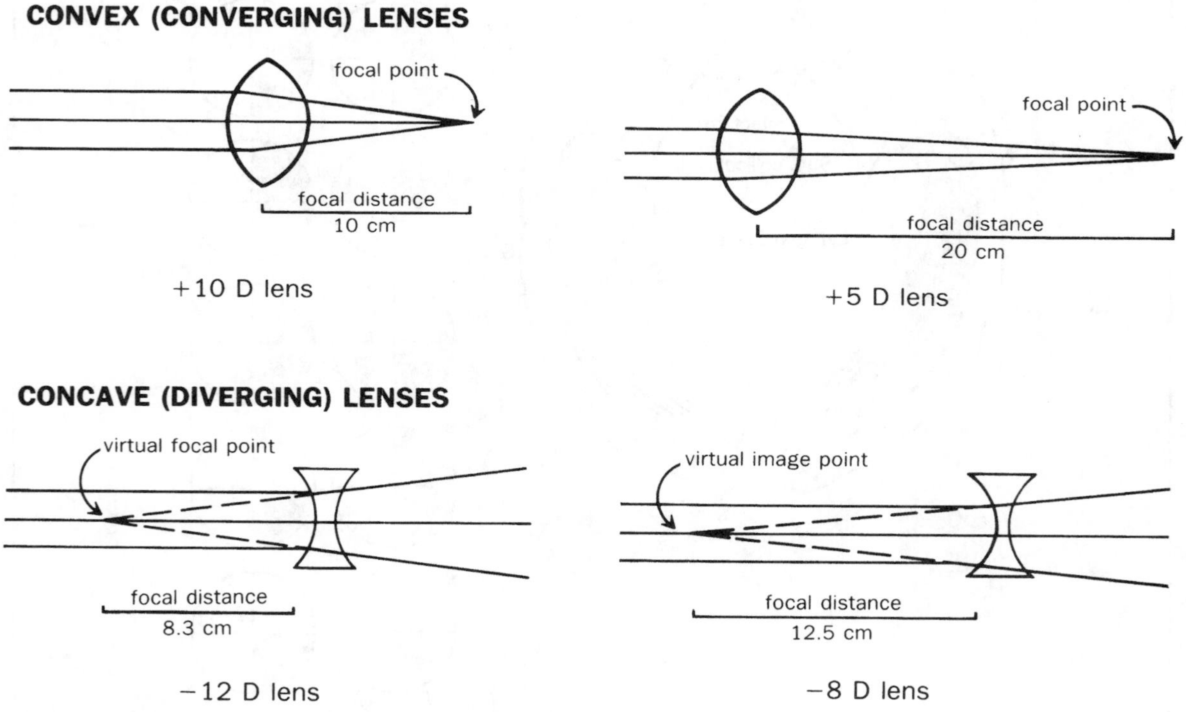

CONVEX (CONVERGING) LENSES

focal point

focal distance
10 cm

+10 D lens

focal point

focal distance
20 cm

+5 D lens

CONCAVE (DIVERGING) LENSES

virtual focal point

focal distance
8.3 cm

−12 D lens

virtual image point

focal distance
12.5 cm

−8 D lens

Figure 3.6. Lenses of Different Powers. Lenses are commonly used to converge or diverge light rays passing through them. The stronger the lens, the shorter the distance required to bring light rays to a point of focus.

Source: Reprinted, by permission, from J. E. Moore, W. H. Graves, and J. B. Patterson, *Foundations of Rehabilitation Counseling with Persons Who Are Blind or Visually Impaired* (New York: AFB Press, 1997), p. 49.

vergent or divergent power to bring light rays to a point of focus on the retina (see Figure 3.6).

To understand the meridians on a lens, one can think of a ball that has a circle drawn around it to represent the vertical axis and another circle to represent the horizontal axis. More circles could be drawn around the ball that pass through the midpoint, where the horizontal and vertical axes cross. These additional circles represent the meridians of a lens, although the lens is biconvex—not round like a ball, but oval like a football. In many cases, the refracting power of all meridians of the lens of the eye is essentially the same, and a spherical corrective lens can be used to correct for myopia or hyperopia because a spherical lens has the same refracting power on all meridians. In cases of astigmatism, however, along one or several adjacent meridians, the bending power of the lenses is prescribed to add bending power for the weaker meridians and to compensate for the stronger meridians so rays of light come to focus *on* the retina, not in front of or behind it.

In many people, visual acuity for near or distant points remains below the normal range even with the best correction. For some of them, generally those over age 18, recently refined surgical procedures to reshape the cornea have dramatically improved vision so that eyeglasses may not even be necessary or if they are, the refractive power of the spectacle lenses is much less than it was before surgery. The procedures include radial keratotomy for myopia, to reduce the curvature of the cornea and thus reduce the refractive power; astigmatic keratotomy, to reduce astigmatism by flattening areas of the cornea to even out the refractive power or the cornea; and eximer laser correction/ablation, to reshape the cornea stroma (*Laser Vision Correction*, n.d.).

Children with refractive errors who are served in programs for students with visual impairments are those whose visual acuity still falls below the normal range in the better eye after the best correction and adversely affects their educational progress. Some of these children may have other ocular conditions that also interfere with functional vision.

Muscle Imbalance

Another problem in eye structure that can lead to possible difficulties with visual function is muscle imbalance. The paired or yoked muscles work together to produce conjugate eye movements in the six cardinal directions of gaze. If these muscles are not innervated equally, that is, if the strength of the muscles is unequal, or if any muscle is paralyzed, then the eyes may not appear straight and may not achieve good, clear, binocular vision.

Strabismus is the condition in which an eye deviates from either the horizontal or vertical axis. It occurs in approximately 2 percent of children (Vaughan et al., 1999) and is sometimes first noticed in infants just several months old. If there is a tendency for misalignment, the turn is referred to as a *-phoria*. If the misalignment is constant, the term used is *-tropia*. The turn may be in toward the nose (*eso-*), toward the temple (*exo-*), or up (*hyper-*) or down (*hypo-*) in relation to the horizontal axis. A person whose right eye tends to turn in, for example, when he or she is tired or has done a lot of close eyework, is said to have a right esophoria. If the turn was constant, it would be called a right esotropia.

If a child has strabismus, there is a danger of diplopia (double vision) in which the child sees two images that may be partially superimposed or totally separated because the image from one eye does not originate from a point on the retina that corresponds to the point on the retina in the other eye. As was discussed earlier, the information from both eyes is carried to both sides of the occipital lobe. Because the two eyes are directed at a visual target from a slightly different position, two slightly different images, one from each eye, arrive in the occipital lobe. The association areas of the lobe fuse the two images into one three-dimensional stereoscopic image in ways that are not clearly understood. If the two images cannot be fused into one clear image, the resulting double vision can be confusing and eventually intolerable. At some point along the visual pathways or possibly in the brain, the bothersome, usually weaker, image is suppressed and ignored. This suppression can lead to amblyopia in the suppressed eye, that is, poor vision from lack of use, rather than from an organic disease. If amblyopia is caught early, at least by age 5 or 6, and treatment of the underlying cause is successful, then vision may improve to within the normal range (*Amblyopia*, 1997).

Options for the treatment of strabismus include the correction of any refractive errors with spectacle or contact lenses; prism lenses to redirect the line of sight; patching or occlusion of the good eye for carefully prescribed periods each day to stimulate use of the weaker eye and equalize the visual acuities; orthoptic eye exercises in selected cases to stimulate the fovea; medication, again to force use of the weaker eye; and surgery. The major goals in the treatment of strabismus are clear vision (acuity), cosmetically straight eyes, and binocular vision (fusion). In many cases, only the first two goals are achieved.

Although refractive errors and muscle imbalance contribute to the population of children and adults who have impaired vision, these conditions are not considered major causes of visual impairment. Most refractive errors can be corrected with lenses and, in some cases, with surgery. Muscle imbalance can be treated successfully in most cases if it is caught early, ideally before a child is one year old. But if these conditions are not diagnosed and treated while a child is still young, or at least before age 5 or 6, then the effects on functional vision and sometimes on social-emotional development may be serious.

CAUSES OF VISUAL IMPAIRMENT

Many conditions contribute to the impairment of eye structures and tissue. Whether the impairment actually leads to limitations in visual function, however, depends on such factors as the site and severity of the tissue damage and the age of the individual at the time the problem occurs. Some conditions originate during the prenatal period, others stem from events that occur during or shortly after birth, and still others develop or occur later as a result of disease or trauma. Conditions that are caused by diseases or accidents after birth are called adventitious.

Some eye conditions are inherited; that is, they are passed on to the affected individuals by a parent or, in some cases, both parents. At times, the inherited condition may appear to skip a generation. A genetic study can help determine a family's pattern of transmission and how the condition might have been passed from one generation to the next and to children within a generation.

There are many ways eye conditions can be inherited. An autosomal dominant pattern means that a condition or disease can be passed to an offspring if one parent transmits the gene responsible for the condition at the moment of conception, as is the case with some types of glaucoma and night blindness. An autosomal recessive pattern means that a recessive gene for the condition must come from each parent, as is the case with some metabolic diseases and at least one type of albinism. In sex-linked patterns, the female carrier, the mother, contributes the affected sex chromosome and the son manifests the condition. Examples of sex-linked diseases are some forms of albinism and color blindness. When inherited conditions are manifest, or expressed, they may appear as mild, moderate, or severe. The variable severity of expression of a disease from one generation to another can complicate attempts to determine penetrance, that is, whether the inherited condition in a particular individual is mild, whether it is skipping a generation, or whether it is genetically present but not manifest. Geneticists who try to determine patterns of transmission of diseases look at expression in previous generations of a family and in members of the same generation of a family and then examine the pedigrees of the individuals of concern in the family (Vaughan et al., 1999).

Some hereditary conditions do not become manifest or obvious until adolescence or even adulthood, while others may be congenital (present at birth). Not all hereditary conditions are congenital, and not all congenital conditions are hereditary. Some hereditary and other later developing conditions, such as retinitis pigmentosa and Usher syndrome, may be diagnosed before their clinical appearance with the aid of sophisticated diagnostic procedures.

This section describes the more common causes of ocular visual impairment; briefly reviews other notable causes, such as cortical visual impairment; and highlights several systemic conditions that can have significant ocular manifestations. In subsequent discussion, diagnostic procedures are reviewed to enhance teachers' understanding of clinical eye reports that are typically required for students who receive special education services because of their visual impairments.

Major Ocular Visual Impairments

The major causes of visual impairments can be described according to their site, type, and etiology. Site refers to the location within the orbit or the eyeball; type indicates the diagnosis, like glaucoma; and etiology refers to the underlying cause, such as an infection.

There are no accurate data on the number of individuals with impaired vision or no vision, let alone on the causes of the visual conditions, because in the United States there is no national registry of individuals who are blind or who have significant low vision (Kirchner & Schmeidler, 1997). The American Printing House for the Blind (APH) collects annual figures to show the number of school-age children and youths who receive educational services because their visual impairments interfere with their learning, but etiology and site are not reported. No national data are available for the number of infants, toddlers, or preschoolers with visual impairments, although efforts are underway in some states with federally funded Project PRISM to establish a multistate registry (Ferrell, with Shaw & Dietz, 1998). For adults over age 40, more accurate and recent estimates are found in *Vision Problems in the U.S.* (1994), published by Prevent Blindness America (PBA), formerly the National Society to Prevent Blindness. These PBA estimates are based on 1990 population data taken from the summary tapes of

the U.S. Bureau of the Census. The best estimates of the prevalence of clinical low vision and blindness are based on data drawn from data pools collected in 1970 from a 16-state region that included approximately 31 percent of the population of the United States in that year. Although there are many questions regarding the accuracy and representativeness of this information, these data are still the best available for overall estimates of prevalence and causes across all ages.

What can be determined from all these data sources with some degree of certainty is that the most common causes of blindness in the United States for people of all ages are macular degeneration, cataracts, glaucoma, and diabetic retinopathy (*Vision Problems*, 1994). In infants and toddlers, including those born prematurely, retinopathy of prematurity (ROP), optic nerve atrophy, and cortical visual impairment account for an increasing number of children with impaired vision.

Macular Degeneration. Macular degeneration is most frequently age related; the more years one lives beyond age 50, the greater the probability that macular degeneration will develop. Because the macular region of the retina and the fovea within the macula are responsible for carrying information about detail and color to the brain for interpretation, problems with blood supply or the removal of old cell tissue can interfere with the work of the cone cells that make up the macular area and degrade the fine resolution a healthy macula can provide. Whether macular degeneration occurs in childhood or is age related, there is no cure for it. In some cases, however, photocoagulation (the use of a high-energy light source to destroy tissue) may stop or delay further neovascularization, capillary seepage, and degeneration. In the case of macular degeneration, photocoagulation with a laser can destroy the fragile and abnormal blood vessels and capillaries that form and seep or leak blood.

Cataracts.   As was explained earlier, a cataract is a lens that has become opaque, so that light rays can no longer pass through it into the vitreous and on to the cells of the retinal layer. Congenital cataracts are found in approximately 1 in 250 live births (Wright, 1997) and may be linked to maternal rubella during the first trimester of pregnancy, to an autosomal-dominant or other inheritance pattern, or to an infection like syphilis or cytomegalovirus. Some cataracts occur as a result of a systemic disease, but for many, the cause cannot be identified.

Glaucoma.   As with cataracts in young children, many attempts to identify the causes of blindness and low vision among the general population or among the school-age population end with "undetermined" or "not specified" or "not clear at this time." The glaucomas, except for those secondary to disease or trauma, fall under this category because the reason for the increase in pressure within the eye is not clearly understood. As was noted earlier, the significant feature of all types of glaucoma is a specific pattern of optic nerve damage, usually coupled with increased pressure in the eye. The eye care specialist can determine the status of the optic disc by using an ophthalmoscope to examine the back of the eye, as long as the cornea, lens, and vitreous are clear. A slit lamp and high-power handheld lens provide an even better magnified stereoscopic view of the optic disc and surrounding retina (Wright, 1997). But the underlying reason, the etiology, for the pattern of damage to the disc and the increase in intraocular pressure is usually not evident.

Retinopathy of Prematurity.   Infants with low birth weight (under 1500 grams, or 3.5 pounds), typically as a result of premature birth, are at risk of developing retinopathy of prematurity (ROP). For many such infants, oxygen is necessary to sustain life. About half the premature infants born at 26 weeks gestation and weighing only 700 grams now survive (Wright, 1997). But the oxygen given to sustain life, even when blood gasses and oxygen uptake are carefully monitored, may stimulate the growth of fragile and abnormal blood vessels in the underdeveloped retina. These tiny vessels may grow in the wrong direction into the vitreous or form a ridge instead of branching out and sometimes break down and cause hemorrhages. Skilled

ophthalmologists can determine the stages of the development of ROP in a careful examination. If Stage 3+, indicating severe and critical disease, is determined, the treatment of choice is laser therapy or cryotherapy (use of extreme cold to freeze tissue). Without treatment, the tiny abnormal vessels that grow may exert enough pull on the retina to lead to retinal detachment. In some babies, ROP resolves with no apparent decrease in visual function as the babies grow and develop. In other babies, ROP is just one of a number of conditions related to prematurity and low birth weight; vision may or may not be compromised, as can be the case with other areas of motor and cognitive development. With the increase in the number of extremely premature infants of low birth weight who survive, the incidence of ROP is growing (Wright, 1997). Children with ROP seem to have a higher-than-normal incidence of myopia, astigmatism, and strabismus (Wright, 1997).

Optic Nerve Conditions.   Optic nerve hypoplasia and optic nerve atrophy, in which the optic nerve either does not develop normally or develops but then degenerates, also contribute to the number of school-age children with visual impairments. Trauma, a tumor causing pressure against the optic nerve, and decreased blood supply may lead to the atrophy. In some cases, if the cause is eliminated, vision may improve. In other cases, the condition is associated with other congenital abnormalities (Vaughan et al., 1999).

Eye Injuries.   Eye injuries account for many known instances of visual impairment among school-age youngsters, but are not considered a major cause of visual impairment because often only one eye is involved. Such injuries are a leading cause of preventable impaired vision, at least monocular impaired vision. Burns, flash burns, contusions, foreign bodies (such as pieces of glass or metal) embedded in the eye, motor vehicle accidents, sharp toys or pencils, sport ball injuries to the orbit when goggles are not worn, exposure to sunlamps, and other items and events are associated with eye accidents that may, but fortunately do not always, lead to blindness in the injured eye. Teachers, parents, and other responsible caregivers can help prevent instances of vision loss by being alert to these potentially hazardous objects and situations when youngsters are under their supervision.

Infectious Diseases. Infectious diseases still account for cases of impaired vision in some children. Rubella, also called German measles, can cause damage to the eyes, ears, heart, and central nervous system of a developing baby if contracted by the mother during her first trimester of pregnancy. These systems and structures are especially vulnerable to infection during the early weeks after conception, and the rubella virus attacks the cells of the developing structures when they are most at risk during those first few months. The mother may not even notice any symptoms, but the virus apparently can interfere with the transcription of genetic information in the cells of the developing structures of her baby. The result can be hearing loss, cardiac malformation, cataracts, and mental retardation in the child. A vaccine to immunize individuals against the disease is available. Although it is of no value to those who have already had rubella or who have been affected by it, this vaccine can decrease the number of persons who may contract the disease and transmit it to any pregnant woman who has not been inoculated against it.

Other infectious diseases besides rubella that may result in damage to the eyes, either before or after birth, include toxoplasmosis, tuberculosis, and trachoma. Trachoma, a leading cause of preventable blindness in Africa, Asia, and the Middle East, is an infection of the conjunctive and cornea that can lead to corneal scarring if not treated but is preventable with the use of antibiotics. Infectious sexually transmitted diseases, such as AIDS and HIV, can lead to eye infections and inflammations with a significant loss of vision.

Tumors. Tumors may cause damage to eye structures and may even necessitate enucleation (removal of the affected eye). Retinoblastoma, a life-threatening malignant tumor that occurs bilaterally in approximately 20 percent of the cases, usually appears before a child reaches his or her third birthday. At present, the treatment generally is enucleation (Wright, 1997). In selected cases when the tumor is small, radiation, chemotherapy, laser photocoagulation, and cryosurgery may be options (Wright, 1997).

Nystagmus. Nystagmus is a condition that is frequently found in children and adults whose vision was impaired at birth or during the first two or three years of life. It is an involuntary, rhythmical oscillating movement of one or both eyes from side to side, up and down, in a rotary pattern, or in some combination. The movement can be pendular and regular or jerky with comparatively slow movement in one direction and a rapid return. Nystagmus may accompany other ocular conditions, usually those that have existed for an extended period; it is not characteristic of cortical visual impairment or post-optic chiasm disorders such as tumors or cerebrovascular disease (Wright, 1997). Treatment is directed at the primary condition if the nystagmus accompanies another condition. Some children and adults may turn or tilt their heads in an effort to decrease the speed, amplitude, or duration of the eye movements. Under certain circumstances, nystagmus can be elicited in individuals with normal vision, for example, by looking as far to the side as possible for a period or by watching a rotating drum marked with alternating dark and light bands or looking at railroad cars moving along the tracks. Since nystagmus can be stimulated in the normal eye with intact ocular motor and visual pathways, some visual tests make use of rotating drums with bands of various thicknesses and intensity in an effort to elicit nystagmus as evidence of some degree of visual function.

Cortical Visual Impairment. As was mentioned earlier, some children have cortical visual impairment, meaning that their decreased visual function is the result of a lesion located somewhere along the visual pathways between the lateral geniculate body and the occipital cortex in the brain. Many of these children (although not all of them) have additional disabilities, including cognitive delays, epilepsy, and cerebral palsy. The incidence of such children seems to be increasing, according to data being collected by Ferrell and her colleagues (Ferrell et al., 1998). Students with cortical visual impairments do not appear to have eye problems, but they demonstrate difficulties with depth perception, the visual detection of objects, estimation of distance, and spontaneous visual learning (Groenveld, Jan, & Leader, 1990).

Systemic Conditions with Possible Ocular Manifestations

Many general systemic diseases that affect the vascular, neurological, and metabolic systems can put the eyes at risk. Diabetes is a prime example of a metabolic disorder that can result in retinopathy with changes in the retinal blood vessels, hemorrhages, and proliferation of blood vessels. The occurrence of diabetic retinopathy seems to be more closely related to the duration and control, rather than to the severity, of diabetes. About 50 percent of those with diabetes for 7 years show some signs of retinopathy, and approximately 90 percent show signs after 20 years. Damage to the retina can occur as a result of tiny leaks from the retinal capillaries that weaken those capillaries or the growth of new but abnormal capillaries in an attempt to bypass areas of poor perfusion (blood flow). Children who develop early-onset diabetes may not experience eye difficulties until years after they leave school, but regular eye examinations need to be a vital part of their ongoing health care.

Another systemic condition that is frequently accompanied by difficulties in ocular movement is cerebral palsy, a disorder of voluntary movement and posture caused by damage to the brain before, during, or soon after birth (Rosen, 1998). Considered a multidimensional disorder because of the variety of daily functions that can be affected by the associated problems, such as seizures, impaired communication, and mental retardation, cerebral palsy also carries with it a high incidence of sensory impairments. Many youngsters have difficulty tracking or visually fixing on objects, and may have strabismus or their eyes may show nystagmus.

Retinitis pigmentosa (RP), an inheritable condition leading to progressive deterioration of the retina with decreased night vision and restricted fields of vision, can occur in just the eyes or may be associated with systemic conditions (*Understanding Retinitis Pigmentosa*, 1996; Wright, 1997). The rods are usually affected first. The loss of night vision typically begins in adolescence, and eventually the cones may be affected. The severity of the visual loss is apparently related to the type of inheritance pattern, with the sex-linked pattern leading to more severe loss (Newell, 1996; Wright, 1997). An individual with Usher syndrome has congenital neurosensory deafness and then later manifests RP. About 90 percent of individuals with Lawrence-Moon-Biedl-Bardet syndrome, which includes such characteristics as mental retardation and obesity, have RP. Although there is no cure for RP, some researchers have suggested that vitamin A supplements and avoidance of exposure to bright sunlight may delay the deterioration. Specialized physiological testing may detect signs of RP in the retina before a person is aware of any decreased function, but since there is no cure and no certainty of the eventual degree of vision loss, some professionals have been reluctant to suggest testing when nothing can be done to improve the condition. Others have noted the value of genetic counseling, along with the use of appropriate visual aids to enhance remaining vision.

Multiple sclerosis, a chronic neurological disease that appears usually between age 15 and 50, is sometimes difficult to diagnose unless magnetic resonance imaging reveals the typical indicators in the brain. It is a demyelinating disease of the central nervous system, but its course is unpredictable, and there are remissions and relapses. If the optic nerve is involved, vision may decrease and then improve, just as motor weaknesses, ataxia, tremors, and other physical symptoms come and go (Vaughan et al., 1999).

Along with multiple sclerosis, disorders of the thyroid gland, certain vitamin deficiencies, and other systemic diseases can lead to severe eye problems and vision loss. Although the total number of children affected may be relatively small, some cases do occur and are of extreme significance to the individuals who are affected.

DIAGNOSIS OF VISUAL IMPAIRMENTS

Parents and teachers may be the first to suspect that something is wrong with a child's eyes. They may notice the child having difficulty accomplishing visual tasks at home or school. Difficulties with vision might also be identified through screening procedures that are commonly conducted in preschool and kindergarten. These screenings provide a gross judgment about how the child sees. If the child's performance on the screening task, such as naming objects at a set distance and size or matching shapes at a set distance and size, does not meet the criteria for "passing" the screening, the child is referred for a clinical eye examination. The real value of such screenings, usually conducted by trained volunteers, lies in the follow-up of those children who are referred for professional eye examinations. If there is no follow-up to ensure children are examined by eye specialists, then the screenings serve little purpose. Screenings can be thought of as sorting children into two groups: those whose visual acuity is probably within the normal range and those who need further evaluation to determine their visual status.

Eye Care Specialists

Various eye specialists—ophthalmologists, optometrists, orthoptists, and opticians—are trained in the use of diagnostic procedures to determine specific causes or rule out problems with children's eyes. An ophthalmologist is a physician who concentrates on the diagnosis and comprehensive treatment of defects and diseases of the eye, prescribes lenses, performs surgery, and uses drugs and other forms of medical treatment. An optometrist is a trained and licensed eye specialist who examines the eyes to detect signs of disease, measures refractive errors and muscle disturbances, and prescribes and fits lenses. In many states, optometrists are permitted to use certain medications to provide a better view into the eye, just as ophthalmologists do. Some optometrists

and ophthalmologists specialize in the evaluation of patients for the possible use of low vision devices (for further information on low vision devices, see Chapter 14 of *Foundations of Education: Instructional Strategies for Teaching Children and Youths with Visual Impairments*). In some low vision clinics, both of these eye specialists are on the staff, as is an orthoptist, who is trained to give eye exercises in cases of muscle imbalance, amblyopia, diplopia, and suppression of foveal stimulation, and who works in conjunction with these eye specialists. An optician is a technician trained to design, fit, and dispense lenses according to optometrists' or ophthalmologists' prescriptions, fit contact and spectacle lenses, and adjust spectacle frames to the wearers. Some opticians may also make low vision aids available (*Common Eye Problems*, 1997).

Anyone who is referred to an eye specialist generally receives a clinical examination that includes a history, a discussion of why the person has come for an examination, and the physical examination itself. Sometimes special procedures are necessary to determine the integrity of the eye structures.

Diagnostic Procedures

Eye specialists use a wide variety of diagnostic procedures and tests to assess the integrity, health, and function of the eyes and the optic pathways that lead to the back of the brain. The following are among the more common procedures, but an eye specialist decides which of these or other more sophisticated procedures are called for in a given situation.

Notation of Symptoms.   The eye specialist notes any symptoms the person exhibits—pain, double vision, tearing, dryness, blind spots, halos around lights, floaters, photophobia (sensitivity to light), poor night vision, blurriness, difficulty reading, and so forth. In combination with a careful and detailed history, this is a rich source of information and helps the eye specialist determine the type and extent of further testing.

Notation of Appearance. The eye specialist pays attention to the size, shape, position, and color of the eyes; the presence of discharge or inflammation; and whether the pupils are of equal size.

Acuity Measurement. Typically, visual acuity is checked with the Snellen Letter or E Chart, the latter preferred for children and others who cannot accurately identify letters. In some cases, special equipment with symbol cards showing objects or shapes other than letters may be used. Acuities are taken for both distance and near vision.

Field Measurement. The normal field of vision covers approximately 150 degrees on the nasal to temporal axis and approximately 120 degrees on the superior to inferior axis (Wright, 1997). (See Sidebar 3.1 for a further explanation of visual field.) A number of different confrontation techniques using grids and screens, as well as computerized software that presents points of light at predetermined spots and intensities and mechanical devices that allow points of light to be presented at selected locations, can be used to determine defects in the central field and the peripheral field of vision in each eye (Wright, 1997).

The eye specialist selects the one most appropriate for the specific situation.

Biomicroscopy. Use of a slit lamp with a high-power magnification and illumination provides the eye specialist with a more detailed view of the eyelids and the inside of the eyeball.

Tonometry. Intraocular pressure may be measured by several techniques. Tonometers require the insertion of a local anesthetic solution in the eye. Most glaucoma screening programs use a technique that does not involve touching the eye directly. This type of screening procedure is satisfactory for initial screening purposes, but indentation and applanation tonometry are considered more precise for clinical purposes. In applanation tonometry, as with the Goldmann tonometer, a variable amount of force is applied directly to the anesthetized cornea to determine how much force is needed to produce a predetermined amount of indentation. In indentation tonometry, such as with the Schoitz tonometer, weights of various amounts are applied to the corneal surface and the amount of indentation is measured. The purpose of all these techniques is to determine the pressure within the eyes, a critical element in the diagnosis of glaucoma.

SIDEBAR 3.1 — Visual Fields

The field of vision refers to the area one can see without shifting one's gaze. Because of the location of the eyeballs in the orbits and the position of the orbits in the head, the normal field of vision is approximately 150 degrees horizontally and 120 degrees vertically (Wright, 1997). The nasal fields of vision from each eye overlap when the eyes look straight ahead, but not the temporal. Field defects are denoted as nasal, temporal, superior, and inferior, terms that refer to space, not to the retinal site. For example, if a person has right superior field loss in the right eye, some of the retinal cells in the inferior nasal retina of the right eye are not functioning adequately or their message is not relayed accurately to the appropriate occipital lobe of the brain. In other words, one way to check retinal function and integrity of the optic pathways is to check visual fields and infer retinal function and integrity from what a person reports in each quadrant of the field. See Figure 3.7 for an illustration of visual field.

Source: Reprinted, by permission, from A. L. Corn and A. J. Koenig, Eds., *Foundations of Low Vision: Clinical and Functional Perspectives* (New York: AFB Press, 1996), p. 73.

Ophthalmoscopic Examination. The ophthalmoscope provides a good view of the retina and the internal structures of the eye. The ophthalmologist routinely instills a drug that dilates the pupil but does not affect accommodation, so as to obtain visual access to the peripheral retina and regions of the fundus.

Gonioscopy. Particularly in suspected cases of glaucoma, gonioscopy is done to examine the angle of the anterior chamber by direct visualization. A local anesthetic, special lighting, a special microscope, and a special lens, called a goniolens, are required for the examination.

Corneal Staining. A dye, frequently fluorescein, may be instilled in the eye to reveal corneal abrasions and irregularities, to help locate foreign bodies in the eye, or to determine the drainage of tears.

Color Perception Tests. Tests for color perception require a person to identify patterns, often numbers, made up of colored dots on a background of dots of a different color. The colors are selected so patterns in the frequencies of these colors are not discernible to persons with defects in color perception. Red-green confusion is the most common problem in both males (8 percent) and females (0.4 percent), whereas blue-yellow confusion is rare in both sexes (Newell, 1996; *True Colors,* 1996). Problems with color vision are almost always sex linked and transmitted by mothers to their sons.

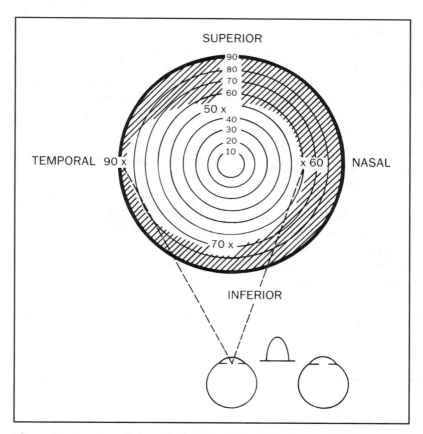

Figure 3.7. Normal Full Visual Field for the Left Eye.
Source: Reprinted, by permission, from R. Jose, *Understanding Low Vision* (New York: American Foundation for the Blind, 1983), p. 98.

Types of Eye Examinations

SIDEBAR 3.2

SCREENING

Not really an examination but, rather, a gross sorting of individuals whose visual performance on a visual task meets a predetermined cutoff from those whose visual performance does not. Examples of screening include:

◆ Preschool vision screening with the E chart,
◆ School-age screening with the Snellen letter chart, and
◆ Glaucoma screening.

CLINICAL EYE EXAMINATION

An eye examination done by an eye specialist to determine the health and integrity of the eyes. Typically, it involves a history; physical examination of the eyes, including a check of visual acuity, appearance of the eyes and surrounding structures; and certain tests, such as for glaucoma or macular degeneration. Treatment may or may not be recommended, depending on what is found. Treatment may include refraction to improve near and/or distant acuity, medication, surgery, referral to another specialist, follow-up care at a later date, or further specialized tests. The following are examples of specialized tests:

◆ Contrast sensitivity to determine sensitivity to size in relation to lightness or darkness of the background (frequency to intensity);
◆ Electrophysiological tests to determine retinal function;
◆ Visually evoked response to check macular function;
◆ Ultrasonography to determine internal structures of the eye and eyeball and changes in the shape, size, position, and density of internal structures;
◆ X-rays, CT scans, or MRI studies to determine the status of internal structures.

FUNCTIONAL EYE EXAMINATION

An assessment carried out by a low vision specialist, teacher of students who are visually impaired, or another individual who is knowledgeable about the development of visual skills and the effects of visual impairment on visual performance. The assessment considers visual performance in a variety of tasks and settings, visual fields, eye movements, and responses to such specific environmental conditions as light and color. The report of a functional vision exam should indicate recommendations for any modifications in instructional procedures, materials, strategies, or conditions for learning that can enhance the use of vision in school, as well as at home and in the community (Corn & Koenig, 1996).

LOW VISION EVALUATION

An evaluation to determine if any low vision devices may enhance visual performance for specific tasks the individual has identified. A low vision evaluation should follow any clinical examination and treatment and may include elements of a functional eye examination if one has not been completed. This evaluation explores ways to carry out tasks, such as reading a book or a newspaper, watching television, locating places on a map, or reading labels on bottles or packages.

Amsler Grid. To detect blind spots or scotomas in the central visual field, an eye specialist may ask a person to focus on a dot on a grid chart and then indicate any area of distortion on the grid or absence of a grid pattern. Blind spots in the field can indicate where on the retina or in other structures of the eye there may be damage, as with macular degeneration.

Once an individual has had a clinical examination and has been fitted with the best possible corrective lenses, his or her functional vision may still not be efficient for some tasks the person would like to do. In these cases, a low vision evaluation may result in the identification of optical aids, magnifiers, closed-circuit television (CCVT), or other adaptations that can enhance visual performance. Sidebar 3.2 summarizes information on three types of eye examinations in addition to screening: clinical, functional, and low vision.

INTERPRETING EYE REPORTS

In most programs for school-age youngsters with visual impairments, an eye examination report completed by an eye specialist, either an ophthalmologist or an optometrist, is required annually for each student who is in or referred to the program. Many school districts, intermediate units, counties, and administrative units have designed forms for this annual report or have adopted or modified the form suggested by PBA (Prevent Blindness America). All annual reports for a student should be retained in the student's permanent record folder.

The information in an annual eye report is clinical and may not appear to be directly useful in determining instructional objectives and teaching strategies. Nevertheless, much of the information is valuable to teachers of students with visual impairments. Therefore, teachers need to be able to interpret the information in these reports to determine what may be relevant for instructional purposes and the signs that may indicate a significant deterioration or improvement in a child's eye condition. The following sections describe the various types of information that are reported on most annual report forms, which are illustrated in Figure 3.8.

Identifying Information

A record of the child's name, age, address, and school placement identifies the child for whom the report is requested. Although in some cases, a parent takes the form to an eye specialist, who completes it at the time of the child's eye examination, in most cases, the report form is mailed to the eye specialist, along with a cover letter that explains why the report is needed. In either case, the identifying information should be filled in before the eye specialist gets the form. If the teacher accompanies the child and parent to the examination, he or she can present the form and request that the information for the other sections be reported at the completion of the examination (for a list of abbreviations that are commonly used in these reports, see Table 3.3).

The information on the eye report should be considered confidential, as is clearly indicated on most such forms, just as are any other records pertaining to the student's achievement, performance, health, behavior, and potential. Teachers, guidance counselors, and administrators who legitimately have access to the student's records must respect this confidentiality. Teachers who serve more than one school district or program need to investigate the procedures for maintaining confidentiality of information for all the programs they serve.

History

A complete and accurate history of previous health problems, treatments, and habits is considered to be one of the most critical components of any type of physical examination. Certain elements of the health history are particularly important for teachers of students with visual impairments to know about, not only for what they may contribute to a better understanding of the present condition of the student who is being

Eye Examination Report

Patient's Name _____ Date of Birth _____ Social Security No. _____

Address _____ City _____ State _____ Zip _____

Ocular History (e.g., previous eye diseases, injuries, or operations)

Age at onset _____ History _____

Visual Acuity

If the acuity can be measured, complete this box using Snellen acuities or Snellen equivalents or NLP, LP, HM, CF.

Without Glasses		With Best Correction	
Near	Distance	Near	Distance
R	R	R	R
L	L	L	L

Acuity with glare testing, if applicable: R _____   L _____

If the acuity cannot be measured, check the most appropriate estimation.

☐ Legally Blind
☐ Not Legally Blind

Extra Ocular Muscle Function   ☐ Normal   ☐ Abnormal   Describe _____

VISUAL FIELD
(Goldmann preferred)

LEFT EYE (O.S.)
Remaining field:
_____ DEGREES
Circle applicable code(s)
H Hemianopsia-like
S Central Scotoma
O Other handicapping
    field loss
N Normal field
I 40° or less
B 20° or less

RIGHT EYE (O.D.)
Remaining field:
_____ DEGREES
Circle applicable code(s)
H Hemianopsia-like
S Central Scotoma
O Other handicapping
    field loss
N Normal field
I 40° or less
B 20° or less

TANGENT SCREEN	
INSTRUMENT	
TARGET SIZE	
COLOR	
INTENSITY	

INTRAOCULAR PRESSURE	RIGHT EYE (O.D.) Tension in mm:	LEFT EYE (O.S.) Tension in mm:
CHECK ONE: ☐ POSITIVE ☐ NEGATIVE ☐ BORDERLINE	Instrument Used:	Instrument Used:

(continued on next page)

Figure 3.8. Eye Examination Report.

Source: Adapted, by permission from the Texas Commission for the Blind, Austin, and the New Jersey Commission of the Blind and Visually Impaired, Newark, and reprinted, by permission of the publisher, from J. E. Moore, W. H. Graves, and J. B. Patterson, Eds., *Foundations of Rehabilitation Counseling with Persons Who Are Blind or Visually Impaired* (New York: AFB Press, 1997), pp. 55–56.

| Color Vision | ☐ Normal | ☐ Abnormal | Photophobia | ☐ Yes | ☐ No |

Colors involved:

Diagnosis (Primary cause of vision loss)

_____

_____

_____

Prognosis ☐ Permanent ☐ Recurrent ☐ Improving ☐ Uncertain
☐ Progressive ☐ Communicable ☐ Can Be Improved

Treatment Recommended

☐ Glasses   Refraction Record: ☐ Surgery

    Sph   Cyl Axis ADD   Prism   ☐ Hospitalization will be needed for approximately

  R   _____ days.

  L   Name of hospital _____

☐ Patches (Schedule):

  R _____   Name of anesthesiologist or group:

  L _____   _____

☐ Medication _____

☐ Refer for other medical treatment/exam:

_____

☐ Low Vision Evaluation

☐ Other _____

Precautions or Suggestions (e.g., lighting conditions, activities to be avoided, etc.)

_____

_____

Scheduling   When should patient be re-examined? _____

          Date of Next Appointment _____ Time

Print or Type Name of Licensed Ophthalmologist or Optometrist | Signature of Licensed Ophthalmologist or Optometrist

Address | Date of Examination

City   State   Zip | Telephone Number

RETURN COMPLETED FORM TO:

Name | Address

Agency | City   State   Zip

Figure 3.8. *Continued*

Table 3.3. Abbreviations Frequently Encountered in Eye Reports

OD	ocular dexter (right eye)
OS	ocular sinister (left eye)
OU	oculi unitas (both eyes)
Δ	prism diopter
+	plus or convex lens
−	minus or concave lens
x	at (used in recording correction for astigmatism to indicate location of added cylindrical power)
X	number of times of magnification, as a 10X magnifier that enlarges 10 times
CF	count fingers
HM	hand movements
LP	light perception
D	diopter

examined but for what they suggest about the student's record of past eye care, the parent's follow-through with care and the possible implications for other family members.

One of the first questions asked when a health history is taken is the probable age of onset of the eye problem. A preschooler who has had little or no functional vision since birth has a considerably different repertoire of experiences (in both quantity and quality) from that of the child who has had normal vision since birth. Children learn much by just watching what others are doing, by visually exploring their surroundings, and by combining their visual examination with tactile investigations of objects they grasp and put in their mouths. Chapter 4 in this volume explains the development of vision and visual perception and its impact on cognitive, psychomotor, and psychosocial development. For the purposes of the present discussion, it is sufficient to point out that a child whose visual impairment and subsequent limitations in functional vision have existed since birth or shortly thereafter generally has learning characteristics and instructional needs that are significantly different from those of a child whose visual impairments and limitations in visual function developed after age 3 or 4 (Lowenfeld, 1981). The instructional needs of both children may call for modifications in the regular school program so these children can receive an appropriate education.

Other aspects of the health history are also important: previous eye problems that have required medical treatment, the age at which these problems occurred, and immediate or extended family members who have the same eye condition as the child or other eye problems that may be hereditary. At some point, the teacher of students with visual impairments needs to discuss with the parents whether other family members have been examined to determine if signs of any hereditary eye problems are evident.

Measurements

Visual Acuity

Clinical measurements of vision include distance and near visual acuities with and without correction, a report of what correction has been prescribed for spectacle or contact lenses, a record of the field of vision for each eye, and information about any problem with color vision. Distance visual acuity is perhaps the measurement that many teachers check first, but all the other measurements, especially near vision, are also important for what they can suggest about functional vision that should be explored in the classroom.

In many programs, eligibility for services because of visual impairment is determined by considering the impact of the visual impairment on the student's ability to benefit from the educational program offered to classmates with no visual impairments. If the visual status after treatment and correction indicates the need for specialized educational programming, then the student is deemed eligible for services. The determination of eligibility for services is sometimes still based on the definition of blindness used for legal purposes: a restricted visual field (20 degrees or less in the better eye) or a limited distance visual acuity (20/200 or less in the better eye after correction). On the eye report, distance acuity may be reported with and without correction, although many children who wear corrective lenses are checked only while wearing their lenses. For those for whom no correction with lenses is possible, no acuity is reported in that portion of the report form.

Near vision acuity is extremely important. Acuity is reported with and without correction for near vision. When a child has been fitted with a low vision device, either some type of telebinocular or monocular aid for distance or a magnifying aid for near work, acuity is reported for vision when using that device.

At times, there may be a discrepancy between the acuity demonstrated in the clinical setting, and the acuity demonstrated at school, or at home. Many factors can contribute to this discrepancy, not the least of which is anxiety. Therefore, teachers need to consider various possible reasons for a student's poor performance in one setting but not in others, as in the following example:

A 5-year-old child in kindergarten was referred to a school program because the eye specialist found her visual acuity to be 20/200 OU and was concerned about her school performance. The teacher of students with visual impairments who received the referral note talked with the girl's kindergarten teacher and with the school nurse who knew the family and then spent time observing the girl draw, color, and do her reading readiness activities. It was clear that although the girl could copy shapes and letters accurately, she did not know the names of the shapes or letters. She appeared to have no problem seeing details or color and worked with materials at the normal distance from her eyes.

As the teacher gave the eye specialist the eye report form to complete when he next examined the girl, she mentioned that the girl did not yet know the names of the letters. When the eye report form was returned to the school several weeks later, the girl's visual acuity was reported to be well within the normal range for a 5 year old. During the first examination, the girl's acuity had been checked with the Snellen Letter Chart, and her performance was, of course, poor because she had not yet learned the names of the letters and could not match them to the shapes of the letters. When the girl had been checked with the Snellen E Chart during the next examination several weeks later, her performance improved dramatically.

It is important to note the distance from the visual target at which visual acuities are taken. For example, in the United States, distance visual acuity is generally based on a 20-foot test distance from the visual target. In some cases, when equipment like the Titmus vision screener is used, the 20-foot distance is simulated by adjusting the size of the target picture or letter. Visual acuity within the normal range is reported as 20/20, meaning that the individual identified the letter or shape at a distance of 20 feet. An acuity of 20/200 indicates that the individual identified the letter or shape at a distance of 20 feet that a person with normal vision could identify at a distance of 200 feet. If the individual cannot identify or even see the visual target from the 20-foot mark, then he or she can move closer to the target. Successful identification at a point closer than 20 feet would be recorded as, for example, 7/200, indicating the individual saw at 7 feet what the person with normal vision would see from 200 feet. These notations are not fractions; they indicate distance from the target and size of the target—two different values. Such information is helpful for some purposes, such as the determination of eligibility for services, but it does not reveal much useful information regarding visual efficiency and performance in a nonclinical setting.

Measurements of near visual acuity are generally reported in inches from the target, with 14 inches considered the standard (14/14); in centimeters from the target with 35 centimeters the standard (35/35); or sometimes in the size of type read, such as J4, a number shown on a Jaeger chart, a chart using graded sizes of letters or numbers for testing. Some eye report forms contain conversion tables that can be helpful in deciphering the specialist's notations if they are not in the anticipated figures. But again, these notations suggest where to start in learning media assessments or functional vision assessments; they do not show what the individual may be able to do in a particular instructional setting.

Visual acuity measures taken in a clinical setting that may be strange or anxiety producing, may certainly be different from those taken in the typical work setting at home or in school. They can give a good idea of visual function in that clinical setting. However, they do not necessarily reveal how efficiently a given child will use his or her vision at school or home. Thus, it is imperative for the teacher of students with visual impairments to determine how each student uses whatever vision he or she has at school; under what conditions the student can work best; and what modifications in the task, time limits, materials, setting, and lighting may increase the student's visual function. A summary of that information should be given to the eye specialist for review before the student's examination.

Lenses

A student's prescription can provide information about the strength or power of the lenses the student is to wear and suggest factors the teacher of students with visual impairments and the general classroom teacher should keep in mind. Although a detailed description of the intricacies of prescription lenses is beyond the scope of this chapter, teachers may find the following basic information helpful.

Prescriptions for corrective lenses are reported in terms of the refractive power, that is, the bending power, of the lenses. The unit of bending power of an optical lens is measured in diopters. For a convex lens, one that converges light rays, as would be necessary to sharpen vision in a hyperopic eye, the shorter the focal distance, the more powerful the lens (see Figure 3.6). A convex, or plus, lens of +10D would have more refractive power than a +2D lens. The same is true for a concave, or minus, lens that diverges light rays, as would be necessary for the myopic eye; the shorter the focal length, the more refraction, in this case diverging, power the lens has. A −10D lens would be more powerful or stronger than a −2D lens.

Corrective lenses can be spherical or cylindrical. A spherical lens has the same refractive power on all axes, while a cylindrical lens has more power or less power along one axis than along another. Spherical lenses are prescribed for simple refractive errors, and cylindrical lenses are used to correct for astigmatism. The eye report form should provide space for recording the power of the spherical lens prescribed for each eye, any cylindrical lens, and the axis or direction in which the cylindrical power is to be set. If an individual has been given a bifocal lens, then that power is usually reported as OU −Add +3D (both lenses will have an added power of +3 diopters for near vision, fixed typically for a comfortable reading distance). With advances in lens technology, correction for astigmatism, as well as bifocal adds, can sometimes be fitted in contact lenses.

What, then, is important for the teacher of students with visual impairments to note when examining the prescription portion of a student's eye report? A number of items should stand out.

Power of the Lens.   The more power, generally the poorer the individual's vision is without correction and the more important it is for the lenses to be worn all the time. The exception to this rule is that some nearsighted students may remove their eyeglasses for near vision tasks, since their natural near vision may be sufficient.

Power of a Lens Greater Than +12D.   This notation could suggest that a student's own lens had been removed. To confirm or reject this supposition, a teacher can check other portions of the report to see if the student is aphakic, which means that the lens has been removed or, in rare cases, did not completely form to begin with. It could also mean that the student is extremely farsighted. In such extreme cases, even distance vision after correction may not be good.

Very Strong Minus Lens.   A −6D to −8D or stronger lens probably mean that the wearer is quite nearsighted.

Disparity in the Strength of Correction in Both Eyes. When the difference between the refractive powers of the two eyes is large, as in the case of a student who is extremely farsighted in one eye and nearsighted in the other (anisometropia), the student may tend to favor one eye for some tasks, like reading. The reason is related to the difference in the size of the image received on the retina of each eye; a plus lens that converges light rays tends to increase the size of the image. A difference in size, if noticeable to the individual, may be resolved by favoring one eye for tasks that require near vision.

Presence of Astigmatism. With astigmatism, it becomes even more important for students not only to keep their eyeglasses on but to keep the eyeglasses properly adjusted on their faces so the power of the corrective lenses matches accurately the power of the eyes on the various meridians. That is, the power of the lenses in the eyeglasses is positioned to provide the power the natural lenses need where they need it.

Safety Lenses. Ideally, all people who wear eyeglasses should have safety lenses that are shatter resistant and frames that are fire resistant. Some tragic accidents have been reported to Prevent Blindness America (PBA) as a result of lenses shattering, cutting the eyelids, or penetrating the cornea or deeper structures of the eye. Members of the PBA-sponsored Wise Owl Club and Wise Owl Jr. Club give ample testimony to the advantages of wearing safety lenses or safety goggles in laboratories and workshops. Each year, new members whose eyesight was saved in industrial or school laboratory accidents as a result of having worn safety lenses or goggles are added to the clubs. Many sports can also be safer when the participants wear safety goggles.

Low Vision Devices. A great variety of low vision devices can be prescribed to help a student who is visually impaired use vision efficiently to perform certain tasks. Low vision devices include handheld, stand, and head-borne magnifiers for en-

larging images; telescopes to see targets at a distance; electronic aids, such as CCTVs, voice output systems, and handheld cameras that enlarge text; nonoptical aids like markers, reading stands, large-print dials, and talking clocks; and filters to reduce glare and improve contrast (Faye, 1999). (For additional information, see Chapter 14, *Foundations of Education: Instructional Strategies for Teaching Children and Youths with Visual Impairments*.) If a low vision device has been prescribed or it has been recommended that the student should be evaluated at a low vision clinic to determine whether a device may be helpful, then the teacher of students with visual impairments needs to be certain either that the student actually has the device and knows how and when to use it or that the appointment for the low vision evaluation has been made and kept.

Field of Vision

Some students have good central visual acuity but limited field or peripheral vision. The field loss may be in one or both eyes and may or may not be in the same location in each field. Students with impaired central vision may have patches or islands of useful vision of various sizes that require that they learn to redirect their gaze to permit rays of light entering the eye to stimulate that portion of their retina that is actually activated by light.

Usually the eye report form contains an illustration to indicate where the fields are restricted and to what degree. The eye specialist shades in the portion of the field that is constricted and the areas of the central field where there are scotomas (blind spots) or macular degeneration has resulted in reduced visual acuity. These field drawings can be useful to explain why students may turn their heads slightly when attempting to see an object or person directly in front of them (see also Figure 3.7).

Several types of tests, as mentioned in the discussion of specialized testing, can determine the extent of any field loss. The purpose of all of the tests is to identify where in the visual field for each eye the individual can see the test objects or light points. The results are generally used to make inferences about what portions of the retina of each eye are sensitive to light simulation. If the field is restricted for some other reason, as may be the case after retinal hemorrhage or optic nerve damage, the test results can indicate from where in the field the light rays can actually pass unimpeded through the various media of the eye to the retina and produce a reaction in the retinal cells.

Students with extensive field losses need to be alert to auditory and other cues that warn of people or objects that are present or approaching from the area in which visual cues are absent. They also must learn to move their heads and eyes to scan their environment in such a way that light rays can reach those portions of the retina that still function (see Figure 3.7).

Contrast Sensitivity

Contrast sensitivity refers to an individual's ability to detect differences in light and dark parallel lines with predetermined changes in both the thickness and darkness of the lines. When visual acuity is tested with the Snellen Chart letters, lighting in the room where the test occurs is held constant and the visual targets, the letters or the letter E, are dark. What changes is the size of the letters. In contrast sensitivity, the visual targets are usually parallel lines. The light in the room is constant, but the lines on the test chart get thinner and lighter, decreasing the contrast and requiring more visual sensitivity to detect them. In some retinal and optic nerve diseases and with cataracts, the sensitivity to these changes decreases (Newell, 1996; Vaughan et al., 1999; Wright, 1997). Contrast sensitivity tests may yield useful information for functional vision assessments because they are sensitive to differences in the lightness and darkness (intensity) as well as size (frequency) of visual targets.

Visual Capacity

Visual capacity refers to an individual's visual endurance. It is one thing to read letters on a chart; it is another to do sustained reading for a long period. A person may be able to read regular or en-

hanced print, as with a CCTV or handheld magnifier, for only a few minutes before tiring. Clinical eye tests typically do not provide information about visual capacity. Visual capacity is mentioned here simply to stress its importance in determining how an individual uses whatever vision he or she has and to highlight that it is different from a measure of either near or distance visual acuity.

Color Perception

Problems discriminating color are much more common in males than in females (Newell, 1996; Vaughan et al., 1999). The complete absence of color vision (achromatopsia) is quite rare, 0.3 per 100,000 in males and lower in females (Jose, 1983), and most people who have difficulty interpreting color have normal visual acuity (Vaughan et al., 1999). Children and adults may confuse colors because their retinal cone receptors lack the pigment necessary or their cones are less sensitive, in general, to light waves and levels of light intensity and do not detect lengths of red-orange, yellow-green, or blue light waves when light waves strike them.

Usually, no serious learning problems are involved as long as a teacher and student are aware that the student has difficulty distinguishing various colors and hues. But beginning readers, for example, whose activities may include "reading" picture stories or drawing their own pictures to illustrate stories they make up or hear, may have difficulty using colors and color words appropriately, which may result in unusual confusion or combinations of colors.

Another area of concern is the recognition of color in traffic lights when a student must cross light-controlled intersections. A student who cannot clearly distinguish red from green can learn which color appears where on the traffic signal and what is correct behavior in response to the red, green, and yellow positions. One second grader who had such a problem and had learned that he was to cross only when the bottom (on the vertical sign) or right (on the horizontal signal) green traffic light was on, asked his teacher what he should do when the middle light switched on. He was advised not to do what his friends did, which was to run. That boy had taught himself to read the names of the colors that were printed on his crayons so he could color his pictures according to the teacher's instructions. He had difficulty, however, when no instructions were given and when the teacher based the questions asked during reading class on color aspects of the pictures, such as "What is the boy in the red shirt doing?"

If a student is suspected of having problems with color perception, the teacher of students with visual impairments should consider them when selecting instructional materials or discussing strategies with the student's general education teacher. Color deficiency can be a serious problem when a person is trying to follow color-coded directions or is seeking employment in occupations that require the best possible perception of all colors. School-age children's problems with color perception usually do not create major difficulties as long as the teacher understands the possible limitations and works with the students to find ways to compensate for them.

Monocular Vision

Some individuals have only one eye because of an injury or birth defect or have normal vision in one eye but limited vision in the other. A student who has poor or no vision in one eye may need assistance to develop compensatory skills but may not require modifications in the instructional program. For example, a student with a right temporal peripheral field loss may need to learn to be alert for sound cues that people or objects are approaching from that side and to turn his or her head in that direction to pick up visual cues. A student with poor central vision in one eye needs to determine where to hold reading materials so he or she can read with comfort and efficiency with the good eye. A student with useful vision in only one eye will need to be particularly alert for auditory signals from his or her blind side and needs to develop strategies to make up for the absence of

depth perception. These strategies may include looking for shadows and intervening objects and using a knowledge of distance perspective to help determine the space between the viewer and other stationary or moving objects. Knowing specific situations (like running on a playground at recess, reaching for objects on a desk or shelf or items in the cafeteria line, or driving behind a pickup truck from which boards or ladders extend) in which it is particularly difficult to judge distance is also important.

Causes of Visual Impairment

Most eye report forms provide space for the eye specialist to report what condition is affecting the eyes at that time and what previous conditions—injuries, diseases, infection, and so forth—may have led to the present condition. For example, a student with degenerative myopia may be extremely nearsighted and at a high risk for retinal detachment or even secondary glaucoma. The degree of degeneration, as determined by a clinical examination of the sclera, optic disk, choroid, retina, and vitreous, may actually have little relationship to the severity of the myopia as measured by the strength of the correction, that is, the dioptric power, needed to bring visual acuity as close to 20/20 as possible. Although functional vision is a prime concern for instructional purposes, the degree of degeneration is a major focus in the clinical examination and in the determination of any restriction on physical activities. The teacher needs to be cognizant of the implications of eye conditions and should examine carefully any information on etiology.

Frequently, the eye specialist indicates if the condition is hereditary and what implications there may be for other family members. If the genetic patterns of transmission are known, the eye specialist may explain what they are. The teacher of students with visual impairments can use this information in discussions with the family of the importance of examinations for other family members who may be at risk because they manifest clinical signs of the condition or because they may be carriers, although not affected. In addition, during adolescence, a student may question whether his or her eye condition can be passed on to offspring and approach the teacher for an answer. Although the teacher is not likely to be trained in genetics or to be an expert on patterns of genetic transmission, frequency of penetrance, degree of expression, or determination of pedigree, he or she needs to know enough to respond to basic questions about dominant, recessive, and sex-linked patterns of transmission and to recognize when additional sources of information or a referral to a genetic counseling clinic may be necessary and helpful. Teachers of students with visual impairments are often called on to explain what certain diagnoses mean; how the eye is affected; or what the educational implications of a particular disease, defect, or hereditary condition are.

If the condition was caused by an injury or poisoning at school that occurred under circumstances that could have been avoided had adequate precautions been taken or supervision provided, school personnel need to do what is possible to prevent a similar event from happening in the future. As was mentioned before, teachers may be able to prevent needless eye injuries and possible loss of vision by anticipating thoughtless actions on the playground; noting where dangerous equipment or supplies are kept; recognizing the improper use or placement of sports, shop, and laboratory equipment; and insisting that protective goggles and safety lenses be used for risky instructional and athletic events.

Many times, the etiology of a student's eye condition is simply not known. Sometimes a condition can be given a name and clearly identified, as in the case of glaucoma or congenital cataracts, but the reason the condition exists in the first place may not be known at the time. Additional research on causes and treatment and more information about the effects of disease, infection, environmental pollution, nutrition, and lifestyle on the human body should lead eventually to the identification of ways to prevent or at least reduce the incidence of visual impairment among both children and adults.

Prognosis and Recommendations

The eye specialist should note for the student's file any information regarding the stability of the student's eye condition. If the condition may deteriorate, the teacher needs to know what signs the student may exhibit in school that could indicate a significant change. For example, a student with Marfan syndrome, an inherited disorder of the connective tissue that can cause subluxated (partially displaced) lenses, among other things, may complain of blurry vision, a possible indication of a dislocated lens. The presence of significant signs calls for immediate contact with the student's family to arrange for an examination by the student's eye specialist. It is better to err on the conservative side than to allow complaints that could indicate serious trouble to go unheeded.

The eye specialist usually reports what treatment has been recommended and when the student's next examination should be scheduled. The teacher should note this information and follow up with the parents to make certain the recommendations are carried out. If medication is to be administered during school hours, the teacher can help obtain the permissions that the school district requires for school personnel to give the prescribed pills or eyedrops. Some medications have side effects that can affect school performance; therefore the time that a student takes them should be scheduled so as not to disrupt school activities, if possible. Teachers should be alerted to any side effects, such as drowsiness or blurred vision, that may affect the student's energy level or quality of work and report these observations to the eye specialist.

Some eye conditions, like degenerative myopia, call for restrictions on certain types of physical activity, primarily activities that may involve hard physical contact with other players, such as football, field hockey, diving, dodgeball, and volleyball. In some cases, wearing polycarbonate spectacle lenses may reduce the danger to acceptable risk levels (but what is acceptable to one person may not be to another).

If limits on physical activity or impact are advisable, then such information needs to be communicated to the student's teachers, especially the physical education teacher. But just because physical contact sports are restricted or ruled out does not mean that the student cannot participate in other types of physical activities and athletic events. This message also needs to be conveyed to the student's teachers as well as to the student.

Eye specialists' recommendations for lighting in the classroom, seating for classroom work, type or mode of reading to be taught, and even school placements may be helpful, but they must be considered in light of the context in which they were determined—the clinical environment, which generally bears little resemblance to the facilities in the student's school. If the teacher of students with visual impairments can send a concise report of the student's current level of visual function in school to the ophthalmologist or optometrist, along with the eye report form, the eye specialist will have additional information that can supplement the clinical information gathered in the clinical setting. Working together, the student and teacher need to determine the most comfortable levels of ambient and task lighting for classwork, the placement of the desk or table and chair for efficient use of functional vision, and the best working distance from a task or visual target to the eyes.

Additional Information to Aid Interpretation

Eye report forms frequently provide space for the eye specialist to report additional information about the student's eye condition or visual functioning. For example, for some individuals who are not able to see the test objects at any distance, notations other than those previously discussed measures that indicate distance from and size of the target (for example, 20/200) may prove informative: HM, to indicate the ability to detect hand movements; light projection, to indicate the ability to detect the direction from which the light comes; light perception, to indicate the ability to tell the difference between light and dark; and no light perception, to indicate no sense of light

(Vaughan et al., 1999; Wright, 1997). In addition, as was mentioned earlier, near visual acuity may be reported in inches or centimeters from the target or the size of type, based on numbers on the Jaeger chart. Furthermore, information on restrictions in fields of vision, discussed earlier, needs to be given to and interpreted for students and their parents to confirm where areas of functional field are and to suggest directions of gaze that may collect more stimuli than a direct gaze could, especially if a student's central vision is not clear or sharp.

As should be clear from this discussion, much information of significance for educational and instructional purposes can be gleaned from clinical eye reports by teachers who have basic knowledge about the anatomy and physiology of the eye, conditions that can interfere with how the eye functions, and implications of eye disorders in school-age children and youths.

RELATIONSHIP BETWEEN VISUAL ACUITY AND PREFERRED READING MODE

Over the years, the percentage of youngsters in school programs for students with visual impairments who have used braille as their primary reading medium has decreased. In the late 1950s, approximately 58 percent of the students who were registered with APH used braille as their chief mode of reading; in 1979, about 16 percent; and in 1997, about 8 percent. Many factors have contributed to this seemingly drastic reduction in the percentage of school-age students whose visual acuity is 20/200 or less in the better eye after correction and whose primary reading medium is braille. Among these factors are changes in the characteristics of some of the students being served. First, many students with disabilities were excluded from neighborhood schools in the 1950s in some states. Second, medical advances have led to the survival of more students with a variety of disabilities, including visual impairments. Third, the development of technology has enabled individuals with low vision (that is, those with severe visual impairments that, even with the best correction, interfere with the performance of daily tasks) to use optical and other aids to enhance their functional vision. Fourth, for many students with low vision who may not have had an opportunity to learn braille, braille reading may be more efficient than print reading. It is essential that a student's most effective way of accessing information be determined early and on a regular basis. For this reason, the performance of learning media assessments has become a critical part of the educational programming for students with visual impairments. (Further information on assessments for determining literacy media is presented in Chapter 4 of *Foundations of Education: Instructional Strategies for Teaching Children and Youths with Visual Impairments*.)

Effects on Functional Vision

The previous section touched on the relationship of visual acuity and preferred reading media to illustrate that many factors can contribute to choice of reading medium. In this section, the discussion is broadened to explore the relationship between visual impairments and clinical information about the impairments, including visual acuity, and an individual's functional vision. It is important for teachers and other professionals who work with students with visual and sometimes additional impairments to understand the relationship and the fact that a visual impairment and clinical information may remain stable while visual function may fluctuate from day to day or even from task to task.

Hoover (1963), whose work with newly blinded veterans of World War II led to the development of the field of orientation and mobility (O&M), identified the major components of visual function as visual acuity measured for near, midrange, and distant objects; visual versatility, meaning accommodative power for switching from near to far to near; convergence, or the ability to focus both eyes on a single visual target; light-dark adaptation, color vision, and binocular vision; and visual capacity, including field of vision, lighting requirements and preferences, and the length

of time an individual can sustain a visual effort. These factors and others discussed in this book play a role in determining the use of vision by an individual who has some vision. (It should be noted that a person who is functionally blind has no usable vision or, at best, can sense light and dark.)

The effects of visual impairment on functional vision and how an individual uses whatever vision he or she has at a particular time or for a particular task can rarely be predicted with much certainty because so many other factors enter into the situation—age of onset of visual impairment, present age, quality of the repertoire of visual experiences, presence of other disabilites, cognitive skills, risk-taking behaviors, and general psychological makeup, to name a few. Other factors in visual function are the specific task and the environment in which the task is to be performed, the amount and quality of available light, the degree of contrast between visual targets and surrounding objects or platforms on which they sit, color, glare, time allotted, the time of day, the individual's degree of interest or engagement in the task, and the time the individual is willing to spend on the task (Blanksby & Langford, 1993; Corn, 1983).

Although little may be altered regarding the visual impairment itself, the professional who understands the relationship of visual impairment to visual function should be prepared to look for environmental adaptations, instructional strategies, learning materials, and conditions for learning that may be modified to enhance a student's opportunities to learn visually as efficiently as possible. The critical factor in determining what can enhance functional vision is the skill of the teacher, counselor, parent, eye care specialist, or O&M specialist in observing the individual's behavior and documenting how the individual is using vision for learning. Careful observation and recording are the first steps in planning appropriate instruction for students who appear to be functionally blind.

Often the teacher of students with visual impairments recommends a low vision evaluation after clinical and functional vision examinations have been completed (see Sidebar 3.1). Among the purposes of such an evaluation are to help students learn to use the vision they have efficiently and to determine whether any low vision devices may further enhance functional vision for specific visual tasks.

SUMMARY

This chapter has provided the groundwork—structures of the eye and their function, causes of visual impairments, and clinical information and its interpretation for instructional purposes—for understanding the process of seeing. The following chapters of this text will address the impact of visual impairment on growth and development through early childhood and adolescence and consider the educational implications accompanying this impact.

STUDY QUESTIONS

1. What is the path of light rays from the environment through the eye to the brain? Describe it.

2. What is the purpose of the bony orbit?

3. Why is it important that teachers of students with visual impairments clearly understand the structure of the eye and terminology used to describe the eye and its functions?

4. What are three types of refractive errors, and how may each be corrected?

5. What are the major causes of visual impairment among the general population? Among school-age children?

6. What do these terms mean?
Ophthalmologist
Optometrist
Visual acuity
Field of vision
Cortical visual impairment

7. What types of information are typically included in an eye specialist's report for an examination of a student who is visually impaired? What is the importance of each section of the eye report for a teacher of students who are visually impaired?

REFERENCES

Amblyopia. (1997). Schaumburg, IL: Prevent Blindness America.

Blanksby, D. C., & Langford, P. E. (1993). VAP-CAP: A procedure to assess the visual functioning of young visually impaired children. *Journal of Visual Impairment & Blindness, 87,* 46–49.

Common eye problems and who's who in eye care. (1997). Schaumburg, IL: Prevent Blindness America.

Corn, A. (1983). Visual function: A theoretical model for individuals with low vision. *Journal of Visual Impairment & Blindness, 77,* 373–377.

Corn, A. L., & Koenig, A. (Eds.) (1996). *Foundations of Low Vision: Clinical and Functional Perspectives.* New York: AFB Press.

Ferrell, K. A., with Shaw, A. R., & Dietz, S. J. (1998). *Project PRISM: A longitudinal study of developmental patterns of children who are visually impaired* (Final Report, CFDA 84.023C, Grant H023C10188). Greeley: University of Northern Colorado, Division of Special Education.

Groenveld, M., Jan, J. E., & Leader, P. (1990). Observations on the habilitation of children with CVI. *Journal of Visual Impairment & Blindness, 84,* 11–15.

Hoover, R. E. (1963). Visual efficiency as a criterion of service needs. *Research Bulletin No. 3.* New York: American Foundation for the Blind.

Jan, J. E., & Groenveld, M. (1993). Visual behaviors and adaptations associated with cortical and ocular impairment in children. *Journal of Visual Impairment & Blindness, 87,* 101–105.

Jose, R. T. (1983). *Understanding low vision.* New York: American Foundation for the Blind.

Kirchner, C., & Schmeidler, E. (1997). Prevalence and employment of people in the United States who are blind or visually impaired. *Journal of Visual Impairment & Blindness, 91,* 508–511.

Laser vision correction: Patient information guide, (n.d.). Dublin, OH: Columbus Eye Consultants.

Lowenfeld, B. (1981). *Berthold Lowenfeld on blindness and blind people: Selected papers by Berthold*

Lowenfeld. New York: American Foundation for the Blind.

Moore, J. E., Graves, W. H., & Patterson, J. B. (1997). *Foundations of rehabilitation counseling with persons who are blind or visually impaired.* New York: AFB Press.

Newell, F. W. (1996). *Ophthalmology: Principles and concepts.* St. Louis, MO: Mosby.

Rosen, S. (1998). Educating students who have visual impairments with neurological disabilities. In S. Z. Sacks & R. K. Silberman (Eds.), *Educating students who have visual impairments with other disabilities* (pp. 221–260). New York: Paul H. Brookes.

True colors: Facts about color vision deficiency. (1996). Schaumburg, IL: Prevent Blindness America.

Understanding retinitis pigmentosa. (1996). Schaumburg, IL: Prevent Blindness America.

Vaughan, D. G., Ashbury, T., & Riordan-Eva, P. (1999). *General ophthalmology.* (15th ed.). Stamford, CT: Appleton & Lange.

Vision Problems in the U.S.: A report on blindness and vision impairment in adults age 40 and older. (1994). Schaumburg, IL: Prevent Blindness America.

Wright, K. W. (Ed.). (1997). *Textbook of ophthalmology.* Baltimore, MD: Williams & Wilkins.

CHAPTER 4

Growth and Development of Young Children

Kay Alicyn Ferrell

KEY POINTS

◆ A young child with a visual impairment faces a set of adaptive tasks in development and brings to those tasks a set of personal capabilities and characteristics; the environment shapes the nature of the tasks.

◆ The greatest impact on developmental outcomes appears to be the presence of additional disabilities.

◆ The traditional assumption that children with visual impairments follow the same sequence of development as do sighted children is being challenged.

◆ The most important values incorporated into early education services are that children should be in high-quality programs, services should address the special learning needs of children with visual impairments, and services should be family centered.

◆ Research on young children with visual impairments is instructive but not always conclusive.

Thanks are extended to Linda Mamer, Department of Educational and Counselling Psychology and Special Education, University of British Columbia, for her contributions to an earlier version of this chapter.

All children are unique, and children with visual impairments are no different in their uniqueness and need for loving home environments that are both stimulating and supportive. Regardless of how vision loss affects growth and development, children who are visually impaired still grow and learn. However, perhaps more than any other disability, visual impairment has the potential to influence dramatically how children develop. Whether it does and how much it does depends on parents' and teachers' knowledge and understanding of the potential impact of the disability.

This chapter focuses on children from birth to age 8. Early childhood has generally covered ages 3–8 years, whereas early childhood special education (ECSE) has traditionally covered the period from birth to age 5. Because ECSE has gradually moved toward and been assimilated into regular early childhood, it now serves children from birth to age 8 (P.L. 105-17, Individuals with Disabilities Education Act (IDEA), amendments of 1997). The following terms are commonly used to describe children in this age range: infant, from birth to walking; toddler, from walking to 35 months; preschooler, from 36 months to 5 or 6 years, depending on each state's mandatory school age; and primary, from 5 or 6 years to 8 years, corresponding to kindergarten to Grade 3. Thus, the term *early childhood* is used in this chapter to refer to the age range of birth to 8 years. Although the term *early intervention* is widely used in the field, it is not used in this discussion to avoid the connotation sometimes accompanying it that families need intervention or that professionals can prevent the consequences of disability or poverty (Turnbull & Turnbull, 1985). Instead, the term *early education* is used to refer to the services provided to children and families before children enter kindergarten.

The field of visual impairment has an impressive record in early education, beginning in the late 1800s with homes for neglected children. "Neglect" was determined simply on the basis of a child's visual impairment. It was assumed at that time that parents were incapable of providing an adequate home environment and that babies who were blind would develop much better in residential programs with trained staff (Koestler, 1976). These programs existed until the late 1930s, when the Arthur Sunshine Home and Kindergarten for Blind Babies in Summit, New Jersey, closed its residential program. The Arthur Sunshine Home continued its home counseling and training functions and established a standard of service to children who were blind and their families that endured for many years.

In the 1950s, as the number of children who were blind from birth dramatically increased as a result of retrolental fibroplasia (Silverman, 1980), now called retinopathy of prematurity (ROP), parents established home counseling services that provided support to parents in raising their children who were blind (Turnbull & Turnbull, 1997). Many of these services still exist—most notably, the Foundation for Blind Children in Phoenix, Arizona. Established by Margaret Bluhm and three other parents in 1952, this agency now has a staff of 83 and serves 1,400 children and 400 adults throughout the state. The foundation remains one of the leading agencies that provides early education services in the United States. Today, early education programs are delivered by a cadre of private service agencies, local school districts, and health agencies across the United States. This combination of private and government funds for early education seems to be repeated in developing countries as well.

At the end of the 20th century, services to infants and preschool children with visual impair-

ments were widespread in the industrialized world. Arguments for and against early education are now moot, particularly since legislation has rendered the debate unnecessary. In the United States, these services are mandated by the 1997 amendments to IDEA. All 50 states participate in this program, which requires early education for preschoolers beginning at age 3 and supports a variety of resources for families of infants and toddlers with and at risk of having disabilities. Children who are visually impaired are eligible for services because of their biological risk; most states have acknowledged that sensory impairments are likely to have substantial effects on early development, to the point that the diagnosis of visual impairment alone determines eligibility for services, with or without evidence of developmental delay.

FOUNDATIONS OF EARLY CHILDHOOD EDUCATION

Early education is rooted in the European child-rearing practices dating back to the early 1800s (Williams, 1992). It was initially the privilege of the children of wealthy parents. Froebel's kindergarten, however, began to change the prevailing notion that young children were simply biding time by demonstrating that young children could rapidly acquire skills if they were taught using materials that took advantage of their natural tendency to play (Froebel, 1887, 1895). Froebel's theories were readily accepted in the United States, but were adapted to meet the political, religious, socioeconomic, intellectual, and cultural ideas of the times. Simultaneously, education, in general, was abandoning metaphysical and classical studies in favor of more scientifically based work, reflected notably by the progressive movement in education and the child study movement in psychology (Williams, 1992).

Early education was greatly influenced by the American experience, democratic ideals, and view of schools as places to socialize a diverse citizenry. As the population of the United States grew, particularly through European immigration, child-rearing practices—dependent as they were on cultural values, traditions, and customs—became increasingly diverse. Tension thus developed between the developmental perspective, with its emphasis on observation, on the typical course of development, and on process curricula, and public education in general, with its orientation toward the acquisition of specific knowledge and skills (Williams, 1992). That tension remains today.

THEORIES OF CHILD DEVELOPMENT

Several theories of how children grow and develop have evolved from the child study movement in psychology. Like other aspects of education, although there may be agreement about research findings, there is much less agreement about the meaning and explanations of the findings. As a result, most early education programs incorporate a variety of theories into their philosophies and curricula. The child development theories that are most frequently used to support the practice of early education include behavioral, cognitive-transactional, psychodynamic, and normative-maturational (Fromberg & Gullo, 1992). For additional information about models of development see Chapter 5.

Behavioral theory is best represented by the work of Skinner (1968). It postulates that learning occurs in response to the environment, and, consequently, by creating the right environment, children's behavior can be "shaped." Skinner believed that children are born with a basic repertoire of responses and that they develop new responses when the environment forces them to move outside the basic repertoire. Behavioral theory has been widely used in special education, but strict adherence to its principles often results in programs that are rigid and inflexible (Fromberg & Gullo, 1992). Instead, most programs incorporate elements of behavioral theory, such as reinforcement, shaping, modeling, imitation, and extinction, into their curricula as teaching strategies.

Cognitive-transactional theory holds that development occurs through a combination of forces: biological maturation, physical experiences, and social interaction. Piaget and Inhelder (1969) stated that children are naturally active, and it is through their actions on the environment (a process called adaptation and assimilation) that learning occurs. Vygotsky (1986) also subscribed to cognitive-transactional theory but emphasized the social role of the adult as the child's teacher. Early education curricula incorporating this theory create environments that match a child's level of development and expect the child to make choices.

Psychodynamic theory has its roots in the work of Sigmund Freud, but in early childhood, it is best known by the work of Erikson (1963). Freud stated that children were born with drives that must be channeled. Erikson postulated that there is a connection between children's capacity to handle emotion and their ability to think, based on biological readiness, psychological readiness, and social interaction. Curricula incorporating the psychodynamic theory address children's abilities to cope with their feelings and interact with their environments. Early education programs attempt to establish a physical and social environment that is emotionally supportive, physically appropriate, socially responsive, consistent, and predictable.

Normative-maturational theory was the basis of many of the developmental studies conducted in the 1940s and 1950s and is perhaps exemplified by Gesell's (1940) classic book, *The First Five Years of Life.* This theory acknowledges the role of the environment, but emphasizes that a child is primarily a product of his or her genetics. Programs using a normative-maturational approach focus on readiness by matching a child's development to the demands of the curriculum. This approach has also been widely used in special education, but has come under attack recently as one way that children with disabilities are held back by well-meaning teachers, who wait for children to demonstrate lower-level skills before they teach the children higher-level skills. Normative-maturational theory seems logical on the surface, but fails to acknowledge that some skills may be beyond a child's capacity specifically because of the nature of the child's disability.

Dewey (1933) wrote that the interaction of work and play is the legitimate realm of education. Play is both a condition of learning and an activity that is worthwhile for its own sake. For children older than 3 years, sociodramatic play is particularly useful in helping them understand others' points of view. Fromberg (1990, p. 223) believed that play builds children's cognitive development through shared language, social negotiations, and imagery and is the "ultimate integrator of human experience." After years of implementing a prescriptive and behavioral approach in special education, ECSE has returned to play as the basis of early education, largely because of Linder's (1990, 1993) work on play-based assessment and intervention. The National Association for the Education of Young Children emphasizes that play is one aspect of developmentally appropriate practice (Bredekamp & Copple, 1997).

BASIS FOR SERVICES

Theories of child development have influenced early education services for children with disabilities, but theories themselves do not provide the rationale for creating the services in the first place. That impetus came from a series of studies conducted since the 1930s and from the federal government's increasing investment in the future of children with and without disabilities.

Effectiveness of Early Education

The first studies that are generally cited as providing the basis for early education examined the effects of institutionalization on the cognitive and socioemotional development of infants. These studies included landmark research by Skeels and Dye (1939), Spitz (1945), and Provence and Lipton (1962). All these studies demonstrated that intelligence, previously thought to be fixed and immutable (Gesell, 1925, 1929), was, in fact, malleable under a program of stimulation and enhanced experience. Skeels (1966) followed the babies in his original study until adulthood and found that the effects of the early stimulation persisted. Kirk's (1958) study, the first to focus on the effects of early education on young children with mental retardation, demonstrated that these children's IQ scores increased after the children participated in a structured ECSE program. Once Hunt (1961) and Bloom (1964) published their research, the child development movement changed its orientation. Whereas the field had talked about a continuum of reproductive casualty, referring to the potential of genetics and medical concerns to lead to developmental failure, it now referred to a continuum of caretaking casualty (Sameroff & Chandler, 1975). "Although reproductive casualties may play an initiating role in the production of later problems, it is the caretaking environment that will determine the ultimate outcome" (Sameroff, 1975, p. 274). Clearly, intelligence was affected by environment, and change was possible.

This preliminary research was followed by a grand experiment in social policy: Lyndon Johnson's Great Society. According to Shonkoff and Meisels (1990), the Great Society was marked by three themes: (1) the belief in the society's responsibility to care for and protect young children, (2) a special commitment to the needs of children who were particularly vulnerable as a result of chronic disabilities or conditions of poverty, and (3) a sense that prevention was better than treatment and that earlier intervention was better than late intervention. Shonkoff and Meisels called these three themes the "spiritual origins of early childhood intervention" (p. 15).

These experiments in social policy were also followed by research. The Head Start synthesis project followed the performance of early participants in Head Start programs. It found that initial improvements in children's intelligence persisted several years after the children graduated from Head Start (McKey et al., 1985). Although there was evidence of some decrement in intellectual functioning over time, other long-term benefits from early education were found: (1) fewer students placed in special education or retained in grade, (2) higher rates of graduation from high school, (3) higher achievement, (4) fewer arrests of adolescents, (5) fewer teenage pregnancies, (6) fewer adults receiving welfare, and (7) lower costs to taxpayers for social services over the long term (Lazar, Darlington, Murry, Royce, & Snipper, 1982; Schweinhart, 1992).

Approximately 10 years after the passage of P.L. 94-142, the Education for All Handicapped Children Act, in 1975 (reauthorized as IDEA in 1990), ECSE began to examine the effectiveness of its programs. Much of the research used meta-analysis to examine a large number of studies for the size of their effect (Shonkoff & Hauser-Cram, 1987; White, Mastropieri, & Casto, 1984; White, Taylor, & Moss, 1992). White (1986) concluded that early intervention appeared to have positive effects, but that the methodologies used in the 300 studies he reviewed were simply too disparate to be certain. Subsequent federally funded intervention studies proved inconclusive (White & Boyce, 1993). Today, it is generally agreed that early education is indeed effective, despite the myriad methodological problems associated with previous studies (Guralnick, 1997). In the mid-1980s, however, Strain (1984) had raised doubts about the emphasis on efficacy and questioned whether efficacy was an important issue at all. Early education, in Strain's view, was critical for children and families; whether those effects could be measured was irrelevant.

CURRENT CONTEXT

Studies of the efficacy of ECSE were indeed made irrelevant by the passage of the Education for All Handicapped Children Act Amendments of 1986 (P.L. 99-457), which mandated early education services to children with disabilities from age 3 and created a comprehensive system of infant and toddler services for children from birth to age 3. Although the infant and toddler program was not mandatory, every state participated by setting up

its own system of early intervention services. This acceptance of early education for children with and at risk for disabilities and the paradigm shift created by the legislation affect the way in which early education services are delivered today.

Legislation

Table 4.1 presents a chronology of federal activities that have affected children and families, beginning in 1909 with the first White House Conference on Children and leading to the 1997 amendments to IDEA. The first federal program to target funds for children and youths with disabilities was created in 1965, and the first federal attention to ECSE occurred in 1968, four years after the beginning of Head Start. The federal government's role in early education for children with disabilities has been one of gentle encouragement, followed by mandated services. Federal funds created demonstration programs in the 1960s, and after these programs were implemented and subsequently valued by professionals and families, early education services later became law.

Delivery of Services

Early education services for infants and toddlers have three principal objectives:

- ◆ To provide information, support, and assistance to families who are dealing with the needs associated with their children's development;

- ◆ To build parents' confidence as the primary facilitators of their children's development and advocates for their children; and

- ◆ To promote interactions between family members that encourage mutual feelings of competence and enjoyment (Raver, 1999, p. 22).

Part C of IDEA (P.L. 105-17) requires states that receive federal funds to establish compre-

Table 4.1. Federal Legislation and Programs Affecting Early Childhood Education

Year	Legislation or Program
1909	The first White House Conference on Children is held. The conference has been held every 10 years since then except in 1980.
1912	The U.S. Children's Bureau is established.
1921	The Sheppard-Towner Act provides support to widowed, divorced, or abandoned mothers.
1935	Title V of the Social Security Act of 1935 provides grants for child welfare services, including child care.
1942	The Lanham Act provides for the care of children whose parents are employed in wartime industries.
1946	The National School Lunch Act provides food for licensed child care facilities, as well as schools.
1954	President Dwight D. Eisenhower signs a bill authorizing tax deductions for work-related child care expenses.
1962	President John F. Kennedy signs Title IV-A, the Social Security Act Amendments of 1962, creating the Aid to Families with Dependent Children (AFDC)–Employed Parent Program and providing work-expense benefits for child care.
	Title V (now Title IV-B), amended to assist states in improving child welfare services, also provides funds for training child care workers.
1964	The Food Stamp Act also subsidizes work-expense benefits for child care.
	President Lyndon B. Johnson signs the Economic Opportunity Act, creating Head Start.
1965	Johnson signs the Medicare and Medicaid law, authorizing the Early and Periodic Screening, Diagnosis and Treatment program.
	The Elementary and Secondary Education Act provides funds for compensatory preschool education for children in low-income families and authorizes grants to state institutions and state-operated schools to serve students with disabilities (the first federal grant program specifically targeting funds for children and youths with disabilities).
1966	The Child Nutrition Act creates the School Breakfast Program and the Special Milk Program in areas with a significant number of low-income children.
	The Elementary and Secondary Education Act amendments provide funds for children with disabilities in local public schools and establish the Bureau of Education of the Handicapped.
1967	The Work Incentive Program extends federal funding for child care to low-income families in jobs or in job training programs.
	Funding is authorized for Follow Through Programs that extend Head Start to kindergarten and the elementary grades.
1968	The Handicapped Children's Early Education Program provides funds for demonstration programs for preschoolers with disabilities.
1969	The Office of Child Development is established (and incorporates the Children's Bureau) to serve as a focal point for children's services in the federal government.
1970	The Education of the Handicapped Act (EHA) establishes a core grant program for local education agencies to serve children with disabilities.
1972	The Special Supplemental Food Program for Women, Infants, and Children provides food supplements for pregnant women, lactating mothers, infants, and preschool children.
1973	Amendments to the Internal Revenue Act permit tax deductions for businesses that provide child care services.
	At least 10 percent of the Head Start enrollment is mandated for children with disabilities.
	The Rehabilitation Act authorizes rehabilitation services, regardless of the severity of disability and includes a basic civil rights provision for individuals with disabilities.
1974	The Elementary and Secondary Act amendments refer to the appropriateness of education for children with disabilities.

Table 4.1. *(Continued)*

Year	Legislation or Program
	The Family Education Rights and Privacy Act (Buckley amendment) gives parents and students the right to examine school records and restricts the dissemination of personal information.
1975	The Education for All Handicapped Children Act (P.L. 94-142) (formerly EHA) provides services for children as young as age 3. It ensures due process, education in the least restrictive environment, the development of Individualized Education Programs, and parental involvement.
1978	The Indian Child Welfare Act subsidizes child care services to Native Americans.
1981	The Omnibus Budget Reconciliation Act restructures eligibility and service coverage for children's programs, eliminates $200 million targeted for child care, and reauthorizes Head Start.
1983	Amendments to P. L. 94-142 establish and fund parent training and information centers and demonstration projects and research in early intervention and early childhood special education.
1984	Head Start is reauthorized to ensure the delivery of comprehensive services. Grants for the care of school-age children are authorized.
1986	Amendments to P. L. 94-142 authorize free and appropriate public education for children aged 3–21 and provide incentive funds to states to establish comprehensive family-centered early intervention programs for infants and toddlers (from birth to age 3).
	The Handicapped Children's Protection Act provides attorneys' fees and costs to parents and guardians who prevail in hearings or in court when disputing their children's right to a free, appropriate public education and related services.
	The Higher Education Act authorizes child care for the children of low-income college students.
1988	The Elementary and Secondary School Improvement amendments create Even Start, a joint parent-child educational program aimed at improving adult literacy and offering early childhood education to children aged 1–7.
	The Family Support Act provides child care assistance for parents in job training or education and for mothers who are ineligible for welfare.
1989	The Children with Disabilities Temporary Care Reauthorization Act provides funds for temporary child care and crisis nurseries for children with disabilities or chronic illnesses.
1990	The Child Care and Development Block Grant constructs a comprehensive federal child care policy. It subsidizes child care for low-income families, provides new and expanded tax credits, and begins to address the issue of the quality of child care.
	The Augustus F. Hawkins Human Services Reauthorization Act reauthorizes Head Start and Follow Through. It sets aside 10 percent of the funds for improvements in the quality of the programs, including staff compensation, and authorizes Head Start to provide full-day, full-year services to children in families who have full-time work, education, or training responsibilities.
	The Claude Pepper Young Americans Act provides funds to states to increase awareness of the needs of young children.
	The Education for All Handicapped Children Act is reauthorized and renamed the Individuals with Disabilities Education Act (IDEA).
	The Americans with Disabilities Act guarantees equal opportunities for individuals with disabilities in employment, public accommodation, transportation, state and local governmental resources, and telecommunications.
1997	The IDEA amendments provide financial incentives to states to provide full services to families of infants and toddlers with and at risk for disabilities.

Source: Adapted from S.G. Goffin, "Federal Legislation of Importance to Early Childhood Education: A Chronology," in L.R. Williams, and F.P. Fromberg, Eds. *Encyclopedia of Early Childhood Education* (New York: Garland, 1992), pp. 58–64.

hensive early education services that include at least the following components: (1) a definition of *developmentally delayed;* (2) a multidisciplinary evaluation; (3) an Individualized Family Service Plan (IFSP) for each child and family; (4) a child-find system; (5) a central directory of early intervention services; (6) a comprehensive system of personnel development; (7) a designated lead state agency, either in education or health care; and (8) a system for interagency agreements. The organization of these services is different from special education services in important ways. First, the lead agency for services for children from birth to age 3 is not necessarily an education agency. Second, these services are organized around the needs of families, rather than children. Although the needs of a child with or at risk for disabilities are certainly paramount, Part C services utilize the family to ensure that these needs are met. The services are thus family centered, rather than child centered, as occurs with services for school-age children.

Services to infants and toddlers are provided mainly in children's homes, although center-based programs are often used because they are efficient for families and the various personnel involved. Services to children aged 3–5 occur primarily in preschool classrooms in day care, nursery school, or public school facilities. Services to children aged 5–8 are generally provided through the local education agency.

IDEA requires the development of an IFSP, similar to the Individualized Education Program (IEP) developed for school-age children. The IFSP is mandatory for children up to age 3 and may be used for children aged 3–5. It differs from the IEP in its orientation to the family and in its period of review (every six months versus every year).

Normalization

The state of the art of early education services in 1990 led Bailey and McWilliam (1990, p. 33) to state that "most early intervention programs for infants and preschoolers with handicaps are not normal" and to propose the adoption of a principle of normalization. In ECSE, normalization refers to three dimensions: the physical environment, teaching strategies, and family-centered services. For the physical environment, Bailey and McWilliam suggested that preschool classrooms for children with disabilities should look like nursery schools and day care centers, with the same types of play areas. Their review of ECSE programs in the late 1980s revealed that programs were not as comfortable as, allowed less time for play than, and were less likely to include areas, activities, and materials typically found in regular preschool classrooms. The materials used for play should look the same, too. One reason the natural environment is so important is that exposure to skills and their later generalization to new environments may affect the child's ability to learn in unfamiliar and novel situations.

The IDEA amendments and regulations since 1986 have grown stronger in their requirement for natural environments for early education services. The emphasis on normalization has led to the increasing use of regular early childhood settings as the primary site for delivering early education services to children with disabilities. Center-based programs, particularly segregated center-based programs, are viewed as unnatural and negative environments for children with disabilities that result in stigmatization. Erwin (1993, 1994) found, however, that there was no difference in social interaction among children with visual impairments in segregated or integrated settings (although there was less isolation and more social initiations in integrated settings, the difference was not statistically significant).

Stratton (1990) raised the issue of normalization regarding the instructional materials often used to teach children with visual impairments, suggesting that their "unusualness" was often as stigmatizing as the disability itself. Mamer (1995) questioned the terminology used with children with visual impairments, pointing out that behaviors that are often praised in children without disabilities (such as "tactile sensitivity") are often described negatively (as "tactile defensiveness") when applied to children with disabilities.

Bailey and McWilliam (1990, p. 41) pointed out that "families of children with handicaps inevitably must assume 'nonnormal' roles and engage in activities not expected of other parents." In addition, children with disabilities and their families are often under increased scrutiny simply because they are identified as needing early education services. Sometimes that increased scrutiny results in misconceptions and assumptions about children's abilities and families' competence that create barriers to strong family-professional relationships (Turnbull & Turnbull, 1997).

Facilitated Learning

Facilitated learning suggests that the role of the teacher is to create learning opportunities for children that the children discover and act on themselves. Less emphasis is placed on the diagnostic-prescriptive approach of the 1970s and early 1980s, and more emphasis is placed on the process of building scaffolds that children can use to move on to the next skill. Davidson and Simmons (1992) referred to the need to mediate the environment for children with visual impairments, rather than to leave learning to chance. Bailey and McWilliam (1990) suggested that more normalized early education programs are those that produce a stimulating and responsive learning environment, provide models for appropriate behavior, allow some errors to occur, and capitalize on children's initiations and interests.

Inclusion

There has been a great deal of debate on the inclusion of children with disabilities in regular early childhood settings, much of which has pointed to the legal, moral, and philosophical values that support the practice, including the principles of normalization suggested by Bailey and McWilliam (1990). Bailey, McWilliam, Buysse, and Wesley (1998) pointed out that although there is strong empirical support for inclusion at the early childhood level, little is known about the inclusion of young children with visual impairments in early childhood settings. They stated:

> In our opinion, placement in inclusive settings should be a goal for all children with disabilities.

The legal, moral, rational, and empirical arguments provide a consistent and compelling foundation which supports this position. However, we temper our recommendation with the caveat that inclusive settings should be of high quality, able to address the special needs of children, and consistent with parents' goals and priorities. (p. 36)

Inclusion in early childhood settings is a strategy, not a condition, and, as Bailey et al. (1998) suggested, it should be used only if the values of high quality, family centeredness, and children's needs are met. These values are often difficult to achieve for children with visual impairments, primarily because most inclusive settings are not prepared to meet these children's needs. Stoiber, Gettinger, and Goetz (1998), for example, found that teachers in early childhood inclusive settings felt less prepared to integrate children with neurological disorders, visual or hearing impairments, and autism. Furthermore, incorporating children with visual impairments into typical early childhood settings requires early childhood educators to adopt a nonvisual teaching approach, one that counteracts all previous teaching experience and includes the idea that incidental learning cannot be left to chance.

Developmentally Appropriate Practice

Developmentally appropriate practice (DAP) has been adopted by the National Association for the Education of Young Children and the Division for Early Childhood of the Council for Exceptional Children as the primary philosophy that should drive programs for young children. DAP ensures that children with and without disabilities are seen as children first and bases the curriculum on how young children learn. It requires practitioners to understand child development and work in partnership with families to deliver services, both in early education and in day care, that support and encourage young children's growth and learning. The guidelines for DAP are as follows:

1. Create a caring community of learners.
2. Teach to enhance children's development and learning.
3. Construct an appropriate curriculum.
4. Assess children's development and learning.
5. Establish reciprocal relationships with families.

The principles of child development and learning are presented in Sidebar 4.1.

CHILDREN WITH VISUAL IMPAIRMENTS

Visual Disorders

According to Ferrell, with Shaw and Dietz (1998), the most common visual disorders in children are cortical visual impairment (20.6 percent of the participants), ROP (19.1 percent), optic nerve hypoplasia (16.6 percent), and structural anomalies (11.1 percent). The findings of an earlier study (Ferrell et al., 1990) were somewhat consistent with these findings, documenting the most common visual disorders as ROP (24.2 percent), cortical visual impairment (17.1 percent), and Leber's congenital amaurosis (6.8 percent) (all other disorders were identified in less than 5 percent of the respondents). A study of worldwide blindness found that there are marked differences in the causes of blindness in children that seem to be related to socioeconomic factors. The leading cause of childhood blindness in the world, for example, is corneal opacification, caused by a combination of measles, xerophthalmia (vitamin A deficiency), and poor eye care (Steinkuller et al., 1999). Steinkuller et al. also determined that the leading causes of childhood visual impairment in the United States were cortical visual impairment, ROP, and optic nerve hypoplasia, findings that are highly consistent with the study by Ferrell et al. (1998).

The high prevalence of children with ROP may seem surprising, given Hatfield's (1975) determination that the leading cause of childhood visual impairment was cataracts and that the proportion of children with retrolental fibroplasia (the precursor to ROP) would gradually decrease to about 2.0 percent of the population of children under age 15. This increase in the proportion of children with ROP is probably due to falling infant mortality rates in the United States, which declined 31 percent for infants with birthweights of 500–745 grams and 53 percent for infants with birthweights of 750–1499 grams between 1985 and 1995 (McNab & Blackman, 1998). About 20 percent of newborns weighing less than 800 grams are eventually diagnosed with neurosensory impairments, including visual impairments. Although this proportion has not increased over the past two decades (O'Shea, Klinepeter, Goldstein, Jackson, & Dillard, 1997), the actual number of children with ROP has increased simply because more infants are surviving.

Understanding the Development of Children with Visual Impairments

Traditional Approaches

Historically, children with visual impairments were compared to sighted children who were developing typically. Two early studies found that in the absence of additional disabling conditions, children with visual impairments generally developed the same skills in the same sequence as did sighted children (Maxfield & Buchholz, 1957; Norris, Spaulding, & Brodie, 1957). However, these studies also concluded that although children with visual impairments developed all the same skills as did children without disabilities, they did so at a slower rate, even given the optimum conditions of parent support and training.

During the 1960s and 1970s, Fraiberg (see Fraiberg, 1977, for a summary of her various studies) conducted her crucial work that documented the development of 10 children who were blind, none of whom had additional disabilities. She determined that children who were visually impaired demonstrated delays in developmental areas that were dependent on or greatly influenced

---

Principles of Child Development and Learning That Inform Developmentally Appropriate Practice

◆ The domains of children's development—physical, social, emotional, and cognitive—are closely related. Development in one domain influences and is influenced by development in the other domains.

◆ Development occurs in a relatively orderly sequence, with later abilities, skills, and knowledge building on those already acquired.

◆ Development proceeds at different rates from child to child, as well as unevenly within the various areas of each child's functioning.

◆ Early experiences have both cumulative and delayed effects on individual children's development; optimal periods exist for certain types of development and learning.

◆ Development proceeds in predictable directions toward greater complexity, organization, and internalization.

◆ Play is both an important vehicle for and a reflection of children's social, emotional, and cognitive development.

◆ Development advances when children have opportunities to practice newly acquired skills and when they experience a challenge just beyond the level of their present mastery.

◆ Children demonstrate different modes of knowing and learning and different ways of representing what they know.

◆ Children develop and learn best in the context of a community in which they are safe and valued, their physical needs are met, and they feel psychologically secure.

Source: Adapted from the National Association for the Education of Young Children (NAEYC) (1997). NAEYC position statement: Developmentally appropriate practice in early childhood programs serving children from birth through age 8—Adopted July 1996. In S. Bredekamp and C. Copple, eds., *Developmentally Appropriate Practice in Early Childhood Programs*. rev. ed. (Washington, DC: National Association for the Education of Young Children, 1997), pp. 3–30.

---

by vision, such as motor skills, perception, concept development, spatial relationships, auditory skills, tactile exploration, and ego development.

The prevailing view in the field of visual impairment thus came to be that the development of children with visual impairments was similar to that of sighted children, but that some children with visual impairments developed some skills at a slower rate. This belief was often referred to as "more alike than different." However, these early studies pointed out that such children would need more time to develop these skills, even under the optimum conditions of high-quality early inter-

vention, educated parents, and knowledgeable caregivers. Fraiberg (1977), Norris et al. (1957), and Maxfield and Buchholz (1957) continue to be cited extensively in examinations of the development of children with visual impairments.

In 1984, Warren reviewed the research comparing children with and without visual impairments and suggested that this "more alike than different" approach might be misleading. He thought that comparative studies were not helpful in understanding the development of children with visual impairments, since the premise of comparability was faulty. As Cutsforth (1951) stated:

Teachers, through an erroneous psychological concept, are compelled to regard the blind pupil as the equivalent of a seeing pupil except that he does not see. They conceive of the child as structurally incomplete, like an automobile engine with one cylinder missing. Therefore education must not only be education, but must also be a remedial therapy that will supply the missing power and also make the car sound as if it were really hitting on all six cylinders. It occurs to but few that a blind child is a complete mental and physical whole, organized to function perfectly upon his level of sensory equipment. (p. 50)

Warren (1984) concluded with a plea for more empirical research: "It is important to establish the range of normal behavior as well as to study the extent to which differences might be traced to differences in early experience." He implored professionals to take up the challenge of conducting empirical studies to clarify the development of children with visual impairments.

Consider what our goal in working with the visually impaired child should be. Should it be to make the child reach developmental milestones at the same age as the sighted child, or should we instead seek to optimize the developmental course of the visually impaired child? Comparative research tends to lead us toward the first goal. I argue that it is the second goal that we should take as a guiding principle. (p. 4)

Ferrell (1986) discussed the limitations of the three major studies and noted that individual differences among children with visual impairments had not been addressed. Furthermore, she pointed to the differences in the population of children studied earlier, most of whom were only visually impaired and had no additional disabilities, and the current population of children being served, who were more likely to exhibit additional disabilities. Ferrell also questioned the use of a standard based on sighted children to judge the development of children with visual impairments.

The problem, however, may rest in the comparison itself: it assumes that the experiences of visually handicapped children are similar to those of nonhandicapped children when in fact they may be totally different. Does the feel and smell of a banana, for example, produce the same concept in a child's mind as the sight and taste of one? Is the sound of an object as motivating to reach out to as the sight of it? (p. 124)

In a later publication, Ferrell (1997) described the problem this way:

Children with blindness and visual impairment learn differently, for no other reason than the fact that in most cases they cannot rely on their vision to provide information. The information they obtain through their other senses is *inconsistent* (things do not always make noise or produce an odor), *fragmented* (comes in bits and pieces), and *passive* (not under the child's control). It takes practice, training, and time to sort all this out. (p. v)

Current Approaches

Warren's (1994) book reexamined the literature on the development of children with visual impairments and provided a rationale for using an individual-differences approach in research with young children with visual impairments. Wanting to move beyond comparing children who were visually impaired to those who were sighted, he looked within the population of children who were visually impaired for variations and the reasons for the differences. He referred to the "adaptive tasks approach," the premises of which are as follows:

1. The developing child faces a set of adaptive tasks;
2. The child faces these adaptive tasks armed with a set of personal capabilities and characteristics;
3. The environment shapes not only the nature of the adaptive tasks but also the child's set of capabilities and characteristics; and
4. For the child with a visual impairment, there are variations on the tasks, the capabilities and characteristics, and the envi-

ronmental circumstances that must be taken into account to understand development and its causality. (p. 6)

VIIRC. The challenges posed by these issues had been met earlier by a group of service providers representing early childhood programs for visually impaired children in the New York City area. Working collaboratively to form the Visually Impaired Infants Research Consortium (VIIRC) (see Ferrell et al., 1990), these practitioners collected information about the children served by their agencies, including demographic data and ages when developmental milestones were achieved. In general, the VIIRC pilot study determined that "the median age for acquisition of these milestones was at or near the age for typical children" (Deitz & Ferrell, 1994, p. 470).

Subsequent analyses of the VIIRC database ($N = 314$), enhanced by the voluntary data submission by service providers across the United States, yielded essentially the same information. Children with visual impairments exhibited delays in the acquisition of certain milestones, particularly fine motor skills, and these delays were even greater for children who had additional disabilities (Ferrell & Mamer, 1993). A perplexing difference in the sequence of reaching milestones was noted and thought to be an artifact of the study's limitations. But the implications of this finding, including the possibility that families and educators were expecting development to proceed along a different path or that the methodology used to teach children with visual impairments might have actually created the difference in sequence, made the need for a scientifically rigorous study more critical.

Project PRISM. The VIIRC pilot study set the stage for a grant from the U.S. Department of Education to conduct the first longitudinal study on the sequence and rate of development of children (from birth to age 5) with visual impairments: Project PRISM: A National Longitudinal Study of the Early Development of Children Who Are Visually Impaired (Ferrell et al., 1998). Project PRISM, housed at the University of Northern Colorado, was a collaborative effort by seven agencies

across the United States that contributed 202 children, almost 60 percent of whom had additional disabilities, over the course of five years. The project trained personnel at each agency to administer a series of standardized assessment instruments, while parents independently completed a packet of questionnaires. One of the project's major findings was that the greatest impact on developmental outcome appeared to be the presence of disabilities in addition to visual impairment, although differences were also found on the basis of gestational age at birth (time elapsed from conception to birth) and some types of visual disorders. Differences were documented in the rate and sequence of acquisition of developmental milestones and developmental inventory scores, but those differences tended to disappear over time (Ferrell et al., 1998, p. 2).

In addition to differences between children with and without disabilities, Project PRISM documented the tremendous variability among the participants. Figures 4.1 and 4.2 illustrate the range of age-equivalent scores on the Battelle Developmental Inventory (BDI) (Newborg, Stock, Wnek, Guidubaldi, & Svinicki, 1984) of the participants at different age levels. The BDI is a standardized developmental instrument that measures young children's behaviors in the personal-social, adaptive, motor, communication, and cognitive domains. It is normed on children with disabilities and includes adaptations for children with various disabilities, including visual impairment. Figures 4.1 and 4.2 utilize box plots to illustrate the median, quartiles, and extreme values for age-equivalent scores on the BDI, grouped by two levels of visual function (Figure 4.1) and three levels of additional disability status (Figure 4.2). For each entry at each age level, each box indicates the semi-interquartile range (25th–75th percentile); the line within the box is the median, and the T-lines at the top and bottom of each box indicate the range of scores at that age interval.

In Figure 4.1, the median age-equivalent scores of the two groups are fairly close until the 18–23 month assessment interval, when they begin to differ sharply. It is important to note, however, that until the 48–59 month assessment interval, the

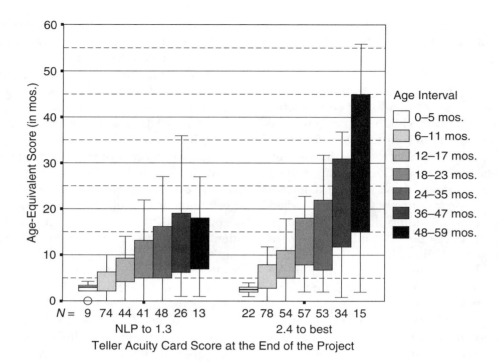

Figure 4.1. Range of Total Scores on the Battelle Developmental Inventory, by Level of Visual Function, at Each Assessment Interval.
The two levels of visual functioning were defined as the last Teller Acuity Card score obtained and were divided into two groups: NLP to 1.3 (poorest vision) and 2.4 to best (best vision).
Source: Generated by SPSS for Windows (release 8.0.0, 1997) using data from Project PRISM; see K.A. Ferrell, with A.R. Shaw and S.J. Dietz, *Project PRISM: A Longitudinal Study of Developmental Patterns of Children Who Are Visually Impaired.* Final Report, CFDA 84.023C, Grant H023C10188. (Greeley: University of Northern Colorado, Division of Special Education, 1998).

ranges of scores in both groups are highly variable but essentially equal, demonstrating not only the variability of the population, but the inability to predict outcomes based on visual function alone.

In Figure 4.2 the median age-equivalent scores of the three groups begin to deviate at 6–11 months, and the ranges of scores differentiate as well. The information in the figure lends support to Ferrell et al.'s (1998) conclusion that additional disability has a more predictable outcome than does visual function.

Whether analyzed by level of visual function or additional disability status, the children in Project PRISM exhibited tremendous variability at each assessment interval. This variability makes predictions about individual outcomes highly suspect

and supports Warren's (1994) conclusions. (For additional information on assessment, planning, and services and on supporting the development of young children who are visually impaired, see Chapter 7, in *Foundations of Education: Instructional Strategies for Teaching Children and Youths with Visual Impairments.*)

Since Project PRISM was an outgrowth of VIIRC, the results were also analyzed for delays in the age and sequence of the acquisition of similar developmental milestones. Table 4.2 compares the data from PRISM and VIIRC (Ferrell & Mamer, 1993), as well as from Fraiberg (1977); Maxfield and Buchholz (1957); and Norris et al. (1957). The columns indicate whether the milestone is delayed (D), out of sequence (S), on target (T), or earlier (E) in comparison to children without disabilities.

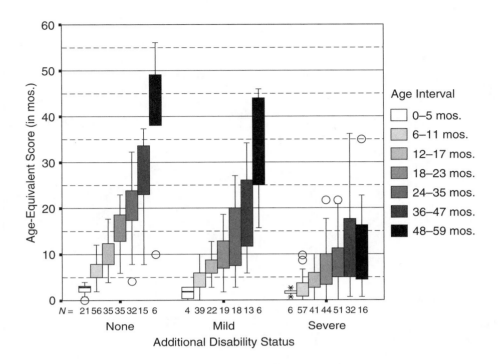

Figure 4.2. Range of Total Scores on the Battelle Developmental Inventory, by Additional Disability Status, at Each Assessment Interval.

Source: Generated by SPSS for Windows (release 8.0.0, 1997), using data from Project PRISM; see K.A. Ferrell, with A.R. Shaw and S.J. Dietz, *Project PRISM: A Longitudinal Study of Developmental Patterns of Children Who Are Visually Impaired.* Final Report, CFDA 84.023C, Grant H023C10188. (Greeley: University of Northern Colorado, Division of Special Education, 1998).

The conclusions of Project PRISM were as follows:

> The age of acquisition for 12 milestones was delayed in comparison to typically developing children.
>
> For 5 milestones [all related to expressive and receptive communication], median age of acquisition was within the range of attainment for typical children.
>
> Two milestones were acquired earlier. . . . Earlier acquisition is somewhat suspect, however, since data are available for less than 10% of the total sample.
>
> Six milestones were acquired in a different sequence than usually acquired by children without disabilities. (Ferrell et al., 1998, pp. 114–115)

Children with additional disabilities were generally delayed in all the developmental mile-stones examined. When the milestones were examined by degree of visual function, however, only one milestone ("plays interactively with adults") resulted in a significant difference among the groups. That is, children with no light perception acquired this behavior significantly later than did those with greater levels of visual functioning.

Ferrell et al. (1998) stressed that even though Project PRISM was conducted with rigor, there were still limitations that must be considered when examining the results of this study. All the children were receiving services from agencies that worked with children with visual impairments, and the level of services varied in "intensity, duration and frequency" (p. 65). Thus, care must be taken to "avoid (a) misinterpretation of the findings, (b) oversimplification of the results or (c) unclear generalizations about the delicate

Table 4.2. Age of Acquisition of Selected Developmental Milestones in Five Studies (in months)

Milestone and Median Age of Attainment by a Typical Child (in Months)	PRISM (Ferrell, 1998) (N = 202)	VIIRC (Ferrell & Mamer, 1993) (N = 314)	Fraiberg (1977) (N = 10)	Maxfield & Buchholz (1957) (N = 398)	Norris, Spaulding, & Brodie (1957) (N = 66)
Reaches for and touches object (5.4)	8.3 (D)	8.0 (D)	8.3 (D)	Median: 0–12 (D)	50 percent at 9.0 (D)
Transfers object from hand to hand (5.5)	9.3 (D)	8.0 (D)			
Searches for a removed object (6.0)	15.0 (D, S)	12.0 (D)			
Sits alone without support for 5 seconds (6.6)	10.9 (D)	9.0 (D, S)	8.0 (D, S)	Median: 13–24 (D)	25 percent at 9.0
Feeds self bite-size pieces of food (7.4)	12.6 (D, S)	12.0 (D)[a]		Median: 13–24 (D)	
Produces 1 or more consonant-vowel sounds (7.9)	10.9 (D)	12.0 (D)		Median: 0–12 (S)	
Moves 3 or more feet by crawling (9.0)	12.8 (D, S)	12.0 (D)[a]		Median: 13–24 (D)	
Plays interactive game (9.7)	11.4 (T)	12.0 (D)			
Walks 10 feet without support (13.0)	19.8 (D)	16.0 (D)[b]	19.3 (D)	Median: 25–36 (D)	50 percent at 24.0
Points to at least 1 major body part when asked (17.5)	19.5 (T)				
Removes a simple garment without assistance (20.5)	22.7 (D)	30.0 (D)		Median: 37–48 (D)	
Generally follows daily-routine directions (20.5)	24.3 (D)	30.0 (D)			
Uses 2-word utterances to express meaningful relationships (20.6)	28.2 (D, S)	24.0 (D, S)[b]	26.3 (D)	Median: 37–48 (D)	
Uses pronouns "I," "you," and "me" (24.0)	25.8 (T)	36.0 (D)[b]		Median: 49–60 (D)	
Controls bowel movements regularly (30.0)	36.5 (D, S)	34.0 (D, S)[b]		Median: 37–48 (D, S)	
Repeats 2-digit sequences (30.0)	33.4 (T)				
Walks down stairs alternating feet (30.0)	33.4 (T)[c]	29.0 (E, S)[b]			
Copies a circle (33.0)	31.8 (E, S)[c]	36.0 (D)[b]		Median: 49–60 (D)	
Relates his or her past experiences (40.0)	37.3 (E)[c]	29.0 (E, S)[b]		Median: 49–60 (D)	

Note: Letters after numbers indicate comparisons with the median for typical children: D = delayed, T = on target, E = earlier, and S = out of sequence.

[a]Less than 50 percent of the VIIRC respondents reported that the children with additional disabilities had acquired this milestone.

[b]Less than 50 percent of the VIIRC respondents reported that the children had acquired this milestone

[c]Of the 16 participants in Project PRISM who were last assessed at 40.5–54.4 months, 14 had not met these milestones at the end of the project; 85.7 percent of the 16 had additional impairments.

interactions between children's development and other variables under investigation" (p. 65).

Historically, comparing children who were visually impaired to children who were sighted gave professionals some guidelines for working with young children who were visually impaired. In the absence of research to the contrary, such comparisons were appropriate. Now, however, the results of Project PRISM support Warren's (1994) call for an "individual differences" approach to intervention.

In the future, early interventionists may wish to reconsider the assumptions that the degree of visual function is related to child developmental outcome and that children with visual impairments follow the same sequence of development as do children without disabilities. The assumption that levels of visual functioning influence early child development did not appear to make a difference in the age-equivalent scores of the PRISM participants. (See, however, Hatton, Bailey, Burchinel, & Ferrell's, 1997, combined PRISM–North Carolina study, which did find differential scores by level of visual function using growth curve analysis.) Perhaps what is more important is that the assumption that children with visual impairments follow the same sequence of development as children without disabilities must be challenged.

Impact of Visual Impairment

Lowenfeld (1973) stated that blindness imposes three basic limitations on the individual: the range and variety of experiences, the ability to get about, and control of the environment and the self in relation to it. Because of restrictions in the range and variety of experiences that are due to the lack of vision, the individual relates to and learns about the world through the remaining four senses, especially hearing and touch. Hearing is the source sense for language and communication and provides information when a person moves about in the environment; however, it does not supply all the necessary information about objects and their shapes. Touch provides information about objects, but a person needs to be close enough to an object to explore it by hand. Thus, an individual who is blind cannot completely experience objects that cannot be fully touched by hand, such as skyscrapers, mountains, and oceans, or touch at all objects that are small, difficult, or dangerous to explore physically, such as insects, soap bubbles, and fire (Lowenfeld, 1981). "A great many experiences which are taken for granted with seeing children are either impossible or much more difficult for blind children" (Lowenfeld, 1981, p. 70).

Restrictions on the ability of an individual who is totally blind to get about have an impact on orientation to the surrounding area, both inside (the type of room and furniture) and outside (the terrain and weather), and mobility (moving about, by crawling, walking, or running). Therefore, a young child who is blind must have formal and informal orientation and mobility (O&M) lessons to compensate for these restrictions.

Restrictions on control of the environment and the self in relation to it include not being able to look around an area and, in a few seconds, gain information about the elements of the space and the people who are present. In addition, individuals who are blind cannot learn by visual imitation; they need to learn by direct teaching or assistance about relationships with others and their own and others' facial expressions and gestures. Thus, Lowenfeld (1981, p. 77) believed that "education must aim at giving the blind child a knowledge of the realities around him, the confidence to cope with these realities, and the feeling that he is recognized as an individual in his own right."

Children with low vision, who have a severe visual impairment that, even with the best correction, interferes with the performance of daily tasks, have some degree of these limitations, although, with a systematic plan to develop their residual vision, the obstacles will not be as great. For example, children who can see color can gain much information about the environment from color cues, and those with light perception only can learn to use their ability to see shadows to help them move around the environment (Barraga & Erin, 1992).

Barraga and Erin (1992) highlighted the impact that visual impairment can have on the development of children by discussing the role that vision plays in early development in general. The following statements summarize important aspects of vision that have the potential to affect the development of children with visual impairments.

Vision gives a reason for movement.   Children see something that is interesting or that they want and move toward it.

Vision provides continuous contact with the environment.   When their eyes are open, children are instantly in contact with all that is going on around them.

Vision is an active sense that is under children's control.   Children cannot turn off their hearing or sense of smell, but they can close their eyes.

Vision gives an estimation of space.   Children can look at a desired object in a room and calculate the movement necessary to obtain it. They can also determine where empty chairs and the food table are located. And they can do all this without moving.

Vision stimulates coordination and control. Although movement in infants is initially reflexive, vision allows infants to monitor and eventually coordinate movements. The infants become aware of their body parts from the visual cues obtained by watching the parts move.

Vision provides feedback for refining patterns of movement.   Vision helps children give meaning to movement. When children reach for a toy, they learn how far and in what direction to extend their arms and then can make any necessary adjustments. Interactive games, such as pat-a-cake, help children make a physical connection to a visual image.

Vision allows for vicarious participation in movement.   With vision children can watch another person's actions and be part of an activity.

Young children can watch others move around and develop an understanding of how to move their body parts. When an adult rolls a ball, for example, a child watches the adult's position, the shape of the hands, the pushing action of the arms, and the movement of the ball. Thus, the child learns a great deal about rolling a ball without ever touching it.

Vision provides information about the sequence and totality of movement patterns in progress—the whole process is visible.   Vision provides the wholeness of actions, the "start-to-finish" aspects of an activity. Young children see other children swinging and gain valuable information about the process of swinging—the position, posture, and acceleration of the swing; the pumping action of the arms and the legs; and expressions of enjoyment.

Vision provides a model for motor skills and gives feedback on the result.   Vision allows children to watch others' movements and see what happens as a result of those actions. The children can then imitate those movements, observe their own movements, and use this feedback to correct their movements.

Vision facilitates body image and perception. By observing the whole and individual parts of the body, children gain an easy sense of where their body parts start and end. Vision also helps children develop a sense of depth, as well as directionality and laterality, as they look at objects and people in all areas of their environment and see how these objects and people relate to them. This perception assists children in forming the concept of objects.

Vision provides consistent, coordinated, and verifiable information.   Vision is not subject to the whims of opportunity—it is always there unless one closes one's eyes. Odors, on the other hand, disappear, and touch can be used only if one is within reach. If a person hears a noise, vision verifies where it came from. Other sensations are discrete, one-time occurrences that are intermittent, inconsistent, and generally unverifiable.

Vision is a strong motivator that stimulates self-initiated exploration of the environment. Vision alone can motivate sighted children to move. If children see a desired toy, they will move to it without needing another person to encourage them. Vision encourages children's curiosity to explore and increases children's motivation to become independent.

Vision provides an incentive for tactile exploration. Tactile exploration is stimulated by the visual dimensions of objects, such as color, pattern, shape, and location.

Vision is a distance sense and is under an individual's control. Individuals can regulate visual input by opening and closing their eyes, and they see both near and far. Hearing is a distance sense, too, but there is no way to control the presence or absence of sound in the environment. Sound without visual verification is only noise coming from some undefined place. It acquires meaning only after sustained tactile, motor, and auditory interaction. In time, sounds become predictable, but a sound must acquire meaning before it can provide information about location, cause, or source.

Vision facilitates cognitive development. Vision is related to the development of concepts, abstractions, and mental representations that are difficult to form without visual memory.

Vision provides an incentive for communication. Young children learn to communicate with the world by developing a bond with the permanent people in their lives. For children who are sighted, vision tells them that their parents are constant and predictable people in their worlds. By responding to the sight of their parents and then turning to their parents' voices, young children begin to communicate by directing visual attention, showing anticipation, and then gesturing and eventually making sounds. The communica-tive intent of the gestures and sounds receives constant feedback and reinforcement from vision. As they observe the faces of adults, children are motivated to continue this ever-increasing cycle of reaching out, response, motivation, reaching out, response, and so on. Adults take advantage of children's visual sense to teach communication by using such phrases as "See this?" "Look at this." "Over here."

Vision helps children develop concepts. Concept development is an ongoing learning process for all children. Children learn the names of items and their function and then how to use the items. Concepts range from concrete (objects and characteristics, such as shapes, sizes, textures, likenesses, and differences) to semiconcrete or semiabstract (colors) to abstract (emotions and thoughts).

These statements about the role of vision in early childhood do not imply that children with visual impairments will not be able to develop concepts, communicate, or move about in the environment. They are presented here to highlight the fact that visual impairment presents a great risk to development. But in looking at Figures 4.1 and 4.2, it is also apparent that there is no guarantee that these risks will develop. All the research to date, from Norris et al. (1957) to Ferrell et al. (1998), has found that some children with visual impairments grow and develop at the same rate as do sighted children. What seems to make the difference are the opportunities available to learn and the presence of additional disabilities.

Impact of Additional Disabilities

Project PRISM found that 59.9 percent of its participants were diagnosed with disabilities in addition to visual impairment. This finding seems consistent with other studies, notably Kirchner's (1980, 1989), and is somewhat less than the 69.5 percent found by Ferrell et al. (1990). Ninety different additional disabilities and health conditions were diagnosed in the 202 PRISM participants, including central nervous system disorders

(42.1 percent), developmental delay (40.1 percent), eating disorders (16.3 percent), and auditory disorders (12.4 percent). Many conditions occurred concurrently; for example, of the 85 children who were diagnosed with central nervous system disorders, 76.5 percent were also diagnosed with developmental delays.

Additional disability clearly affects early development. The children who were categorized as having no additional disabilities performed better on developmental tests than did the children with mild additional disabilities, who performed better than the children with severe additional disabilities. Although differences in the acquisition of skills based on the degree of functional vision were apparent for only one milestone, the age of acquisition was significantly later for children with additional disabilities for 63.2 percent of the milestones studied. This impact of additional disabilities was consistent across the various measures used in Project PRISM and has been replicated in other studies (see, for example, Hatton et al., 1997).

Certainly, the range of performance is as great among children with additional disabilities as it is among children without additional disabilities (see Figure 4.2). But it seems clear that additional disabilities may have a greater impact on development than does the degree of visual impair-

---

SIDEBAR 4.2

Suggestions for Families and Educators

- Make no assumptions.
- Understand that learning proceeds from parts to wholes.
- Use concrete objects.
- Adopt the child's point of view.
- Address the child by name.
- Allow time.
- Use the body as a reference point.
- Capitalize on past experiences.
- Make a doer, not a "done-to-er."
- Tie together all the separate pieces of information that the child receives.
- Provide physical contact and guidance often.
- Keep the child engaged.
- Change the child's position and objects of interest often.
- Create situations that facilitate the next developmental milestone.
- Encourage the child to follow walls with his or her hands.

- Increase the amount of sensory input.
- Describe what the child cannot see.
- Recognize that all objects in the home are potential toys for learning.
- Encourage the child to run, climb, and play with other children.
- Help the child experience something new every day.

Sources: Adapted from K.A. Ferrell, "Preface. What Is It That Is Different About a Child with Blindness or Visual Impairment?" In P. Crane, D. Cuthbertson, K.A. Ferrell, and H. Scherb (Eds.), *Equals in Partnership. Basic Rights for Families of Children with Blindness or Visual Impairment.* (Watertown, MA: Perkins School for the Blind and the National Association for Parents of the Visually Impaired), pp. v–vii, and K.A. Ferrell, S.A. Raver, and K.A. Stewart "Techniques for Infants and Toddlers with Visual Impairments," in S.A. Raver, (Ed.), *Intervention Strategies for Infants and Toddlers with Special Needs: A Team Approach.* 2nd ed. (Upper Saddle River, NJ: Merrill, 1999), pp. 298–330.

ment. For the field of visual impairment, this conclusion, if it is supported by future studies, may necessitate a paradigm shift from viewing visual impairment as a disability to viewing it as a risk that can be ameliorated and mastered.

Implications for Families and Educators

A change in outlook cannot occur without high-quality early education programs that are family centered and address the special learning needs of children with visual impairments (Bailey et al., 1998). All the children in Project PRISM were, after all, enrolled in early education programs for various amounts of time and services. Unless further analyses identify factors that would suggest otherwise, it must be assumed that early education for children with visual impairments is, indeed, effective.

Ferrell (1997) and Ferrell, Raver, and Stewart (1999) presented several principles for families and professionals in providing early education services to young children with visual impairments. These principles include capitalizing on incidental learning, recognizing that children with visual impairments learn from parts to wholes, and providing concrete experiences. The suggestions for families and educators listed in Sidebar 4.2 can be reviewed in Chapter 7, Early Childhood, in *Foundations of Education: Instructional Strategies for Teaching Children and Youths with Visual Impairments*.

A final implication for families and professionals who work with young children with visual impairments may be to avoid developmental checklists that list various skills by age level in favor of more process-oriented approaches to understanding development. Two examples of a process-oriented approach are Lueck, Chen, and Kekelis's (1997) *Developmental Guidelines for Infants with Visual Impairment* and Ferrell's (1985) *Reach Out and Teach*. Ferrell used a corequisite-skills approach that postulates a minimal number of discrete skills that are related to and incorporated into higher-level behaviors. These corequisite skills are as follows:

Motor Skills

◆ Absence of atypical or abnormal reflexes

◆ Balance

◆ Rotation

◆ Protective reactions

◆ Muscle tone

Fine Motor and Self-Help Skills

◆ Reach

◆ Grasp

◆ Wrist rotation

Social and Communication Skills

◆ Attention

◆ Imitation

◆ Imagination

◆ Interaction

Cognitive Skills

◆ Percepts

◆ Concepts

◆ Object permanence

◆ Object constancy

◆ Categorization

◆ Symbolization

SUMMARY

Teachers who work with young children who are visually impaired must keep in mind that research on this population is only a tool. Studies seldom conclude without posing more questions than they sought to answer, so they should not be allowed to become self-fulfilling prophecies. Teachers, parents, and school administrators should use the results of research to gain a greater understanding of the development of children with visual impairments and to develop new ways of responding to the children's unique learning needs. It is important to remember that "generalizations about stages and structures never capture all the nuances of child development, and . . . the possibilities often do outrun the predictions" (Greene, 1992, p. 37).

STUDY QUESTIONS

1. Why is it important to study the unique developmental patterns of young children with visual impairments?

2. What are the components of an early intervention program that takes into account the developmental needs of a young child who is visually impaired? List and describe them.

3. How have services to young children with visual impairments changed over the past 60 years?

4. What is meant by an "individual differences" approach to studying young children with visual impairments?

5. How are the impact of visual impairment and the impact of additional disability on the development of children with visual impairments different?

6. What role has the federal government played in fostering services to young children and their families?

7. How have attitudes toward parents changed since the passage of P.L. 94-142?

REFERENCES

Bailey, D.B., Jr., & McWilliam, R.A. (1990). Normalizing early intervention. *Topics in Early Childhood Special Education, 10*(2), 33–47.

Bailey, D.B., Jr., McWilliam, R.A., Buysse, V., & Wesley, P.W. (1998). Inclusion in the context of competing values in early childhood education. *Early Childhood Research Quarterly, 13,* 27–47.

Barraga, N.C., & Erin, J.N. (1992). *Visual handicaps and learning* (3rd ed.). Austin, TX: Pro-Ed.

Bloom, B.S. (1964). *Stability and change in human characteristics.* New York: John Wiley & Sons.

Bredekamp, S., & Copple, C. (Eds.). (1997). *Developmentally appropriate practice in early childhood programs* (rev. ed.). Washington, DC: National Association for the Education of Young Children.

Cutsforth, T. (1951). *The blind in school and society.* New York: American Foundation for the Blind.

Davidson, I.F.W.K., & Simmons, J.N. (1992). Mediating the environment for young blind children: A conceptualization. In I.F.W.K. Davidson & J.N. Simmons (Eds.), *The early development of blind children: A book of readings* (pp. 83–91). Toronto: Ontario Institute for Studies in Education.

Deitz, S.J., Ferrell, K.A. (1994). Project PRISM: A national collaborative study on the development of children with visual impairment. *Journal of Visual Impairment & Blindness, 88,* 470–472.

Dewey, J. (1933). *How we think.* Lexington, MA: D.C. Heath.

Erikson, E. (1963). *Childhood and society.* New York: W.W. Norton.

Erwin, E.J. (1993). Social participation of young children with visual impairments in specialized and integrated environments. *Journal of Visual Impairment & Blindness, 87,* 138–142.

Erwin, E.J. (1994). Social competence in young children with visual impairments. *Infants and Young Children, 6*(3), 26–33.

Ferrell, K.A. (1985). *Reach out and teach: Meeting the training needs of parents of visually/multiply handicapped young children.* New York: American Foundation for the Blind.

Ferrell, K.A. (1986). Infancy and early childhood. In G.T. Scholl (Ed.), *Foundations of education for blind and visually handicapped children and youth* (pp. 119–135). New York: American Foundation for the Blind.

Ferrell, K.A. (1997). Preface. What is it that is different about a child with blindness or visual impairment? In P. Crane, D. Cuthbertson, K.A. Ferrell, & H. Scherb (Eds.), *Equals in partnership. Basic rights for families of children with blindness or visual impairment* (pp. v–vii). Watertown, MA: Perkins School for the Blind and the National Association for Parents of the Visually Impaired.

Ferrell, K.A., & Mamer, L.A. (1993). *Visually impaired infants research consortium, March 1993 analysis.* Unpublished manuscript, University of Northern Colorado, Division of Special Education.

Ferrell, K.A., Raver, S.A., & Stewart, K.A. (1999). Techniques for infants and toddlers with visual impairments. In S.A. Raver (Ed.), *Intervention strategies for infants and toddlers with special needs: A team approach* (2nd ed., pp. 298–330). Upper Saddle River, NJ: Merrill.

Ferrell, K.A., Trief, E., Dietz, S.J., Bonner, M.A., Cruz, D., Ford, E., & Stratton, J.M. (1990). Visually impaired infants research consortium (VIIRC): First-year results. *Journal of Visual Impairment & Blindness, 84,* 404–410.

Ferrell, K.A., with Shaw, A.R., & Deitz, S.J. (1998). *Project PRISM: A longitudinal study of developmental patterns of children who are visually impaired* (Final Report, CFDA 84.023C, Grant H023C10188). Greeley: University of Northern Colorado, Division of Special Education.

Fraiberg, S. (1977). *Insights from the blind.* New York: Basic Books.

Froebel, F.W.A. (1887). *The education of man* (W.N. Hairmann, Trans.). New York: Appleton.

Froebel, F.W.A. (1895). *Education by development: The second part of the pedagogies of the kindergarten* (J. Jarvis, Trans.). New York: Appleton.

Fromberg, D.P. (1990). Play issues in early childhood education. In C. Seefeldt (Ed.), *Continuing issues in early childhood education* (pp. 223–243). Columbus, OH: Merrill.

Fromberg, D.P., & Gullo, D.F. (1992). Perspective on children. Introduction. In L.R. Williams & D.P. Fromberg (Eds.), *Encyclopedia of early childhood education* (pp. 191–194). New York: Garland.

Gesell, A. (1925). *The mental growth of the preschool child.* New York: Macmillan.

Gesell, A. (1940). *The first five years of life: A guide to the study of the preschool child.* New York: Harper & Row.

Goffin, S.G. (1992). Federal legislation of importance to early childhood education: A chronology. In L.R. Williams & F.P. Fromberg (Eds.), *Encyclopedia of early childhood education* (pp. 58–64). New York: Garland.

Greene, M. (1992). Beyond the predictable: A viewing of the history of early childhood education. In L.R. Williams & F.P. Fromberg (Eds.), *Encyclopedia of early childhood education* (pp. 31–39). New York: Garland.

Guralnick, M.J. (1997). *The effectiveness of early intervention.* Baltimore, MD: Paul H. Brookes.

Hatfield, E.M. (1975). Why are they blind? *Sight-Saving Review, 45*(1), 3–22.

Hatton, D.D., Bailey, D.B., Jr., Burchinel, M.R., & Ferrell, K.A. (1997). Developmental growth curves of preschool children with visual impairments. *Child Development, 68,* 788–806.

Hunt, J.M. (1961). *Intelligence and experience.* New York: Ronald Press.

Individuals with Disabilities Education Act (IDEA) Amendments of 1997, PL 105–17. Title 20, U.S.C. 1400 et seq.

Kirchner C. (1989). National estimates of prevalence and demographics of children with visual impairments. In M. C. Wang, M. C. Reynolds, & H. J. Walberg (Eds.), *Handbook of special education: Research and practice. Vol. 3. Low incidence conditions* (pp. 135–153). Oxford: Pergamon.

Krichner, C., & Peterson R. (1980). Multiple impairments among noninstitutionalized blind and visually impaired persons. Statistical brief No. 7. *Journal of Visual Impairment & Blindness, 74,* 42–44.

Kirk, S.A. (1958). *Early education of the mentally retarded.* Urbana: University of Illinois Press.

Koestler, F. (1976). *The unseen minority: A social history of blindness in the United States.* New York: David McKay.

Lazar, I., Darlington, R., Murry, H., Royce, J., & Snipper, A. (1982). Lasting effects of early education. *Monographs of the Society for Research in Child Development, 47* (1–2, Serial No. 194).

Linder, T. (1990). *Transdisciplinary play-based assessment: A functional approach to working with young children.* Baltimore, MD: Paul H. Brookes.

Linder, T. (1993). *Transdisciplinary play-based intervention: Guidelines for developing a meaningful curriculum for young children.* Baltimore, MD: Paul H. Brookes.

Lowenfeld, B. (Ed.). (1973). *The visually handicapped child in school.* New York: John Day.

Lowenfeld, B. (1981). *Berthold Lowenfeld on blindness and blind people: Selected papers by Berthold Lowenfeld.* New York: American Foundation for the Blind.

Lueck, A.H., Chen, D., & Kekelis, L.S. (1997). *Developmental guidelines for infants with visual impairments.* Louisville, KY: American Printing House for the Blind.

Mamer, L. (1995). Tactile defensiveness. *Journal of Visual Impairment & Blindness, 89,* 9–10.

Maxfield, K.E., & Buchholz, S. (1957). *A social maturity scale for blind preschool children: A guide to its use.* New York: American Foundation for the Blind.

McKey, R.H., Condeli, L., Ganson, H., Barrett, B.J., McConkeyt, C., & Plantz, M.C. (1985). *The impact of Head Start on children, families, and communities* (Final report of the Head Start Evaluation, Synthesis, and Utilization project). Washington, DC: Administration for Children, Youth, and Families, Head Start Bureau.

McNab, T.C., & Blackman, J.A. (1998). Medical complications of the critically ill newborn: A review for early intervention professionals. *Topics in Early Childhood Special Education, 18,* 197–205.

National Association for the Education of Young Children (NAEYC). (1997). NAEYC position statement: Developmentally appropriate practice in early childhood programs serving children from birth through age 8—Adopted July 1996. In S. Bredekamp & C. Copple (Eds.), *Developmentally ap-*

propriate practice in early childhood programs (rev. ed., pp. 3–30). Washington, DC: Author.

Newborg, J., Stock, J.R., Wnek, L., Guidubaldi, J., & Svinicki, J. (1984). *Battelle developmental inventory.* Allen, TX: DLM Teaching Resources [Available from Riverside Publishing Company].

Norris, M., Spaulding, P.J., & Brodie, F.H. (1957). *Blindness in children.* Chicago: University of Chicago Press.

O'Shea, T.M., Klinepeter, K.L., Goldstein, D.J., Jackson, B.W., & Dillard, R.G. (1997). Survival and developmental disability in infants with birth weights of 501–800 grams born between 1979 and 1994. *Pediatrics, 100,* 982–986.

Piaget, J., & Inhelder, B. (1969). *The psychology of the child.* New York: Basic Books.

Provence, S., & Lipton, R.C. (1962). *Infants in institutions.* New York: International Universities Press.

Raver, S.A. (1999). *Intervention strategies for infants and toddlers with special needs: A team approach* (2nd ed.). Upper Saddle River, NJ: Merrill.

Sameroff, A.J. (1975). Early influences on development: Fact or fancy? *Merrill-Palmer Quarterly of Behavior and Development, 21,* 267–294.

Sameroff, A.J., & Chandler, M.J. (1975). Reproductive risk and the continuum of caretaking casualty. In F.D. Horowitz, M. Hetherington, S. Scarr-Salapatek, & G. Siegel (Eds.), *Review of child development research* (Vol. 4, pp. 187–244). Chicago: University of Chicago Press.

Schweinhart, L. (1992). Sociocultural studies of the effectiveness of early childhood education. In L.R. Williams & D.P. Fromberg (Eds.), *Encyclopedia of early childhood education* (pp. 187–188). New York: Garland.

Shonkoff, J.P., & Hauser-Cram, P. (1987). Early intervention for disabled infants and their families: A quantitative analysis. *Pediatrics, 80,* 650–658.

Shonkoff, J.P., & Meisels, S.J. (1990). Early childhood intervention: The evolution of a concept. In S.J. Meisels & J.P. Shonkoff (Eds.), *Handbook of early childhood intervention* (pp. 3–31). New York: Cambridge University Press.

Silverman, W. A. (1980). *Retrolental fibroplasias: A modern parable.* New York: Grune & Stratton.

Skeels, H.M. (1966). Adult status of children with contrasting early life experiences. *Monographs of the Society for Research in Child Development, 31,* 1–65.

Skeels, H.M., & Dye, H.B. (1939). A study of the effects of differential stimulation on mentally retarded children. *Proceedings of the American Association of Mental Deficiency, 44,* 114–136.

Skinner, B.F. (1968). *Science and human behavior.* New York: Free Press.

Spitz, R.A. (1945). Hospitalism: An inquiry into the genesis of psychiatric conditions in early childhood. In R.S. Eissler (Ed.), *Psychoanalytic study of the child.* New Haven, CT: Yale University Press.

Steinkuller, P.G., Du, L., Gilbert, C., Foster, A., Collins, M.L., & Coats, D.K. (1999). Childhood blindness. *Journal of the American Association for Pediatric Ophthalmology & Strabismus, 3,* 26–32.

Stoiber, K.C., Gettinger, M., & Goetz, D. (1998). Exploring factors influencing parents' and early childhood practitioners' beliefs about inclusion. *Early Childhood Research Quarterly, 13,* 107–124.

Strain, P.S. (1984). Efficacy research with young handicapped children: A critique of the status quo. *Journal of the Division for Early Childhood, 9*(1), 4–10.

Stratton, J.M. (1990). Comment: The principle of least-restrictive materials. *Journal of Visual Impairment & Blindness, 84,* 3–5.

Turnbull, A.P., & Turnbull, H.R. (1985). Stepping back from early intervention: An ethical perspective. *Journal of the Division for Early Childhood, 10,* 106–117.

Turnbull, A.P., & Turnbull, H.R. (1997). *Families, professionals, and exceptionality: A special partnership.* Upper Saddle River, NJ: Merrill.

Vygotsky, L.S. (1986). *Thought and language.* Cambridge, MA: MIT Press.

Warren, D.H. (1984). *Blindness and early childhood development* (2nd ed. rev.). New York: American Foundation for the Blind.

Warren, D.H. (1994). *Blindness and children: An individual differences approach.* Cambridge, England: Cambridge University Press.

White K.R. (1986). Efficacy of early intervention. *Journal of Special Education, 19,* 401–416.

White, K.R., & Boyce, G.C. (Eds.). (1993). Comparative evaluations of early intervention alternatives [Special issue]. *Early Education and Development, 4.*

White, K.R., Mastropieri, M., & Castro, G. (1984). An analysis of special education early childhood projects approved by the Joint Dissemination Review Panel. *Journal of the Division for Early Childhood, 9*(1), 11–26.

White, K.R., Taylor, M.J., & Moss, V.D. (1992). Does research support claims about the benefits of involving parents in early intervention programs? *Review of Educational Research, 62,* 91–125.

Williams, L.R. (1992). Historical and philosophical roots of early childhood practice. In L.R. Williams & D.P. Fromberg (Eds.), *Encyclopedia of early childhood education* (pp. 7–10). New York: Garland.

CHAPTER 5

Growth and Development in Middle Childhood and Adolescence

Karen E. Wolffe

KEY POINTS

◆ Four major theoretical models guide an understanding of the developmental process: the maturational model, the psychoanalytic model, the behavioral model, and the cognitive-developmental model.

◆ During later childhood and adolescence, students undergo major physical, cognitive, and emotional changes.

◆ Students with visual impairments face unique challenges during adolescence.

◆ Parents and teachers can help adolescents with visual impairments by providing opportunities for them to participate in important milestones and rites of passage.

◆ Adolescents with visual impairments who are given honest, sensitive feedback are more likely to have the tools they need to develop into strong, healthy, productive adults.

Although various authors (Anderson & Clarke, 1982; Fenwick & Smith, 1996; Tanner, 1962; Weiner, 1970) have defined adolescence as extending from approximately age 10 or 11 to age 18 or 21, it is difficult to divide human beings' lives neatly into limited periods like childhood, adolescence, or adulthood. The time limits of adoles-cence have changed from one historical period to another, from one culture to another, and from one social class to another. Adolescence appears to be a phenomenon of modern Western society—a culture that indulges its youths in an extended time for education and growth that was unheard of even a century ago when children as young as 10 were often expected to assume adultlike responsibilities at home and in the community. There is, however, one aspect of adolescence that is common to all cultures, social classes, and historical eras—the biological phenomenon (Dasberg, 1983). This chapter presents models of human development and then specifically discusses the development of adolescents, including the biological phenomenon. The similarities and differences between youngsters from about age 10–21 with unimpaired vision and those with visual impairments are described in the context of physical, cognitive, and emotional characteristics. The chapter concludes with a look at some of the key studies that have explored the impact of visual impairments on adolescents.

MODELS OF DEVELOPMENT

A review of the literature on children's typical developmental sequences reveals four major theoretical models: the maturational model, the psychoanalytic model, the behavioral model, and the cognitive-developmental model (Bee, 1997; Dworetzky, 1981; Salkind, 1985). These four theoretical models attempt to explain human behavior in different ways; some explain or try to predict behavior on the basis of environmental factors, whereas others emphasize the interaction between the environment and an individual's genetic makeup. In the following sections, each model is briefly discussed; a comparison of the four models is presented in Table 5.1.

Maturational Model

Developmental psychologists who support the maturational model believe that heredity (innate biological strengths and weaknesses) is paramount in an individual's development—much more influential than nurturing or the impact of the environment. In short, they believe that a child's development is governed by a pattern built in at birth. Arnold Gesell, a physician whose work in the 1920s was strongly influenced by Charles Darwin's studies of biological evolution, and Konrad Lorenz were two early theorists who espoused the maturational model. Lorenz is perhaps best remembered for his experiments with newborn

ducklings where he described imprinting—the innate process in which a duckling (or other animal) follows the first thing that moves and perceives that "thing" as "mother," guardian, and teacher.

Both Gesell (1928, 1956) and Lorenz (1958, 1965) believed that the sequence of human development was determined by the biological and evolutionary history of the species. In other words, they thought that a child progresses through a series of stages that recount the developmental sequence characterized by his or her ancestors. In addition to the contributions Gesell made to the maturational model, he made significant contributions in research on human development by introducing studies of twins to compare the effects of nature (heredity) versus nurture (environmental factors) and documenting his efforts on film (Gesell & Thompson, 1929, 1941). His work chronicled the development of "normal" children and greatly influenced mid- to late 20th-century child-rearing patterns, most notably through its incorporation in the work of Dr. Benjamin Spock (Salkind, 1985).

Psychoanalytic Model

Freud (1905) introduced the psychoanalytic model at the beginning of the 20th century. His

Table 5.1 An Overview of Models of Human Development

Models	Maturational Model	Psychoanalytic Model	Behavioral Model	Cognitive-Developmental Model
Assumptions	Development is determined by biological factors.	Development is based on a person's need to satisfy basic instincts.	Development occurs as a person learns from his or her environment.	Development is contingent on the modification of a person's cognitive structures over time.
Implications for practitioners	Importance of biological determinants and how children are reared.	Impact of early parent-child relationships on personality development.	Understanding of behavioral analysis, modification of behavior, and extinction of maladaptive behavior.	Understanding of cognitive processes and how to engage children in appropriate tasks to match their developmental level.

basic assumption was that human development consists of dynamic, structural, and sequential components that are distinct and influenced by a continual need to gratify basic instincts. Freud defined the dynamic component of the model as the psyche, or the mind, which he characterized as fluid and energized. The structural component of the model consisted of the id, ego, and superego, three separate but interdependent psychological structures. The sequential component of the model focused on the notion that human beings progress developmentally through different stages (oral, anal, phallic, latency, and genital) that correspond to erogenous zones of the body. Freud believed that people encountered psychological conflicts (weaning, toilet training, identification with the same-sex parent, development of ego defenses, and mature sexual intimacy) at each of these stages that had to be resolved for them to become healthy adults.

According to Freud, biological needs were paramount in development and behaviors were expressions of unconscious psychological and social conflicts. Resolution of these conflicts, he thought, was an ongoing process. Although Freud's work met with resistance from the scientific community because of its focus on the unconscious and his attempts to tap into the unconscious through hypnosis, Freud's efforts to document and systematically organize a theory of development were a significant contribution (Salkind, 1985).

Many modern psychoanalytic theorists have gravitated to the work of Erikson (1963, 1980), who de-emphasized the centrality of the sexual drive. Although he shared many of Freud's assumptions, Erikson focused on the gradual emergence of self-identity, rather than the sexual drive, as the primary motivation for growth and development. He proposed the following eight psychosocial stages, five of which occur in childhood:

◆ *Basic trust versus mistrust (birth to 1 year).* At this stage, children bond with their primary caregiver and realize that they can make things happen.

◆ *Autonomy versus shame, doubt (2–3 years).* At this stage, children engage in motor skills to make choices and are toilet trained; they learn control but may develop shame if training in skills is not handled well.

◆ *Initiative versus guilt (4–5 years).* At this stage, children organize activities around goals and become more assertive; conflict with their same-sex parents may lead to guilt.

◆ *Industry versus inferiority (6–12 years).* At this stage, children are absorbed in learning cultural mores and acquiring academic and tool-usage skills.

◆ *Identity versus role confusion (13–18 years).* At this stage, youths adapt to the physical changes of puberty, make career choices, achieve a sexual identity, and clarify values.

◆ *Intimacy versus isolation (19–25 years).* At this stage, people form intimate relationships, marry, and start families.

◆ *Generativity versus stagnation (26–40 years).* At this stage, individuals raise children, perform life work, and prepare the next generation.

◆ *Ego integrity versus despair (40 and older).* At this stage, people integrate the earlier stages and accept their basic identities.

Both Freud and Erikson emphasized the critical importance of the early years of children's lives and focused attention on children's need for positive emotional support from caregivers, underscoring the impact of good parenting and positive family relationships on children's lives. The difficulty with this model is the lack of empirical evidence to support its various hypotheses (Bee, 1997).

Behavioral Model

The work of Ivan Pavlov, who introduced the behavioral model in the early 20th century, focused on classical conditioning. In Pavlov's (1927) most famous experiment, classical conditioning occurred when a dog learned a new behavior (salivating) in response to the pairing of an unconditioned stimulus (food) with a previously neutral stimulus (a bell); in time, the dog salivated at the sound of the bell without seeing food. The dog was already programmed (innately) to salivate at the presentation of food, which is considered an unconditioned response. Salivating at the sound of the bell was the conditioned response. In summary, classical conditioning involves attaching an old response to a new stimulus.

Adherents of the behavioral model view development as a function of learning that proceeds according to certain laws or principles. The human being is seen as reactive, not active, and behavior is considered a function of its consequences. If the consequences of a given behavior are good or positive, then the behavior is reinforced and is likely to continue. However, if a behavior is punished or ignored, then it is likely to diminish or be extinguished.

The behavioral model is a mechanistic model that assumes that the environment is more important in development than a person's hereditary attributes. Behaviorists (Bandura, 1977, 1979, 1986, 1989; Skinner, 1938, 1957, 1976) believe that children's behaviors are modified or learned over time with both positive and negative reinforcement. They have shown, through extensive scientific study, the power of consistent and intermittent reinforcement schedules, intermittent reinforcement being the most powerful. Consistent or scheduled reinforcement occurs when a behavior is reinforced at specified times, for example, rewarding a child who gets to school on time every day in a semester. Intermittent reinforcement occurs when a behavior is reinforced, but not always and not at any particular time, for instance, rewarding a child who gets to school every day on time at the end of the first, fourth, and tenth weeks of the semester. The child is more likely to continue getting to school on time in the latter scenario because he or she is waiting to be reinforced, rather than expecting a reinforcement at a scheduled time. Providing the reinforcement on a consistent schedule requires diligence by the giver of the reinforcement that is often not possible to maintain, and if the child becomes dependent on the reinforcement, the behavior may not

continue when the reinforcement is withdrawn. Therefore, intermittent schedules of reinforcement are the most powerful. Perhaps the greatest contributions of the behaviorists have been an emphasis on the scientific study of behavior, systematic analysis of behavior, specific techniques to modify deviant behaviors, and encouragement of programmed instruction (Salkind, 1985).

Cognitive-Developmental Model

Piaget (1932, 1952, 1977), a psychologist, presented the cognitive-developmental model in response to the behavioral model. In his theory, he stressed the individual's active, rather than reactive, role in the developmental process. Cognitive-developmentalists believe that development occurs in a series of qualitatively distinct stages and that all people undergo the same stages in the same sequence but not necessarily at the same chronological time. The stages are considered hierarchical, and the later stages subsume the characteristics of the earlier stages, so that what children learn in the earlier stages is used to develop more complex and mature sensory motor schemas to use in life.

Piaget's four proposed stages of development are as follows:

- *Sensorimotor (birth to 18 months).* At this stage, children respond to the world almost entirely through sensory and motor schemas, operate entirely in the present and without intentions, and have no internal representation of objects.

- *Preoperational (18 months to approximately age 6).* At this stage, children begin to use symbols and language, engage in pretend play, exhibit egocentrism, and can perform simple classifications but cannot understand that two amounts that look different can be the same (conservation).

- *Concrete operational (from about age 6 to age 12).* At this stage, children discover strategies for exploring and interacting with the world and master internal schemas that enable them to perform mathematical functions, categorize objects and entities into related groupings, and perform feats of logic.

◆ *Formal operational (from approximately age 12 onward).* At this final stage, youngsters can apply complex mental operations to ideas and thoughts, as well as to objects and experiences, and exhibit deductive reasoning.

Piaget believed that children actively participate as they develop an understanding of the world in which they live. He thought that babies are born with a small repertoire of basic sensory schemas, such as tasting, touching, looking, hearing, and reaching, and that they develop mental schemas, such as categorizing, over time. Schemas are often loosely defined as concepts or a "complex of ideas," but Piaget used the term to denote the action of categorizing in some particular mental or physical fashion (Bee, 1997).

According to Piaget, children shift from the simplistic schemas of infancy to increasingly complex mental schemas through assimilation, accommodation, and equilibration. Assimilation is the process of absorbing an experience or an event into a schema—connecting the concept to whatever other concepts are similar. Accommodation (the reorganization of thoughts) is a complementary process that requires changing a schema because of the assimilation of new information. Equilibration is the means by which children achieve balance in their lives between what they know and the new things they are learning.

Although some of Piaget's ideas have been called into question and errors in his theory, such as his description of the timing of the development of cognitive skills, have been identified, Piaget's notion that a child is actively engaged in constructing an understanding of his or her world has been widely accepted (Bee, 1997). An important outgrowth of Piaget's work is the emphasis by contemporary developmental theorists on qualitative change—how an adolescent approaches a problem or a task is not only faster than but qualitatively different from how an infant, toddler, or child approaches a similar problem or task.

Table 5.1 presents an overview of the four developmental models just discussed. Although there are adherents of all four models, there is no consensus in the field of human development that one model is better or more accurate than another. Many contemporary child psychologists borrow from the array of models and consider the interaction between nature and nurture to be the real answer to the question of how children develop (Bee, 1997).

In the sections that follow, three significant areas of development in adolescence are detailed: physical, cognitive, and emotional. In each section, the attributes that are universal to youngsters at this age are described. Any differences or concerns pertinent to children and youths with visual impairments are then discussed.

OVERVIEW OF ADOLESCENT DEVELOPMENT

Physical Attributes

During the later years of elementary school, girls and boys typically experience a growth spurt. This growth spurt, which usually begins at age 10 or 11 in girls and at age 12 or 13 in boys, includes considerable physical changes. For girls, these physical changes include the development of breasts; the appearance of pubic, underarm, and body hair; menstruation; and the production of underarm perspiration. For boys, the changes include growth of the testes; darkening of the skin of the scrotum; lengthening and thickening of the penis and the onset of ejaculation; the appearance of pubic, underarm, body, and facial hair; the production of underarm perspiration; and a deepening of the voice (Fenwick & Smith, 1996). Although these physical changes often begin in the late elementary school years, they continue through middle school and often extend into high school.

Perhaps the greatest physical changes occur during the middle school (6th, 7th, 8th grades) or junior high school (8th and 9th grades) period. For many young people, this period is truly a transition from childhood. Many young women reach physical maturation at age 14 or 15, and many young men do so at age 15 or 16, while they are in high school. Young people may continue to gain height and weight in their 20s, but, for the most part, they complete the bulk of their physical development before they leave high school.

These physical changes and milestones in growth are usually the same for youths with and without visual impairments. However, Western society adheres to a "body-perfect" tenet that basically presupposes that being intact physically is critical to life satisfaction (Buscaglia, 1975). The most popular children, youths, and adults are often those who look most attractive to others; they have no apparent cosmetic flaws. This notion of a perfect body causes many adolescents significant stress. Young sighted girls and boys spend an inordinate amount of time in front of their mirrors, scrutinizing their appearance. They gain and lose weight as they judge themselves to be too skinny or too fat to fit the body-perfect image presented in the popular press and on film. They paint their faces and dye their hair, tattoo and pierce their body parts, and dress differently from adults in their midst as they emulate popular musicians, athletic superstars, and film characters. Adolescence is a time to experiment with matching one's body and appearance to whatever the popular image of the body-perfect is (Elkind, 1984; Fenwick & Smith, 1996; Wolf, 1991).

Without good, functional vision (vision that is reliable and useful for performing activities of daily living), this task is difficult, if not impossible. It is difficult for children and youths with visual impairments to discern what their cosmetic liabilities may be—unless someone with good vision gives them feedback on their appearance. If youngsters have any kind of overt cosmetic flaw, such as damaged eyes or facial scarring, the task of fitting the body-perfect mold is nearly impossible. Often children with cosmetic flaws are teased at school and at play, which contributes to their poor body image and, in turn, lowers their self-esteem (Tuttle & Tuttle, 1996). Positive self-esteem is the first internal capacity or resource for developing social competence (Peterson & Leigh, 1990). Studies of the impact of visual impairment on self-concept and self-esteem have been contradictory (Beaty, 1991, 1994; Head, 1979; Huurre, Komulainen, & Aro, 1999; Meighan, 1971). However, what these and other studies have consistently indicated is that young people who are visually impaired and who have positive support from their families and strong peer networks have higher levels of self-esteem than do those without such supports (Huurre et al., 1999; Kef, 1997; Rosenblum, 1997; Wolffe & Sacks, 1997).

In addition to cosmetic or surface appearance, how one presents oneself "in total" is a significant issue in adolescence. Teenagers often adopt certain ways of walking, sitting, standing, and posturing that are indicative of how they feel, how they want to be seen, and how they see themselves. In some cases, their movements and mannerisms may identify them as belonging to specific cliques or social groups. Certainly, how they walk or move through space tells others about their level of comfort and how well they "fit in" to the social milieu.

For children who are congenitally blind or severely visually impaired, this may be another area of concern. If children with visual impairments skip early developmental stages, such as the critical crawling stage, they may demonstrate differences in gait, posture, and fluidity of movement (Ferrell, 1986). These observable differences between students who are sighted and students who are visually impaired may cause difficulties for children who are trying to fit in. Likewise, the tendency of some students with visual impairments to engage in stereotypic mannerisms, such as rocking, eye poking, or flicking their hands in reaction to the lack of visual sensory input, negatively influences their sighted peers (MacCuspie, 1996) because these behaviors do not conform to the socially age-appropriate behaviors demonstrated by sighted teenagers. Teenagers do not necessarily conform to the adult world in which they live, but they conform avidly to the teenage world they aspire to join. Thus, the behaviors and mannerisms they adopt must fit the behaviors and mannerisms demonstrated by their friends or the groups they wish to join because anything that sets people apart from the strictures of those cliques or groups will be disdained.

Issues surrounding physical limitations, particularly the inability to drive, are particularly poignant for teenagers with visual impairments. Getting a driver's license is a rite of passage for many teenagers in Western society, and being physically restricted from doing so imposes many hardships on teenagers with visual impairments (Chase, 1986; Corn & Sacks, 1994; Erin & Wolffe, 1999; Lowenfeld, 1971). Driving is an important milestone in the developmental process of adolescents, and youngsters who are not able to drive need support from their families and friends to participate actively in social and vocational activities. These youngsters also need to learn how to negotiate and solve transportation problems that will only increase with the demands of adult responsibilities. Sidebar 5.1 discusses clinical interventions for adolescents who are faced with this difficult issue.

An additional area of concern for young people with visual impairments is whether to use the tools that enable them to improve their functional abilities, such as optical devices or speech and braille output devices for reading and writing and a long cane or guide dog for mobility. Since these tools obviously set them apart from their sighted peers, adolescents with visual impairments often abandon these tools when the desire to fit in overwhelms the desire to see or improve functionality (Warnke, 1991b).

Cognitive Attributes

Cognitively, children in the late elementary and middle school years begin to think more abstractly and creatively. For example, most cognitively intact youngsters appear to enter Piaget's formal operational stage at about age 12. Thus, as teenagers, they can use their reasoning abilities to think abstractly and not *only* consider real things or actual occurrences. Although they can understand more than one point of view and are able to solve problems on their own, they tend to see global issues in terms of just or unjust or black or

white, with little room for compromise. By the time young people are in high school, most of them are well into thinking independently and making decisions about matters like clothing, friends, and where they want to spend their time. There is evidence that students with visual impairments have considerable academic success; as a group, they tend to receive fairly good grades and enter into higher education settings in numbers comparable to their sighted peers (Wagner et al., 1991, 1992). However, a closer inspection of youngsters with visual impairments in this age range indicates that their parents do not necessarily believe that their grades or acquisition of skills are truly comparable to those of their sighted classmates and that their exposure to the community and world around them may be inhibited by their lack of active participation in activities of daily living, leisure pursuits, and vocational experiences (Sacks & Wolffe, 1998; Sacks, Wolffe, & Tierney, 1998; Wolffe & Sacks, 1995, 1997). These concerns are discussed in further detail later in this chapter.

Similar to the description in the classic poem by John Godfrey Saxe (Felleman, 1936) about the blind men and the elephant, children and youths without functional vision or with severely limited eyesight have great difficulty acquiring a "whole-picture" perspective. Rather, their world is at their fingertips, and if they happen to encounter only a portion of an object, that portion may be their perception of the object. For example, each man in the poem approached the elephant and felt a different part of it—its side, tusk, trunk, knee, ear, and tail—and each thought that what he had felt was the elephant in its entirety. Therefore, the man who felt the ear thought that the elephant was like a fan, the man who felt the tusk thought the elephant was hard and sharp like a spear, the man who felt the trunk thought the elephant was like a snake, and so forth. This is the challenge, in a nutshell, for students who are blind—how to know the whole when they have the opportunity to come into contact with only a part of something.

Children with severe visual impairments develop in an environment that is proximate and serial, rather than in the environment of their

Clinical Notes: Driving

The age at which a person may obtain a driver's license varies from state to state, but whatever the age, high school students throughout the country eagerly anticipate this "rite of passage" into adulthood for about a year before they take the required driving tests. Most adults can remember the feelings associated with learning to drive and the excitement and fear the process aroused.

Transportation provides independence. People in cities are able to travel to desired locations on buses, trains, and streetcars, but as the suburban culture has expanded, Americans have become far more dependent on automobile transport. Furthermore, cars are marketed as objects of desire and beauty. These factors lead young people to yearn for cars of their own and the ability to drive them. Unfortunately, the same factors lead young people with visual impairments to feel left out and sad when they consider a life without driving a car. Although some people with visual impairments are able to operate vehicles safely (Jose, 1983; Corn, Lippmann, & Lewis, 1990), this note refers to those who cannot, particularly students in local high schools whose friends are learning to drive. Visual impairment can raise feelings of deprivation and incompetence when a teenager cannot do everything his or her friends are doing.

Discussions in groups for adolescents with visual impairments invariably include transportation and the students' dependence on others for rides. Counselors, teachers, and other professionals may find that some teenage group members, including many who are totally blind, admit to having driven friends' cars. One can only hope that such experiments take place in the safety of open, untraveled areas, but the attempt represents teenage desire and daring at its starkest. Friends of students who are blind are

willing accomplices to these actions, partly because they want to help their classmates and partly because of their desire for thrill seeking.

What clinical interventions are helpful when the dilemma of automobile travel arises in discussions? Several guidelines may be followed:

1. Although teenagers with visual impairments need to feel some self-pity because driving is not possible, it is not helpful to generalize this feeling to a "poor-me" attitude toward all forms of transportation. In fact, the group discussion is often timed so that each person is given a two-minute period of sorrow about one or another deprivation and then is encouraged by the group to move on. This technique is used in many groups, not just those for people with disabilities.

2. Each student should be helped to become an optimal traveler. Orientation and mobility (O&M) training is an essential ingredient of independence, and each person with a visual impairment should strive for excellence in travel, whatever the terrain. Sophisticated use of a cane, along with sensitive interaction with helpful others, such as family members and teachers, can ensure that the person is viewed as competent and independent in most settings. Teenagers may shun aspects of O&M training, but firm instruction for safety and smooth movement is essential and expresses true concern for students' well-being and respect for students' independent strivings.

3. Similarly, each teenager with a visual impairment should consider all available options for public transportation. If mass transportation is not available, it is usually possible to

(continued on next page)

Clinical Notes: Driving *(Continued)*

obtain special taxi passes and privileges so one can get where one wants to go without always depending on others.

4. Many young people who are totally blind are unaware of the nature of streets and highways and how complex traffic patterns can be. Rides on carnival bumper cars, for example, may give them some idea of the jolting they may experience while riding in cars in heavy, stop-and-go traffic. Furthermore, tactile traffic maps and other aids can help them become aware of the nature of driving. Slowly driving old cars in open fields may provide a meaningful simulation for adolescents with visual impairments if there is a sighted guide along.

5. Family members, school personnel, and friends can offer consistent schedules for transportation. A serious problem arises when drivers offer rides as rewards or teenagers who are visually impaired lose rides because of negative interactions with the drivers. Each time a person must be assisted, he or she loses a measure of independence. To ensure interdependence, teenagers with visual impairments may exchange rides for helping the drivers in other ways, such as assistance with homework. There is a delicate balance between needing help and feeling helpless at one end of the continuum and wanting to do things totally on one's own at the other end. The emotional aspects of transportation must be considered. A colleague who is blind once said, "The worst days begin when I must ask my wife for a ride to work after having had an argument the night before."

6. Find alternative means of marking the onset of adulthood. For example, one family arranged for their visually impaired 16-year-old to visit a friend in a distant city, a trip that entailed solo airline travel. The young person had a chance to feel "grown up" and on her own. Other methods of making an adolescent gain a sense of having "arrived" at adulthood might be considered. Election day provides an excellent "marker" for attaining an age of responsibility. A person who is visually impaired can apply for an identification card, a voter registration card, and a sample ballot. Most communities provide transportation to the polls. Alternatively, independent shopping trips, unescorted prevocational job-site interviews or a local volunteer job, such as at a hospital, allow adult role opportunities. Students should be encouraged to share their experiences with others, so that they provide the "bragging rights" that accompany coming of age.

Clinically, tension is produced in relation to movement even under the best circumstances, since people leave the security of their homes and face risks whenever they go out. Because risk-taking behavior is such a central feature of adolescence, it is not surprising that automobile travel is the source of such pleasure for teenagers and such worry for the adults who care about them. When a visual impairment is a factor in the process, transportation becomes a complicated issue.

JOAN B. CHASE
Psychologist
Dunedin, FL

sighted peers that includes input from afar as well as input that is near and serial. Sighted children can also receive input that is sometimes disjointed or multifaceted and still make sense of it, whereas for children with visual impairments, such input may be confusing or overwhelming. Thus, youngsters who are visually impaired may view the environment narrowly and in fragments, rather than as whole gestalts. Although children who are totally blind evidence the greatest experiential consequences of this phenomenon, any degree of visual impairment will affect learning (Chase, 1986; Lowenfeld, 1987).

Difficulty acquiring abstract concepts without good, functional vision is another cognitive issue for children and youths. If something is too distant, such as a planet or a star, or if something is inaccessible through touch, such as a color, body language, or facial expression, the concepts may be too abstract for many children with severe visual impairments truly to understand. A child who is blind may form a concept based on a stereotypic understanding of what something is. For example, one child reported to her teacher that the color black was a poor choice for clothing because only bandits and outlaws wore black. An adult asked her friend to show her the hinges on an airplane's wings that enabled it to fly like a bird.

Another cognitive concern frequently seen in children and youths with severe visual impairments is the tendency to be rigid in their thinking patterns. This rigidity in thinking may be due to the lack of consistent and realistic input from others, coupled with limited incidental learning. It has been estimated that the average child learns 60 percent to 80 percent visually, through scanning the environment and observing what people and things are doing (MacCuspie, 1996). Without constant and casual access to information, children who are visually impaired can easily come to believe that there are fewer choices than children with unimpaired vision recognize. This problem is often exacerbated by well-meaning people in the lives of children who are visually impaired, who attempt to protect them from the evils and hardships of daily life by filtering the information they share with them. Rather than provide uncensored information about what choices are available, sighted informants sometimes tell a child who is blind only about the available choices that they believe are good or right for him or her based on their own value systems. This filtering can lead to the child's misunderstanding of the full spectrum of choices, and, consequently the child may appear rigid.

Emotional Attributes

Although teenagers sometimes act in ways that seem to be selfish and egocentric, their outward appearance of bravado often masks feelings of insecurity. Their acting-out behaviors may be irksome to parents and other adults, but for teenagers, they are an important part of confidence building (Fenwick & Smith, 1996). By acting as if they are in control and comfortable with themselves, teenagers can influence the people around them to think of them in a similar way. Ideally, they receive positive feedback from their peers and families that builds their self-esteem. They need to know that they look good, that they are performing well, and that the people in their lives care about them even when they misbehave. If they do not receive constructive positive input, their insecurities multiply, and they tend to act out more and more outrageously.

This lack of self-confidence is often compounded for youngsters with visual impairments because their efforts to act out and behave in rebellious ways are often thwarted by their inability to see who is around to notice or to observe how other teenagers are presenting themselves. A consequence of this inability to rebel effectively or mold themselves to the style of a particular group is that teenagers with visual impairments often find it difficult to fit into social groups or cliques.

In terms of how children view and come to understand other people's feelings, it is important to understand that sighted children can visually discern the difference between positive and negative facial expressions in the first year of life. This ability to "read" people's facial expressions appears to be cross-cultural, meaning that there is a great similarity in people's expressions of basic emotions, such as fear, happiness, anger, and sadness, throughout the world (Ekman, cited in Bee, 1997).

Children and youths with severe visual impairments often have difficulty understanding the impact of their behavior on others because they cannot see the reaction of others—they miss visual cues, particularly facial expressions and body language. Just as they cannot see what is going on in the environment, they cannot see how people look and evidence their approval or disapproval of what they see and hear through facial expressions and body language when they are communicating with them or others. This inability to read body language and facial expression cannot be fully compensated for through auditory means, so youngsters with visual impairments need to be taught to interpret verbal messages (Matsuda, 1984; Minter, Hobson, & Pring, 1991; Wolffe & Sacks, 2000).

Compounded by other people's unwillingness to provide realistic, honest feedback, this inability to observe others' reactions to their behaviors puts teenagers with visual impairments at risk in social situations. For teenagers, involvement with peer groups is an important developmental process that sets the stage for future separation from their parents and other family members. Emotional issues surrounding dependence, independence, and interdependence are often at the crux of many adolescents' seemingly rebellious and self-centered behavior. There is an almost constant struggle between wanting to stay safely within the dependent structure of their families and wanting to experiment with self-rule early in adolescence. In this regard, Sidebar 5.2 discusses the various tensions in families of adolescents with visual impairments and how parents can provide the supports that the adolescents need. Then, as youngsters mature, they move toward mutually beneficial, interdependent relationships. Involvement in peer groups is perhaps the most intense in the junior high school years, before interest in members of the opposite sex begins to encourage the partnering that is more common in high school (Fenwick & Smith, 1996; MacCuspie, 1996; Scholl, 1986).

Difficulty with peer relationships and dating may be partly due to the delays in perspective taking (the ability to comprehend that another person may perceive a situation differently from the way one does) in children who are visually impaired (MacCuspie, 1996). Since relationships are built on reciprocity, it is critical for partners in a relationship to be able to understand each other's needs and wants. For teenagers with visual impairments, this concept of reciprocity may be delayed, along with the delay in perspective taking, and dating activity may subsequently be delayed as well.

Again and again, the inability to observe others incidentally and casually seems to threaten the socialization process of children and youths with visual impairments and may have its greatest negative impact on teenagers in relation to dating. Much of the preliminary behavior in dating centers on nonverbal communication: ogling, smiling, winking, nodding, and other ways of noticing and expressing interest in one another. In addition to noticing one another and indicating interest, observational skills are used routinely to identify where individuals of interest are in relation to others—on the bus, outside the classroom, in the cafeteria, and so forth. Without vision to direct one into close proximity with someone of interest, a young person must rely on others to know both who is in the vicinity and who is available. Once all the obstacles are overcome, teenagers who are interested in dating another must muster the assertiveness skills to ask and have something to offer in the way of an activity of interest. In Sidebar 5.3, a clinician discusses the impact of blindness on sexuality.

Difficulties expressing intent through nonverbal communication and interpreting the intent of others are frequently mentioned as outcomes of growing up with a severe visual impairment (MacCuspie, 1996; Wolffe & Sacks, 2000). In addition, eccentric behaviors or mannerisms, unusual language patterns, self-centeredness, and preference for interaction with adults are negative social behaviors that some children and youths with visual impairments evidence (Sacks, Kekelis, & Gaylord-Ross, 1992). These behaviors are a source of concern because they inhibit acceptance by same-age

Clinical Notes: Families

Families respond to visual impairment in the myriad ways they respond to all challenges in life. For some, the experience of having a family member with impaired vision strengthens bonds and relationships, but for others, it is a source of tension. For most, the emotional impact falls somewhere in between. In many instances, the quality and quantity of intervention at the time of diagnosis or onset can have dramatic effects on the way in which people adapt to changed circumstances. Families manifest unique interactive patterns and modes of communication. They process the "news" of a visual impairment (Scott, Jan, & Freeman, 1995) in ways that create reverberations for all family members.

Families operate as systems (McGoldrick & Gerson, 1985), and changes in one part of a system affect all the other parts. Chase (1993) applied family systems theory to families with young children who are visually impaired, citing parents' response to any disability as a source of a shift in relationships. As youngsters reach middle childhood, they have an increased impact on their families. They begin to bring home new ideas from school and peers who may differ from those raised in the family circle (Fine, 1995). Furthermore, youngsters with visual impairments recognize that they may be viewed as "different" by people outside their families.

Adolescence is a period of turmoil for many young people. Because teenagers often bring intense energy into their homes, charged in both positive and negative ways, they may engage in a struggle for independence from their parents and for autonomy that surprises and raises anxiety in their parents. All family members experience many emotions in rapid succession (Larson & Richards, 1994). The father of a 12-year-old may wonder: "How did my sweet young daughter learn to be sarcastic?" Some struggles for independence are particularly intense when a young person has a visual impairment because the parents tend to feel more protective than with other children in the family.

Families often exercise extreme caution when their children with visual impairments want to explore on their own out of fear of the many risks to safety when young people travel alone unless they have had expert instruction in orientation and mobility. Suddenly, it seems, the youngsters want to gallivant around with friends or by themselves in ways that strike terror in the parents' hearts. Such anxiety about separation and individuation is typical among parents of adolescents with visual impairments, but it is exacerbated when the parents fear for their youngsters' safety (Nixon, 1991). A blind colleague recalled that he purposely "lost" his mother in the New York subway system to prove to her that he could get home on his own.

Other issues that create family tension include transportation, self-initiated activities, and routines. Parents continue to transport their adolescents with visual impairments long after sighted adolescents are driving on their own or with friends who own cars (Tuttle & Tuttle, 1996). This added symbol of dependence may exacerbate the tension caused by any high school student "pulling away" from his or her family. In addition, other family members may view teenagers with visual impairments as more pliable or passive, so when the teenagers strike out on their own, the family members may be surprised and sometimes impose restrictions on them that are not imposed on other teenagers.

Routines are a source of contention in most families, particularly because middle school and high school students prefer activities of their choice to those required at home. Even the neatest, most compliant child may become less concerned with the state of his or her things than with the state of his or her friendships as adolescence approaches (Crary, 1995). For a young

(continued on next page)

Clinical Notes: Families *(Continued)*

person with a visual impairment, neatness counts, in that things that are moved or in disorder are more difficult to find again when needed, so conflicts arise that are more intense in a family with a child who has problems with vision.

None of the issues raised is specific to families in which there is a teenager with a visual impairment, but the presence of such a complicating factor adds to the tension of adolescence. Cowen et al. (1961) found that although the adjustment variables for teenagers with visual impairments were the same as those for teenagers who were sighted, parents' (in their study, mothers') understanding was a significant contributor to the teenagers' ultimate adjustment. For those with visual impairments, parents and other family members have the task of understanding the disability, along with all the other ingredients that combine to make the complex beings called adolescents.

JOAN B. CHASE
Psychologist
Dunedin, FL

---

peers. It is important for youths with visual impairments to be taught the attributes demonstrated by popular and unpopular teenagers so they can strive to assimilate the attributes of popular teenagers that are feasible in their lives.

Fenwick and Smith (1996) described popular teenagers as those who are cheerful and friendly, those who like to joke and suggest games or activities, and those who are physically attractive or have athletic ability (especially boys). Attributes that contribute to rejection are restlessness and overtalkativeness, being quiet or shy, being unattractive (especially fat), and being "different." Obviously, teenagers with visual impairments have some attributes over which they have little or no control, such as being or looking "different," that may have negative social consequences. However, they can develop many positive attributes that can contribute to the likelihood of their acceptance by peers.

Another emotional concern is that because parents, teachers, and other well-meaning adults tend to shelter or overprotect many teenagers who are visually impaired, these teenagers are often socially immature. In addition, Western society tends to support the notion that people with disabilities are "children" for life. Behavior is contextual, meaning that people act in ways that re-

flect the expectations or perceived expectations of those around them (Chase, in press). By overdoing or doing for young people with visual impairments, adults send these youngsters the message that they are expected to do little or nothing for themselves and that they are unable or unworthy (Wolffe, 1999). The consequence of overprotectiveness is that it impedes the social and emotional development of young people with visual impairments. As Scott, Jan, and Freeman (1995) noted, youngsters who lose their vision in adolescence may suffer greater emotional and physical effects than those who lose vision earlier in life. Together with adjustment to adolescence, the struggles with peer pressure, social acceptance, and concerns about life and work in the future, the loss of vision may exacerbate teenagers' emotional concerns.

IMPACT OF VISUAL IMPAIRMENT

Studies of the impact of visual impairment on child development (Deitz & Ferrell, 1994; Ferrell, 1996; Fraiberg, 1977; Norris, Spaulding, & Bradie, 1957; Warren, 1984, 1994) have found evidence of

Clinical Notes: Sexuality

Most people gradually become aware of the nature of sexual differences, behaviors, acts, and intimacies through observation. Young people "surf" the Internet and television stations and are exposed electronically to stimulating material. Many such images are purely visual. For the adolescent who is severely visually impaired or blind, the visual aspect of this dawning awareness is absent or altered, so that much of what is learned is vicarious, through talk with adults or peers, and through exploration of one's own body.

Years ago, when most visually impaired young people were educated in more segregated settings, either residential or day programs, they tended to be more innocent than their sighted age-mates. Cutsforth (1951) decried the lack of meaningful information for youngsters who were visually impaired during his era, and described the resulting tendency for students in special schools to internalize fantasies and practice autoeroticism and/or homosexual experimentation. Even today, the self-stimulatory behavior and body rocking that sometimes accompany early development in children who are blind creates discomfort among those observers who interpret the activity as early masturbation or deviant behavior. The emotional reactions that sexuality and visual impairment can evoke are compounded by the myth about masturbation causing blindness, a myth that persists in spite of modern science. Welbourne (1982) describes one situation in which an adolescent believed that self-stimulation was responsible for his decreasing vision. She proceeds to describe other associations between guilt over sex (viewed as sin) and visual impairment.

In today's media-drenched society, few young people are unsophisticated about sexual information, whether or not they have any experience. Students with disabilities are often as theoretically "savvy" about the facts of life as their classmates. However, visual impairment intensifies anxieties for parents and youngsters, as a child or adolescent who is visually impaired may be more vulnerable than others to offers of friendship and affection, and may truly fail to "see trouble ahead." Therefore, discussion of human sexuality is even more urgent in families in which a growing child has a visual impairment than in those where disability is not an issue.

Sexual awakenings occur in even the most disabled adolescents (Heslinga, 1974), so that open attitudes toward any individual struggling with intimacy issues are essential. People with disabilities, regardless of challenges, seek sexual gratification. Warnke (1991a) candidly described his tendency to spend time and energy obsessing about sexual matters as an adolescent, and his inward tendency to focus, with guilt, on his own emotional and physical state. Professionals often bear a heavy responsibility to assure that the knowledge and attitudes that students develop will be accurate, wholesome, and nonjudgmental.

How can primary sexual knowledge be acquired by touch and hearing alone? Webourne (1982) recommends guided touch with realistic plastic models and dolls, with demonstrations performed in the privacy of a physician's office. Van't Hooft and Heslinga (1975) recommend the use of live artists' models and statuary to provide insight into anatomy and physiology, along with sensitive teaching for insight into intimacy. Foulke and Uhde (1975) raise the need for wider exploration so that a congenitally blind child learns about the "variety of physical characteristics manifested by the human species . . . fat bodies, muscular bodies, thin bodies, tall bodies, short bodies. . . ." They describe a research

(continued on next page)

Clinical Notes: Sexuality *(Continued)*

study in which they queried students with visual impairments and found that both misinformation and adherence to negative myths were pervasive among them. Other authors in the same book (School, 1975; Torbett, 1975) and in a companion volume (Dickman, 1975) provide guidelines about sex education curricula for those with visual impairments, so that students may have access to accurate information.

Visual impairment does not limit a person's potential for meaningful and pleasurable sexual experiences. Sex researchers discuss the extent to which sexual expression occurs mentally as well as physically (Fisher, 1992). Inactivity may increase the extent of sensual fantasy, making so-

cial and recreational undertakings, both in and out of school, particularly crucial during adolescence. Sexual acting-out, teen pregnancy, sexually transmitted disease, and other risks observed among teenagers may also occur in those with disabilities. Teachers and counselors will wish to establish relationships with their students/clients that permit frank and open adolescent group discussion and instruction regarding this important, life-affirming area of development.

JOAN B. CHASE
Psychologist
Dunedin, FL

---

similarities and differences in the early development of children who are visually impaired and sighted. Initially, there appears to be little, if any, difference in the physical development of infants with and without vision, but later in infancy and toddlerhood, the differences between the two groups of children seem to increase; for example, babies who are blind are often delayed in walking, reaching, and pulling up (Ferrell, 1996; Warren, 1984, 1994). However, longitudinal studies, such as the Canadian follow-up study that is described later in this chapter, have presented empirical evidence that these differences dissipate and may well disappear over an individual's life span (Freeman, Goetz, Richards, & Groenveld, 1991; Freeman et al., 1989).

Age at onset of visual impairment must also be considered because the older children are when they lose vision, the more likely they will have acquired basic psychomotor skills through visual channels and, therefore, less retardation in skills will be evident. In other words, the earlier the onset of visual impairment, the greater the effect on all areas of development, including spatial aware-

ness, mobility, nonverbal communication, personality, and general information. Making up for early developmental deficits is qualitatively and quantitatively different from restoring or substituting for abilities that have been acquired (Freeman, 1987; Scholl, 1986). Sidebar 5.4 discusses some effects of the time at onset of visual impairment on development.

By adolescence, many behaviors and patterns are in place. However, the developmental process does not end at a particular age for anyone. In fact, many developmental milestones are achieved during and beyond adolescence. Only a few studies have looked closely at the development of adolescents with visual impairments; three that have done so are described in the sections that follow.

Study of Adjustment to Visual Disability in Adolescence

Cowen, Underberg, Verrillo, and Benham (1961) undertook one of the earliest and most comprehensive empirical studies of social and emotional

Onset of Visual Impairment

When a visual impairment is diagnosed, it has a profound effect on a person. Congenital conditions require specialized interventions early in life, so children have opportunities to learn gradually about the environment using residual sensory pathways (Scott, Jan, & Freeman, 1995). Furthermore, families in which children with visual impairments are born may benefit from developmental counseling and training. Thus, they "grow up" with their children with visual impairments, gaining awareness of what support activities may be needed and accepting the children as family members with possible special needs (Bolinger & Bolinger, 1996; Ferrell, 1996; Langley, 1996).

When older children and teenagers become visually impaired, they have the advantage of having seen well during their formative years. Educationally, such experience with sight is helpful in that the young people have learned environmental features by visual observation and pictures. Children who are congenitally visually impaired must rely on their other senses or the vicarious experiences that others provide to learn concepts. But for those who lose their vision later, even a brief period of vision allows for association and incidental learning (Barraga, 1986).

Emotionally, however, older children and teenagers who lose vision must adapt to altered learning circumstances, and the adaptation may not be smooth. For those who are beginning to establish body images, any newly acquired feature can lead to conflict. Many middle school-aged children begin spending hours before mirrors or in situations that reflect their senses of self. Visual data are often primary in these efforts, and "How do I look?" becomes a frequent query to parents and friends. When vision is impaired at that age, the developmental sequence of self-reference is interrupted. Furthermore, the youngsters may have to undergo treatments or use visual aids that affect their self-percepts and may be embarrassed by the new circumstances.

In adolescence, depression is a common response to a newly diagnosed visual impairment and is a widespread problem (A. C. Peterson et al., 1993), often triggered by changing life circumstances. A compounding element in this society, is the likelihood that visual impairments may result from at-risk behaviors, such as automobile accidents, the use of firearms, drug overdoses, and sports injuries. These etiologies during the teenage years exacerbate the tendency for diagnoses of visual impairments to lead to severe emotional reactions.

If the etiology is an illness or physical condition, such as a brain tumor or severe infection, the young person often has a string of "Why me?" questions. Family members are often so pleased that the person has lived through the health ordeal that they are unprepared for the emotional aspects of the situation. Families need time to express their reactions, as with any health crisis, in such a way as to open communication channels for adolescents.

Other issues arise around the onset of visual impairments in middle childhood and adolescence. In some instances, the eye disease or condition, such as childhood-onset macular degeneration, is hereditary. The parents may not have been aware that they both carried the gene for the particular eye disease or condition until the child reached the age at which the symptoms are expressed. Siblings may also be affected. At about age 11 or 12, when visual acuity drops, the child is becoming aware of biology and may even be studying genetics at school. Family members then become aware that other children or future generations might be affected, which may have social and emotional consequences. For such reasons, open communication is crucial.

(continued on next page)

Onset of Visual Impairment *(Continued)*

Dealing with the depression that accompanies any health problem that arises in adolescence is never easy. It is best addressed in a group setting because teenagers are far more likely to share their feelings with peers than with adults, even trained counselors. Family counseling is critical in hereditary disorders, so that all affected members of the family can be screened, tested, and advised about the probability of off-spring being affected. Whatever the diagnosis, allowing adolescents to express feelings of sadness and other emotions and to share their struggles with their altered circumstances is essential.

JOAN B. CHASE
Psychologist
Dunedin, FL

---

adjustment of adolescents with visual impairments. Their study included 167 adolescents aged 13–18 in Grades 7–12 and their 167 mothers. Although efforts were made to include the fathers, only 66 ultimately participated.

The study encompassed two distinct phases of data collection. In the first phase, the experimental group consisted of 71 adolescents with visual impairments who attended public schools in New York state. In the experimental group, there were three subgroups according to degree of visual impairment: totally blind ($n = 12$), legally blind ($n = 28$), and partially sighted ($n = 31$). In this study, the researchers defined the legally blind group as those with visual acuities no better than 20/200 to no worse than 20/400 in the better eye after correction. The partially sighted group had visual acuities that ranged from 20/70 to 20/100 in the better eye after correction. The control group ($n = 40$) consisted of sighted adolescents of comparable age, sex, intelligence, socioeconomic level, and educational status. In the second phase, the experimental group consisted of 56 adolescents with visual impairments from residential schools for students who are blind: 30 who were totally blind and 26 who were legally blind.

The investigators used three instruments—the Self-Ideal Sort, Teachers' Behavior Rating Scale, and Child Perception: The Situations Projective Test-B (SPT-B) that they developed. The tests were designed to evaluate adolescent adjust-ment and elicited seven adjustment indices. The Self-Ideal Sort included 10 groups of six statements each (three indicating "good" and three indicating "poor" adjustment) on each form. The participants were asked to choose one statement of the six that they felt was most like them and then to choose from the remaining five the one that was least like them. The same procedure was followed until all the items had been chosen and was then repeated for all the blocks. The researchers derived two scores from the participants' responses: a self-ideal discrepancy score and a self-concept adjustment score.

The researchers developed the Teachers' Behavior Rating Scale and the SPT-B because they were unable to find appropriate standardized instruments to serve their purposes. The Teachers' Behavior Rating Scale was presented as a behavior-rating instrument, rather than an adjustment measure, in an effort to minimize bias and focus on concrete aspects of behavior. The SPT-B was developed as a multiple-choice projective-type test that incorporated perceptions of pity, overprotection, rejection, and acceptance (Cowen et al., 1961).

In addition to the assessment of the youngsters' acceptance, the researchers evaluated parents' attitude and parental understanding, using instruments that they designed, items borrowed from standardized measures, and subscales of standardized tests. The study's findings were as follows:

◆ Basically, no differences in adjustment among the adolescents who were sighted and those who were visually impaired were indicated on the three test instruments.

◆ Better adjustment tended to be associated with greater visual impairment, that is, adolescents with low vision evidenced greater adjustment difficulties than those who were totally or legally blind. However, these differences were not statistically significant.

◆ Strong relationships were found between parental, particularly maternal, understanding and adolescent adjustment across all the groups (blind, low vision, and sighted participants).

The study was the first to question some of the traditional ideas concerning the psychosocial development and adjustment of children and youths with visual impairments. The researchers studied both adolescents who were blind or visually impaired who were living at home or in residential settings and compared them to a group of sighted youngsters. Until this study was reported, many people assumed that maladjustment was unavoidable when visual impairment occurred. Cowen and his colleagues disputed this notion and pointed out that although there were individual differences, the groups of youngsters they studied were more alike than different in their social and emotional adjustment to adolescence.

Canadian Follow-up Study

Another important study was the Canadian follow-up study of children with visual impairments when they were young adults (Freeman et al., 1991). Freeman, the primary investigator who had participated in the original 1973–74 study of young children, and his colleagues initiated this longitudinal follow-up study to determine the status of those individuals as adults. Of the 92 individuals who were legally blind who were included in the original study, 69 participated in the follow-up study. With the exception of cognition, the follow-up study looked at the same aspects as the

original study: social-emotional functioning, health, vision, mannerisms, and family (Freeman et al., 1989, 1991). These are the highlights of the researchers' findings:

◆ Just over half (54.5 percent) the 57 participants who could be questioned on the subject of marriage and sexuality reported having had a romantic relationship.

◆ Except for a few participants who had multiple disabilities, almost all stereotypic mannerisms had disappeared from the sample. Some participants said that they still engaged in their mannerisms when they were alone, but that they understood the negative social effect of mannerisms on people who were sighted. No participant credited any systemic treatment program with having helped him or her eliminate such behaviors; most of them indicated that they had stopped because family members and friends had told them that their mannerisms were unacceptable.

◆ Many participants had taken a longer time than usual to complete their secondary school programs.

◆ Thirty-nine percent of the participants were employed (46.7 percent of the men and 32.7 percent of the women).

◆ Seventy-one percent of the participants engaged in some regular sports or physical fitness program.

The researchers pointed out that most of these young adults were doing remarkably well without the help of sophisticated and systematic intervention; in fact, they were performing better than anticipated. However, they cautioned that they were unable to locate the original control group for comparisons. Another interesting point the researchers mentioned was that many of the participants with severe visual impairments refused to acknowledge their visual differences and tended to "pass" as normally sighted. Finally, the researchers suggested that there may well be some benefit to developing interactive programs to improve the social skills of both people who are blind and people who are sighted in their dealings with individuals with visual impairments. The perceived benefit would be to decrease the social isolation the researchers discerned in their participants, especially during the junior high school years (Freeman et al., 1991).

Social Network Pilot Project Study

Only one study in the 1990s looked specifically at how adolescents with visual impairments compared in major life areas to their sighted peers: the Social Network Pilot Project (SNPP). The results of the SNPP (Sacks & Wolffe, 1998; Sacks et al., 1998; Wolffe & Sacks, 1995, 1997) are detailed in the following sections. Although there were only 48 participants in SNPP, the researchers made a considerable effort to achieve acceptable levels of representation on demographic variables, such as sex, ethnicity, socioeconomic level, and age. In addition, the participants were recruited from urban, suburban, and rural settings; reported no other disabling conditions; and were functioning close to grade level (within one year). However, because of the small sample, it is important not to overgeneralize the results but, rather, to consider them *possible* indicators of adolescents' behaviors.

SNPP comprised two studies that compared the lifestyles and social support networks of adolescents who were blind, who were partially sighted, and who were sighted. The first study provided comprehensive quantitative data. The second study, which used ethnographic methodology, techniques borrowed from the field of anthropology to describe specific cultures, yielded qualitative data and validated the findings of the first study. Taken together, the two studies provided documentation for an in-depth analysis of the social lives of adolescents with visual impairments.

In the first study, four separate student-interview and parent-interview questionnaires were designed to examine academic involvement and performance, as well as involvement in daily living and personal care activities, recreation and leisure activities, and work or vocational experi-

ences. In addition, a time diary format was designed and used to obtain data from the participants on how they were spending their time. The time diary format for this study was modified from the one used by Kirchner and her colleagues (1992) to obtain information about the use of time by visually impaired adults in their daily lives. In the second study an observation protocol was used to gather data.

Highlights of SNPP: Study 1

Study 1 included the major data collection process for the research project (interview questionnaires and time-diary formats). A series of three telephone interviews were conducted with each adolescent in the study and separate interviews were conducted with their parents. The parents and adolescents responded to the questionnaires during the interviews and the adolescents also reported for the time diaries. The interviews were conducted at different times during the academic and social year: spring semester, summer vacation, and fall semester. Data consolidation and analyses occurred following each stage of the interviewing process.

Academic Questionnaire. The results of the academic questionnaire were as follows:

- ◆ The adolescents and their parents were in close agreement about the adolescents' grades in school. (Most of the adolescents who were blind or sighted were receiving As and Bs, and most of the adolescents with low vision were receiving Bs and Cs.)

- ◆ The greatest discrepancy between the adolescents' and parents' reports of grades was in the group with low vision, where most of the adolescents reported receiving As, and their parents reported that they were receiving Bs.

- ◆ The differences between youths who were sighted and those who were visually impaired were evident in reports of whom they received help from with their homework.

The youths who were blind reported receiving help from six sources: a parent, sibling, friend, tutor, paid reader, and volunteer. Those with low vision reported receiving help from four sources: a parent, sibling, friend, and tutor. Although one-fifth of the students who were sighted reported receiving no assistance, those who did receive help identified three sources: a parent, friend, or tutor.

- Another difference between adolescents who were sighted and those with visual impairments was where they studied. Only the adolescents who were blind or had low vision reported studying in classrooms with the guidance of their teachers. The sighted adolescents studied at home, in the public library or school library, and at friends' houses. In addition to studying in classrooms, those who were visually impaired reported studying in the same settings as the sighted adolescents: home, libraries, and at friends' houses.

Vocational Questionnaire.   These were the results of the vocational questionnaire:

- Almost all the adolescents (88 percent of those who were blind and 94 percent of those with low vision and those who were sighted) had worked for pay.

- Whereas 81 percent of the adolescents who were sighted had found their own jobs, only 31 percent of the adolescents with low vision and 19 percent of those who were blind had done so. (For the most part, teachers and counselors found jobs for the adolescents with visual impairments.)

- The majority of the adolescents who were blind (75 percent) had jobs in the office-clerical area at school.

- Overall, there was a more even distribution of work activities among the adolescents who were sighted.

Activities of Daily Living Questionnaire.   The following were the results of the questionnaire on activities of daily living:

- The adolescents with visual impairments were more like than different from their sighted peers when performing money-management, time-management, and personal-management tasks.

- The most obvious differences between the groups of adolescents were in the home-management area: performing household chores, grocery shopping, cleaning, cooking, and general housekeeping. Those with low vision reported having the least amount of responsibility for performing home management tasks, and those who were blind reported having only slightly more responsibility. On the other hand, the sighted adolescents reported having considerably more responsibility at home. The greatest discrepancies were in activities centered on cooking, helping with yardwork, and simple clothing repairs.

- In response to probes about what kinds of assistance the adolescents and their parents anticipated was necessary for youths to live independently in the future, all the parents and adolescents anticipated an ongoing need for financial assistance. However, financial assistance was the only kind of assistance anticipated by the sighted adolescents and their parents. In contrast, 50 percent of the parents of the adolescents with visual impairments (both those who were blind and those with low vision) anticipated that their children would need assistance in the financial area, in the household- and personal-management areas, and with transportation. The youths who were blind likewise thought they would need assistance in all the areas identified, and those with low vision thought they would need assistance in all the areas except personal management.

Social Questionnaire.   The results of the social questionnaire were as follows:

- According to both the adolescents and parent reports, the students who were sighted in this sample were the most active socially.

◆ The types of social interactions the adolescents were involved in after school differed by the amount of vision they had. The sighted adolescents and their parents reported that the adolescents spent their time almost exclusively with their friends and only occasionally with their parents or siblings. On the other hand, the majority of adolescents who were blind or had low vision and their parents reported that the adolescents spent their time after school alone. Only 25 percent of the adolescents with visual impairments and their parents reported that the adolescents spent time after school with friends.

◆ Overall, the adolescents with low vision appeared to be involved in the fewest activities and were the least likely to be in social situations that involved many other people (high-level activities).

Time Diaries. These were the results of the time diaries:

◆ Of significance were the differences among the groups of adolescents at each of the three interviews in how long it took them to prepare for activities. The adolescents with visual impairments tended to take longer to prepare for activities than did the adolescents who were sighted.

◆ There were also differences among the groups in their friendship networks and levels of interaction within these networks. Overall, the adolescents with visual impairments reported fewer social interactions than did the adolescents who were sighted.

◆ At each of the three interviews, the adolescents with low vision reported greater amounts of time devoted to sleeping than did those who were blind or sighted.

◆ The adolescents with low vision engaged in the most passive leisure activities, followed by those who were blind. The adolescents who were sighted were the least involved in such passive activities.

Highlights of SNPP: Study 2

Study 2, a qualitative study of three adolescents (two who were blind and one with low vision) from Study 1, involved an in-depth ethnographic analysis, or social history, of each participant. In addition to the social histories, a series of observations of each participant were undertaken in a variety of school, home, and community environments. An observation protocol was designed to target specific academic, social, vocational, and daily living indicators that influence transition planning. The following results were obtained:

◆ All three participants required additional time and support to complete their academic assignments, class projects, and homework. They spent the additional time receiving assistance from teachers, parents, and teacher aides.

◆ The participants' ability to gain access to adaptive technology was dependent mostly on the availability of the participants' special education teachers, except for one participant whose parents helped support his educational endeavors.

◆ The participants were not exposed to a range of adaptive equipment and tended to depend on expensive equipment for note taking, rather than use more common means (such as a mechanical braillewriter or slate and stylus).

◆ All the participants performed a range of independent living tasks that were similar to those of their sighted age-mates. They took care of their personal hygiene, performed chores around the house and in the dormitory, prepared simple snacks, and assisted with laundry. None used the range top or oven without the support of an adult.

◆ The greatest difference observed between the participants with visual impairments in Study 2 and the participants who were sighted in Study 1 was independent travel. Most of the sighted adolescents had reasons to travel independently and were autonomous from their families. The adolescents with visual impairments seemed more protected by their families and teachers; as a result, they spent more time at home by themselves.

◆ Despite attempts to interact socially with their sighted age-mates all three participants in Study 2 preferred to interact with peers with visual impairments. They felt more relaxed, at ease, and shared a greater sense of closeness with them than they did with their friends who were sighted.

◆ Observations indicated that the adolescents who were visually impaired, particularly the adolescents with low vision, had to work harder to maintain social relationships with their sighted friends than with their visually impaired friends.

◆ The participants with visual impairments spent more time on the telephone, engaged in more sedentary activities, spent more time alone, and were bound to their homes by their inability to travel independently. Although one participant's travel skills were more typical of a sighted adolescent, the reason appeared to be that he lived in an urban area where public transportation was more readily available. Also, his family encouraged him to travel independently because they did not have a family car.

◆ All three participants who were observed during Study 2 had limited vocational experiences.

SUMMARY

This chapter presented an overview of the four major developmental models: maturational, psychoanalytic, behavioral, and cognitive-developmental. Although it noted that youths with visual impairments develop in ways much like their sighted peers, it addressed some disability-specific considerations for those who work with young people who are visually impaired. These considerations or issues centered on three aspects: physical attributes (how a person looks), cognitive attributes (how a person learns), and emotional attributes (how a person feels). The common thread that ran through these issues was the importance of access to incidental information—information picked up casually through observation by children with good, functional vision—for children and youths with visual impairments.

Finally, the chapter described three studies of adolescents with visual impairments and their levels of adjustment and involvement in various aspects of life. As evidenced in these studies, adolescents with visual impairments are performing in many ways like their sighted peers. However, their families and others who care for them need to provide supports, such as assistance with transportation, instruction in social skills, and feedback on objects, people, and events in the environment that they may miss because they are unable to see or see well. At the same time, significant adults need to allow adolescents who are visually impaired to take the risks inherent in adolescent development, socialize with their peers, and experience life as independently as possible.

STUDY QUESTIONS

1. Reflect on your own adolescence. What challenges did you face as you moved from elementary to secondary school settings? How important were the opinions of your peers?

2. Describe the theoretical models of development presented in this chapter. What impact would a visual impairment have in each model?

3. Carefully read the clinical notes presented in the sidebars of this chapter. What information from them would be useful for a teacher of students with visual impairments?

4. This chapter addresses the "body-perfect" notion that is prevalent in adolescence. It is important to address this notion with adolescents who are visually impaired. What can parents and teachers do to help adolescents with visual impairments address concerns in this area?

5. Driving is so important during adolescence. What can parents and teachers do to help adolescents who will not be able to drive because of their visual impairment?

6. It is important to provide honest, direct feedback to adolescents who are visually impaired. How can a teacher of students with visual impairments help other instructional personnel understand and implement this concept?

7. What effects do visual impairments have on the physical, cognitive, and emotional attributes of adolescence?

8. Briefly describe the results of the studies presented in this chapter. These studies are important to teachers who work with adolescents who are visually impaired. How can parents and teachers use this information?

REFERENCES

Anderson, E. M., & Clarke, L. (1982). *Disability in adolescence.* London: Methuen.

Asher, S. R., & Gottman, J. M. (1981). *The development of children's friendships.* Cambridge, England: Cambridge University Press.

Bandura, A. (1977). *Social learning theory.* Englewood Cliffs, NJ: Prentice Hall.

Bandura, A. (1979). *Principles of behavior modification.* New York: Holt, Rinehart, & Winston.

Bandura, A. (1986). *Social foundations of thought and action: A social cognitive theory.* Englewood Cliffs, NJ: Prentice Hall.

Bandura, A. (1989). Social cognitive theory. *Annals of Child Development, 6,* 1–60.

Barraga, N. C. (1986). Sensory perceptual development. In G. T. Scholl (Ed.), *Foundations of education for blind and visually handicapped children and youth: Theory and practice* (pp. 83–98). New York: American Foundation for the Blind.

Beaty, L. A. (1991). The effects of visual impairments on adolescents' self-concept. *Journal of Visual Impairment & Blindness, 85,* 129–130.

Beaty, L. A. (1994). Psychological factors and academic success of visually impaired college students. *RE:view, 26,* 131–139.

Bee, H. (1997). *The developing child* (8th ed.). New York: Addison-Wesley.

Bolinger, R., & Bolinger, C. (1996). Family life. In M. C. Holbrook (Ed.), *Children with visual impairments: A parent's guide* (pp. 129–157). Bethesda, MD: Woodbine House.

Buscaglia, L. (1975). *The disabled and their parents: A counseling challenge.* Thorofare, NJ: Charles B. Slack.

Chase, J. B. (1986). Psychoeducational assessment of visually-impaired learners. In P. J. Lazarus & S. S. Strichart (Eds.), *Psychoeducational evaluation of children and adolescents with low-incidence handicaps* (pp. 41–74). Orlando, FL: Grune & Stratton.

Chase, J. B. (1993, Fall) Family systems. *EnVision: A publication of the Lighthouse National Center for Vision and Child Development,* pp. 1–5.

Chase, J. B. (in press). Technology and the use of tools: Psychological and social factors. In B. Silverstone, M. A. Lang, B. P. Rosenthal, & E. E. Faye (Eds.), *The Lighthouse handbook on vision impairment and vision rehabilitation.* New York: Oxford University Press.

Corn, A. L., Lippmann, O., & Lewis, M. C. (1990). Licensed drivers with bioptic telescopic spectacles: User profiles and perceptions. *RE:view, 21,* 221–230.

Corn, A., & Sacks, S. Z. (1994). The impact of nondriving on adults with visual impairments, *Journal of Visual Impairment & Blindness, 88,* 53–68.

Cowen, E. L., Underberg, R. P., Verrillo, R. T., & Benham, F. G. (1961). *Adjustment to visual disability in adolescence.* New York: American Foundation for the Blind.

Crary, E. (1995). *Pick up your socks and other skills growing children need.* Seattle, WA: Parenting Press.

Cutsforth, T. N. (1951). *The blind in school and society: A psychological study.* New York: American Foundation for the Blind (originally published in 1933).

Damon, W. (Ed.). (1983). *Social and personality development.* New York: W. W. Norton.

Dasberg, L. (1983). A historical and transcultural view of adolescence. In W. Everaerd, C. B. Hindley, A. Bot, & J. J. van der Werff ten Bosch (Eds.),. *Development in adolescence: Psychological, social and biological aspects* (pp. 1–15). Boston: Martinus Nijhoff.

Deitz, S. J., & Ferrell, K. A. (1994). Project PRISM: A national collaborative study on the early development of children with visual impairments. *Journal of Visual Impairment & Blindness, 88,* 470–472.

Dickman, I. R. (1975). *Sex education and family life for visually handicapped children and youth: A resource guide.* New York: American Foundation for the Blind.

Dworetzky, J. P. (1981). *Introduction to child development.* St. Paul, MN: West.

Elkind, D. (1984). *All grown up and no place to go: Teenagers in crisis.* Reading, MA: Addison-Wesley.

Erikson, E. H. (1963). *Childhood and society* (2nd ed.). New York: Norton.

Erikson, E. H. (1980). *Identity and the life cycle.* New York: Norton (originally published in 1959).

Erin, J. N., & Wolffe, K. E. (1999). *Transition issues related to students with visual disabilities.* Austin, TX: PRO-ED.

Felleman, H. (1936). *Best loved poems of the American people.* New York: Doubleday.

Fenwick, E., & Smith, T. (1996). *Adolescence: The survival guide for parents and teenagers.* London: Dorling Kindersley.

Ferrell, K. A. (1986). Infancy and early childhood. In G. T. Scholl (Ed.). *Foundations of education for blind and visually handicapped children and youth* (pp. 119–135). New York: American Foundation for the Blind.

Ferrell, K. A. (1996, October). *PRISM update.* Paper presented at American Printing House for the Blind annual meeting, Louisville, KY.

Ferrell, K. A. (1996). Your child's development. In M. C. Holbrook (Ed.). *Children with visual impairments: A parent's guide* (pp. 73–96). Bethesda, MD: Woodbine House.

Fine, M. J. (1995). Family-school intervention. In R. H. Mikesell, D. D. Lusterman, & S. H. McDaniel (Eds.), *Integrating family therapy: Handbook of family psychology and systems theory* (pp. 481–495). Washington, DC: American Psychological Association.

Fisher, H. E. (1992). *The anatomy of love.* New York: Norton.

Foulke, E., & Uhde, T. (1975). Do blind children need sex education? In *Sex education for the visually handicapped in schools and agencies . . . Selected papers* (pp. 8–16). New York: American Foundation for the Blind.

Fraiberg, S. (1977). *Insights from the blind.* New York: Basic.

Freeman, R. D. (1987). Psychosocial interventions with visually impaired adolescents and adults. In B. Heller, L. Flohr, & L. S. Zegans (Eds.), *Psychosocial interventions with sensorially disabled persons* (pp. 153–166). Orlando, FL: Grune & Stratton.

Freeman, R. D., Goetz, E., Richards, D. P., & Groenveld, M. (1991). Defiers of negative prediction: A 14-year follow-up of legally blind children. *Journal of Visual Impairment & Blindness, 85,* 365–370.

Freeman, R. D., Goetz, E., Richards, D. P., Groenveld, M., Blockberger, S., Jan, J. E., & Sykanda, A. M. (1989). Blind children's early emotional development: Do we know enough to help? *Child: Care, Health and Development, 15,* 3–28.

Freud, S. (1905). *The basic writings of Sigmund Freud* (A. A. Brill, Trans.) New York: Random House.

Gesell, A. (1928). *Infancy and human growth.* New York: Macmillan.

Gesell, A. (1956). *Youth: Years ten to sixteen.* New York: Harper & Row.

Gesell, A., & Thompson, H. (1929). Learning and growth in identical infant twins: An experimental study of individual differences by the method of co-twin control. *Genetic Psychology Monographs, 6,* 1–124.

Gesell, A., & Thompson, H. (1941). Twins T and C from infancy to adolescence: A biogenetic study of individual differences by the method of co-twin control. *Genetic Psychology Monographs, 24,* 3–121.

Head, D. (1979). A comparison of self-concept scores for visually impaired adolescents in several class settings. *Education of the Visually Handicapped, 10,* 51–55.

Heslinga, K. (1974). *Not made of stone: The sexual problems of handicapped people.* Leyden, the Netherlands: Stafleu Scientific Publishing.

Huurre, T. M., Komulainen, E. J., & Aro, H. M. (1999). Social support and self-esteem among adolescents with visual impairments. *Journal of Visual Impairment & Blindness, 93,* 26–37.

Jose, R. T. (1983). Treatment options. In R. T. Jose (Ed.), *Understanding low vision* (pp. 211–248). New York: American Foundation for the Blind.

Kef, S. (1997). The personal networks and social supports of blind and visually impaired adolescents. *Journal of Visual Impairment & Blindness, 91,* 236–244.

Kirchner, C., McBroom, L., Nelson, K., & Graves, W. (1992). *Lifestyles of employed legally blind people: A study of expenditures and time use.* Mississippi State: Mississippi State University Rehabilitation Research and Training Center on Blindness and Low Vision.

Langley, B. (1996). Daily life. Your child's development. In M. C. Holbrook (Ed.), *Children with visual impairments: A parent's guide* (pp. 97–127). Bethesda, MD: Woodbine House.

Larson R., & Richards, M. H. (1994). *Divergent realities: The emotional lives of mothers, fathers and adolescents.* New York: Basic Books.

Lorenz, K. Z. (1958). The evolution of behavior. *Scientific American, 199,* 67–78.

Lorenz, K. (1965). *Evolution and modification of behavior.* Chicago: University of Chicago Press.

Lowenfeld, B. (1971). *Our blind children: Growing and learning with them* (3rd ed.). Springfield, IL: Charles C Thomas.

Lowenfeld, B. (1987). The influence of blindness and visual impairment on psychological development. In B. Heller, L. Flohr, & L. S. Zegans (Eds.), *Psychosocial interventions with sensorially disabled persons* (pp. 99–114). Orlando, FL: Grune & Stratton.

MacCuspie, P. A. (1996). *Promoting acceptance of children with disabilities: From tolerance to inclusion.* Halifax, NS: Atlantic Provinces Special Education Authority.

Matsuda, M. M. (1984). A comparative analysis of blind and sighted children's communication skills. *Journal of Visual Impairment & Blindness, 78,* 1–5.

McGoldrick, M., & Gerson, R. (1985). *Genograms in family assessment.* New York: W. W. Norton.

Meighan, T. (1971). *An investigation of the self-concept of blind and visually handicapped adolescents.* New York: American Foundation for the Blind.

Minter, M. E., Hobson, R. P., & Pring, L. (1991). Recognition of vocally expressed emotion by congenitally blind children. *Journal of Visual Impairment & Blindness, 85,* 411–415.

Nixon, H. L. (1991). *Mainstreaming and the American dream: Sociological perspectives on parental coping with blind and visually impaired children.* New York: American Foundation for the Blind.

Norris. M., Spaulding, P. J., & Brodie, F. H. (1957). *Blindness in children.* Chicago: University of Chicago Press.

Pavlov, I. P. (1927). *Conditioned reflexes.* London: Oxford University Press.

Peterson, A. C., Compas, B. E., Brooks-Gunn, J., Stemmler, M., Ey, S., & Grant, K. E. (1993). Depression in adolescence. *American Psychologist, 48,* 155–168.

Peterson, G. W., & Leigh, G. K. (1990). The family and social competence in adolescence. In T. P. Gullotta, G. R. Adams, & R. Montemayor (Eds.). *Developing social competency in adolescence* (pp. 97–138). Newbury Park, CA: Sage Productions.

Piaget, J. (1932). *The moral judgement of the child.* New York: Macmillan.

Piaget, J. (1952). *The origins of intelligence in children.* New York: International Universities Press.

Piaget, J. (1977). *The development of thought: Equilibration of cognitive structures.* New York: Viking Press.

Rogers, D. (1977). *Issues in adolescent psychology* (3rd ed.). Englewood Cliffs, NJ: Prentice Hall.

Rosenblum, L. P. (1997). Adolescents with visual impairments who have best friends: A pilot study. *Journal of Visual Impairment & Blindness, 91,* 224–235.

Sacks, S. Z., Kekelis, L. S., & Gaylord-Ross, R. J. (Eds). (1992). *The development of social skills by blind and visually impaired students.* New York: American Foundation for the Blind.

Sacks, S. Z., & Wolffe, K. E. (1998). Lifestyles of adolescents with visual impairments: An ethnographic analysis. *Journal of Visual Impairment & Blindness, 92,* 7–17.

Sacks, S.Z., Wolffe, K. E., & Tierney, D. (1998). Lifestyles of students with visual impairments: Preliminary studies of social networks. *Exceptional Children, 64,* 463–478.

Salkind, N. J. (1985). *Theories of human development* (2nd ed.). New York: John Wiley & Sons.

Scholl, G. T. (1975). The psychosocial effects of blindness: Implications for program planning in sex education. In *Sex education for the visually handicapped in schools and agencies . . . Selected papers* (pp. 20–28). New York: American Foundation for the Blind.

Scholl, G. T. (1986). Growth and development. In G. T. Scholl (Ed.), *Foundations of education for blind and visually handicapped children and youth* (pp. 65–85). New York: American Foundation for the Blind.

Scott, E., Jan, J., & Freeman, R. (1995). *Can't your child see?* (3rd ed.). Austin, TX: PRO-ED.

Skinner, B. F. (1938). *The behavior of organisms: An experimental analysis.* New York: Appleton-Century-Crofts.

Skinner, B. F. (1957). *Verbal behavior.* New York: Appleton-Century-Crofts.

Skinner, B. F. (1976). *Walden two.* New York: Macmillan.

Tanner, J. M. (1962). *Growth at adolescence* (2nd ed.). Oxford, England: Blackwell.

Torbett, D. S. (1975). A humanistic and futuristic approach to sex education for blind children. In *Sex education for the visually handicapped in schools and agencies . . . Selected papers* (pp. 29–34). New York: American Foundation for the Blind.

Tuttle, D., & Tuttle, N. (1996). *Self-esteem and adjusting with blindness* (2nd ed.). Springfield, IL: Charles C Thomas.

Van't Hooft, F., & Heslinga, K. (1975). Sex education and blind-born children. In *Sex education for the visually handicapped in schools and agencies . . . Selected papers* (pp. 1–7). New York: American Foundation for the Blind.

Wagner, M., D'Amico, R., Marder, C., Newman, L., & Blackorby, J. (1992). *What happens next? Trends in postschool outcomes of youth with disabilities.* Menlo Park, CA: SRI International.

Wagner, M., Newman, L., D'Amico, R., Jay, E. D., Butler-Nalin, P., Marder, C., & Cox, R. (1991). *Young people with disabilities: How are they doing?* Menlo Park, CA: SRI International.

Warnke, J. W. (1991a). *Becoming an everyday mystic.* St. Meinrad, IN: Abbey Press.

Warnke, J. W. (1991b). Special needs of children and adolescents. In S. L. Greenblatt (Ed.), *Meeting the needs of people with vision loss* (pp. 37–45). Lexington, MA: Resources for Rehabilitation.

Warren, D. H. (1984). *Blindness and early childhood development* (2nd ed. rev.). New York: American Foundation for the Blind.

Warren, D. H. (1994). *Blindness and children: An individual differences approach.* New York: Cambridge University Press.

Weiner, I. (1970). *Psychological disturbance in adolescence.* New York: John Wiley & Sons.

Welbourne, A. K. (1982). Sexual education of the blind adolescent. *Sexual Medicine Today,* 10–14.

Wolf, A. E. (1991). *Get out of my life but first could you drive me and Cheryl to the mall?* New York: Noonday Press.

Wolffe, K. (1996). Career education for students with visual impairments. *RE:view, 28,* 25–32.

Wolffe, K. E. (Ed.). (1999). *Skills for success: A career education handbook for children and adolescents with visual impairments.* New York: American Foundation for the Blind.

Wolffe, K. E., & Sacks, S. Z. (1995). *Social Network Pilot Project: Final report.* (Department of Education grant H023A30108). Unpublished manuscript.

Wolffe, K., & Sacks, S. Z. (1997). The Social Network Pilot Project: A quantitative comparison of the lifestyles of blind, low vision, and sighted young adults. *Journal of Visual Impairment & Blindness, 91,* 245–257.

Wolffe, K. E., & Sacks, S. Z. (Eds.). (2000). *Focus on: Social skills.* New York: American Foundation for the Blind.

CHAPTER 6

Psychosocial Needs of Children and Youths

Dean W. Tuttle and Naomi R. Tuttle

KEY POINTS

◆ Children who are visually impaired have the same needs and drives as do all children.

◆ Children with visual impairments can and do develop positive and wholesome attitudes toward themselves, others, and their visual impairments, despite the prevailing negative and devaluing attitudes often encountered in society.

◆ Children constantly revise their self-concepts according to the reflections they observe in others or to their revised measure of their own competence.

◆ A child's self-concept is not only influenced by every life experience, but is a determiner of how every life experience is perceived and interpreted.

◆ With the confidence that competence brings, children and youths with visual impairments develop healthy self-esteem, especially when they begin to think of themselves as persons of worth with many attributes, only one of which is visual impairment.

To understand and respond adequately to the psychosocial needs of children and youths with visual impairments, teachers and families need to grasp the significance of the interaction between the developmental patterns of the individual and the social context within which development occurs. Since the number of people who are visually impaired is relatively small, the general public has few opportunities to know, let alone befriend, someone with a visual impairment. This chapter explains how children with visual impairments can and do develop positive and wholesome attitudes toward themselves, others, and their visual impairments.

Several assumptions underlie this chapter. There is no unique psychology of blindness, no special personality attributable to someone solely on the basis of a visual impairment (Foulke, 1972; Kirtley, 1975; Lowenfeld, 1981; Schulz, 1980; Tobin & Hill, 1987; Tuttle & Tuttle, 1996). Children who are visually impaired are, first of all, children and have the same needs and drives as do all children. The psychological principles that have been developed to understand the thoughts and behaviors of all children can be used to understand the thoughts and behaviors of children with visual impairments. Therefore, the educational, sociological, and psychological literature on all children and youths can be used as a framework for understanding the psychosocial needs of those with visual impairments. This does not mean that there are no differences between children who are sighted and those who are visually impaired. Differences in psychosocial development do, indeed, exist, but they can be explained through conventional models and theories.

Chapter 5 contains a general discussion of theoretical models used to explain development. Erikson's (1950) model of psychosocial developmental needs is an example of a general work that can be applied to individuals with visual impairments. Erikson theorized that development proceeds through eight psychosocial stages that aggregate one upon the other as infants grow into childhood, then adolescence, and finally adulthood (see Sidebar 6.1). The extent to which each succeeding need can be met is dependent on the extent to which the preceding need was satisfied. Children who are visually impaired, like all children, require positive interactions with their parents and others in their environment and need to be supported as they are exposed to a variety of rich and new experiences. For example, Erikson believed that, during the second year of life, children who have appropriate experiences will develop independence. Parents who teach and encourage their children to pick up toys, help put toothpaste on a toothbrush, and so forth, promote the acquisition of the stage of independence. As children and youths who are visually impaired acquire the necessary multisensory information and interact experientially with their environment, they may be better able to satisfy the demands of each developmental level.

Obtaining and processing essential environmental information and interacting appropriately with the environment require children who are visually impaired to develop some compensatory or adaptive skills and alternative techniques (such as the use of low vision devices, braille and other communication skills, and orientation and mobility techniques). These skills enable the children to satisfy the demands of each developmental level, although perhaps in a different way from their sighted peers.

Age, intelligence, parental support, and other factors help determine the type and extent of the needs and drives felt by any child at any given moment. Still other factors influence the ability of children who are visually impaired to gather essential multisensory information about their environment and interact with their world. Learning that there is a world to experience beyond the immediate surroundings, learning to conceptualize a whole by integrating the perception of many parts, and learning about the nature and function of vision are examples of some unique factors for children with visual impairments, especially those who are congenitally visually impaired. Also, the degree of visual impairment, the stability of the eye condition, the presence of additional disabilities (hearing, orthopedic, or other health impairments), the availability of blindness-specific services and resources, and other factors combine to produce the climate and potential for growth.

Learning to live with a visual impairment involves three aspects of adjustment:

- ◆ Cognition—the awareness and knowledge of coping;
- ◆ Action—the behaviors and skills of coping; and
- ◆ Affect—the feelings and attitudes of coping (Tuttle & Tuttle, 1996).

When children and youths who are visually impaired master and integrate all three areas, their psychosocial needs are met. The ability to meet life's demands with a visual impairment is further enhanced when a student learns to use all available resources (including student's self-motivation, parental support, community resources, and specialized services).

Another factor in the ability to meet life's demands is the quality of a person's self-concept: the mental image or set of perceptions and feelings that a person has of himself or herself. Both cognitive and affective dimensions are included in self-concept. Individuals with healthy self-concepts expect to be successful, whereas those with poor self-concepts are often unable to imagine positive interactions or outcomes.

A child's self-concept is reinforced or modified by every life experience, especially those that occur during the developmental years when parents play a primary role (Hattie, 1992). One's self-concept is formed "in social intercourse, private reactions to himself, mastery in solving developmental tasks, and competence in dealing with

Erikson's Stages of Psychosocial Development

STAGE	AGES	STAGE	AGES
Basic trust versus basic mistrust	0–1 years	Identity versus role confusion	12–18 years
Autonomy versus shame and doubt	1–3 years	Intimacy versus isolation	Young adulthood
Initiative versus guilt	4–6 years	Generativity versus stagnation	Middle adulthood
Industry versus inferiority	7–11 years	Ego integrity versus despair	Later adulthood

life's situations" (Coopersmith, 1967, p. 20). It is not only influenced by every life experience, but is a determiner of how every life experience is perceived and interpreted. People with healthy self-concepts usually have the ability to see the good side of things, whereas those with poor self-concepts may more often view themselves as victims, feeling that they are unable to exert much control over their circumstances. A self-concept is not acquired in a vacuum; it emerges from repeated social interactions. The prevailing attitudes of family members, educators, and peers toward visual impairments that a child perceives and assimilates have a strong influence on the child's developing self-concept.

Many inconsistencies in prevailing societal attitudes still exist, as discussed in Chapter 2. Thus, although some individuals in the general public have positive attitudes toward persons with visual impairments (Kent, 1989), not everyone in a community necessarily subscribes to attitudes that foster assimilation. Some would prefer to separate, protect, and educate children who are visually impaired without acknowledging the fundamental right of every person to be a fully participating member of society (Kirchner et al., 1992). These inconsistencies simply compound the problem of developing a strong, healthy self-concept.

The companions to negative and devaluating attitudes are erroneous myths and unfair stereo-types. Persons who are visually impaired are not automatically endowed with better hearing or touch as a compensation for their lack of vision. If their hearing and touch seem better than normal, it is because of training and their greater reliance on these other sensory modalities. Contrary to popular opinion, individuals who are visually impaired do not live in a world of darkness or blackness. Furthermore, people with visual impairments do not live "in their own world" but share the same world with everyone else. They are not all gifted with special musical abilities or endowed with some extraordinary sixth sense or extrasensory perception. (See Chapter 2 for a detailed discussion of myths and realities related to visual impairment.) The perpetuation of such myths and stereotypes further complicates the development of a healthy self-concept.

To illustrate this interaction between a child who is visually impaired and his or her social environment, it is interesting to analyze the types of social encounters that the child experience. Some people hardly recognize the child as a person, talking over the child's head as if he or she could not hear or comprehend. Others choose to ask the companion about the child's interests or desires, rather than to talk directly to him or her. Some encounters are based on demeaning myths and stereotypes, so that the child is seen as one of "them," not one of "us." Others are oversolicitous offers of help that are rooted in condescending pity. Any of these exchanges places the child who is visually impaired in an inferior status position, leaving him or her feeling like a second-class citizen. With positive interactions and specialized instruction, children who are visually impaired develop satisfying social connections that enable them to experience the healthy give-and-take of strong relationships built on mutual respect.

IMPACT OF A VISUAL IMPAIRMENT

Kirtley (1975, pp. 137–138) described two extreme, opposite views of the impact of blindness held by the general public and even by some children and adults who are visually impaired:

> On the one hand, there are those who see blindness as a virtual disaster. This group stresses the physical, psychological, and social limitations associated with blindness and considers it a tragic fate that can never be substantially overcome without superior ability and/or unusually favorable environmental circumstances. The blind person is seen as essentially different from the seeing individual. . . . At the opposite pole, there are others who assess blindness as nothing more than a physical nuisance or practical inconvenience. They contend that the problems traditionally linked to blindness are almost totally the product of social prejudice and discrimination, that blindness, in itself, is at most only a minor handicap. Indeed the proponents of this view resent the very use of such words as handicap, disability, and impairment in connection with blindness.

The first view fosters in those who accept it unrealistic expectations of an unproductive life dominated by such characteristics as passivity, gloomy resignation, and childlike dependence on others. The opposite extreme reflects an unfounded sense of idealistic positivism, since certain obvious effects of blindness are simply denied or ignored. When the child, his or her peers, family members, or educators hold either of these extreme views, the child can become trapped by and enslaved to the negative consequences. Recognizing the challenges that people who are blind face while believing in one's abilities to meet these challenges results in a view of blindness that is in the middle of these two extreme positions.

It seems clear that a visual impairment influences or alters the lifestyle of an individual in meeting the practical day-to-day demands of living, particularly in the areas of personal and home management, reading and writing, travel, recreation, and employment. What is less obvious are the ways in which the visual impairment may affect a child's social and emotional development. The following possible social effects of a visual impairment must be viewed not as absolutes or generalizations, but as guardedly stated tendencies that deserve some consideration (Tuttle & Tuttle, 1996).

Immaturity.   Children and youths who are visually impaired may remain egocentric longer, be more socially immature, and be more self-conscious than their sighted peers (Tuttle & Tuttle, 1996). With their visual restrictions, they have more difficulty learning to view events from another person's vantage point. Social maturity comes with social experiences, and children who are visually impaired often have fewer social contacts with children their own age.

Self-consciousness.   Self-consciousness results from feeling different. Since children who are visually impaired may have eyes that appear different or may use adaptive techniques, aids, and devices that they feel set them apart, they are sometimes self-conscious. One strategy that children and youths with visual impairments use to avoid the stigma of being different is to play the "as if" game (Wright, 1983). When out in public or with their peers, they play as if they could see, pretending to function with normal vision. This strategy may work for a while, but psychologically, it is a costly practice because they are living with the threat that, at any moment, the pretense may be exposed. Those who have learned to accept themselves and who use their alternative skills naturally and efficiently are much more comfortable and relaxed with their peers and others.

Social Isolation.   To a certain extent, social isolation is inherent in interpersonal relationships for individuals with visual impairments. People who are visually impaired may find it more difficult to locate friends in a crowded room, determine who is talking to whom in a small group, or receive complete or correct messages because they may have difficulty communicating nonverbally or cannot do so at all. Since social interactions are often more energy consuming than they are for sighted peers, some children and youths with visual impairments prefer to withdraw into more secure comfort zones, like remaining at home rather than contending with the supposed difficulties of attending a social function.

Dependence.   Frequently, children and youths with visual impairments are in greater danger of becoming more passive and dependent than their sighted peers, and are rewarded for being docile and compliant (Lowenfeld, 1975; Tuttle & Tuttle, 1996). Parents and others who are not knowledgeable about visual impairment may believe that children with visual impairments who are curious and active and enjoy exploring are more likely to hurt themselves. Far too many decisions are made for children, and they are not encouraged to investigate alternative courses of action and to make choices for themselves. Often, others complete tasks for children with visual impairments that they could have done for themselves. Although some children react by insisting that they be allowed to "do it for themselves," children who tend to be compliant may sense that they are expected to be helpless and end up learning to play the game of helplessness—expecting and even demanding that others do for them what they could do for themselves. This "learned helplessness," if unchecked, can become a habit, a way of life.

Inadequate Social Role Models.   Children and youths who are visually impaired generally have more limited exposure to appropriate social role models than do their sighted peers. All children learn by modeling the behaviors of others, but those who are visually impaired are typically more restricted in their ability to observe, and therefore to model, desired behaviors. The tendency of some people to excuse children's inappropriate behavior because they are visually impaired must be avoided. To be socially accepted, children with visual impairments need to learn socially acceptable behaviors.

REFINING THE SELF-CONCEPT

Younger, less mature, and more dependent individuals rely on feedback or reflections from their social environment to establish and validate their perceptions of themselves (Tuttle & Tuttle, 1996). Whether they realize it or not, the expectations of family members, educators, and friends play a powerful role in shaping their emerging self-concepts. When a child encounters high, realistic expectations and receives constructive feedback from significant people in the environment, he or she is likely to develop a positive self-concept. On the other hand, when a child senses that other people believe him or her to be socially inept or overly dependent, he or she is much more likely to incorporate those ideas into the developing notions about self. As the child perceives conflicting messages, he or she will give greater weight to those that agree with his or her own perceptions, those from more credible or respected sources, or those that occur more frequently.

For older, more mature, and more independent individuals, shaping and reshaping the self-concept becomes more internally oriented. Affirmation and approval from others lack sustaining potency. "Sooner or later [affirmation and approval have] to be supported by proof of one's worth, by one's becoming competent, productive and responsible, and this proof of worth in turn feeds into one's interpersonal relationships and enriches them" (Stringer, 1971, p. 119). These individuals tend to have a stronger internal locus of control; make their own decisions; and are more desirous of establishing and reaching personal goals, rather than simply meeting the expectations of others. They tend to be more self-directed, confident, and assertive.

The measurement of competence involves the application of standards for determining a person's performance of a task or achievement of a goal. Some commonly used standards are these:

- The social-comparison standard—comparing oneself to others' performances,

- The personal standard—comparing oneself to oneself, and

- the unique standard for blindness—using separate standards solely on the basis of a visual impairment.

There are two ways to apply the social-comparison standard. The first is to compare the *outcome* of a person's efforts. This comparison relies on the predetermined criterion that everyone achieves the same outcome (such as completing the same number of multiplication problems on a worksheet or running the same number of laps around a track). If a student who is visually impaired achieves the same outcome, regardless of the strategies by which that outcome is achieved (such as using an abacus to complete multiplication problems or using a sighted runner to run laps), then his or her achievement is comparable to everyone else's. This is a positive and productive application of the social-comparison standard. The second way the social-comparison standard may be used is to compare the *process* by which outcomes are achieved. However, this way presents a dilemma in evaluating the competence of individuals who are visually impaired because they often rely on alternate (but just as valid) techniques or use modifications to complete tasks. When the social-comparison standard is used this way, it often puts the individual with a visual impairment at a disadvantage, especially for those tasks requiring vision, and threatens the development of healthy self-esteem. Thus, the more appropriate use of the social-comparison standard

is to focus on the outcome of a task, rather than the process used to achieve it, which builds an accurate self-concept and enhances self-esteem.

In many respects, the personal standard is a more productive way to measure competence, since it compares self with self, measuring today's performance with previous performances. From an educational standpoint, it provides students with a way to measure their achievement on an ongoing basis and to take satisfaction in the gains that are documented from day to day, thereby enhancing their self-concepts and self-esteem. Such a standard is an excellent way to measure the mastery of unique compensatory skills that students who are visually impaired need.

Using a unique standard solely on the basis of a visual impairment is perhaps the most destructive and devaluing way to measure competence. A statement like, "You're doing pretty good for a blind person" reflects this damaging standard. When students who are visually impaired are treated differently or are given different assignments from their classmates, it can foster unrealistic lifelong expectations that tasks and assignments will always be adjusted, even in the workplace (for an example, see Sidebar 6.2). Lowering standards usually results in a threatened self-concept and lowered self-esteem.

The successful completion of a goal or task does not always result in an improved self-concept. To have any effect on self-esteem, the goal or task must be important to and valued by the person. Thus, successes in valued areas have a positive effect, while failures in valued areas have a negative impact. For example, if a child values academic achievement, then a high mark on a class test will have a positive effect on his or her self-esteem; conversely, if the same child fails an important test, it will have a negative impact on his or her self-esteem. On the other hand, successes or failures in nonvalued areas have little or no impact. What family members and educators value may not be valued by the child, making it possible for a high mark on a mathematics or spelling test to please a parent and teacher but not the child. Therefore, to enhance a child's self-esteem, parents and teachers need to identify and

---

One Person's Reflections on the Consequences of Using a Unique Standard

I don't know when it began, this pervasive expectation that others would naturally give me a break because I am blind—probably as a very young child. I do remember in first grade the teacher asked for volunteers to help me during recesses "so I wouldn't get hurt." I didn't need the help, but I have to admit I enjoyed the extra attention.

In fourth and fifth grades the teachers let me complete only even-numbered problems in arithmetic homework while my classmates had to do them all. They told me they were making this exception because I was blind and it took me longer to do my work. I had a teacher in seventh grade who required six book reports during the year for an A, but then turned to me and announced that four would be good enough for an A. Who was I to argue with such good fortune?

Through high school, I guess I began to work the system to my advantage. I learned that if I looked uncomfortable, I wouldn't be called on in class; if I turned in partial work, I would often get full credit; if I happened to be late turning in assignments, it was OK because I was blind. Before long, I expected everyone to give me a break because of my blindness.

My first summer job after my junior year in high school really jolted me to reality. I was hired by a used car dealer to wash, wax, and vacuum six cars a day. At the end of the first week I questioned my paycheck—I thought they had short-changed me. My boss didn't pull any punches. "You serviced four cars a day this week, so I paid you for four cars a day. If and when you get up to speed and you finish six cars, I'll pay you what we agreed upon." I didn't argue—I knew he was right. I got myself organized, hustled a bit more, and put in some extra time that next week. I was proud to get my full paycheck on Friday; I knew I had earned it fair and square.

---

improve the child's competence in areas the child values. One of the best ways to help a child improve his or her self-concept is to recognize accomplishments viewed from the child's perspective, whether or not the parent or teacher agrees with their significance. These accomplishments can be used to motivate the child to attain other desired short- and long-term goals.

RESPONDING TO A CRISIS

As children and youths interact with their social and physical environments, they encounter and respond to unexpected difficulties and thus find it necessary to work their way through a variety of issues related to their visual impairments. They may experience the sting of being made to feel different and the emotionally unsettling self-consciousness of needing to use adaptive techniques that their sighted peers do not use. Teenagers may undergo a crisis when they are unable to participate fully in a rite of passage, as when friends obtain their learner's permits to drive, or are excluded from participating in an activity, such as a ball game.

For many children and youths, such a crisis is short-lived because they have learned to turn their attention to other more positive thoughts or activities that do not put them at a disadvantage. However, others have a difficult time wrestling with these troublesome areas. They may be stunned or numb, unable to make any response for a time, or they may simply deny that the crisis ever occurred, unable and unwilling to talk about it. Within reason, both shock and denial are normal and healthy because they allow the youngsters to buy time to sort things out before dealing with the consequences of the psychological trauma.

Children who are seriously struggling with crises may express feelings of sadness and need to vent their frustrations over painful encounters. According to Moses (1987), grieving is essential because it enables people to separate from their sense of loss, from their unrealized dreams, so they can establish new dreams. To be effective, grieving a loss must be shared with others, especially those who are close to one (Moses, 1994). This may be a time of self-pity and loneliness for some children, who may withdraw from family members and friends. Along with feeling sad, children may express their anger and hostility indiscriminately to anyone who may be physically or emotionally close.

Sooner or later, children and youths may begin to verbalize, one by one, the activities or relationships they feel they have lost or can no longer achieve. Frequently, these perceptions of presumed inabilities or losses are not grounded in fact, and a child may need assistance to sort the real from the imagined. For example, after being teased on the playground, a child may conclude, "I will never have another friend in my whole life." Or a teenager may say, "If I can't drive, I'll never be able to date." The phrase "I can't . . ." begins to creep into their conversations, which reflect a more negative and pessimistic outlook. This is the time to establish some short-term goals that are easily attainable, such as playing a game with a friend or inviting a friend out for pizza.

After struggling with some of these issues, children and youths with visual impairments may go through a period when they question the meaning and purpose of life and then take time to establish the things they consider important. They may say, "It's more important that I get my work done accurately than it is to be embarrassed about using my slate and stylus in public." or "It's more important to develop friendships than it is to drive." Clear messages of affirmation that the children are individuals of value and worth are essential for those children who are searching and questioning.

Some children are ready and willing to develop some additional specialized techniques and strategies for coping with life's demands only after they have wrestled with issues and crises related to their visual impairments. As a result of this struggle, they are more willing to identify themselves as "different" with respect to vision, which frees them to learn to use the adaptive skills and devices that are essential for a productive, satisfying life and to use available resources, services, and organizations related to visual impairments.

With the confidence that competence brings, children and youths will begin to develop or regain self-esteem as persons of dignity and worth. Rather than see themselves as "blind persons," they will see themselves as individuals with many characteristics and traits, only one of which is related to their visual impairments. When their perceptions and feelings of themselves as persons who happen to be visually impaired become incorporated into their self-concepts, then visual impairment is not the focal point of their life. They are comfortable with themselves and discover that they have important and valuable individual traits (Tuttle & Tuttle, 1996).

Acceptance of others is predicated on self-acceptance. Children find it difficult to appreciate and accept others until they have first learned to appreciate and accept themselves. Self-acceptance is facilitated by warm and caring relationships, by unconditional acceptance, by constructive feedback, and by the freedom to express thoughts and feelings.

THE DEPENDENCE–INDEPENDENCE CONTINUUM

An understanding of independence has a critical influence on how a child or youth learns to respond to life's demands with a visual impairment. Many people tend to view independence and self-sufficiency as measures of maturity and worth. For most individuals, there is a constant tension between desired independence and required assistance. Anyone on the dependent-receiving end of a relationship is often deemed less valued and less acceptable. Because of the nature of visual impairment, the areas of dependence for persons with a severe visual impairment are more obvious than those of others, making them more vulnerable to the effects of these negative attitudes.

Perceived dependence is both a threat to the self and a temptation to succumb to the limiting and devaluating expectations of oneself and others. With society's prevailing attitudes regarding the helpless and dependent state of children and youths with visual impairments, many family members and friends, without thinking, cater to and thus perpetuate these perceived needs for dependence, robbing the young people of being in control and exercising choices. Naturally, the dependence needs of young children or others who recently became visually impaired are more pronounced until their adaptive behaviors and coping skills are established.

All people find themselves at some point on the independence–dependence continuum. Unrealistically dependent individuals may seek emotional and physical security by demanding total care. Unrealistically independent persons may find themselves attempting dangerous and foolish tasks, placing themselves and others in awkward and embarrassing situations.

In responding to the dependence aspects of visual impairments, children and youths may react with hostility and aggression, with submissiveness and compliance, or with a more balanced willingness to accept needed assistance when the circumstances of a given situation seem to warrant the help. The willingness to accept assistance when needed requires a strong self-concept that is insightful enough to recognize when assistance is unnecessary and strong enough to resist gracefully the offered unneeded assistance (Lowenfeld, 1975).

Society tends to overglorify independence and condemns normal interdependence. Interdependence is cooperative, not competitive. Interdependent individuals, building on the joint efforts and strengths of all involved, are able to recognize their own value and worth and the need to give and receive love and forgiveness. "Interdependence is a choice only independent people can make. Dependent people cannot choose to become interdependent. They don't have the character to do it; they don't own enough of themselves" (Covey, 1990, p. 51). Healthy interdependence reflects a more realistic and satisfying resolution of the tension between independence and dependence. "Dependent people need others to get what they want. Independent people can get what they want through their own effort. Interdependent people combine their own efforts with the efforts of others to achieve their greatest success" (Covey, 1990, p. 49).

NURTURING AND MAINTAINING A HEALTHY SELF-CONCEPT

During the years when children and youths are in school, parents and educators have expectations that their children will do well. Much effort, time, and resources are directed toward the satisfactory completion of daily classroom activities and assignments. Often, this focus on schoolwork is made at the expense of other, perhaps more significant, aspects of personal growth. For professionals, family members, and friends, developing and maintaining the integrity of the whole child and nurturing healthy self-esteem should be the highest priorities. When all else is said and done, the most crucial and vital contributors to a full, rich, and satisfying life are broader and more basic than completing one academic grade after another, as rewarding and necessary as that may be. Maintaining an appropriate balance among the five ingredients discussed next will foster the skills, attitudes, and climate so essential to the development of a wholesome well-rounded individual with a healthy self-concept (Luckner, 1988; Tuttle, 1994).

Self-Acceptance

For any person, a positive, wholesome outlook on oneself and life begins with self-acceptance. Children need to learn to accept themselves as individuals with many attributes, only one of which is their visual impairment. In some ways, children with visual impairments are similar to other people, but in other ways, they are distinctive. This recognition is essential to the nurturing process. Children with visual impairments need many opportunities to interact with others, both sighted and visually impaired, in both integrated and segregated settings to learn about their attributes, abilities, and strengths and about their similarities with and differences from others. As a result, students who are visually impaired are able to learn about, appreciate, and respect their unique mix of personal attributes and individual qualities. It is essential to self-acceptance that each child receives respect and approval from others for these qualities and traits. In addition, it is important to affirm that the child's nonvisual experiences are real and valid without attempting to superimpose a visual frame of reference on the child. The child's nonvisual experiences must be respected, a respect that should not be undermined by constant reminders that he or she lacks the visual imagery available to most people.

Social Connectedness

Another basic ingredient of a positive self-concept is to be socially connected with others. Students with visual impairments need to develop respectful, courteous, and cordial relationships with and positive attitudes toward others (McCallum & Sacks, 1993; Sacks & Wolffe, 1992). All individuals need to feel valued, loved, and cared for. They must feel that what they think, say, and do matters to others and that others appreciate the people and things they hold in high regard.

Informed Choices

A healthy self-concept and wholesome outlook are also associated with the ability to make choices for oneself. All people have a need to feel that they have some control over themselves and the events in their lives. Making choices involves knowing alternative courses of action and the consequences of each. The ability to take charge by making personal choices fosters a sense of responsibility for one's actions. The choices made are based on one's personal set of values and the belief statements one holds to be true about oneself and others. Other people must respect the choices that children and youths make, even if they think the choices are "wrong." Individuals with visual impairments learn responsibility for their own actions only when they experience both the positive and negative consequences of their choices.

Genuine Productivity

The successful completion of important tasks and achievement of valued goals foster a strong sense of personal accomplishment. Feeling productive also involves contributing to the welfare of another. Therefore, to be genuinely productive, children and youths with visual impairments need to demonstrate their personal and social competencies, showing that they have knowledge, skills, and attitudes that are appreciated and valued by others.

Relaxing and Having Fun

The ability to relax and have fun is another key ingredient for nurturing a healthy self-concept. All individuals, whether visually impaired or sighted, need periods when they can set aside the stresses of day-to-day living. They need to learn and engage in recreational and leisure-time skills, such as sports and other physical activities, table games, puzzles and brain teasers, arts and crafts, and other hobbies.

Fuller enjoyment of life also comes with the development of a healthy sense of humor, and the ability to laugh at oneself, which is a sign of healthy self-esteem. Children and youths who are visually impaired need to learn how to appreciate the comical or absurd, but avoid the kind of sarcastic humor that deprecates them or others. They need to learn how to relax and enjoy life, how to fit play and work (in their case, school) together without sacrificing either.

SUMMARY

The psychosocial development of children and youths with visual impairments can best be understood as students interact with their physical and social environments, learning to meet the day-to-day demands of living with a visual impairment. Many factors affect the ability of these students to interact with and gain knowledge about their environment. The quality of a person's self-concept is influenced by life experiences, which, in turn, determine how these experiences are perceived. A child's self-concept is constantly being revised by the reflections the child observes in others or by the measure of the child's own competence. Unfortunately, many in society still hold negative and devaluating attitudes toward blindness and visual impairments. A visual impairment may, at times, affect a person's ability to initiate and participate in social relationships.

Children and youths with visual impairments may struggle with a wide variety of issues and emotions before they are able to use specialized techniques and strategies for coping with life's demands and become comfortable with themselves as people who happen to be visually impaired. They may be working through dependence-independence issues and need to be encouraged to develop a healthy attitude of interdependence. A positive self-concept needs to be nurtured and encouraged to form the foundation of a wholesome, well-rounded person.

STUDY QUESTIONS

1. What are some common attitudes toward and misconceptions about individuals who are visually impaired in this society?
2. What are four possible consequences of a severe visual impairment for social interactions?
3. What is meant by the term *self-concept*? How is *self-concept* different from *self-esteem*?
4. Which external and internal factors are likely to influence a person's self-concept and self-esteem?
5. What damage may result from applying a unique standard for "the visually impaired" or excusing unacceptable behavior on the basis of a visual impairment?
6. How would you respond if your students expressed feelings of sadness or anger about a blindness-related difficulty or challenge?
7. Why is asking for assistance so difficult for some students with visual impairments?
8. What role do fun and humor play in maintaining a healthy, well-balanced outlook on life?

REFERENCES

Coopersmith, S. (1967). *The antecedents of self-esteem.* San Francisco: W. H. Freeman.

Covey, S. R. (1990). *The seven habits of highly effective people.* New York: Simon & Schuster.

Erikson, E. H. (1950). *Childhood and society.* New York: W. W. Norton.

Foulke, E. (1972). The personality of the blind: A nonvalid concept. *New Outlook for the Blind, 66,* 33–37, 42.

Hattie, J. (1992). *Self-concept.* Hillsdale, NJ: Lawrence Erlbaum.

Kent, D. (1989). Shackled imagination: Literary illusions about blindness. *Journal of Visual Impairment & Blindness, 83,* 145–150.

Kirchner, C., McBroom, L., Nelson, K., & Graves, W. (1992). *Lifestyles of employed legally blind people.* Mississippi State: Rehabilitation Research and Training Center on Blindness and Low Vision, Mississippi State University.

Kirtley, D. D. (1975). *The psychology of blindness.* Chicago: Nelson-Hall.

Lowenfeld, B. (1975). *The changing status of the blind*

from separation to integration. Springfield, IL: Charles C Thomas.

Lowenfeld, B. (1981). *Berthold Lowenfeld on blindness and blind people: Selected papers.* New York: American Foundation for the Blind.

Luckner, J. (1988). Enhancing self-esteem of hearing impaired students. *Association of Canadian Educators of the Hearing Impaired Journal, 14,* 83–90.

McCallum, B. J., & Sacks, S. Z. (Eds.). (1993). *Social skills curriculum for children with visual impairments.* Santa Clara, CA: Score Regionalization Project.

Moses, K. (1987). The impact of childhood disability: The parent's struggle. *Ways Magazine, 1,* 6–10.

Moses, K. (1994 July). Grief groups: Rekindling hope. *Voices, Journal of the American Academy of Psychotherapists,* pp. 70–77.

Sacks, S. Z., & Wolffe, K. (1992). The importance of social skills in the transition process for students with visual impairments. *Journal of Vocational Rehabilitation, 2(1),* 46–55.

Schulz, P. (1980). *How does it feel to be blind?* Van Nuys, CA: Muse-Ed.

Stringer, L. A. (1971). *A sense of self: A guide to how we mature.* Philadelphia: Temple University Press.

Tobin, M., & Hill, E. (1987). Visually impaired teenagers: Ambitions, attitudes, and interests. *Journal of Visual Impairment & Blindness, 81,* 414–416.

Tuttle, D. W. (1994). Contemporary issues: Impact on self-esteem. *DVI Quarterly, 39,* 15–19.

Tuttle, D. W., & Tuttle, N. R. (1996). *Self-esteem and adjusting with blindness* (2nd ed.). Springfield, IL: Charles C Thomas.

Wright, B. A. (1983). *Physical disability—A psychological approach.* New York: Harper.

CHAPTER 7

Children and Youths with Visual Impairments and Other Exceptionalities

Rosanne K. Silberman

KEY POINTS

- Many students who are visually impaired also have other disabilities.

- Students with visual impairments and other exceptionalities are a diverse group with a wide variety of strengths and needs.

- Teachers of students with visual impairments and additional disabilities work in a variety of service delivery systems with a variety of professionals.

- The additional disabilities of students who are visually impaired represent the range of disabilities present in students who are sighted. However, some syndromes or disabling conditions are attended by a greater prevalence of visual impairments.

- Students who are visually impaired and gifted present unique challenges in identification and intervention.

Children and youths with visual impairments often have a range of other exceptionalities that have an impact on their development, on decisions regarding their educational placement, and on the formulation of Individualized Family Service Plans (IFSPs) and Individualized Education Programs (IEPs) to meet their unique needs. Combinations of two or more disabilities are sometimes referred to as multiple disabilities. Those that include visual impairments may be caused by prenatal, perinatal, or postnatal factors. Prenatal factors include congenital infections and abnormalities, hypoxia (a low amount of oxygen in the blood and lungs), chromosomal and genetic defects, and parental alcohol and drug abuse (Heller, Alberto, Forney, & Schwartzman, 1996). Factors that cause multiple impairments during the perinatal period (shortly before, during, or right after birth) and the postnatal period include trauma, hypoxia, infection, and prematurity (Batshaw, 1997).

The combined exceptionalities result in unique characteristics that are not present in children and youths with only visual impairments. Although the types of combinations of these exceptionalities are numerous, this chapter discusses the characteristics and medical and educational impacts of the following combinations that a teacher may find among students with visual impairments:

- Visual impairments and mental retardation,

- Visual impairments and learning disabilities,

◆ Visual impairments and neurological disabilities,

◆ Visual impairments and orthopedic and health impairments,

◆ Visual impairments and auditory impairments (deaf-blindness),

◆ Visual impairments and behavioral disorders, and

◆ Visual impairments and giftedness.

PREVALENCE

Estimates of the number of students with visual impairments and additional disabilities vary, depending on the source. However, the reported increase in the percentage of these students is significant (Hatlen, 1998). According to his source (Home Counselors of the Blind Babies Foundation, San Francisco, personal communication, 1997), since the mid-1980s, the prevalence of these children has increased an estimated 50 percent to as high as 75 percent of the total number of children with visual impairments.

Regardless of the source, information on the prevalence of children and youths with visual impairments and other exceptionalities is limited and frequently inaccurate because students with visual impairments may be counted in several disability areas other than visual impairments, including mental retardation, multiple disabilities, hearing impairment, and neurological disabilities. Child counts are further influenced by factors such as placement, administrative decisions, and lack of knowledge about the identification of visual impairments. Underestimating child counts has led to implications that relate to shortages of personnel needed to teach this low-incidence population. (For a more detailed discussion of the general problem of child counts, see Chapter 2.)

TYPES OF SERVICE DELIVERY SYSTEMS

Children and youths with visual impairments and other exceptionalities can receive an appropriate education in a variety of service delivery systems, depending on such factors as their families' preferences, unique educational needs, recommendations of the IFSP or IEP team, and the availability of qualified personnel. It is important to note that placement decisions should be reevaluated regularly because no one placement is necessarily appropriate throughout a student's schooling.

The variety of placement options for children and youths with other exceptionalities range from disability-specific environments, such as schools for students who are blind; to public and private day programs for students who are blind; to specialized classes, resource rooms, and itinerant programs in public schools. In addition, this population can also be served in inclusive general education classes and in special programs for students with other disabilities, such as cerebral palsy centers and classes for students with severe disabilities, deaf-blindness, or neurological impairments. The teacher of students with visual impairments must be a key member of the professional team, regardless of where a student who has a visual impairment and other exceptionality is placed. (See Chapter 9 for a more detailed discussion of placement options.)

COLLABORATIVE TEAMING

A range of expertise is needed to meet the unique challenges that children and youths with visual impairments and other exceptionalities present. No one professional can be expected to be totally competent in providing for all the distinct needs of these students. Depending on the types of additional disabilities, participants on a collaborative team may include a teacher of students with visual impairments; an orientation and mobility (O&M) specialist; a rehabilitation teacher; other special educators; and general education teachers of specific subjects. They may also include related-services personnel, such as a physical therapist to assist with gross motor development; an occupational therapist to assist with fine motor development, particularly daily living skills; a speech and language therapist to assist in developing appropriate augmentative communication systems; a psychologist; and a social worker. Other significant members of the collaborative team may be the audiologist to assess hearing, a nurse and physician to address medical concerns, and a behavioral interventionist to address emotional difficulties. In addition, every collaborative team must include the student's parents and relevant paraeducators to participate in decisions regarding educational placement, assessment, program planning and development of IEPs, and program evaluation (Orelove & Sobsey, 1996; Sacks, 1998; Silberman, Sacks, & Wolfe, 1998). (For additional information on working in educational teams, see Chapter 1 in *Foundations of Education: Instructional Strategies for Teaching Children and Youths with Visual Impairments.)*

The three types of teams that are evident in educational programs for children and youths with visual impairments and other exceptionalities are the multidisciplinary team, the interdisciplinary team, and the transdisciplinary team. The model that is highly recommended as being effective with students with multiple disabilities is the transdisciplinary model (Orelove & Sobsey, 1996; Rainforth & York-Barr, 1997). Therapists and other specialists with unique expertise provide direct services to students in classrooms and other natural environments as part of the daily routine, rather than in isolated therapy rooms. An example of this practice is a speech-language therapist assisting a student with a visual impairment and mental retardation to interact with his peers at lunch using an augmentative communication device.

The transdisciplinary model also enables a related-service professional gradually to provide lesser amounts of direct services and to serve as a consultant to the classroom teacher once the teacher learns to implement a specific strategy. An example of this "role release" is when an O&M specialist shows a special education teacher how to help a student trail a wall in her wheelchair to go from the classroom to the cafeteria. Then the O&M specialist observes the teacher instructing the student and gradually fades from the activity.

(For a more thorough explanation of various team models, see Chapter 1 in *Foundations of Education: Instructional Strategies for Teaching Children and Youths with Visual Impairments.)*

VISUAL IMPAIRMENTS AND MENTAL RETARDATION

Definitions and Characteristics

Some children and youths with visual impairments also have various degrees of mental retardation. As defined by the American Association on Mental Retardation (AAMR, 1992, p. 5),

> Mental Retardation refers to substantial limitations in present functioning. It is characterized by significantly subaverage intellectual function, existing concurrently with related limitations in two or more of the following applicable adaptive skill areas: communication, self-care, home living, social skills, community use, self-direction, health and safety, functional academics, leisure and work. Mental retardation manifests before age 18.

Unlike earlier definitions from professional organizations, the current definition focuses on the strengths, needs, and types and degrees of supports that an individual needs. The level of supports can be intermittent, limited, extensive, or pervasive, and the type of support varies across environments and depends on the skills of a specific student.

The Association for Persons with Severe Handicaps (TASH) adopted the following definition of the people whom they serve:

> These people include individuals of all ages who require extensive ongoing support in more than one major life activity in order to participate in integrated community settings and to enjoy a quality of life that is available to citizens with fewer or no disabilities. Support may be required for life activities such as mobility, communication, self-care, and learning as necessary for independent living, employment, and self-sufficiency. (1989)

Both the AAMR and the TASH definitions are based on the following assumptions:

1. The deficits are not a result of cultural or linguistic diversity;
2. A student's adaptive performance must be compared with that of the student's chronological age-peers in community environments, and the necessary supports should be identified;
3. Students have strengths in addition to limitations; and
4. In most cases, improvements will be noted when appropriate supports are provided over time. (AAMR, 1992)

Impact on Development and Learning

Children and youths with visual impairments and mental retardation have difficulty attending to certain stimuli, dimensions, and cues. Without the ability to observe visually, they also have difficulty imitating others and synthesizing separate skills into meaningful wholes. They are unable to learn skills incidentally, and generalize from one environment to another (Silberman, Sacks, & Wolfe, 1998; Westling & Fox, 2000). In addition, because they have limited access to information, they are less motivated to explore, initiate interactions, or participate in everyday situations (Chen, 1995b). These students learn at slower rates, need more time to learn new skills, and learn fewer skills than their peers with only visual impairments or those without disabilities (Sacks, 1998).

In the area of gross motor development, these children and youths frequently exhibit motor delays because of the combination of visual impairment and mental retardation. For example, many have difficulties rotating parts of their bodies, such as their heads and trunks. A child with a central visual loss who is unable to rotate his or her head cannot turn to locate an object placed on the left side of his or her desk. Some are also unable to ambulate independently from place to place in their environment. In the area of fine motor development, these children and youths have delays in fine motor skills involving the use of arms, hands, and fingers. They have difficulty reaching for, grasping, and releasing objects because vision plays an extremely significant role in encouraging physical contact with the hands or near objects (Silberman, 1986). In addition, delays in fine motor skills prevent these children from acquiring skills in activities of daily living, such as dressing, eating, and grooming.

In the area of social development, students with visual impairments and mental retardation may be isolated until specific interventions are provided to enable them to interact with other peers with and without disabilities. With regard to the development of communication skills, many of these students are unable to acquire speech and need to use a combination of unaided and aided augmentative and alternative communication techniques. Unaided techniques include touch cues, manual signs, tactile signs, and gestures. Aided techniques can be nonelectronic, such as real objects, tangible symbols that feel or sound like what they represent, photographs, black-and-white enlarged line-drawing symbols, and textured symbols. Other aided techniques incorporate external electronic devices such as computers, microswitches, or voice-output communication aids (Mirenda, 1999).

Common Syndromes

Chromosomal and genetic defects, caused by missing or extra chromosomes or interactions of different types of genes, can result in syndromes that have combinations of disabilities that include visual impairments. One example is Cri-du-chat syndrome, a chromosomal defect that causes mental retardation, microcephaly (an abnormally small head), hypotonia (low muscle tone), myopia, glaucoma, microphthalmos (abnormally small eyes), optic atrophy, and corneal opacity. Another example is Laurence-Moon-Bardet-Biedl syndrome, which is an autosomal recessive disorder characterized by night blindness, progressive central field loss, and photophobia, as well as developmental delays and spastic paraplegia (Levack, Stone, & Bishop, 1994). Still another example is Down syndrome, a chromosomal defect that causes mental retardation, endocrine abnormalities, hypotonia, congenital heart defects, refractive errors, cataracts, strabismus, and keratoconus (for a complete list of ocular changes in pediatric syndromes, see Nelson, 1984). Several syndromes that result in visual and auditory impairments are described in the section on deaf-blindness.

VISUAL IMPAIRMENTS AND LEARNING DISABILITIES

Definitions and Characteristics

Students with visual impairments and learning disabilities have a sensory loss combined with significant difficulties in listening, speaking, reading, writing, reasoning, or mathematical abilities (Silberman & Sowell, 1998). As defined by the Individuals with Disabilities Education Act (IDEA) Amendments (1997) (Lerner 1997; Silberman & Sowell, 1998), the definition of learning disabilities includes the following concepts:

1. The student has a disorder in one or more of the basic psychological processes, such as memory, auditory perception, visual perception, oral language, and thinking.

2. The student has difficulty learning, that is, in speaking, listening, writing, reading (word-recognition skills and comprehension), and mathematics (calculation and reasoning).

3. The student's difficulty is not due primarily to other causes, such as visual or hearing impairments; motor impairments; mental retardation; emotional disturbance; or economic, environmental, or cultural disadvantage.

4. A severe discrepancy exists between the student's potential for learning and his or her low level of achievement.

Students with visual impairments and learning disabilities have myriad limitations that vary from individual to individual. The most frequent limitations are in information processing, language, mathematics, attention, motor abilities, organizational skills, test taking, and social interactions. Although no student with a learning disability has difficulties or limitations in all areas, it is important to note that these characteristics are heightened or intensified in a student who also has a visual impairment. See Silberman and Sowell (1998) for a more detailed discussion of students with visual impairments and learning disabilities.

Impact on Learning in School

Some of the difficulties that students with visual impairments and learning disabilities may experience relate to such areas as information processing, language skills (both oral and written expression), reading (decoding and comprehension), and mathematics, which affect their learning in school.

In the area of information processing, the lack of visual cues hinders these students from integrating the elements of the environment into a meaningful whole, and their learning disability may hinder their development of short-term memory. Therefore, the students with both of these disabilites may become confused and unable to follow directions to get from one place to another (such as from the cafeteria or gym back to the classroom).

In the area of language, these students may experience difficulties with oral expression, since they may not have all the salient details of a particular experience because of their visual impairment. Furthermore, they may find it more difficult to write a high-quality composition because they lack the visual experience of reading the plethora of information presented in newspapers and magazines. In the area of reading, they may find it difficult to decode unfamiliar words, a common difficulty of students with learning disabilities (Lyon, 1996). This difficulty is heightened for students with low vision who use their vision as their primary sensory channel because it takes them longer to decode print letters read with a low-vision device or in large print. The difficulty may also be heightened for students who are also blind with a learning disability who read braille and have to decode letters and words in two different formats (uncontracted and contracted form) (Silberman & Sowell, 1998). With regard to reading comprehension, students with visual impairments and learning disabilities have difficulty because of their reduced experiential background. They have problems bringing together all the parts into a meaningful whole and sometimes are unable to find the appropriate line, to track words on a line, and to shift to the next line (Silberman & Sowell, 1987).

In the area of mathematics, many children and youths with visual impairments and learning disabilities have difficulty solving word problems because of their difficulties with oral language and reading just described. Because of blindness or low vision, they may find it difficult to learn concepts that relate to one-to-one correspondence, groups of items, or number relationships at a glance. In addition, many of these students have not had enough opportunities to manipulate objects, and because of the combined disabilities, they have problems understanding concepts related to space, form, order, time, distance, and quantity (Silberman & Sowell, 1998). Many are unable to remember geometric shapes, memorize basic mathematics facts, and perform mathematics tasks that require recalling steps and sequences (Miller, 1996). Furthermore, these students may have difficulties with visual-motor tasks related to mathematics. Many are unable to read, copy, and align numbers in the appropriate columns to do various types of numerical operations and, as a result, make errors in computation (Mercer & Mercer, 1997).

VISUAL IMPAIRMENTS AND NEUROLOGICAL DISABILITIES

Some students with visual impairments also have neurological disabilities that affect the brain,

spinal cord, and peripheral nerves that connect the spinal cord to the skin and muscles of the body (Rosen, 1998). Three of the most prevalent neurological conditions that affect this population in educational programs are seizure disorders, cerebral palsy, and traumatic brain injury. The following section describes these common neurological disorders and discusses their medical and educational impacts on learning in the classroom.

Seizure Disorders

A seizure is a sudden, involuntary, disruption of the normal functioning of the nervous system that may be characterized by changes in consciousness, motor activity, sensory phenomena, or inappropriate behavior that occur alone or in combinations (Berkow, 1992; Holmes, 1992). Seizures usually last a few seconds to a few minutes and end spontaneously. A seizure that is continuous and lasts for 30 minutes or more is known as status epilepticus and is considered a medical emergency, since it may result in brain damage or death if immediate intervention is not provided. A seizure may be caused by a short-term condition, such as a high fever or meningitis; when it occurs at least two times and is unrelated to a short-term condition or is ongoing, the condition is considered to be a seizure disorder.

Seizures are classified into two major types: partial seizures and generalized seizures. Partial seizures occur in one area of the brain in one cerebral hemisphere, and generalized seizures occur in both hemispheres or begin in one area and then move to both hemispheres.

Partial Seizures

Partial seizures are divided into three types: simple partial, complex partial, and complex partial with secondary generalization. Forty percent of seizures that occur in children are simple partial seizures (Behrman, 1992). Simple partial seizures usually last 10–30 seconds, and children remain awake and alert during them. The localized electrical discharge commonly occurs in the neurons in the motor area of the brain, and depending on the location of the abnormal discharge in the motor area where movements are controlled, the arm may make a jerking motion or the foot may move. When a simple partial seizure moves from one motor area of a limb to another, the foot may move, then the lower leg, and then the upper leg. The sequential involvement of body parts is referred to as a Jacksonian march (Holmes, 1992). Sometimes small muscles that control the movements of the face or fingers may be affected as well.

Simple partial seizures that involve abnormal electrical discharges along the sensory strip or sensory area of the brain result in somatosensory symptoms, such as numbness or tingling in the affected body part, certain odors or tastes, visual hallucinations (lights or color) and a feeling of falling or floating (Heller et al., 1996; Rosen, 1998). Simple partial seizures that are caused by involvement of the autonomic nervous system can result in a fast heart rate; dilation of the pupils; goose bumps; and psychic symptoms, such as hallucinations, certain emotions, and other disturbances in cognitive functioning. All simple partial seizures can occur as an "aura" that precedes complex partial seizures or generalized seizures (Keller et al., 1996; Rosen, 1998).

Complex partial seizures, known as temporal lobe or psychomotor seizures, usually last from 30 seconds to several minutes during which a student's consciousness is affected. These seizures are often multisymptomatic and usually involve involuntary motor movements and psychic behaviors. The motor behaviors include chewing, blank staring, scratching, laughing, gesturing, or repeating a phrase. The student may look dazed and engage in random, purposeless activities such as walking in a circle or picking up objects; the student usually repeats the same behaviors each time he or she has a seizure. The psychic behaviors include illusions, hallucinations, and flashbacks to earlier events or feelings; certain emotions, such as fear, joy, or embarassment, may also be present (Heller et al., 1996). When the seizure is over, the student may feel confused, be tired, or sleep (known as the postictal phase). Sometimes a partial complex seizure may spread to other parts of the brain and result in a generalized seizure.

Generalized Seizures

Generalized seizures occur in both hemispheres of the brain. The two most common are absence seizures and tonic-clonic seizures.

Absence Seizures. Absence seizures, previously called petit mal seizures, cause a child suddenly to stop whatever activity he or she is doing, lose consciousness, and either stare ahead or roll the eyes upward. In addition, the child may make involuntary movements, such as blinking the eyes or twitching the mouth. These seizures last from a few seconds to 30 seconds. At the end of a seizure, a child will resume the activity as if nothing had happened (Keller et al., 1996; Rosen, 1998).

Tonic-clonic Seizures. Tonic-clonic seizures previously called grand mal seizures, usually start after an aura, which begins minutes or seconds before the onset of the seizures. A headache, mood change, irritability, difficulty sleeping, or change in appetite may also occur hours or days before a seizure and serve as a warning that a seizure is going to occur (Holmes, 1992). The seizure begins with a sudden loss of consciousness. During the tonic (rigid) phase, which occurs first and lasts less than a minute, a child may fall and his or her muscles become rigid, the arms and legs extend, and the back arches. In addition, the eyes may roll upward, and the lips, skin and, nailbeds may turn blue. The next phase, the clonic (jerking) phase, begins with rhythmic, jerking motions of the body that gradually lessen. During this phase, a child may lose bladder or bowel control, saliva may pool in the mouth and breathing becomes noisy and shallow. The child also may aspirate saliva, bite the tongue, and vomit. The entire seizure lasts from 2 to 5 minutes, then the child wakes up confused and sleeps for 30 minutes to 2 hours (Heller et al., 1996; Rosen, 1998). There are several other types of seizures that are less common; for additional information see Heller et al. (1996) and Rosen (1998).

Medical Implications

It is extremely important for the teacher to follow specific procedures if a student in the class has a seizure. It is essential to observe the student while the seizure is taking place and to submit an accurate report of the seizure. (See Table 7.1 for information on types of seizures, ways to recognize them, and what to do and what not to do during a seizure.)

Most seizure disorders are treated effectively with medications. However, it is important to be aware of the side effects that the different antiepileptic medications may cause. Some of these drugs that are given to children and youths to control seizures (e.g., dilantin) may affect visual functioning by causing blurry or double vision.

Effects on Learning and Social Behavior

Students with disabilities have a higher prevalence of seizure disorders that may result in the need to modify academic content. According to Brown (1997), they may miss information while seizures are occurring and afterward if they become fatigued or disoriented. In addition, high dosages of medication that they are given to prevent future seizures sometimes cause drowsiness, a reduced attention span, and loss of short-term memory. Since the occurrence of seizures is unpredictable, students with seizures may feel dependent and have a sense of loss of control and decreased self-worth (Heller et al., 1996).

Cerebral Palsy

Cerebral palsy is a nonprogressive disorder of voluntary movement and posture that is caused by damage to the brain before or during birth or within the first few years of life (Pellegrino, 1997). The majority of the cases are due to problems during intrauterine development and to prematurity (Scher et al., 1991).

Visual impairments are common and diverse in children with cerebral palsy (Black, 1982; Schenk-Rootlieb, van Nieuwenhuizen, & van der Graaf, 1992). They include retinopathy of prematurity, homonomous hemianopsia, and strabismus.

There are several classifications of cerebral palsy. One classification system that is frequently used is based on the predominant type of motor impairment and the region of the brain that is affected (Blair & Stanley, 1985). Damage to the pyramidal motor system of the brain causes spastic cerebral palsy. A child with spastic cerebral palsy will have increased muscle tone (hypertonicity) and difficulty with voluntary gross motor and fine motor movements (of the hands and fingers). Depending of the actual part (or parts) of the body that is affected and the extent of the injury, this type of cerebral palsy is further categorized according to the specific limbs involved. These classifications are as follows:

- ◆ Monoplegia: increased muscle tone in one extremity.
- ◆ Hemiplegia: increased muscle tone or paralysis of the arm and leg on one side of the body. A child with right-side hemiplegia would have damage to the left side of the brain.
- ◆ Diplegia: increased muscle tone in the legs more than in the arms. A child with diplegia may have knees that come together tightly and legs that cross over (scissoring).
- ◆ Paraplegia: increased muscle tone or paralysis of the legs only.
- ◆ Quadriplegia: increased muscle tone or paralysis of all four limbs, as well as of the trunk and muscles that control the mouth, tongue, and pharynx.

The types of cerebral palsy that are caused by damage to the extrapyramidal system of the brain involve abnormalities of muscle tone that affect the entire body. One type, athetoid cerebral palsy, is caused by damage to the basal ganglia; a student with this type of cerebral palsy has abnormal, involuntary movements that may be slow and writhing or quick and jerky. Another type is dystonic cerebral palsy, which is characterized by rigidity and tenseness in the trunk and neck; a student with this type shows greater rigidity or resistance (no release of tension) to slow movement than to rapid movement. Still another type, ataxia, is caused by injury to the cerebellum and results in either decreased or increased muscle tone. A student with ataxia has difficulty coordinating voluntary movements and balance and walks with a wide-based, unsteady gait. He or she may also have problems controlling his or her hand and arm while reaching for an object and timing motor movements.

Other types of cerebral palsy caused by damage to the extrapyramidal system include tremor (regular and rhythmical involuntary shaking movements) and atonia (no tone or extremely low muscle tone). There are also cases of mixed cerebral palsy in which there is more than one type of motor pattern, neither of which predominates (Heller et al., 1996; Pellegrino, 1997; Rosen, 1998).

Effects on Development

Children and youths with cerebral palsy have varying difficulties with motor movements, resulting in abnormal patterns and problems with coordination. Many retain primitive reflexes that interfere with the achievement of higher-level postural reactions, such as changing positions, and motor milestones, such as voluntary sitting and walking. Some also develop contractures, that is, permanently shortened muscles that reduce their range of motion and ability to move limbs fully. Because of limited range of motion and abnormal movement patterns, students with visual impairments and cerebral palsy may have difficulty moving their heads or eyes (or both) to track across their midline and scan the environment.

These students also have difficulty with expressive and nonverbal forms of communication that are exacerbated when they also are blind or have low vision. Some who retain primitive reflexes have difficulty with the muscles that control the mouth; as a result, they may be unable to develop speech or have difficulty articulating and slur their words. The combination of lack of vision and the inability to move facial muscles and maintain eye contact causes problems with social interactions as well as communication.

In the area of daily living skills, some students with visual impairments and cerebral palsy with severe motor involvement have great difficulty dressing, toileting, feeding themselves, taking care of their personal hygiene, and grooming. Visual impairment, combined with poor motor coordination and range of motion, and difficulty with balance and fine motor control all adversely affect a student's ability to become independent (Heller et al., 1996).

Traumatic Brain Injury

Characteristics

Traumatic brain injury (TBI) refers to acquired injuries to the brain that present at least one or more of the following symptoms: changes in the level of consciousness, posttraumatic amnesia for 5 or more minutes, and physiological documentation that is determined by a physical examination or diagnostic testing (Heller et al., 1996). The most frequent causes of TBI are falls from heights; sports and recreation-related injuries; motor vehicle crashes; and assaults, such as shaken infant syndrome that results from child abuse (Michaud, Duhaime, & Lazar, 1997).

The nature and extent of impairments depend on the specific part of the brain that was injured, the type of force that caused the injury, and the severity of the injury (Michaud et al., 1997). Impact forces, when the head strikes a surface or is struck by a moving object, result in scalp injuries, skull fractures, bruises to the brain (contusions), or collections of blood beneath the skull (epidural hematomas). Inertial forces, when the brain undergoes violent motion inside the skull and tears the nerve fibers and blood vessels, result in injuries that range from mild concussions to more severe injuries, such as subdural hematomas (blood clots that form beneath the duramater, the hard, outer membrane covering the brain and spinal cord) and diffuse injuries to axons (nerve fibers). Most brain injuries are the result of both impact and inertial forces. See Michaud et al. (1997) and Heller et al. (1996) for more detailed descriptions of the specific types of brain injuries.

TBI may cause several types of visual impair-

Table 7.1. Seizure Recognition and First Aid

Seizure Type	What It Looks Like	What to Do	What Not to Do
Generalized Tonic Clonic (Also called Grand Mal)	Sudden cry, rigidity, followed by muscle jerks, shallow breathing or temporarily suspended breathing, bluish skin, possible loss of bladder control, usually lasts a couple of minutes. Normal breathing then starts again. There may be some confusion and/or fatigue, followed by return to full consciousness.	Look for medical identification. Protect from nearby hazards. Loosen ties or shirt collars. Protect head from injury. Turn on side to keep airway clear unless injury exists. Reassure as consciousness returns. If single seizure lasted less than 5 minutes, ask if hospital evaluation wanted. If multiple seizures, or if one seizure lasts longer than 5 minutes, call an ambulance. If person is pregnant, injured, or diabetic, call for aid at once.[a]	Don't put any hard implement in the mouth. Don't try to hold tongue. It can't be swallowed. Don't try to give liquids during or just after seizure. Don't use artificial respiration unless breathing is absent after muscle jerks subside, or unless water has been inhaled. Don't restrain.
Absence (Also called Petit Mal)	A blank stare, beginning and ending abruptly, lasting only a few seconds, most common in children. May be accompanied by rapid blinking, some chewing movements of the mouth. Child or adult is unaware of what's going on during the seizure, but quickly returns to full awareness once it has stopped. May result in learning difficulties if not recognized and treated.	No first aid necessary, but if this is the first observation of the seizure(s), medical evaluation should be recommended.	
Simple Partial	Jerking may begin in one area of body, arm, leg, or face. Can't be stopped, but patient stays awake and aware. Jerking may proceed from one area of the body to become a convulsive seizure. Partial sensory seizures may not be obvious to an onlooker. Patient experiences a distorted environment. May see or hear things that aren't	No first aid necessary unless seizure becomes convulsive, then first aid as above. No immediate action needed other than reassurance and emotional support.	

Seizure Type	Description	First Aid
(continued)	there, may feel unexplained fear, sadness, anger, or joy. May have nausea, experience odd smells, and have a generally "funny" feeling in the stomach.	Medical evaluation should be recommended.
Complex Partial (Also called Psychomotor or Temporal Lobe)	Usually starts with blank stare, followed by chewing, followed by random activity. Person appears unaware of surroundings, may seem dazed and mumble. Unresponsive. Actions clumsy, not directed. May pick at clothing, pick up objects, try to take clothes off. May run, appear afraid. May struggle or flail at restraint. Once pattern established, same set of actions usually occur with each seizure. Lasts a few minutes, but post-seizure confusion can last substantially longer. No memory of what happened during seizure period.	Speak calmly and reassuringly to patient and others. Guide gently away from obvious hazards. Stay with person until completely aware of environment. Offer to help getting home. Don't grab hold unless sudden danger (such as a cliff edge or an approaching car) threatens. Don't try to restrain. Don't shout. Don't expect verbal instructions to be obeyed.
Atonic Seizures (Also called Drop Attacks)	A child or adult suddenly collapses and falls. After 10 seconds to a minute he recovers, regains consciousness, and can stand and walk again.	No first aid needed (unless he hurt himself as he fell), but the child should be given a thorough medical evaluation.
Myoclonic Seizures	Sudden brief, massive muscle jerks that may involve the whole body or parts of the body. May cause person to spill what they were holding or fall off a chair.	No first aid needed, but should be given a thorough medical evaluation.
Infantile Spasms	These are clusters of quick, sudden movements that start between 3 months and two years. If a child is sitting up, the head will fall forward, and the arms will flex forward. If lying down, the knees will be drawn up, with arms and head flexed forward as if the baby is reaching for support.	No first aid, but doctor should be consulted.

Source: Reprinted, by permission, from Epilepsy Foundation of America. *Seizure Recognition and First Aid.* (Landover, MD: Author, 1998).

[a]*No need to call an ambulance:* (1) If medical I.D. jewelry or card says "epilepsy," *and* (2) If the seizure ends in under five minutes, *and* (3) If consciousness returns without further incident, *and* (4) If there are no signs of injury, physical distress, or pregnancy.

ments that can affect a student's visual acuity and/or visual fields, and the severity can range from mild visual impairment to total blindness (Gerring & Carney, 1992). Two common visual impairments are diplopia (double vision), caused by eye-muscle palsy, and nystagmus (rapid, involuntary movement of the eyeballs), caused by injury to the cerebellum. Two less common injuries that affect the eyes are a crush injury (from a blow by a blunt object) and a missile injury (from a gunshot), both of which sever a portion of the visual pathway and cause irreversible damage. Severe brain swelling caused by a TBI can result in cortical blindness that may go away fully or partially over time (Michaud et al., 1997). Since the vision of students with TBI may fluctuate, ongoing visual evaluations are essential to help students function visually as efficiently as possible.

Students with visual impairments and TBI may also have a unilateral sensorineural hearing loss, caused by a fracture of the temporal bone or transverse fractures of the cochlea of the ear, and a unilateral conductive hearing loss, caused by fractures of the middle-ear structures (Healy, 1982; Michaud et al., 1997). Therefore, hearing assessments are important so the student can obtain amplification, if necessary, to use all his or her remaining senses.

Impact on Learning

Children and youths with visual impairments and TBI can have myriad difficulties that have an impact on their learning. Depending on the nature and the severity of the TBI, some of these difficulties may be minimal or last for a short period, while others may be significant and last indefinitely. Recovery from TBI usually occurs rapidly during the first few months; then significant improvements continue during the first year. This progress becomes slower, and a gradual recovery of deficits may occur up to 5 years following the injury (Behrman, 1992). This section describes specific difficulties that may occur in students' cognitive, communication, motor, and behavioral areas of functioning.

Students with visual impairments and TBI usually have cognitive impairments that result in problems with both short-term memory, essential for new learning, and long-term memory, needed for retaining previously learned material. They also have difficulty returning to a specific task after a pause or interruption and become confused or misinterpret what is required of them because of their inconsistent memory function (National Task Force, 1988). In addition, like students with learning disabilities, they may be easily distracted and have poor concentration. These students also find it difficult to follow instructions and shift attention from one activity to another and to organize and process information (and therefore have problems with summarizing, sequencing, outlining, and problem solving) (Dalby & Obrzut, 1991; Hanson & Clippard, 1992; Kreutzer, Devany, Myers, & Marwitz, 1991; National Task Force, 1988; Rosen, 1998).

Students with visual impairments and TBI may have speech and language impairments that accompany cognitive impairments following their injuries that cause a slower rate of speech, dysarthria (slurred speech), and aphasia (impairment of receptive or expressive language) (Chapman, 1995). They have difficulty naming things, retrieving words, abstracting, distinguishing relevant from less relevant information, and organizing ideas expressively. In addition, when required to read and write information, they tend to respond at a slower rate and need extra time beyond that of students with only visual impairments (Heller et al., 1996; Rosen, 1998).

In the area of motor functioning, these students may have some of the same motor impairments as those with cerebral palsy discussed previously. These include abnormal muscle tone, reduced motor speed, and loss of motor coordination (Rosen, 1998). They may also exhibit behavioral challenges, such as hyperactivity or hypoactivity, inattention, emotional swings (for example, laughing or crying inappropriately) and aggression (for instance, hitting or talking out of turn), and a lower tolerance for stress and frustration. Some may overreact; become restless, irritable, and destructive; have temper tantrums; and lack goal-directed behavior. Others may become withdrawn and apathetic and be poorly motivated. Frequently, these students are unaware of their inappropriate behaviors, have poor relationships with their peers, and lack the internal feedback to correct their behavior (Hanson & Clippard, 1992; Michaud et al., 1997).

VISUAL IMPAIRMENTS AND ORTHOPEDIC AND HEALTH IMPAIRMENTS

Several orthopedic and health impairments are associated with visual impairments. They include juvenile rheumatoid arthritis, sickle-cell anemia, acquired immunodeficiency syndrome (AIDS), and Type I (juvenile-onset) diabetes.

IDEA (1990, sec. 300.5) defined orthopedic disabilities and health impairments as follows:

Severe orthopedic impairments adversely affect a child's educational performance and include impairments caused by congenital anomaly (e.g., clubfoot, absence of some member, etc.), impairments caused by disease (e.g., phliomyelitis, bone tuberculosis, etc.), and impairments from other causes (e.g., cerebral palsy, amputations, and fractures and burns which cause contractures). . . . Health impairments comprise physical conditions that affect educational performance, including limited strength, vitality, or alertness, due to chronic health problems such as heart conditions, tuberculosis, rheumatic fever, nephritis, asthma, sickle cell anemia, hemophilia, or diabetes.

Juvenile Rheumatoid Arthritis (JRA). JRA refers to chronic inflammation of the joints that affects children and youths under age 22. Sometimes called Still's disease, it is characterized by inflammation of the joints, pain when joints are moved, stiffness after immobility, limitations in the motion of joints, and sometimes fever (Heller et al., 1996). The severity of the symptoms can vary greatly from one time of the day to another, from day to day, and from month to month. Some stu-

dents with JRA develop iritis (inflammation of the iris) that causes photobia (hypersensitivity to light) and blurred vision (Rosen, 1998). It is important for these students to use nonglare materials and to be positioned so that they do not face bright light.

Although no cognitive impairments are associated with JRA, the academic performance of students with JRA may vary, depending on the amount of pain and discomfort they feel. Sometimes students with visual impairments may need extended keys for computers or braillewriters to reduce the pressure in the fingers.

Sickle-cell Anemia. Sickle-cell anemia is an inherited disorder whereby red blood cells, instead of being round, have pinched-in sides and are shaped like sickles, resulting in their inability to flow smoothly through blood vessels. The walls of these red cells rupture, destroying the blood cells. This reduction in blood cells and their reduced ability to carry oxygen cause students to be chronically anemic, which retards their growth and leads to other developmental disorders (Rosen, 1998). Some students with this disorder who also have had an injury to the brain may have damage to the optic nerve or cortex. They may have central vision or peripheral vision losses that require the assistance of trained teachers of students with visual impairments.

Acquired Immune Deficiency Syndrome (AIDS). AIDS is the final stage in the progression of the human immunodeficiency virus (HIV), which weakens the body's immune system and gradually infects and destroys important cells that protect the body from disease. HIV infection in infants frequently occurs either prenatally or during birth and sometimes through breast-feeding. Two-thirds of the children who are born with HIV do not have symptoms until they are age 2–5 (Mintz, 1996). Then they develop opportunistic infections (those that generally do not affect the general population) that damage both the immune system and the central nervous system. Some of these infections cause the loss of cognitive abilities, seizures, and visual impairments (Turnbull, Turnbull, Shank, & Leal, 1999).

Some children with AIDS develop cytomegalovirus, which damages the retina and results in severe visual impairment and blindness. Others develop severe infections of the central nervous system, such as toxoplasmosis and cryptoccoccal meningitis, that damage the optic nerve and result in diplopia or difficulty in moving the eyes (Rosen, 1998).

Type I, or Juvenile-onset Diabetes. Type I diabetes usually develops between the ages of 10 and 16. The pancreas stops producing insulin or sufficient insulin, and injections of insulin are necessary to prevent unused sugar from building up in the blood. Monitoring blood sugar is critical to prevent diabetic emergencies and reduce some long-term effects that include blindness, kidney failure, and poor circulation. Students with Type I diabetes sometimes develop diabetic retinopathy in their teens and early 20s, characterized by scotomas (patches of vision loss in the visual field where the retina has been damaged by the disease) (Rosen, 1998); the associated vision losses become worse over time, leading to total blindness. Students who have vision losses frequently need adaptive devices to monitor their sugar levels and administer their own insulin injections. (See Rosen, 1999, and Heller et al., 1996, for more detailed information on these conditions that are associated with visual impairments.)

VISUAL AND AUDITORY IMPAIRMENTS (DEAF-BLINDNESS)

Definition

The definition of deaf-blindness in IDEA (1990) states:

> [T]he term "deaf-blind," with respect to children and youth, means having auditory and visual impairments, the combination of which creates such severe communication and other develop-

ment and learning needs that they cannot be appropriately educated in special education programs solely for children and youth with hearing impairment, visual impairment, or severe disabilities, without assistance to address the educational needs due to these dual, concurrent disabilities.

Characteristics

According to the 1997 National Deaf-blind Census, conducted by the U.S. Department of Education, Office of Special Education Programs (Baldwin & Hembree, 1998), 11,176 children and youths were identified as deaf-blind in that year. This number has increased in recent years, possibly because of improved child-count procedures. In rare instances, some children are born with significant hearing and vision losses or acquire both losses early. For these children, called congenitally deaf-blind, visual and auditory information is inaccessible, and they need to rely on their other senses for gaining information about the environment. Most children and youths who are identified as deaf-blind at birth or in infancy, or early childhood have either some useful vision or some useful hearing (Prickett & Welch, 1995b). Distance sensory information is accessible to them, although it is limited and distorted. They can acquire information from these senses (vision or hearing), as well as their other senses of touch, smell, taste, and movement. Other children are born with the loss of one distance sense and lose the other distance sense later in childhood after they have acquired basic early childhood concepts. These students have either early visual impairment and later hearing impairment or early hearing impairment and later visual impairment (Prickett & Welch, 1998; Sauerburger, 1993).

In addition to the types of combinations of visual and auditory impairments just described, some students have sensory losses that are progressive or fluctuate daily. Therefore, their sensory access to information from the environment may be irregular and unpredictable or is gradually reduced as the student gets older (as in Usher syndrome, described in the next section).

Frequently, students who are deaf-blind also have additional disabilities. These disabilities include cognitive impairments, cerebral palsy, and seizure disorders.

Common Syndromes

The eyes and the ears develop during the first 12 weeks of pregnancy, both originate from some of the same types of embryonic cells and tissue, and are anatomically similar in some ways (Heller & Kennedy, 1993; Regenbogen & Coscas, 1985). Therefore, it is easy to understand why some prenatal syndromes and conditions cause injury to both organs and result in deaf-blindness. This section describes several genetic disorders and syndromes that are associated with both auditory and visual impairments.

CHARGE Association

Children with CHARGE association are a heterogeneous group who exhibit at least four of the six abnormalities indicated by the letters of the acronym. The cause of this syndrome is unknown. The critical features are these:

- Coloboma: an ocular deformity involving absence of part of the eye. It is a slit or groove in the iris, ciliary body, choroid, or retina that is caused by the failure of the optic cleft to close completely at about 6 weeks of fetal life. It can range from no visual impairment to a small eye (microphthalmia) to a missing eye (anophthalmia). Coloboma of the iris may reduce a child's ability to adjust to bright light; coloboma of the retina will cause blank areas in a child's visual field.

- Heart defects: defects in the heart present from birth, including ventricular septal defects, patent ductus arteriosus, and bicuspid aortic valve.

- Atresia of the choanae (nasal passage): refers to a narrowing or blockage of the passages between the nasal cavity and the na-

sopharynx (windpipe). If it is bilateral (both sides), an infant will be in severe respiratory distress and will die from asphyxiation unless it is corrected.

- Retardation of growth and/or development: low physical growth norms and/or mental retardation. Children are short and/or mentally retarded.

- Genital hypoplasia: incomplete or underdevelopment of the external genitals in males; it is rare in females.

- Ear malformations: abnormal shape (large or small) or absence of the outer ear, smallness of the ear canal, malformation of the bones in the middle ear, and/or high-frequency sensorineural hearing loss as a result of damage to the inner ear. Mixed hearing loss (a combination of conductive and sensorineural losses), from mild to profound is the most common type of hearing loss in children with this disorder (Heller & Kennedy, 1993; Regenbogen & Coscas, 1985).

Cockayne Syndrome and Cornelia de Lange Syndrome

Cockayne syndrome is an autosomal-recessive progressive disorder, characterized by retinitis pigmentosa (RP) with optic atrophy, deafness, dwarfism, and mental retardation. In one form of the syndrome, symptoms appear after birth, and children live only until age 5 or 6. In the second form, the symptoms develop during the second year, and the syndrome progresses for 20 years (Regenbogen & Coscas, 1985). In the second form, hearing is usually normal at birth, but a progressive sensorineural loss develops in both ears and results in a moderate-to-severe hearing loss. Visual impairments caused by RP result in a gradual loss of vision in the peripheral field, night blindness, and eventually total blindness when the person is in his or her 20s (Heller & Kennedy, 1993).

Cornelia de Lange syndrome is a genetic syndrome that results in visual impairments, including hyperopia (farsightedness); sensorineural hearing impairments, and mental retardation. Children who are born with this syndrome have common physical appearances that include excessive body hair, thick continuous eyebrows, and possibly cleft palates.

Usher Syndrome

Usher syndrome, a hereditary condition, is the leading cause of deaf-blindness in adults. It is autosomal recessive and consists of a combined congenital hearing loss and slowly progressive RP. In Type 1, children are born profoundly deaf and develop RP usually in adolescence or early adulthood. In Type 2, children are born with a moderate hearing loss and develop RP usually in adolescence or in early adulthood. The loss of vision begins with night blindness and progresses to tunnel vision and sometimes to total blindness in adulthood (Heller & Kennedy, 1993; Mar, 1991–92).

Intrauterine Infections—STORCH

Intrauterine infections that are passed from the mother to the embryo via the placenta may cause fetal malformations. A group of the most prevalent infections are referred to by the mnemonic acronym, STORCH—syphillis (S), toxoplasmosis (T), varicella and other congenital infections (O), rubella (R), cytomegalovirus (C), and herpes simplex virus (H). If these infections occur early in a pregnancy, they are likely to cause visual and auditory impairments as well as other anomalies. (See Table 7.2 for frequently found impairments of STORCH congenital infections.)

Congenital Rubella Syndrome

Congenital rubella syndrome (CRS), a STORCH infection, is described in detail here, since it was the most common viral cause of birth defects in infants whose mothers had the rubella virus during their first three months of pregnancy. Infants who are born with CRS are those most likely to have visual and auditory impairments and other multiple disabilities. Since the development of the rubella vaccine, which is given to all infants aged 12–15 months, the incidence of maternal rubella has decreased substantially. Fewer than 100 cases occur annually in the United States (Miller et al., 1994). It is important to note that infants with this syndrome can transmit the virus up to age 2; therefore, nonimmunized women who are health care workers and become pregnant are at great risk of contracting rubella.

The types of visual impairments in children with CRS include cataracts; keratoconus; pigmentary retinopathy; and sometimes secondary glaucoma, microophthalmia, strabismus, and optic nerve atrophy. In addition to visual impairments, some children with CRS whose mothers contracted the virus during the first trimester may have sensorineural hearing losses in both ears, from mild hearing impairment to profound deafness, and mild conductive losses. Other defects that children with CRS have include cardiac defects; mental retardation; movement problems; balance difficulties caused by vestibular involvement; excessive behaviors, such as self-injury, aggression, sensory stimulation, and emotional difficulties; specific learning problems; and delayed-onset problems, such as diabetes (Heller & Kennedy, 1993; Mar, 1991–92). (See Heller and Kennedy (1993) for a detailed description of syndromes and disorders that result in combined visual and auditory impairments.)

Impact on Learning

The degree, type, and age of onset of the visual and auditory impairment influence how an individual gains access to, obtains, and uses information for learning (Prickett & Welch, 1995b). Students with a progressive form of deaf-blindness continuously have to find alternate ways to acquire sensory information throughout their lives. They can become frustrated in activities that need to be modified because of changes in visual or auditory functioning and grieve for each major change (Duncan, Prickett, Finkelstein, Vernon, & Hollingsworth, 1988).

The combined losses of vision and hearing severely affect numerous areas of learning, including communication skills, concept development,

Table 7.2. Frequently Found Impairments of STORCH Congenital Infections

	Syphilis	Toxoplasmosis	Rubella	CMV	Herpes
Eye/vision impairments	X	X	X	X	X
Ear/auditory impairments	X	X	X	X	X
Anemia	X	X	X	X	X
Brain calcifications		X		X	
Bone abnormalities			X		
Congenital heart defects			X		
Encephalitis	X	X	X	X	X
Hydrocephalus		X	X	X	X
Jaundice	X	X	X	X	X
Liver/spleen enlarged	X	X	X	X	X
Low birth weight	X	X	X	X	X
Low platelet count	X	X	X	X	X
Microcephaly	X	X	X	X	X
Pneumonia			X	X	X
Seizures	X	X	X	X	X
Skin rash	X	X	X	X	X

Source: Reprinted, with permission, from K. Heller and C. Kennedy, *Etiologies and Characteristics of Deaf-Blindness.* (Monmouth, OR: Teaching Research Publications, 1994).

O&M, social skills, and academic skills. In the area of communication, students with deaf-blindness do not receive the language input from caregivers that they learn to interpret meaningfully in relation to their experiences. Because of the lack of eye contact, body language, tone of voice, inflection, and other nonverbal cues, they are unable to acquire satisfactory communication skills (Chen, 1995a; Chen & Haney, 1995). Difficulty gaining access to important environmental information because of the lack of or reduced vision and hearing also causes significant delays in the development of concepts. In the area of O&M, these students are unable to use auditory cues that assist those with only visual impairments to move from one location to another or to locate a person or object. Without visual and auditory cues, they are unable to use modeling and imitation to interact socially with their families and peers. In addition, these combined disabilities significantly hamper their abilities to acquire academic skills in written language and specific content areas, such as mathematics and science.

Support Personnel

Students with deaf-blindness need assistance from others to enable them to participate effectively with their teachers, peers, and other people in school and the community. Since both auditory information and visual information are totally or minimally inaccessible to them, they require specialized services from an interpreter or an intervenor (Prickett & Welch, 1998).

An interpreter for a student who is deaf-blind has an additional role besides conveying auditory information. He or she also may serve as a sighted guide to help the student move from class to class and may present visual information, such as material on a chalkboard or a printed handout, to the student (Prickett & Welch, 1998). Such an individual may have fewer formal qualifications than an interpreter for individuals who are deaf and may be hired as an "educational interpreter" or an "interpreter-tutor" or an "interpreter-teaching aide" (Prickett & Welch, 1995a).

Intervenors, who are used primarily in Canada and other countries, are "individuals who assist people who are deaf-blind to gather information for daily living" (Prickett & Welch, 1995a, p. 185). In addition to their roles as interpreters, they may read a person's mail, drive a person to a physician's office, and interpret for the person during medical appointments.

VISUAL IMPAIRMENTS AND BEHAVIORAL DISORDERS

Characteristics

Children and youths with visual impairments may have various types of behavioral disorders that interfere with their educational functioning. Many are served in programs for students with visual impairments, with and without the necessary support personnel who are qualified to work with students with behavioral disorders (Scholl, 1986). Emotional disturbance, as defined in IDEA (1999), includes five major criteria for identification:

i. The term means a condition exhibiting one or more of the following characteristics over a long period of time and to a marked degree, which adversely affects educational performance.

a. An inability to learn which cannot be explained by intellectual, sensory and health factors;

b. An inability to build or maintain satisfactory interpersonal relationships with peers and teachers.

c. Inappropriate types of behavior or feelings under normal circumstances;

d. A general pervasive mood of unhappiness or depression; or

e. A tendency to develop physical symptoms or fears associated with personal or school problems.

ii. The term includes children who are schizophrenic. The term does not include children who are socially maladjusted unless it is determined that they have an emotional disturbance.

It is important to identify behavioral problems and their causes accurately in students with visual impairments. For example, a teacher may label a specific student inattentive because the student is not paying any attention to visual cues of an activity. Since students who are blind or who have low vision may not orient visually or maintain eye contact with objects or individuals, they may become distracted easily when the visual information has no meaning or is unrelated to their concrete experiences. This behavior should not be misconstrued as an inattentiveness problem. A student with a visual impairment may exhibit hyperactivity (does not stay in his or her seat without constant reminders or jumps up when he or she hears a loud, unfamiliar sound). These disruptive behaviors may be a result of missing visual cues, such as modeling and imitation, rather than of severe emotional problems (Mar & Cohen, 1998; Van Hasselt, 1987).

Some students with visual impairments have such severe behavioral and emotional problems that they are unable to attend or relate socially to others and therefore cannot participate in any structured activities or daily routines in school. These students are described as having a pervasive developmental disorder, and some are diagnosed as having autism or autistic-like behaviors. The characteristics of these conditions include the inability to respond when addressed by name, the failure to respond to an interaction initiated by a teacher or peer, lack of interest in activities that are popular with other students, and the persistent refusal to be in close proximity or physical contact with others.

Although no direct relationship between visual impairments and autism has been documented, some studies have found a relatively high incidence of autistic-like behaviors in students with visual impairments and other disabilities (Fraiberg, 1977; Rogers & Newhart-Larson, 1989). Autism, is defined as follows in IDEA (1999):

> A developmental disability significantly affecting verbal and nonverbal communication and social interaction, generally evident before age 3, that adversely affects a child's educational performance. Other characteristics often associated with autism are engagement in repetitive activities and stereotyped movements, resistance to environmental change or change in daily routines, and unusual responses to sensory experiences. The term does not apply if a child's educational performance is adversely affected primarily because the child has an emotional disturbance. . . .

Effects on Learning

Teachers of students with visual impairments may observe various types of emotional and behavioral problems in their students that will have an impact on the students' learning. When these behaviors become relentless, they prevent students from acquiring knowledge and skills and from participating in structured activities, such as cooperative groups. These problems include self-stimulatory behaviors; hyperactivity, inattention, and impulsivity; disruptive behaviors, including acting-out and oppositional behaviors; social interaction problems; behaviors that threaten the safety of a student and/or peers; and problems of mood, affect, and emotional adjustment (Mar & Cohen, 1998). Some behaviors, such as hand flapping or waving fingers in front of the eyes, may interfere with both attending to a task and interacting with peers.

Students with visual impairments may express emotional and behavioral difficulties during daily routines in the classroom in infinite ways. There may be great variability in the frequency, duration, or intensity of these difficulties, as well as in the academic and social consequences to the student and his or her classmates (Mar & Cohen, 1998). In addition, a teacher may observe different behaviors in the class from those observed by a clinician in an isolated setting. These students frequently exhibit self-stimulatory or stereotypical behaviors that interfere with attending to and staying on tasks. The term sometimes used is blindisms; however, this term is inappropriate since these behaviors are not unique to this population (Freeman et al., 1989; Mar & Cohen, 1998; Warren, 1994). Some examples include eye pressing or flicking fingers in front of the eyes near fluorescent lights; body swaying, rocking, or twirling; head nodding. These may occur as a result of missing visual cues such as modeling. Others include twisting or pulling hair; and repeatedly manipulating objects (such as tapping or hitting an object or hand on oneself). One explanation of why students with visual impairments exhibit these behaviors is that they either increase or decrease the general level of stimulation (Freeman et al., 1989).

Some students with visual impairments experience fluctuations in their visual functioning from day to day, and some gradually lose their vision. These changes may cause a variety of severe emotional reactions and consequent behaviors. These students can become depressed, fearful, or angry and exhibit noncompliant behaviors, such as angry outbursts, refusal to participate in a learning activity, and exaggerated responses. They may need specific individual counseling or therapy (Mar & Cohen, 1998).

VISUAL IMPAIRMENTS AND GIFTEDNESS

Definitions and Characteristics

Children and youths with visual impairments also may have characteristics that would identify them as being gifted and talented. This group of exceptional children has superior ability or talent in certain areas of development that results in unique educational challenges for them, their families, and their educational programs (Kirk, Gallagher, & Anastasiow, 1993). During the past few decades, the term *giftedness* has been broadened to include other descriptors besides intellectual ability. According to the 1994 reauthorization of the Jacob K. Javits Gifted and Talented Students Education Act of 1988 (P.L. 103–382, Title xiv, p. 388):

> The term "gifted and talented" when used in respect to students, children or youth means students, children or youth who give evidence of high performance capability in areas such as intellectual, creative, artistic or leadership capability, or in specific academic fields, and who require services or activities not ordinarily provided by the school in order to fully develop such capabilities.

Children who have "high performance capability" may have superior ability but do not demonstrate it in their performance. Children who have "specific academic ability" may have exceptional ability in one academic field, but not in others. Furthermore, the terms *creative, artistic,* and *leadership capability* expand the definition of giftedness beyond the cognitive domain (Kirk et al., 2000).

Another definition that some researchers and practitioners use in schools, particularly in relation to some students with disabilities, is the one proposed by Gardner (1993). Gardner described eight specific intelligences; these multiple intelligences are musical, bodily-kinesthetic, linguistic, logical-mathematical, spatial, interpersonal, intrapersonal, and naturalistic. This theory moves educators away from emphasizing limitations and remediation; instead, it emphasizes finding personal strengths in all individuals and finding ways to compensate for their limitations to enhance learning outcomes (Eichinger & Downing, 1996; Silberman et al., 1998). By applying Gardner's theory, more children and youths with visual impairments could be identified more appropriately as gifted and talented. Students who are

blind can demonstrate superior intelligence by using a variety of alternate strategies. For example, a student who is blind can demonstrate linguistic intelligence by verbally responding to taped stories or by accessing technological devices that produce voice output. A student with low vision and mental retardation could demonstrate spatial intelligence by acquiring concepts through three-dimensional objects. Lawrence A. Becker (Hogg Foundation, 1981) described a student who was legally blind. The boy's early test results indicated that he had an IQ in the 30s, and his parents were advised to put him in an institution. His artwork was later appraised by a professor who was "thunderstruck by Richard's precise and inspiring realism" (Corn, 1986). This legally blind student was identifed as gifted (talented); however if the theory of multiple intelligence was used, he would be identified as having exceptional spatial intelligence.

Identification

It is difficult to identify students with visual impairments who also would be considered gifted and talented, since some of the characteristics of these students may mask their potential gifts. Obstacles to the identification of these students include stereotypic expectations, developmental delays, incomplete information about the students, inappropriate test instruments, and the lack of opportunities for students to demonstrate superior abilities (Corn, 1986; Johnsen & Corn, 1989; Whitmore & Maker, 1985). For example, a student with a visual impairment may not have had sufficient concrete experiences, rather than a lack of cognitive abilities, to respond to object words on a vocabulary test. This lack of prior experience would inhibit the emergence of gifts and talents. Corn (1986) noted that although it is easy to identify those who excel in all endeavors, for those whose gifts and talents have not been identified, educators must provide and interpret appropriate assessment processes to search for giftedness. In addition, some children may be overlooked in the referral process if an assessment instrument is not adapted for students with visual impairments. For example, a checklist that includes "is visually perceptive of the environment" and "understands abstract concepts" would not be a reliable indicator of giftedness for students with visual impairments (Johnsen & Corn, 1989).

Other characteristics of these students that would delay or prevent the recognition of their giftedness are learned helplessness, problems with social interactions and communication, and lack of attention to certain activities in their environment because of their lack of vision. Furthermore, a critical concern that affects the identification of this population is the need for students with visual impairments to learn both the general education curriculum as well as an expanded core curriculum that is disability specific (Corn, 1999) to enable them to lead independent lives and fulfill their maximum potential. The nature of the core curriculum and the expanded core curriculum is explored further in Chapters 9 and 10 of this volume, which also discuss the importance of educational teams in work with students with visual impairments, including those with additional exceptionalities.

SUMMARY

Students with visual impairments often have a range of other exceptionalities in addition to their visual impairment. The combinations of visual impairment with other disabilities or giftedness present unique challenges that must be met by a collaborative educational team that will work closely together to address all the needs of each student. This chapter has presented general characteristics of students with various exceptionalities including mental retardation, learning disabilities, neurological disabilities, orthopedic and health impairments, deaf-blindness, behavior disorders, and giftedness. While an understanding of the characteristics associated with each disability is important, it is critical to remember that it is the combination of these exceptionalities with blindness or low vision that must be examined and addressed individually for each student.

STUDY QUESTIONS

1. Why is it important for teachers of students with visual impairments to understand the range of other disabilities that may accompany visual impairment?

2. In what ways will the role of the teacher of students with visual impairments change when students have additional disabilities?

3. Why may students with visual impairments and additional disabilities be educated in a wider range of service delivery systems?

4. Interview a teacher of students with visual impairments. Ask the teacher what challenges he or she faces when working with a team of professionals to address the needs of students with additional disabilities. What are two concrete suggestions for meeting these challenges?

5. What impact does mental retardation have on the development of a student who also has a visual impairment?

6. What practical difficulties does cerebral palsy present to students who are visually impaired?

7. Why is deaf-blindness more than just a combination of blindness and deafness?

8. Why is it difficult to identify and serve students who are visually impaired and also gifted?

REFERENCES

American Association on Mental Retardation. (1992). *Mental retardation: Definition, classification, and systems of supports* (9th ed.). Washington, DC: Author.

Association for Persons with Severe Handicaps. (1989, May). *TASH resolutions and policy statements.* Seattle, WA: Author.

Baldwin, V., & Hembree, R. (1998). *Annual deaf-blind census: National deaf-blind child count summary.* Monmouth, OR: Teaching Research.

Batshaw, M. L. (Ed.) (1997). *Children with disabilities* (4th ed.). Baltimore, MD: Paul H. Brookes.

Behrman, R. E. (1992). *Nelson textbook of pediatrics.* Philadelphia: W. B. Saunders.

Berkow, R. (1992). *The Merck manual of diagnosis and therapy.* Rahway, NJ: Merck, Sharp & Dohme Research Laboratories.

Black, P. (1982). Visual disorders associated with cerebral palsy. *British Journal of Ophthalmology, 66,* 46–52.

Blair, E., & Stanley, R. (1985). Intraobserver agreement in the classification of cerebral palsy. *Developmental Medicine and Child Neurology, 25,* 615–622.

Brown, L. W. (1997). Seizure disorders. In M. L. Batshaw (Ed.), *Children with disabilities* (4th ed., pp. 553–594). Baltimore, MD: Paul H. Brookes.

Chapman, S. B. (1995). Discourse as an outcome measure in pediatric head-injured populations. In S. H. Broman & M. E. Michel (Eds.), *Traumatic head injury in children.* New York: Oxford University Press.

Chen, D. (1995a). The beginnings of communication: Early childhood. In K. M. Huebner, J. G. Prickett, T. R. Wedlch, & E. Joffee (Eds.), *Hand in hand: Essentials of communication and orientation and mobility for your students who are deaf-blind* (pp. 159–184). New York: AFB Press.

Chen, D. (1995b). Who are young children whose multiple disabilities include visual impairment? In D. Chen & J. Dote-Kwan (Eds.), *Starting points: Instructional practices for young children whose multiple disabilities include visual impairment* (pp.1–14). Los Angeles: Blind Children's Center.

Chen, D., & Haney, M. (1995). An early intervention model for infants who are deaf-blind. *Journal of Visual Impairment & Blindness, 89,* 213–221.

Corn, A. L. (1986). Gifted students who have a visual handicap: Can we meet their educational needs? *Education of the Visually Handicapped, 18,* 71–84.

Corn, A. L. (1999). Intellectually gifted children with sensory impairments. In S. Cline & D. Schwartz (Eds.), *Populations of gifted children.* Upper Saddle River, NJ: Merrill.

Dalby, P. R. & Obrzut, J. E. (1991). Epidemiologic characteristics and sequelae of closed head-injured children and adolescents: A review. *Developmental Neuropsychology, 7,* 35–68.

Duncan, E., Prickett, H., Finkelstein, D., Vernon, M., & Hollingsworth, T. (1988). *Usher syndrome: What it is, how to cope, and how to help.* Springfield, IL: Charles C Thomas.

Eichinger, J., & Downing, J.E. (1996). Instruction in the general education environment. In J. E. Downing (Ed.), *Including students with severe and multiple disabilities in typical classrooms: Practical strategies for teachers* (pp. 15–34). Baltimore, MD: Paul H. Brookes.

Fraiberg, S. (1977). *Insights from the blind.* New York: Basic Books.

Freeman, R. D., Goetz, E., Richards, D. P., Groenveld, M., Blockberger, S., Jan, J. E., & Sykanda, A. M. (1989). Blind children's early emotional development: Do we know enough to help? *Child: Care, Health, and Development, 15,* 3–28.

Gardner, H. (1993). *Multiple intelligences: The theory in practice.* New York: Basic Books.

Gerring, J. P., & Carney, J. (1992). *Head trauma: Strategies for educational reintegration.* San Diego: Singular Publishing.

Hanson, S. L., & Clippard, D. (1992). Assessment of children with traumatic brain injury: Planning for school reentry. *Physical Medicine and Rehabilitation: State of the Art Reviews, 6,* 483–494.

Hatlen, P. (1998). Foreword. In S. Z. Sacks & R. K. Silberman (Eds.), *Educating students who have visual impairments with other disabilities* (pp. xv–xvi). Baltimore, MD: Paul H. Brookes.

Healy, G. B. (1982). Current concepts in otolaryngology: Hearing loss and vertigo secondary to head injury. *New England Journal of Medicine, 306,* 1029–1031.

Heller, K. W., Alberto, P. A., Forney, P. E., Schwartzman, M. N. (1996). *Understanding physical, sensory, and health impairments.* Pacific Grove, CA: Brooks/Cole.

Heller, K. W., & Kennedy, C. (1993). *Etiologies and characteristics of deaf-blindness.* Monmouth, OR: Teaching Research.

Hogg Foundation for Mental Health. (1981). *A conversation with Lawrence A. Becker on the gifted-handicapped,* adapted from a radio series, "The Human Condition," produced by the Communication Center of the University of Texas, Austin. Author.

Holmes, G. L. (1992). The epilepsies. In R. B. David (Ed.), *Pediatric neurology* (pp. 185–228). Norwalk, CT: Appleton & Lange.

Individuals with Disabilities Education Act, P.L. 101–476. (1990). 20 U.S.C. 1400 et seq.

Johnsen, S. K., & Corn. A. L. (1989). The past, present, and future of education for gifted children with sensory and/or physical disabilities. *Reoper Review, 12.*

Kirk, S., Gallagher, J., & Anastasiow, N. (2000). *Educating exceptional children.* Boston: Houghton Mifflin.

Kreutzer, J. S., Devany, C. W., Myers, S. L., & Marwitz, J. H. (1991). Neurobehavioral outcome following traumatic brain injury. In J. S. Kreutzer & P. H. Wehman (Eds.), *Cognitive rehabilitation for persons with traumatic brain injury: A functional approach* (pp. 55–73). Baltimore, MD: Paul H. Brookes.

Lerner, J., (1997). *Learning disabilities: Theories, diagnoses, and teaching strategies* (7th ed.). Boston: Houghton Mifflin.

Levack, N., Stone, G., & Bishop, V. (1994). *Low vision: A resource guide with adaptations for students with visual impairments* (2nd ed.). Austin: Texas School for the Blind.

Lyon, G. R. (1996). Learning disabilities. *The Future of Children, 6,* 54–76.

Mar, H. (1991, December–1992, January). Deaf-blindness: Some causes and challenges. *California Deaf-Blind Services reSource, 4.*

Mar, H. H., & Cohen, E. J. (1998). Educating students with visual impairments who exhibit emotional and behavioral problems. In S. Z. Sacks & R. K. Silberman (Eds.), *Educating students who have visual impairments with other disabilities.* (pp. 263–302). Baltimore: Paul H. Brookes.

Mercer, C. D., & Mercer, A. R. (1997). *Students with learning disabilities* (5th ed.). Upper Saddle River, NJ: Prentice Hall.

Michaud, L., Duhaime, A. C., & Lazar, M. F. (1997). Traumatic brain injury. In M. L. Batshaw, (Ed.), *Children with disabilities* (4th ed., pp. 595–617). Baltimore, MD: Paul H. Brookes.

Miller, E., Tookey, P., Morgan, C. P., Hesketh, L., Brown, D., Waight, P., Vurdien, J., Jones, G., & Peckham, C. (1994). Rubella surveillance to June 1994: Third joint report from the PHLS and the National Congenital Rubella Surveillance Programme: Communicable disease report. *CDR Review, 4,* 146–152.

Miller, S. P. (1996). Perspectives on mathematics instruction. In D. D. Deshler, E. S. Ellis, & B. K. Lenz (Eds.), *Teaching adolescence with learning disabilities: Strategies and methods* (2nd ed., pp. 313–367). Denver: Love.

Mintz, M. (1996). Neurological and developmental problems in pediatrc HIV infection. *Journal of Nutrition, 10* (Suppl.), 2663S–2673S.

Mirenda, P. (1999). Augmentative and alternative communicative techniques. In J. E. Downing, *Teaching communication skills to students with severe disabilities.* (pp.). Baltimore, MD: Paul H. Brookes.

National Task Force on Special Education for Students and Youths with Traumatic Brain Injury. (1988). *An educator's manual: What educators need to know about students with traumatic brain injury.* Framingham, MA: National Head Injury Foundation.

Nelson, L. B. (1984). *Pediatric ophthalmology.* Philadelphia: W. B. Saunders.

Orelove, F. P., & Sobsey, D. (Eds). (1996). *Educating children with multiple disabilities: A transdisciplinary approach* (3rd ed.). Baltimore, MD: Paul H. Brookes.

Pellegrino, L. (1997). Cerebral palsy. In M. L. Batshaw (Ed.), *Children with disabilities* (4th ed., pp. 499–528). Baltimore, MD: Paul H. Brookes.

Prickett, J. G., & Welch, T. R. (1995a). Adapting environments to support the inclusion of students who are deaf-blind. In N. G. Haring & L. T. Romer (Eds.), *Welcoming students who are deaf-blind into typical classrooms: Facilitating school participation, learning, and friendships* (pp. 171–193). Baltimore, MD: Paul H. Brookes.

Prickett, J. G., & Welch, T. R. (1995b). Deaf-blindness: Implications for learning. In K. M. Huebner, J. G. Prickett, T. R. Welch, & E. Joffee (Eds.), *Hand in hand: Essentials of communication and orientation and mobility for your students who are deaf-blind* (pp. 25–60). New York: AFB Press.

Prickett, J. G., & Welch, T.R.(1998). Educating students who are deaf-blind. In S. Z. Sacks & R. K. Silberman (Eds.), *Educating students who have visual impairments with other disabilities* (pp. 139–160). Baltimore, MD: Paul H. Brookes.

Public Law 103-82-Title XIV. (1988). Jacob K. Javits Gifted and Talented Students Education Act.

Rainforth, B., & York-Barr, J. (1997). *Collaborative teams for students with severe disabilities* (2nd ed.). Baltimore, MD: Paul H. Brookes.

Regenbogen, L., & Coscas, G. (1985). *Oculo-auditory syndromes.* New York: Masson.

Rogers, S. J. & Newhart-Larson, S. (1989). Characteristics of infantile autism in five children with Leber's congenital amaurosis. *Developmental Medicine and Child Neurology, 31,* 598–608.

Rosen, S. (1998). Educating students who have visual impairments with neurological disabilities. In S. Z. Sacks & R. K. Silberman (Eds.), *Educating students who have visual impairments with other disabilities* (pp. 221–262). Baltimore, MD: Paul H. Brookes.

Sacks, S. Z. (1998). Education of students who have visual impairments with other disabilities: An overview. In S. Z. Sacks & R. K. Silberman (Eds.), *Educating students who have visual impairments with other disabilities* (pp. 3–38). Baltimore, MD: Paul H. Brookes.

Sauerburger, D. (1993). *Independence without sight or sound.* New York: American Foundation for the Blind.

Schenk-Rootlieb, A. J. F., van Nieuwenhuizen, O., & van der Graaf, Y. (1992). The prevalence of cerebral visual disturbance in children with cerebral palsy. *Developmental Medicine and Child Neurology, 34,* 473–480.

Scher, M. S., Belfar, H., Martin, J., & Painter, M. J. (1991). Destructive brain lesions of presumed fetal onset: Antepartum causes of cerebral palsy. *Pediatrics, 88,* 898–906.

Scholl, G. T. (1986). Growth and development. In G. T. Scholl (Ed.), *Foundations of education for blind and visually handicapped children and youth: Theory and practice* (pp. 65–81). New York: American Foundation for the Blind.

Silberman, R. K. (1986). Severe multiple handicaps. In G. T. Scholl (Ed.), *Foundations of education for blind and visually handicapped children and youth: Theory and practice* (pp. 145–164). New York: American Foundation for the Blind.

Silberman, R. K., Sacks, S. Z., & Wolfe, J. (1998). Instructional strategies. In S. Z. Sacks & R. K. Silberman (Eds.), *Educating students who have visual impairments with other disabilities* (pp. 101–138). Baltimore, MD: Paul H. Brookes.

Silberman, R. K., & Sowell, V. (1987). The visually impaired student with learning disabilities: Strategies for success in language arts. *Education of the Visually Handicapped, 18,* 139–149.

Silberman, R. K., & Sowell, V. (1998). Educating students who have visual impairments with learning disabilities. In S. Z. Sacks & R. K. Silberman (Eds.), *Educating students who have visual impairments with other disabilities* (pp.161–185). Baltimore, MD: Paul H. Brookes.

The Association for Persons with Severe Handicaps. (1989, May). *TASH resolutions and policy statements.* Seattle, WA: Author.

Turnbull, A., Turnbull, R., Shank, M., & Leal, D. (1999). *Exceptional lives: Special education in today's schools.* Upper Saddle River, NJ: Merrill/Prentice Hall.

Tuttle, D. W. (1986). Educational programming. In G. T. Scholl (Ed.), *Foundations of education for blind and visually handicapped children and youth: Theory and practice* (pp. 239–254). New York: American Foundation for the Blind.

Van Hasselt, B. B. (1987). Behavior therapy for visually impaired persons. In M. Hersen, P. Miller, & R. M. Eisler (Eds.), *Progress in behavior modification* (Vol. 32, pp. 13–44). Thousand Oaks, CA: Sage Publications.

Warren, D. H. (1994). *Blindness and children: An individual differences approach.* New York: Cambridge University Press.

Westling, D. L., & Fox, L. (2000). Teaching students with severe disabilities (2nd ed.). Upper Saddle River, NJ: Prentice-Hall.

Whitmore, J.R., & Maker, C. J. (1985). *Intellectual giftedness in disabled persons.* Rockville, MD: Aspen Systems Corporation.

CHAPTER **8**

Multicultural Issues
Madeline Milian

KEY POINTS

◆ Teachers of students with visual impairments, like all teachers, will encounter students who come from diverse cultural, religious, and language groups, regardless of the geographic area in which they work.

◆ It is essential for teachers to develop sensitivity to students' diversity and learn effective teaching strategies to work with culturally and linguistically diverse students.

◆ Teaching culturally and linguistically diverse students with visual impairments requires a great deal of professional collaboration.

◆ When students are learning English as a second language (ESL), programs need to be modified to address their language needs.

◆ University programs and school districts need to provide opportunities for preservice and in service teachers to obtain knowledge and skills that will facilitate their work with culturally and linguistically diverse students.

> *We do not really see through our eyes or hear through our ears,*
> *but through our beliefs.*
> —Lisa Delpit (1995, p. 46)

As the student population continues to become more diverse, professionals need to prepare them-

selves to gain a better understanding of the implications of diversity when working with students with visual impairments and their families. Cultural values and beliefs influence the manner in which students and families perceive their needs and interact with teachers and other school personnel. They also influence the ways in which students and families perceive visual impairment and the degree to which they accept recommendations from medical personnel or teachers. Consequently, to be more effective, teachers need to be sensitive to the cultural diversity of students who attend their schools.

This chapter has three major goals. The first goal is to remind practicing teachers, college professors, administrators, and future teachers of their responsibility to educate themselves about and advocate for the educational rights of students who come from diverse ethnic and racial backgrounds, which, in many communities, constitute the majority of the teachers' caseload. The second goal is to challenge all professionals to examine their views and beliefs about educating students from diverse backgrounds. Although it is important to learn effective teaching strategies for working with this population, it is equally important to examine one's beliefs and expectations about these students' abilities and potential. The third goal is to show that diversity offers unlimited opportunities for professionals to learn more about themselves, their students, their colleagues, and other members of their communities. When they view diversity as an asset, professionals learn to incorporate aspects of it into their teaching, and thus their instruction becomes more culturally relevant and appropriate to their students.

DEFINITION OF DIVERSITY

Diversity has come to signify the heterogeneous nature of this society. It has a broad meaning that can refer to human characteristics, such as culture, language, race, class, disability, age, and sex; personal affiliations to religious and political groups or ideologies; or sexual orientation. Diversity has always existed in U.S. schools, but the assimilationist philosophy that long ruled the educational system either ignored or tried to eradicate it. In the case of students with disabilities, appropriate education was often denied. Today, the term *diversity* implies a positive view of the differences of students and often the desire to integrate students' unique differences into the curriculum so they can be validated.

The shift in the view of diversity can be attributed partly to the social changes that took place in the 1960s and 1970s and the expansion of the legal, educational, and civil rights of students and their parents. In 1954, *Brown v. Board of Education* established that racially segregated schools were unequal; in 1964, Title VII of the Civil Rights Act prohibited discrimination based on race, color, religion, or national origin; in 1974, *Lau v. Nichols* ruled in favor of Chinese students in San Francisco by stating that the civil rights of students who did not understand the language of instruction were being violated when the students were provided with the same facilities, textbooks, teachers, and curriculum as students who spoke English. In 1975, perhaps the most significant legislation on behalf of students with disabilities, the Education for All Handicapped Children Act, now known as the Individuals with Disabilities Education Act (IDEA), mandated educational services for all students with disabilities in public schools and ended decades of educational neglect for many stu-

dents (Nieto, 1996; Schwartz & Dunnick Karge, 1996; Sleeter & Grant, 1993).

DIVERSITY AND VISUAL IMPAIRMENTS

Included in the notion of diversity are a number of human characteristics that may not be easily quantified and hence for which limited or no information is available. Statistics on other personal characteristics, such as sex, age, race, ethnicity, and language status, have been collected in a number of studies and are included here.

Using data from the 1994–95 U.S. Bureau of the Census's Survey of Income and Program Participation (SIPP) section on Disability Status of Persons, McNeil (1997) reported that 8.8 million people over age 6 have difficulty seeing and 1.6 million are unable to see at all. Although information was not provided according to sex, an earlier report by McNeil (1993), based on 1991–92 data from SIPP, stated that there were 11.2 million people with visual impairments, including 4.6 million men and 6.6 million women. Kirchner and Schmeidler (1999) compared the rates of visual impairments among whites, blacks, and Hispanics in the United States using data from the National Center for Health Statistics. They explained that age is a critical factor to consider in comparing these three groups, since differences among the groups are not as evident when one compares the overall rates of visual impairments as when one compares the rates of specific age groups older than age 22.

According to information gathered for the federally funded Project PRISM (Ferrell, 1998) on 202 infants and toddlers with visual impairments in Arizona, California, Colorado, Kentucky, New Mexico, Massachusetts, and Texas, 61 percent of the children were white, 15.9 percent were Hispanic, 4.9 percent were African American, 1.1 percent were Native American, and 17.0 percent were of mixed races or ethnicities. In Milian and Conroy's (1999) study, 32 administrators of programs for students with visual impairments in 24 states, including 16

Schools for the Blind, stated that they provided services to 3,614 students. Of the 2,764 students whose race and ethnicity were reported, 1,761 (63.7 percent) were white, 658 (23.8 percent) were African American, 223 (8.0 percent) were Hispanic, 51 (1.8 percent) were Native American, 31 (1.1 percent) were Asian American, 32 (1.1 percent) were of other ethnicities, and 8 (2 percent) were of mixed ethnicities or races.

With regard to linguistic diversity, of the 202 children in Project PRISM (Ferrell, 1998), 88.0 percent of the children came from English-speaking homes; 5.5 percent came from Spanish-speaking homes; 2.6 percent came from homes in which both English and Spanish were spoken; and 3.6 percent came from homes in which other languages were spoken, along with some degree of English. In Milian and Ferrell's (1998) study, a higher proportion of children came from non-English-speaking homes. The 361 educators who participated reported that of the total of 4,640 students with visual impairments with whom they worked, 1,267 (27.3 percent) lived in homes where a language other than English was spoken, and 382 (8.2 percent) were learning English.

Patterns in the distribution of visual impairments by race and ethnicity have also been found. For example, in Project PRISM (Ferrell, 1998), the most frequent visual impairments for African American children were colobomas and other structural anomalies; for European American children, cortical visual impairment; for Hispanic children, retinopathy of prematurity; and for children of mixed ethnicity, optic nerve hypoplasia. While these differences were not statistically significant, the patterns are worth noting.

The race and ethnicity of children with visual impairments that were just reported may be compared to those of the overall student population and to the population of special education students. For instance, the Digest of Education Statistics (National Center for Education Statistics, 1996) reported that in the general population of students, 65.6 percent were white, 16.7 percent were African American, 13.0 percent were His-

panic, 3.6 percent were Asian American, and 1.1 percent were Native American. With regard to special education students, Cook and Boe's (1995) study noted that 68 percent were white, 16 percent were African American, 12 percent were Hispanic, and 4 percent were of other races and ethnicities. Thus, in these studies, there were lower proportions of African American students and higher proportions of Hispanic students in the general and special education populations of students than Milian and Conroy (1999) reported for the population of students with visual impairments.

CONTRIBUTIONS OF IMMIGRATION TO DIVERSITY

As the number of immigrants and refugees entering the United States increases, so does the linguistic, cultural, racial, and religious diversity of students in schools.

Since the United States first started keeping records of the nationalities of immigrants and naturalized citizens in the 1820 census (Rose, 1995), more than 60 million immigrants have entered the United States. In 1997, 25.8 million foreign-born people were living in the United States, or 9.8 percent of the population (Schmidley & Alvardo, 1998). Not all immigrants have been greeted, ranked, and treated with the same degree of acceptance and equality. Factors such as the time of arrival, region of origin, cultural attributes, religious preference, and physical appearance have influenced how immigrants are treated (Takaki, 1979).

Evidence of the selective nature of immigration policies can be found in a number of laws that were aimed at restricting immigration. Chinese people were the first to be singled out for separate treatment in the Chinese Exclusion Act of 1882, followed by those with questionable mental capacities, those who were likely to become public charges, the poor, those with contagious diseases, and those who were convicted of crimes in the Immigration Act of 1891. In 1917, Congress further restricted immigration by requiring every immigrant to pass a literacy test to demonstrate the ability to read. The Immigration Act of 1924, also called the National Origins Act, created immigration quotas on the basis of national origin that favored northern Europeans and closed the doors to immigration from Asia. This act was not changed until the passage of the Immigration and Nationality Act of 1952 (McCarran-Walters Act), which tightened national quotas but allowed token quotas for Asians. Consequently, from 1924 to 1965, when the Immigration and Nationality Act Amendments of 1965 abolished national quotas and restrictions against Asians, immigration fell to its lowest level since the mid-1800s (Brown University, 1997; Rose, 1995).

Since 1948 a number of acts have been passed to accommodate people who were left homeless after World War II and those who were escaping from communist countries in Eastern Europe. Other refugees, such as Cubans, Soviet Jews, and people from Southeast Asia have been given asylum as well (Rose, 1995). However, the 1996 Immigration Act restricted the kinds of public benefits to which legal immigrants have access, increased their chances for "removal" (a new term for deportation), and made it more difficult for legal immigrants to sponsor family members to immigrate to the United States (Becker & Bonesatti, 1997).

Significant shifts in immigration patterns have taken place since the 1820 census. The most important change has been the countries from which immigrants have come. In 1997, individuals from Central America, South America, or the Caribbean accounted for 51 percent of the total foreign-born population; 27 percent came from Asia; and 17 percent came from Europe (Schmidley & Alvarado, 1998). However, immigrants have come from almost every corner of the world for religious, political, professional, or economic reasons. They have also selected certain states as their permanent residence. In 1998, nearly 70 percent of the immigrants lived in California, New York, Texas, Illinois, and New Jersey ("Study Finds Immigrants Doing Well," 1999).

Immigrant students who are visually impaired might perform at, above, or below grade level, and some may never have attended school before. These students have different levels of English fluency and may need to be placed in bilingual education or ESL programs in addition to special education services for their visual impairments. Moreover, although some immigrant students come from affluent or middle-class families and may have had typical childhoods, others have come from areas with political or religious conflicts and may have confronted extremely stressful situations and the loss of family members. Students' experiences before they entered schools may have an impact on their adjustment to the new situation; hence, it is useful for school personnel to understand individual students' circumstances. However, this is an area that requires extreme sensitivity because some immigrant families have precarious legal statuses and may be hesitant to provide personal information that, if divulged, may threaten their chance of staying in the United States. Immigrants' fears, intensified by anti-immigrant sentiments reflected from time to time in recent years in the media and various legislative initiatives and attempts to cut back services, may also inhibit some families from requesting needed services.

The following questions are examples of possible areas to explore with recent immigrant families and their children with visual impairments.

Medical Issues: Previous Care and Current Needs

- When was the student diagnosed with the visual impairment?
- Are there medical records available that could be shared with the school?
- What type of treatment (modern or traditional) has the student received to improve or maintain vision?
- Has the student visited an ophthalmologist in the United States?
- Has the student ever used low vision devices to assist with school-related or functional activities?
- Are there other medical concerns in addition to the visual impairment?

Language: Home Language and Language of Instruction

- What are the family's language expectations for the student?

- How does the family view the student's language skills in the native language in comparison to the skills of other children in the family?

- How important is it to the family that the student maintain the native language?

- What opportunity does the student have to continue to develop the native language at home or in the community?

- How important is it for the family that the student learn English?

- What type of opportunities does the student have to practice English at home and in the community?

Literacy: Previous Exposure and Present Needs

- What was the last grade the student completed in the native country?

- If the student is blind, did he or she receive braille instruction in the native country?

- How does the family view the student's ability to read and write?

- Does the student read and write independently at home?

- Does the student enjoy reading or listening to family members read?

- What opportunities does the student have to read and write at home?

- Has the student been introduced to any type of technology that facilitates literacy?

Social Skills: Past and Present

- How important is it for the family that the student make friends in school or in the community?

- What types of opportunities does the student have to make friends in the community?

- How are people typically greeted in the student's culture?

- What may be some of the differences between the socially acceptable norms of the student's culture and those of the United States?

- What is the nature of relationships between teachers and students in the student's country of origin?

Daily Living Skills: Current Levels and Cultural Conflicts

- What daily home responsibilities are typically assigned to children from this culture?

- Are there sex-based differences in the assignment of chores that are usually found in the student's culture?

- Does the family think that it is not appropriate for children to perform some daily living skills?

- What responsibilities does the family expect the student to perform in relation to feeding, dressing, cleaning, and other developmentally appropriate skills?

- Does the family expect their sighted children and their child with a visual impairment to perform or contribute differently in areas related to daily living skills?

Other Areas

- What do families from the student's culture think about the role of the school?

- How do families from the student's culture view their involvement in the formal education of children with visual impairments?

- Does the family expect to stay in the current neighborhood or city, or are they there only temporarily?

◆ What are some of the family's most immediate needs?

Students who are recent immigrants, particularly those who speak languages other than English, require services that target both their disability-specific and language needs. Special education programs that do not to take into consideration the language needs of students who are learning English fail to provide an appropriate education for these students.

LINGUISTIC DIVERSITY

It has been estimated that 6.3 million students in kindergarten to grade 12 (K–12) or 14 percent of the population of students nationwide, live in homes where languages other than English are spoken. This includes 2.3 million students, or 5 percent of the student population, whose English language skills are limited and hence need ESL programs (Gonzalez, Brusca-Vega, & Yawkey, 1997). These percentages may be higher or lower in individual school districts, depending on the demographics of the local communities.

Students who are learning English and whose skills are not equivalent to those of native speakers of English are commonly referred to in studies and government reports as limited-English-proficient (LEP) students. However, a new label that is a more adequate description of the experiences of students who enter school speaking languages other than English has emerged in the literature. That label—English Language Learners (ELL)—emphasizes what students are in the process of learning, not what they cannot do well (Rivera, 1994). For additional terms frequently used to discuss concepts of language learning, see Sidebar 8.1.

A longitudinal study by Moss and Puma (1995), of first- and third-grade students who were identified as ELLs, found that students other than Asian ELLs are likely to attend schools where at least 75 percent of the students are eligible for free or reduced-price lunches, that more than three-quarters of the students are Hispanic, and that 50 percent of their mothers did not complete high

school. It also reported that although most of these children rely on classroom paraprofessionals to help them, fewer than half the students have aides who speak their language.

Although these findings may be discouraging for teachers who work with ELLs, the results of another study provide some key predictors of academic success for the students. Thomas and Collier (1997) studied the records of 700,000 language-minority students in K–12 in five large school districts and found that three key predictors of academic success are the most important and can overcome such factors as poverty and the school's location in an economically depressed area. These predictors include (1) using cognitively complex, on-grade-level academic instruction in a student's first language for as long as possible and cognitively complex on-grade-level academic instruction in English for part of the school day in each grade throughout a student's schooling; (2) using current approaches to teaching the academic curriculum in two languages, such as thematic units, cooperative learning strategies, incorporating students' diversity into the curriculum, combining the teaching of language and academic content, and developing oral and written language simultaneously; and (3) transforming the sociocultural context for language-minority students' schooling to create a supportive environment for learning in two languages.

The presence of students who are ELLs requires schools to follow state and federal regulations on identification, assessment, placement, programming, and parental consent and notification that apply to this population. Many of the regulations are the results of the requirements of Title VI of the Civil Rights Act of 1994 (Section 601), which states:

> No person in the United States shall, on the ground of race, color, or national origin, be excluded from participation in, be denied the benefits of, or be subject to discrimination under any program or activity receiving federal financial assistance.

The regulations require school districts to identify students who need assistance on the ba-

Useful Terms in the Area of ESL

Basic interpersonal communicative skills (BICs): The language skills one needs for face-to-face or other informal communication when meaning is negotiated through contextual cues (see Cummins, 1981).

Bilingual education: An educational approach that aims to develop a student's native language, helps the student acquire a second language, and uses the native and the second languages for instruction in the areas. There are a number of bilingual education models, including the transitional model, in which only non-English-speaking students participate and instruction in the native language is used only until the students have achieved a certain level of fluency in English, and the dual-language model, in which native English speakers and non-English speakers participate to learn each other's languages and instruction is provided in both languages until the students leave the school.

Bilingual special education: The combination of bilingual education approaches in the special education setting. A student's native language is used to provide instruction.

Cognitive academic language proficiency (CALP): The language skills required to perform the cognitive demanding tasks of schoolwork (see Cummins, 1981).

English as a second language (ESL): A component of a bilingual program that aims to develop the English listening, speaking, reading, and writing skills of students who speak languages other than English.

English language learners (ELL): A term used to describe students who are in the process of learning English.

Limited English proficient (LEP): The federal term used to identify students who need specialized language instruction because they have not yet achieved the required language proficiency to function in an English-only environment.

---

sis of their language, develop a program for these students that has a reasonable chance of success; provide appropriate staff and curricular materials, develop appropriate standards for measuring the students' progress, and evaluate programs and implement necessary modifications (U.S. Department of Education, 1992). However, even with these regulations, many students do not receive any ESL or bilingual assistance because they attend schools that do not have these services. To deal with the schools that clearly are not complying with the regulations, the Office of Civil Rights needs to increase its monitoring and enforcement activities and states need more technical assistance to help them monitor schools' compliance with federal statutes (Moss & Puma, 1995).

Language Programs

School districts across the nation offer a number of programs to meet the needs of ELLs. These programs differ in their overal goals, the degree to which they include the students' native languages, the duration of instruction in the native languages, and whether native English speakers also participate. Schools can offer a given program or a combination of programs, depending on their population. For example, while some students in a school may participate in a dual-language program because their parents want them to become bilingual, others may receive only ESL because the dual-language program is not available at their grade level or their parents prefer an English-only program. Some of the program options are as follows:

Programs That Include Instruction in Native Language

Two-Way Bilingual Programs or Dual-Language Programs.   Students in these programs are native English-speaking students who want to learn a second language and students who speak another language who are learning English. Instruction is provided in both languages, and the goal is to produce students who are bilingual. These programs are becoming popular throughout the United States because many English-speaking families welcome the opportunity to have their children learn a second language in the early grades.

Maintenance Bilingual Education.   Students in these programs are ELLs who belong to the same language group. Instruction is provided in the native language and in English. The aim of these programs is to develop English language proficiency and academic proficiency in the native language.

Transitional Bilingual Education.   Students in these programs are ELLs. Instruction is provided in the native language and in English. However, the students are expected to move out of the bilingual program and into an English-only program within a certain period. The goal of the program is to develop English-language skills.

English-Only Programs

Structured Immersion.   Students in these programs are ELLs who generally belong to different language groups. Instruction is provided in English with modifications, so students can understand the content being taught.

Content-Based ESL.   The ESL program is structured around academic content, rather than the traditional grammar-based approach. Language is taught through instruction in science, mathematics, social studies, and other academic areas.

ESL. Students are instructed for specific periods (daily or weekly) in English-language skills: grammar, vocabulary, and communication. These programs are implemented either as pull-out programs in which students go to an ESL classroom or as integrative programs in which teachers go to the students' classrooms.

ELLs with disabilities, including those with visual impairments, are entitled to participate in the program models just described. Typically, programs with native-language components exist in schools in which a large number of students belong to the same language groups. Consequently, the program offered to a student may be limited by what is available at the school the student attends.

Students who are visually impaired present a special challenge to ESL instructors or bilingual teachers who often rely on visual presentations as instructional strategies. However, methodological concerns should not prevent students who are visually impaired from attending programs that best meet their language needs, nor should programs be substituted because the students are receiving special education services. Consultations between the ESL teacher and the teacher of students with visual impairments can yield positive results for both. The former can learn how to modify material and instruction, and the latter can learn about the sequence of acquiring a second language.

ELLs who use braille should also be able to participate in language programs in the schools they attend. When a program offers a native-language component, some modifications are necessary if the teacher of students with visual impairments is not bilingual in the child's native language. The long-term benefits of maintaining the native languages of students are worth any apparent challenge that teachers have to face to achieve this goal. Teachers of students with visual impairments can play important roles even when they are not able to provide direct instruction in reading and writing in the students' native languages. They can (1) arrange for the transcription of materials in braille in the students' native languages, which is frequently a problem because braille textbooks in languages other than English are usually not available in the United States; (2) work with the bilingual teacher, ESL teacher, and bilingual paraeducator to modify the instruction and to help them understand the braille system; (3) provide specialized equipment and materials to support the program; and (4) provide instruction in English that will support or extend the ESL teacher's efforts.

Clearly, some creativity is required in providing appropriate services to ELLs who are visually impaired. These students have the right to services that address both their visual impairments and their language needs.

ETHNIC AND RACIAL DIVERSITY

Before embarking on a description of ethnic and racial groups, it is important to emphasize that ethnicity or race is only one of the many characteristics that define and influence the beliefs and values of students and their families. Although important, membership in a specific racial or ethnic group does not imply that all members of the group hold the same opinions or values about education, disability, and the roles of professionals. Thus, the following discussion is presented to provide basic historical and demographic information about specific racial and ethnic groups and to share relevant research that is applicable to teaching students from these groups.

African American Students and Families

Selected terms, such as indentured servants, slavery, the Emancipation Proclamation, Reconstruction Era, Jim Crow laws, *Plessy v. Ferguson*, "separate but equal," the Harlem Renaissance, *Brown v. Board of Education*, the Civil Rights Act of 1964, the Voting Act of 1965, and affirmative action have not only become an important part of history, but define, at least partly, the experiences of the over 33 million African Americans in the United States.

Racism and discrimination are still daily factors in the lives of African American children and adults and still hamper their ability to make use of available opportunities.

Knowledge of the historical burden and the consequences of the denial of education, educational segregation, and unequal education helps teachers understand the poor academic achievement of many African American students. However, these historical factors should not be used to justify and accept the failures. Instead, better practices to teach African American students should be implemented so that educational achievement becomes a reality, rather than an elusive dream.

The first educational program for African American students who were blind began in North Carolina in 1869. It was called the "Colored Department" and it was located in a separate building in southeast Raleigh. In 1929, 345 acres southeast of Raleigh were purchased for new facilities for African American students, known as the Garner Road Campus. Exchanges between white and African American students and teachers who attended the two separate campuses began in 1967, but it was not until 1977 that full racial integration was achieved and the Garner Road campus was closed (Governor Morehead School, 1995).

Concerns for the education of African American students with sensory impairments were first recorded in Alabama in 1881, when the issue was presented to the board of the Alabama Institute for Deaf and Blind (Couch & Hawkins, 1983). However, it was not until 1891 that the state legislature approved a bill establishing a school for African American students with sensory impairments and construction began in Talladega. The Alabama School for Negro Deaf and Blind opened on January 4, 1892, with 9 students. Enrollment grew quickly, so that by the end of 1892, 13 students who were deaf and 21 students who were blind were enrolled, and by 1894, 52 students were enrolled. African American students who were blind and those who were deaf continued to be educated at the same school until 1947, when a new campus for students who were deaf was opened. Desegregation efforts began in 1967, when a suit was filed and the U.S. District Court ordered the

Alabama Institute to develop a desegregation plan by the end of that year. In 1968, the Institute submitted the final plan for desegregation of the school, ending the long history of racial segregation of students with sensory impairments.

In Tennessee, African American students who were blind were taught by Susan M. Lowe at her home in Nashville until the Colored Department of the Tennessee School for the Blind opened in 1883 with 8 students and Mrs. Lowe was appointed matron (Waddey, 1996). In 1898, the Colored Department was moved to a new building because the original building was old and not well suited to be a school. By 1927, 52 African American students were attending the school. During the 1950s, the campus of the Colored Department was moved twice in search of more suitable locations. In 1954, the American Foundation for the Blind's (AFB's) evaluation of the school (at the request of Superintendent Mr. E. J. Wood) was not favorable; problems were found in the programs for both the African American and the white students. For the Colored Department, the study indicated the following problems: overcrowding, poor conditions in the infirmary, lower salaries for the African American teachers than for their white counterparts, and the lack of secretarial help for the principal. The report encouraged the school to live up to the claim of "separate, but equal facilities." In 1965, the two departments of the school were combined, and the white and African American students began learning under the same roof.

Much of what is known about the educational concerns of the African American community has been written specifically about students who are sighted; however, many of the same problems, although not as well documented, have existed for African American students who are visually impaired. For example, in the 1940s, when Helen Keller addressed a committee that was studying the public and private aid given to students who were physically disabled, she emphasized the needs of two groups—African American students who were blind and students with deaf-blindness. With regard to African Americans who were blind, she said:

In my travels up and down the continent I have visited their shabby school buildings and witnessed their pathetic struggle against want. I have been shocked by the meagreness of their education, lack of proper medical care, and the discrimination which limits their employment chances. I feel it is a disgrace that in this great wealthy land such injustices should exist to men and women of a different race—and blind at that! (quoted in Koestler, 1976, p. 184)

Another source of information on the quality of education for African American students who were blind in racially segregated schools in the South was a 1939 survey conducted by AFB. The survey revealed that schools for African American children who were blind were given hand-me-downs from schools for white children who were blind, including not only furniture and building supplies, but old classroom materials and braille books with worn-out braille cells. The survey also noted that racial segregation prevented African American teachers from attending training courses at white colleges in the South and that the teachers' salaries did not allow the teachers to attend summer programs in unsegregated colleges in the North. The need to train African American teachers who taught in segregated schools for students who were blind was the driving force behind a pilot summer training program at a southern college for African Americans. In 1939, AFB established the first course at West Virginia State College and contributed a grant to cover the instructors' salaries and materials and provided scholarships for some of the teachers to travel to West Virginia (Koestler, 1976).

Today, African American students who are blind are educated in racially integrated classrooms and are typically taught by white teachers. However, as is true for other minority groups, little is known about the needs and educational gains and concerns of African American students or areas that need to be improved to provide better opportunities for these students and their families. But it is known that there are few African American teachers in the field of visual impairments (Milian & Ferrell, 1998). African American teachers can share aspects of their culture with students who are blind, educate other school personnel about the African American community, and serve as role models for all students who are blind.

One area that concerns educators is the disparity in the scores of African American and white students on achievement tests. This disparity is evident even when students from the same socioeconomic levels are compared. For example, in 1990, the average combined scores on the SAT for students who came from homes where the parents' income was below $10,000 was 683 for African Americans and 866 for whites, compared to 854 for African American and 998 for white students who came from homes where the parental income was above $70,000. In 1995, the combined SAT scores for students whose parents did not have high school diplomas were 655 for African Americans versus 792 for whites. The scores of students who had at least one parent with a graduate degree still differed by race: 844 for African American students compared to 1,035 for white students (Belluck, July 4, 1999).

In her book *The Dreamkeepers,* Ladson-Billings (1994) described teachers, both African American and white, who have found culturally relevant ways to educate African American students as having high self-esteem and high regard for others and viewing teaching as an art and themselves as artists. These teachers consider themselves part of the community, believe that teaching contributes to the community, and encourage their students to make connections among their community, national, and global identities. Moreover, they believe that all students can succeed and see teaching as "digging" knowledge out of students. In addition, these teachers have relationships with students that are fluid and equitable and extend interactions with students beyond the classroom and into the community, demonstrate a connectedness with all students, encourage a community of learners, and encourage students to learn collaboratively. They view knowledge as something that is continuously re-created, recycled, and shared; are both passionate and critical about knowledge; help students develop necessary skills; and see excellence as a complex standard that takes students' diversity and individual differences into account.

Landson-Billings (1994) also presented suggestions of ways that teacher preparation programs could assist preservice teachers in developing attitudes that will lead to successful teaching experiences with African American students. Although these suggestions were specific to one group of culturally diverse students, they may apply to other diverse groups as well. They include the following:

- Recruit preservice teachers who have expressed an interest and desire to work with African American students.

- Provide educational experiences that help preservice teachers understand the central role of culture.

- Give preservice teachers opportunities to critique the system in ways that will help them choose to be either agents of change or defenders of the status quo.

- Require preservice teachers to have a prolonged immersion in African American culture.

- Provide preservice teachers with opportunities to observe culturally relevant teaching.

- Conduct student teaching over a longer period in a more controlled environment.

Overall, it is essential that teachers find ways to gain a better understanding of the needs of African American students who are visually impaired and to identify areas that are relevant to the students in schools. The stories of African Americans, both past and present, need to be shared with professionals in the field of visual impairments so that the professionals can identify and design more successful educational practices for these students.

Native American Students and Families

Native Americans are a heterogeneous group with diverse languages and cultures. However, they share a common history of social and cultural oppression and native-language attrition as a result of their conquest by European and American settlers and the later policies of the U.S. Government. Those who belong to one of the Native American communities occupy a unique place in American history.

Although the presence of Native American students varies by geographic area, teachers may encounter Native American students both in areas with large concentrations of Native Americans and in cities. Teachers who work in residential schools in states with Indian reservations have many opportunities to work with students who are visually impaired from the reservations because these students typically attend residential state schools for blind students.

In many cases, teachers who educate Native American students may not be familiar with aspects of the students' culture that may be important for providing culturally sensitive practice. Robinson-Zañartu (1996) recommended a number of cultural factors that teachers should attend to when working with this population, some of which are discussed next.

Cultural Factors

Worldviews. Worldviews are the beliefs and principles that guide individuals' understanding of the world and their place in it. Native Americans value the present, patience, extended family, "we" thinking, few material possessions, being in balance with nature, holistic thinking, and the spiritual. A core principle of their beliefs is that all aspects of life are integrated or related.

Acculturation and Acculturation Stress. Historically, aggressive measures were taken to assimilate Native Americans into the mainstream culture and to pressure them to abandon their traditional lifestyles. Native Americans' experiences with the U.S. government, educational system, and religious institutions have created a population that varies significantly in their identification with Western culture and Native American traditional culture, thus creating acculturation stress. Acculturation stress can lead to alienation that disrupts the transmission of culture from generation to generation and results in the loss of linguistic traditions and other important cultural knowledge.

School-Home Discontinuity. When children enter school, they bring the values they learned at home through socialization with adults and peers. Ideally, these values are validated and supported at school. However, most school practices follow the values and beliefs of the majority culture, which creates conflicts for Native American students. Examples of discontinuity that may be evident in the classroom include Native American families' practice of discouraging competition, respecting teachers and the elderly by not questioning them, and placing more importance on the present and the needs of the group than on the future or deadlines.

Parent Involvement. The relationships between Native American parents and schools have frequently been adversarial. In some instances, teachers have considered the cultures and languages of Native Americans detrimental to children's education and future. However, Native American parents and leaders generally place a great emphasis on education. Two cultural principles are important to discuss because they are related to the overall topic of parental involvement in education. First, many Native American parents believe in the principle of noninterference, which assumes that children are not their parents' property and are responsible for making their own choices. In other words, parents do not overtly teach or punish, but expect children to learn from the consequences of their actions. Second, the principle of avoiding disharmony may keep parents away from schools because they may perceive visits to schools as predicting disharmony which could lead to the depletion of spiritual energy and, consequently, illness.

Suggestions for Working with Navajo Students

Dufort and Reed (1995) offered the following helpful suggestions for teachers who work with Navajo students with disabilities, particularly those who conduct home visits.

Native American Belief Systems Regarding Disability, Illness, and Healing. The understanding of disability may be shaped by both the mainstream American system and the more traditional belief system. By combining the two belief systems, Native Americans can have a biological understanding of and a cultural explanation for the cause of disability. Many Native Americans believe in the power of words, thoughts, and actions to cause illness, disability, and other misfortunes. Therefore, they believe that parents and other family members are responsible for causing and preventing illness or disability in their children. As is the case with other cultural groups, members of Native American communities differ widely in their belief systems, ranging from those who have traditional beliefs to those who have abandoned the traditional views.

Navajo Parenting Styles. Navajo parents openly nurture their young children; smiles, laughter, hugs, and gentle teasing are often observed. When they discipline their children, they avoid name-calling or comparing them to other children. Caretakers quickly respond to crying children, since it is believed that crying children can "cry themselves out," which is associated with dying, or that crying can lead to illness. Navajo traditional parenting styles have been classified as adult centered; in other words, Navajo children are expected to fulfill adult-like roles at a much younger age than are other children.

Role of the Extended Family. Extended family members are involved in child care and decision-making. Grandmothers and aunts often provide short- and long-term care for children. Older family members are often consulted about decisions regarding the care of children. The term *multiple mothering* has been used to describe the sharing of child-care responsibilities in Navajo families.

Communication Styles. Aspects of communication, such as turn taking, information sharing, emphasizing important points, and applying rules of politeness, differ in Native American conversations from what is typical in Euro-American conversations. When a Navajo person is speaking, others wait without interrupting, asking questions, or making comments. Then, after an extended pause, others may ask questions or make comments about the points the speaker addressed. Navajo people share information by using personal vignettes and brief narratives and emphasize important points by repeating them and using quotations. Loud talking is viewed as rude behavior, and the rules about making direct or indirect eye contact vary with age. A slight handshake or touching of the hands is a symbol of polite greeting and leave taking.

The pressures that Native Americans experienced in the past to abandon their traditional culture and language, coupled with more recent efforts to use students' culture and language to improve educational outcomes, led to the conclusion that programs for Native American students with visual impairments should incorporate the students' language and culture into the curriculum to help the students maintain their culture and become bilingual.

Asian American and Pacific Islander Students and Families

Although Asian Americans and Pacific Islanders are grouped together as a single ethnic group, there are significant differences in their immigration histories, physical characteristics, geographic origins, languages, and cultural practices. Three general groups have been identified as being part of this larger ethnic group (Huang, 1993). They are Pacific Islanders (mostly Hawaiians, Samoans, and Guamanians), Southeast Asians (largely Indochinese from Vietnam, Thailand, Cambodia, and Laos; Burmese; Filipinos), and East Asians (including Chinese, Japanese, and Koreans). Groups from other Asian countries, such as India and Pakistan, also have visible representation within the Asian American community. One significant difference among these groups is social class. For example, although some groups entered the United States with monetary and human capital, which gave them a significant advantage in attaining upward mobility, others came directly from refugee camps, where they were placed as the result of war and were forced to leave all their possessions behind. The consequences of socioeconomic class can also be observed in levels of education; for example, 5.6 percent of Japanese Americans report having only an elementary school education as compared to 61 percent of Hmong Americans ("A Literature Review," 1997). The diversity within this ethnic group makes the following comment by Hodgkinson and Obarakpor (1994, p. 13) essential for teachers to remember: "Almost all generalizations about Asian Americans will prove to be incorrect for some, if not most, member groups. This makes for great complexities in the provision of health care, education, criminal justice and community development services for Asian Americans."

As with other members of diverse groups, teachers who work with Asian American students and family members may need to learn important cultural aspects of the specific group with whom they are working to establish a more productive educational environment. Views on education and perceptions of healing and disabilities are two important areas that deserve some attention. However, given the previously mentioned difficulties of making generalizations among the many groups within the Asian American population, statements in the following discussion are attributed to specific groups as they apply.

Views on Education

Hidalgo, Siu, Bright, Swap, and Epstein (1995) reviewed the literature on Chinese American families' views on education and came to the following conclusions:

◆ Chinese Americans define their cultural identity in terms of academic achievement.

To do well in school is to be Chinese, and education is perceived as an avenue for upward social mobility.

◆ Chinese American parents value grades and believe that effort is more of a factor in success in school than is innate ability.

◆ Chinese American families support their children's school performance at home by reducing the number of household chores the children are required to perform; using proverbs and folk stories to motivate the children to study; purchasing workbooks, establishing study times and helping the children with homework; scheduling children's free time; taking the children to the library; and enrolling the children in language schools and music classes on weekends or after school.

◆ Chinese American parents are concerned about the lax discipline, lack of moral education, poor mathematics training, and insufficient homework in the schools.

◆ Chinese American parents take compensatory measures, such as inventing homework, sending children to church or to Chinese-language school to learn discipline and moral values, hiring tutors, or enrolling children in after-school programs, instead of sharing their concerns with school authorities.

An interview by Lai (1994) with Jane, a Chinese student in British Columbia who was blind, illustrates some of the values just mentioned. Jane's comments suggest how she views her parents' expectations: "If I do well, I'll tell my parents. If not, I'll not tell them because I don't want to disappoint them. My parent do not tell me, but I know they expect. They know I will not disregard their wishes . . . because they know I know" (Lai, 1994, p. 129).

With regard to Southeast Asian children, Bempechat and Omari (1990) pointed out that these children may have difficulty expressing themselves and being assertive in the classroom. Respect for authority may inhibit them from discussing their views and any problems they may have. A proverb taught to children by parents exemplifies this concept: "First you learn respect, then you learn letters." Cheng (1993) summarized some prevailing views about learning that many Asian American families hold: Education is formal, so teachers are expected to be formal and to lecture; teachers are to be highly respected and not challenged or interrupted; humility is an important virtue, so students are not to show off or volunteer information; reading factual information is studying, therefore, fiction is not valued as serious reading; order and obedience are important, so students need to sit quietly and listen; since learning is done by observation and memorization, rote memory is an effective teaching strategy; and since pattern practice and rote learning are valued, homework that reinforces memorization is expected.

Views on Healing and Disability

The following views on healing and disability are held by Asian Americans in general or specific groups.

◆ Illness may be treated with a number of traditional methods, including acupuncture, rubbing coins, wearing amulets filled with sacred healing herbs, heating crushed wormwood or other herbs directly on the skin (moxibustion), applying balms, or eating a combination of hot or cold foods (Cheng, 1993; Dresser, 1996; Fadiman, 1997).

◆ The Hmong believe that if the soul is separated from the body, illness can result. Therefore, they view surgical intervention as invasive because the spirit may leave the body during surgery. They also tie a string around their wrists to bind their souls to their bodies. They attribute causes of illness to eating the wrong food, failing to make offerings to one's ancestors, pointing one's finger at the full moon, being punished for one's ancestors' transgression, or being cursed (Fadiman, 1997).

◆ Many Hmong families believe that if parts of the body are removed, as in the case of the eyes in retinoblastoma, the person will be reincarnated with an incomplete body. This belief may lead to their rejection of surgery and illustrates the need to develop mediation systems that will result in mutual compromises and consequent agreements (Fadiman, 1997).

◆ Asian American parents may have difficulty accepting such concepts as learning disabilities and depression. As Huang (1993) explained, they may believe that an individual is either being physically sick or simply lacks motivation.

◆ Since traditional Asian families expect children to do well in school, they may feel ashamed and responsible when their children do poorly or need special attention (Cheng, 1998).

◆ Some Asian American and Pacific Islander families believe that the cause of disability may be a curse or fate (Cheng, 1993). For other causes ascribed to disabilities, see Chan (1998).

Finally, teachers are reminded that given the multiplicity of factors that create differences within the group of individuals who are considered to be Asian Americans and Pacific Islanders, caution should always be exercised when trying to apply generalizations to a specific student or family. Certainly, such factors as levels of education, acculturation to the mainstream society, and social class influence the manner in which any given group perceives education, healing, and disabilities.

European American Students and Families

Most of the focus of this section on race and ethnicity has been on ethnic and racial minority groups—a focus based on the reality that the number of students from these groups is growing and that most teachers come from nonminority communities. However, there is also great diversity among the groups that originated from European countries. Some of these differences are religious affiliations, political views, educational levels, connection to ethnic traditions and food, linguistic variations, contact with the countries of ancestors, socioeconomic status, loyalty to the language of ancestors, generations removed from original ancestors, geographic locations that have led to rural or urban lifestyles, and intermarriages.

Although most European American teachers feel comfortable when working with other European American students and families, social class, linguistic variations, religious differences, and urban versus rural upbringing sometimes present challenges in the classroom and to an otherwise amicable relationship with family members. In recent years, immigrants from Eastern Europe who have been educated under a different political system have challenged the skills of teachers who have been relatively secure in their ability to work with students with European roots. Consequently, it is important to recognize the different groups that have been clustered under the umbrella of European Americans and the many factors that create variations within this large group.

Hispanic American Students and Families

Hispanics in the United States, also known as Latinos, include those whose families have been in this country for centuries, as well as those who are relatively new immigrants. Although Mexican Americans have always been the largest group of Hispanics in the United States, other groups have sizable numbers. These groups are Puerto Ricans, Cubans, Dominicans, and those who trace their origins to the many countries in South and Central America. Although Latino families can be found in all states, concentrations of certain groups live in different geographic areas of the country. For example, Mexicans and Mexican-Americans are found in large numbers in Texas,

Arizona, New Mexico, and California; Puerto Ricans and Dominicans tend to live in northeastern states, such as New York, Connecticut, and Massachusetts; Cubans are concentrated primarily in Florida; and large numbers of Central and South Americans are found in California and Florida. Many Hispanics also live in Illinois. The Hispanic population has experienced a dramatic growth since the 1960s for two reasons: increased levels of immigration and high birth rates (Schlesinger, 1998).

The family's immigration history, experiences in the native country, use of Spanish and English at home, length of time living in the United States, legal status, income level, educational level, religious beliefs, family structure, intention to return to the native country, and reasons for living in the United States are among the factors that create much diversity within the population of Hispanics. These factors may determine the familiarity or unfamiliarity of individuals with the educational system and influence how they react to service providers. For example, a third-generation Hispanic who was educated in the United States and is fluent in English is able to gain access to resources and information with much greater ease than is an immigrant from a rural area in Central America who is new to the community and speaks only Spanish. Whereas the U.S.-born Hispanic may have values that are similar to those of the teachers, the new immigrant may have more traditional values that will not be as easily understood by school personnel.

At the national level, Latino students make up about 13 percent of the school population. However, the percentages living in various states range from a low of less than 1 percent in Alabama, Kentucky, Mississippi, Missouri, North Dakota, South Carolina, South Dakota, and Vermont to over 20 percent in Arizona, California, New Mexico, and Texas (National Center for Education Statistics, 1996). It is typically assumed that the number of Latino students with visual impairments resembles the number in the general population of students attending public schools, but, as was mentioned earlier, there is only limited demographic data to confirm this assumption, especially in relation to determining the over- or underrepresentation of Latino students in these types of programs.

Latino families have been studied by a number of researchers in general and special education. In special education, studies have suggested that these families often have difficulty with the printed information that schools send home because it is written in English or in technical terms even when Spanish is used. These families frequently feel that they should not question the decisions made by school personnel. In addition, despite their children's placement in special education, the parents want their children to be better educated and have better jobs than they had (Gallegos & Gallegos, 1988; Harry, 1992; Hayes, 1992; Lynch & Stein, 1987; Mary, 1990). With regard to visual impairments, Milian (1999) stated that students' characteristics, such as age and reading mode, and parents' characteristics, including educational level and language spoken, are associated with differences in families' attitudes toward teachers and school programs for families, ability to help their children with schoolwork, and perception that they need to participate in their children's education.

In general education, studies have suggested that as Latino parents become more knowledgeable through interactions with other parents, they are able to improve their relationships with schools and that programs to increase collaboration between families and schools require sensitivity to their staff's implicit and explicit assumptions about working with these families. These studies have also found that family members' efforts to support their children's education go unnoticed by schools because they do not fit into the model of traditional involvement and that family-involvement programs need to understand, appreciate, and respect the families' internal dynamics (Delgado-Gaitán, 1992; Powell, 1995; Torres-Guzmán, 1991; Valdés, 1996).

The Latino families of students with visual impairments who participated in a study on family involvement and attitudes toward schools were asked to list the best thing that their children's schools could do for them the following school year (Milian-Perrone, 1994). Some of their answers, such as "improving materials and equipment," "helping the child improve," "give child more homework," and "continuing with the services," reflected requests that would directly benefit the children or programs the children attended. Other answers including "inform families of child's progress," "create programs for families," and have "meetings in the evenings," were more directly connected to what schools could do for and with families. It is interesting that the most frequent responses directly addressed the quality of education, rather than schools' efforts to create programs for families. In other words, the answers indicated that the best thing schools can do for families is to provide good educational programs for children.

Some Latino students with visual impairments and their families require school programs that are different from those offered to English-speaking families or families who have been in the United States for a number of years and are familiar with the school culture. Certainly, many school programs are better equipped than others to develop successful programs because they have bilingual programs and personnel and ESL programs, as well as other knowledgeable professionals who can work effectively with these families. Other school programs may be less familiar with Latino children and families and may lack the support systems that are needed to provide appropriate services. In any case, all programs need to develop plans to better meet the educational needs of this growing population of students.

DEVELOPING CULTURAL COMPETENCE

Bau (1999) proposed that culturally competent services for individuals with visual impairments can be developed through an examination of cultural values, such as communication, health beliefs and practices, family structure, attitude toward authority, etiquette, expectations of "helping," and time orientation. A framework based on specific cultural values guides teachers to investigate certain cultural aspects without having to become experts in all cultures in the United States, which is clearly an impossible task. Rather, teachers can concentrate on learning about important cultural factors that are relevant to the specific students with whom they work.

Wayman, Lynch, and Hanson (1990) presented helpful guidelines specifically to teachers who work with young children. The guidelines include categories and specific areas which assist teachers' need to collect information about the students they work with, including these:

Family Structure

- Members of the family, decision makers, relationship of friends to the family; and status given to members of the family.

- The primary caregiver, other people who are responsible for caring for the child, and issues related to the care of the child.

Child-Rearing Practices

- Feeding, mealtime rules, foods eaten, beliefs about breast-feeding and bottle feeding, transition to solid foods, and views on independent feeding.

- Sleeping patterns: sleeping in the same room or separate rooms from parents, the age at which a child is moved to another room, established bedtime, response to an infant when he or she awakes at night and daytime napping.

- Disciplinary practices: responses to disobedience and aggression, the family member who sets disciplinary standards, acceptable child behaviors, and the form of discipline practiced by the family.

- Responses to a crying infant or child: how long it takes before the caregiver picks up the child and ways of calming a crying baby.

Family Perceptions and Attitudes

- Does the family assign responsibility for the disability to something supernatural or to a force (God), rather than to a medical factor? What are the family's views on intervention to help improve the child's condition?

- Health and healing practices: Western medical approaches, holistic approaches, a combination of medical and holistic approaches, and which family member is responsible for relating medical information to service providers.

- Help-seeking patterns: information sought from other family members, community agencies, or religious organizations; which family member seeks help; direct or indirect ways of seeking help; the family's feelings about seeking help; the best method of communicating with the family; and which family member is in charge of following up on communicating.

Language and Communication Style

- The language that the family feels most comfortable using when communicating feelings or sensitive information on the family or the child's disability and the service provider's fluency in the language that the family feels most comfortable using.

- Translators: use of a translator who is of the same culture as the family, or who is of a different culture but is familiar with colloquialisms used by the family; comfort level of the family in using a translator.

- Whether the family shares their feelings when discussing emotional events and asks direct questions, the family members' interaction style with each other (loud, quiet, turn taking) and the family members' practice of asking service providers about their personal lives.

◆ The family members' use of body language and silence in communicating.

The presence of culturally and linguistically diverse students with visual impairments in schools requires teachers to become much more aware of the linguistic and cultural aspects of students' lives that can influence students' educational progress. Although it may not be easy to acquire such awareness, it is a necessary task.

SUMMARY

Since multicultural diversity among the population of students with visual impairments is a growing trend, changes need to be made at different levels in the field of visual impairments. University training programs need to incorporate content into the curriculum that will provide new teachers with the knowledge and skills they need to teach students from diverse backgrounds. Program administrators need to support teachers and provide opportunities for them to strengthen their skills when teaching students from multicultural communities. Teachers need to identify areas in their programs that require improvement and share their ideas with colleagues and administrators so that changes can be made. Agencies that are responsible for developing instructional and informational materials need to become more involved in creating materials that can be used with students and families who speak languages other than English. In general, all professionals in the field need to increase their level of awareness and involvement if they want to improve services for students with visual impairments and their families who are members of diverse groups.

STUDY QUESTIONS

1. Interview school personnel on the topic of educating culturally or linguistically diverse students with visual impairments. What factors were identified as important? What important areas do you believe were not mentioned by the teachers you interviewed?

2. Develop a list of words, phrases, and sentences in a language other than English that will facilitate the process of conducting a functional vision assessment with students who are learning English as a second language.

3. Conduct an Internet search to identify five Web sites that provide information on cultural or religious groups, and summarize what you learned about the groups you identified. How will this information help you as a teacher of students with visual impairments?

4. Contact five local, state, or national disability organizations and find out if they have printed information available in languages other than English. Develop a resource file containing information for parents in languages other than English.

5. Interview a braille reader who reads in a second language. What are the differences and similarities between English braille and the braille code used in the particular second language the person reads?

6. Obtain state or local data about the racial, ethnic, religious, and socioeconomic characteristics of the students in your current or future teaching location. What implications will these characteristics have for students with visual impairments and for you as a teacher in that state or community?

REFERENCES

Bau, A. M. (1999). Providing culturally competent services to visually impaired persons. *Journal of Visual Impairment & Blindness, 93,* 291–297.

Becker, A., & Bonesatti, D. (1997). The 1996 welfare and

immigration legislation and U.S. permanent residents. *TESOL Matters, 7*(5), 1, 5.

Belluck, P. (1999, July 4). Reason is sought for lag by blacks in school effort. *New York Times,* pp. 1, 12.

Bempechat, J. , & Omari, M. C. (1990). *Meeting the educational needs of Southeast Asian children* (Digest No. 68). New York: ERIC Clearinghouse on Urban Education.

Brown University. (1997). *U.S. immigration policy in an unsettled world: Public policy debate in the classroom.* Providence, RI: Choices for the 21st Century Education Project, Brown University.

Chan, S. (1998). Families with Asian roots. In E. W. Lynch & M. J. Hanson (Eds.), *Developing cross-cultural competence* (pp. 251–344). Baltimore, MD: Paul H. Brookes.

Cheng, L. L. (1993). Asian-American cultures. In D. E. Battle (Ed.), *Communication disorders in multicultural populations* (pp. 38–77). Stoneham, MA: Butterworth-Heinemann.

Cheng, L. L. (July 1998). *Enhancing the communication skills of newly-arrived Asian American students* (Digest No. 136). New York: ERIC Clearinghouse on Urban Education.

Cook, L. H. , & Boe, E. E. (1995). Who is teaching students with disabilities? *Teaching Exceptional Children, 28,* 70–72.

Couch, R. H. , & Hawkins, J. (1983). *Out of silence and darkness: The history of the Alabama Institute for Deaf and Blind, 1853–1983.* Troy, AL: Troy State University Press.

Cummins, J. (1981). The role of primary language development in promoting educational success for language minority students. In California State Department of Education, *Schooling and language minority students: A theoretical framework.* Los Angeles: Evaluation, Dissemination and Assessment Center, California State University.

Delgado-Gaitán, C. (1992). Involving parents in the schools: A process of empowerment. *American Journal of Education, 100,* 20–46.

Delpit, L. (1995). The silenced dialogue: Power and pedagogy in educating other people's children. In L. Delpit, *Other people's children: Cultural conflict in the classroom* (p. 46). New York: New Press.

Dresser, N. (1996). *Multicultural manners: New rules of etiquette for a changing society.* New York: John Wiley & Sons.

Dufort, M. , & Reed, L. (1995). *Learning the way: A guide for the home visitor working with families on the Navajo reservation.* Watertown, MA: Perkins School for the Blind.

Fadiman, A. (1997). *The spirit catches you and you fall down: A Hmong child, her American doctors, and the collision of two cultures.* New York: Moonday Press.

Ferrell, K. A. (1998). *Project PRISM: A longitudinal study of developmental patterns of children who are visually impaired.* Greeley: University of Northern Colorado.

Gallegos, A. , & Gallegos, R. (1988). The interaction between families of culturally diverse handicapped children and the school. In H. S. Garcia & R. Chavez Chavez (Eds.), *Ethnolinguistic issues in education* (pp. 125–132). (ERIC Document Reproductive Service No. ED316044).

Gonzalez, V., Brusca-Vega, R., & Yawkey, T. (1997). *Assessment and instruction of culturally and linguistically diverse students: With or at-risk of learning problems.* Needham Heights, MA: Allyn & Bacon.

Governor Morehead School. (1995). *150th anniversary edition: Exclusive one-time issue.* Raleigh, NC: Author.

Harry, B. (1992). Making sense of disability: Low-income Puerto Rican parents' theories of the problem. *Exceptional Children, 59,* 27–40.

Hayes, K. G. (1992). Attitudes toward education: Voluntary and involuntary immigrants from the same families. *Anthropology & Education Quarterly, 23,* 250–267.

Hidalgo, N. M., Siu, S. F. , Bright, J. A. , Swap, S. M., & Epstein, J. L. (1995). Research on families, schools, and communities: A multicultural perspective. In J. A. Banks & C. A. McGee Banks (Eds.), *Handbook of research on multicultural education* (pp. 498–524). New York: Macmillan.

Hodgkinson, H. L., & Obarakpor, A. M. (1994). *Immigration to America: The Asian American experience.* Washington, DC: Institute for Educational Leadership Center for Demographic Policy.

Huang, G. (December 1993). *Beyond culture: Communicating with Asian American children and families* (Digest No. 94), New York: *ERIC* Clearinghouse on Urban Education.

Kirchner, C. , & Schmeidler, E. (1999). Life chances and ways of life: Statistics on race, ethnicity, and visual impairment. (USABLE Data Report #3). *Journal of Visual Impairment & Blindness, 93,* 319–324.

Koestler, F. A. (1976). *The unseen minority: A social history of blindness in America.* New York: American Foundation for the Blind.

Ladson-Billings, G. (1994). *The dreamkeepers: Successful teachers of African American students.* San Francisco: Jossey-Bass.

Lai, Y. (1994). Dual challenge in the classroom: The case of Chinese students with special needs. *B.C. Journal of Special Education 18,* 124–131.

A literature review focuses on Asian American students at risk. (1997, September). *CRESPAR Newsletter* No. 2. Washington, DC: Center for Research on the Education of Students Placed at Risk, Johns Hopkins University and Howard University.

Lynch, E. W., & Stein, R. C. (1987). Parent participation by ethnicity: A comparison of Hispanic, black and Anglo families. *Exceptional Children, 54(2),* 105–111.

Mary, N. L. (1990). Reactions of black, Hispanic, and white mothers to having a child with handicaps. *Mental Retardation, 28*(1), 1–5.

McNeil, J. (1993). *Americans with disabilities 1991–92: Current Population Reports (Series P-70, No. 32).* Washington, DC: U.S. Department of Commerce.

McNeil, J. (1997). *Americans with disabilities 1994–95: Current population reports (Series, P-70, No. 61).* Washington, DC: U. S. Department of Commerce.

Milian, M. (1999). Schools and family involvement: Attitudes among Latinos who have children with visual impairments. *Journal of Visual Impairment & Blindness, 93,* 277–290.

Milian, M., & Conroy, P. (1999). *Preparing teachers to educate culturally and linguistically diverse students with sensory impairments: A survey of administrators.* Greeley: Division of Special Education, University of Northern Colorado.

Milian, M., & Ferrell, K. A. (1998). *Preparing special educators to meet the needs of students who are learning English as a second language and are visually impaired: A monograph.* ERIC Document No. ED426545.

Milian-Perrone, M. (1994). *Family involvement and attitudes about school programs among Latino families of students with visual impairments.* Unpublished doctoral dissertation, Teachers College, Columbia University.

Moss, M. , & Puma, M. (1995). *Prospects: The congressionally mandated study of educational growth and opportunity. First year report on language minority and limited English proficient students.* Washington, DC: U.S. Department of Education, Office of the Under Secretary.

National Center for Education Statistics. (1996). *Digest of Education Statistics 1996.* Washington, D.C.: U.S. Department of Education, Office of Educational Research and Improvement.

Nieto, S. (1996). *Affirming diversity: The sociopolitical context of multicultural education* (2nd ed.). White Plains, NY: Longman.

Powell, R. D. (1995). Including Latino fathers in parent education and support programs: Development of a program model. In R. E. Zambrana (Ed.), *Understanding Latino families* (pp. 85–105). Thousand Oaks, CA: Sage.

Rivera, C. (1994). Is it real for all kids? *Harvard Educational Review, 64,* 55–75.

Robinson-Zuñartu, C. (1996). Serving Native American children and families: Considering cultural variables. *Language, Speech, and Hearing Services in Schools, 27,* 373–384.

Rose, I. P. (1995). *They and we: Racial and ethnic relations in the United States* (5th ed.). New York: McGraw-Hill.

Schlesinger, R. (1998, March). *Republicans debate how to court Hispanic vote.* http://www.ljx.com/Government/hisvote.htm

Schmidley, D., & Alvarado, H. A. (March 1998). *Current population reports: The foreign-born population in the United States: March 1997 (Update)* (pp. 20–507). Washington, DC: U.S. Department of Commerce.

Schwartz, S. E., & Dunnick Karge, B. (1996). *Human diversity: A guide for understanding* (2nd ed.). New York: McGraw-Hill.

Sleeter, C., & Grant, C. A. (1993). *Making choices for multicultural education: Five approaches to race, class, and gender.* New York: Macmillan.

Study finds immigrants doing well in America. (1999, July 3). *New York Times,* p. A9.

Takaki, R. (1979). *Iron cages: Race and culture in nineteenth century America.* New York: Alfred A. Knopf.

Thomas, W. P., & Collier, V. (1997). *School effectiveness for language minority students..* Washington, DC: National Clearinghouse for Bilingual Education.

Torres-Guzmán, M. (1991). Recasting frames: Latino parent involvement. In M. E. McGroarty & C. J. Faltis (Eds.), *Languages in school and society: Politics and pedagogy* (pp. 529–552). Berlin: Mouton de Gruyter.

U. S. Department of Education. (1992). *The provision of an equal education opportunity to limited English proficient students.* Washington, DC: U. S. Department of Education, Office of Civil Rights.

Valdés, G. (1996). *Con respeto: Bridging the distances between culturally diverse families and school.* New York: Teachers College Press.

Waddey, J. H. (1996). *Tennessee School for the Blind 1844–1994: The first 150 years.* Nashville: Tennessee School for the Blind.

Wayman, K. I. , Lynch, E. W. , & Hanson, M. J. (1990). Home-based early childhood services: Cultural sensitivity in a family systems approach. *Topics in Early Childhood Special Education, 10,* 65–66.

CHAPTER 9

Educational Programming

Sandra Lewis and Carol B. Allman

KEY POINTS

◆ The provision of educational services for students with disabilities has been federally mandated since the passage of the Education for All Handicapped Children Act of 1975. When this legislation was reauthorized in 1990, its name was changed to the Individuals with Disabilities Education Act (IDEA).

◆ It is important to follow all the steps in the process of educational programming to make sure that students receive appropriate services.

◆ Each student who receives special education services has a specially designed plan, called an Individualized Education Program (IEP), to guide the efforts of the student's educational team.

◆ When determining appropriate placement for students with visual impairments, the IEP team must consider the environment in which identified benchmarks can best be met.

◆ Parents of students with visual impairments have a critical role to play in the educational process.

The foundation of educational programming for students with visual impairments is based on the philosophies described throughout this book.

Educational programming, the focus of this chapter, involves planning through the identification and assessment of a student, development of the student's Individualized Education Program (IEP), and determination of the appropriate placement for implementing the IEP. Also addressed are issues related to the administration of educational programming, including accountability, placements in private schools, legal rights of parents, collaboration with family members, liability, determination of caseloads, use of paraeductors, and links to postschool rehabilitation services. Each component of educational programming interacts with the others to provide direction for the desired outcome for students with visual impairments: development into healthy, happy adults who can function in and contribute to society with the interdependence typical of the general population of adults.

PROCESS OF EDUCATIONAL PROGRAMMING

In 1975, President Gerald R. Ford signed P.L. 94-142, the Education for All Handicapped Children Act, into law. This groundbreaking law mandated that students with disabilities must be educated in the public school system, ensured parents of their right to participate in the development of pro-

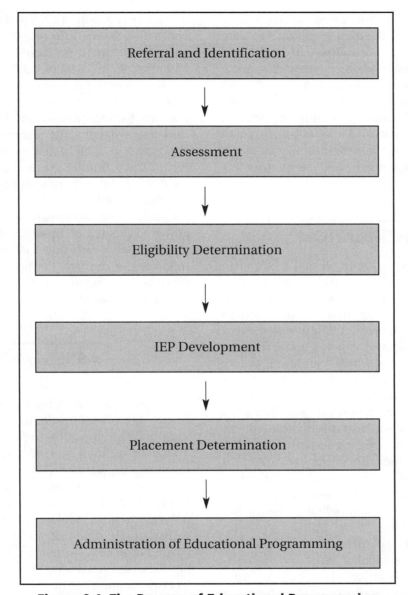

Figure 9.1. The Process of Educational Programming

grams for their children, and established a process for the determination and provision of an appropriate education. Through the reviews and reauthorizations of the law (1990 and 1997), Congress has evaluated these requirements and confirmed their key importance for implementing the law, which is now known as the Individuals with Disabilities Education Act (IDEA).

The process of determining educational programming, depicted in Figure 9.1, begins with the identification of a student with a potential disability, receipt of permission from the parents to assess their child, and the creation of a collaborative educational team to evaluate the student and plan the student's IEP. This team evaluates the student and on the basis of the results of the evaluation, determines if the child is eligible for services. Once the student is deemed eligible, the team then determines his or her abilities, strengths, and needs; develops goals and objectives to ensure the student's educational progress; and identifies the educational placement in which the student will receive special education and related services. Each step is important, and it is essential that all the steps are followed in order, to ensure that a student's individual needs are adequately addressed.

IDENTIFICATION

School districts are required to make efforts to identify students who may have disabilities that interfere with learning. Most states have extensive "child-find" activities that are designed to meet this component of IDEA. These activities include the distribution of general public notices or brochures in places where parents of young children tend to spend time, such as day care centers, pediatricians' offices, and libraries; presentations at public meetings; and door-to-door canvassing of neighborhoods to inform residents of the availability of services for students with disabilities. Parents and others may disclose to school districts their suspicions of a child's need for special education services, and given this information, districts are compelled to honor the request for evaluation.

A child's visual impairment is usually identified by an eye care specialist, either an ophthalmologist or an optometrist, who ideally informs the parents of the availability of services from the local education agency (LEA) or school district. Sometimes, a visual impairment is identified through a child's participation in a vision screening offered to all students of a certain age in a school district. Some students, particularly those with multiple impairments, are not appropriately identified as having visual impairments because their unusual and often unreliable response patterns make it difficult for eye specialists without experience with these children to test them.

There is some concern that parents may delay contacting the LEA for several months after a visual impairment is identified (Corn, Hatlen, Huebner, Ryan, & Siller, 1995), even though immediate referral for appropriate services is critical to the family's adjustment and the child's progress (Council for Exceptional Children, 1991). The period immediately after parents learn that their child has a visual impairment is often one of confusion and turmoil. Frequently, the family's efforts are directed toward understanding and managing the child's medical condition and confirming the diagnosis. Some families need time to process and adjust to this unanticipated change in their lives and are not aware that this adjustment can be made easier through the intervention of educators who are trained in working with children with visual impairments.

ASSESSMENT

Given a referral and signed permission by the parent or guardian, the school district must identify members of the educational team who will assess the child. The educational team usually consists of a school psychologist, educational diagnostician, teachers, support services personnel, and the child's parent or parents. In most cases, the team has two primary responsibilities: (1) to determine if the student is eligible for special education and related services and (2) to identify the student's current level of performance, including strengths, abilities, and needs. Team members should collect information about the student and be familiar with curricula, instruction, related services, and special considerations that are beneficial to the student's education. IDEA specifies the following guidelines for assessing the eligibility of students with disabilities for services:

◆ Evaluations must be completed in a timely manner.

◆ The parents must give permission for assessments and must be informed of the specific evaluations to be conducted.

◆ The child must be assessed in all areas related to the suspected disability or disabilities.

◆ Assessments must be provided and administered in the child's native language and must not be racially or culturally discriminatory.

◆ Assessments must be conducted by a team of trained personnel and based on the needs of the student.

◆ Assessment instruments must be valid and reliable.

◆ Educational decisions cannot be based on the results of a single test.

The assessment of the abilities, strengths, and needs of students with visual impairments is extremely complex, and in some cases, it is difficult to adhere to the IDEA guidelines. For example, there are few tests that have been designed specifically for use with this population, and the validity and reliability of tests designed for sighted students are usually questionable for use with students who are visually impaired. Similarly, it is often difficult to find personnel (such as, speech-language specialists, school psychologists, and occupational therapists) who are trained to assess students who are visually impaired. These circumstances make it essential for an assessment of a student with a visual impairment to be conducted by a team of individuals who work closely together and that includes a teacher of students with visual impairments. Team members should share findings, observations, and insights throughout the collection and interpretation of data. The teacher of students with visual impairments frequently serves as the coordinator of the assessment team, helps the other team members to understand the impact of visual impairment on learning, and facilitates appropriate accommodations and interpretation of the tests.

Because a visual impairment often limits a child's access to visual information and results in limited opportunities to engage in everyday activities, an educational evaluation of a student with a visual impairment will involve much more than the typical academic and achievement testing. Much of the evaluation of a student with visual impairments, including one with multiple disabilities, involves careful observations of the student in a variety of environments. In addition, surveys, interviews, and inventories that are completed by the student, parents, and teachers help the team members assess the student's level of mastery of the components of a comprehensive curriculum for students with visual impairments. This consists of the general curriculum and, as listed below, the expanded core curriculum (Hatlen, 1996):

◆ Compensatory academic skills, including modes of communication;

◆ Orientation and mobility (O&M);

◆ Social interaction skills;

◆ Independent living skills;

◆ Recreation and leisure skills;

◆ Career education skills;

◆ Technology; and

◆ Visual efficiency skills.

DETERMINATION OF ELIGIBILITY

A student is eligible for special education services if his or her disability "adversely affects [the student's] educational performance" (IDEA, 20 U.S.C. § 1401[a]; 34 C.F. R. § 300.7[a][1]-[b][13]). Most students whose visual acuities are not correctable to typical levels or who have visual field limitations are eligible for services, since significant visual impairments are known to interfere with learning (Bishop, 1996). Children with visual impairments for whom a comprehensive assessment reveals no educational needs (academic and functional) technically do not require or qualify for special education and related services, but they may be eligible for services under Section 504 of the Rehabilitation Act. See Sidebar

SIDEBAR 9.1

The Differences Between Section 504 and IDEA

Section 504 of the Rehabilitation Act of 1973 prohibits discrimination against people with disabilities who participate in programs that receive funding from the federal government, including public schools. Under Section 504, *discrimination* is defined as any unequal treatment solely on the basis of a disability. Students who are protected by Section 504 are entitled to an equal opportunity to benefit from their education, and schools must take action to provide the appropriate aids and services that allow for this equal opportunity to occur.

Under Section 504, a person is considered to have a disability if he or she "has a physical or mental impairment which substantially limits one or more . . . major life activities, . . . has a record of such an impairment, . . . or is regarded as having such an impairment." (Sections 504, 29 U.S.C. § 706 (7) (B))

IDEA lists the specific types of disabling conditions that entitle children to receive special education. In addition, for children to be entitled to

receive services under IDEA, their disabling conditions must result in the need for special education services.

Section 504 is much broader than IDEA, since it contains no categorical listing of disabling conditions. However, if a child is eligible for services under IDEA, he or she will also be protected under Section 504. The regulations also make clear that certain conditions, such as drug or alcohol addiction and heart disease, that would not qualify a child under IDEA may be handicapping conditions under Section 504. While Section 504 requires that the condition "substantially limit a major life activity," such as seeing, hearing, speaking, breathing, learning, and walking, it need not necessarily adversely affect a student's educational performance.

Source: Adapted from *Meeting the Needs of Students: Section 504 of the Rehabilitation Act of 1973* (Tallahassee: Florida Department of Education, 1992).

9.1 for an explanation of the differences between Section 504 and IDEA.

DEVELOPMENT OF THE IEP

After a student is determined to be eligible for special education, the education team begins to establish priorities among the student's needs and to determine goals and objectives for the student based on the results of the assessment of eligibility. In some instances, the team develops goals and objectives, which form the basis of the IEP, at its eligibility meeting. At other times, membership on the team changes to include additional personnel who may be providing services to the child.

The IEP is the one document that describes the curriculum, instruction, and assessment that

is to be provided to the student with a disability so that a free, appropriate public education can be implemented. This document is jointly created by school personnel, the student (when appropriate), and the student's parents or guardians.

Basic Tenets of the IEP

Plans for instructing children with disabilities have been the focus of legislation since the Education for All Handicapped Children Act (P.L. 94-142) was passed in 1975. During the past quarter century, IEPs for students with disabilities have included descriptions of goals and objectives agreed upon by members of the student's IEP teams, on the basis of appropriate assessments of the student. In 1990, when P.L. 94-142 was amended and its name changed to IDEA, emphasis was placed on expanding programs, mandating that transition services be included in IEPs, and including assistive technology devices and services as items to be considered in the education of students with disabilities (Florida Department of Education, 1995).

In 1997, IDEA was reauthorized to reflect an emphasis on educational programming with necessary accommodations for students with disabilities in the general education (core) curriculum. It also stressed the identification of needs based on assessments, the reporting of students' progress to parents at least as often as progress is reported for students without disabilities, and the inclusion of all students in the state and local testing designed to measure student learning for purposes of school accountability. The process of developing an IEP is discussed in the next section.

IDEA requires that a student with a disability must have an IEP at the beginning of the school year and that the IEP must be revised at least annually. More frequent revisions should take place whenever a change in the student's placement occurs and as necessary to address the student's programming needs. A revised IEP must note any lack of expected progress toward the annual goals and objectives the results of any reevaluation that has been conducted, information about the child provided to or by the parents, and the child's anticipated needs.

A parent or guardian must be invited to the IEP meeting, afforded due process rights, and guaranteed that evaluation procedures are nondiscriminatory, and that the child's records are kept confidential. The IEP team, as defined by IDEA, must include the following:

◆ The child's parent(s) or guardian(s),

◆ At least one general education teacher if the child is expected to participate in the regular education environment,

◆ At least one special education teacher (who should be a specialist in visual impairments if the student is visually impaired),

◆ A representative of the local school district (or LEA),

◆ An individual who can interpret the results of the evaluation, and

◆ Other individuals at the discretion of the family or the school district.

The student should participate in the development of the IEP, when appropriate, especially as he or she advances in school. Each member of the IEP team is responsible for reporting any information that will be helpful in determining the student's abilities and educational needs at the IEP meeting.

The Process of Formulating the IEP

The teacher of students with visual impairments may be the most appropriate person to lead the IEP team's discussion of the student's strengths and needs. He or she will also inform the other team members of the results of appropriate assessments of the student's progress, needs for modifications (changes in the level of material being taught) and accommodations (changes in the presentation of materials), and unique skill areas. The strength of these assessments will lead to the writing of an IEP that team members can agree to and implement.

At the IEP meeting, other members of the IEP team must also inform the team about the curriculum, instruction, and related services they recommend and provide explanations of how these educational components may be implemented. For example, the general education teacher provides information on the scope and sequence of the curriculum and on typical instructional methodologies that the team may find valuable as they discuss how the student with a visual impairment can best gain access to the general curriculum. The parents provide insights on the strengths and needs of their child from the perspective of their home life and observations of their child in family activities. The representative of the local school district supplies information about general program elements and can assist in determining the setting that may be appropriate for the student to receive the best services and instruction that he or she needs.

For students with visual impairments, the IEP team must consider "the strengths of the child and the concerns of the parents for enhancing the education of their child" (IDEA, 20 U.S.C. § 1401 (a) Sec. 614 (d)(3)(A)(i)). Also, the need for instruction in braille must be considered, depending on an evaluation of the child's reading and writing skills, needs, and appropriate reading and writing media (including an evaluation of the child's future needs for instruction in braille or the use of braille) (IDEA, 20 U.S.C. § 1401 (a) Sec. 614 (d)(3)(B)(iii)). Other factors that must be considered by the IEP team are these:

◆ In the case of a child whose behavior impedes his or her learning or that of others, strategies, including positive behavioral interventions, and support to address that behavior;

◆ In the case of a child with limited English proficiency, the language needs of the child as the needs relate to the IEP;

◆ The communication needs of the child and, in the case of a child who is deaf or hard of hearing, the child's language and communication needs, opportunities for direct communication with peers and professional personnel in the child's language and communication mode, academic level, and full range of needs including opportunities for direct instruction in the child's language and communication mode; and

◆ The child's need for assistive technology devices and services.

If the student with a visual impairment attends the IEP meeting, it may be helpful for the teacher of students with visual impairments to practice with the student so that he or she can effectively contribute to the meeting. Practice sessions may involve having the student list his or her perceived strengths, abilities, and weaknesses and identify desired postschool outcomes. Some special educators have investigated the notion of self-directed IEPs; in such cases, the student is actually in charge of the IEP meeting and conducts the meeting so that the desired postschool outcomes can be addressed from his or her perspective (Martin, Marshall, Maxson, & Jerman, 1993).

Contents of the IEP

Although the format of IEPs varies from one local area to another, as well as from state to state, each IEP must contain the elements mandated by IDEA. There are generally three types of individualized plans: the Individualized Family Service Plan (IFSP), written for a young child from birth to age 3; the general IEP, written for a student in prekindergarten (age 3) through the seventh or eighth grade; and the Transition IEP, written for a student age 14 and older, which addresses the need for transition services.

IFSP

The IFSP is a written document that is developed by the parents and appropriate providers of school and community services. It must include the components listed in Sidebar 9.2.

For a young child with a visual impairment, the IFSP should address the unique skill areas that are necessary for success in prekindergarten and the skills that will be reinforced throughout the child's school experience. Of particular importance to the development of an IFSP for a child with a visual impairment are input from the parent or guardian and identification of the family's priorities and concerns. For families of children with visual impairments, the understanding of how these youngsters experience their world and of the necessary modifications to instruction, skill building, and experiential activities that facilitate learning in children with visual impairments is critical. The IFSP may need to identify specific training for the family to accommodate these concerns.

IDEA states that an IFSP may be used for a child from age 3 to age 5 if the agency implementing the IEP provides the parent with a written

Required Components of an IFSP

- A statement of the infant's or toddler's present levels of physical development, cognitive development, communication development, social or emotional development, and adaptive development, based on objective criteria;

- A statement of the family's resources, priorities, and concerns related to enhancing the child's development;

- A statement of the major outcomes expected to be achieved for the infant or toddler and family and the criteria, procedures, and time lines used to determine the degree to which progress toward achieving the outcomes or services is necessary;

- A statement of specific early intervention services necessary to meet the unique needs of the infant or toddler and the family, including the frequency, intensity, and method of delivering services;

- A statement of the natural environments in which early intervention services shall appropriately be provided, including a justification of the extent to which the services will not be provided in a natural environment;

- The projected dates for initiation of services and the anticipated duration of the services;

- The identification of the service coordinator from the profession most immediately relevant to the infant's or toddler's or family's needs (or who is otherwise qualified to carry out all applicable responsibilities) who will be responsible for the implementation of the plan and coordination with other agencies and persons; and

- The steps to be taken to support the transition of the toddler with a disability to preschool or other appropriate services.

statement describing the difference between the components of IFSPs and IEPs. The agency must ensure that the parents understand their rights and are protected by the requirements of the IEP when the child turns 3 years old.

General IEP

The general IEP for a student in preschool (age 3) through the grade of his or her 14th birthday must contain the written components as defined in the 1997 reauthorization of IDEA, which are described in Sidebar 9.3.

All seven components of the IEP must be addressed for the IEP team to make carefully considered decisions about the appropriate setting or settings for the IEP's implementation. Each component necessarily relates to the others. Each

component is a building block of the entire program for the student and should form a plan for the student that addresses his or her needs related to access to general education and the student's desired school or postschool outcomes. The following section discusses each of the seven components.

Present Level of Educational Performance. If the assessment thoroughly and specifically identifies the student's strengths and needs and the modifications needed for instruction and assessment, the IEP team can write an accurate statement describing present levels of educational performance, a statement that will guide the team in completing the remaining components of the IEP. For a student with a visual impairment, the assessment must include information on the child's

SIDEBAR 9.3

Required Components of the IEP

- A statement of the child's present levels of educational performance, including how the child's disability affects the child's involvement and progress in the general curriculum or, for preschool-age children, how the disability affects the child's participation in appropriate preschool activities;

- A statement of measurable annual goals, including benchmarks or short-term objectives, to enable the child to be involved in and progress in the general curriculum and to meet each of the child's other educational needs that result from his or her disability;

- A statement of the special education, related services, and supplementary aids and services to be provided to the child and a statement of the program modifications or supports for school personnel that will be provided for the child to advance appropriately toward attaining the annual goals, to be involved and progress in the general curriculum, to participate in extracurricular and other nonacademic activities, and to be educated and participate with other children with disabilities and nondisabled children in these activities.

- An explanation of the extent, if any, to which the child will not participate with nondisabled children in the general education class and in the activities described;

- A statement of any individual accomodations in the administration of state or districtwide assessments of students' achievement that are needed for the child to participate in such assessments, and, if the IEP team determines that the child will not participate in a particular state or districtwide assessment of achievement (or part of an assessment), a statement of why that assessment is not appropriate for the child and how the child will be assessed;

- The projected date of the beginning of the services and modifications described and the anticipated frequency, location, and duration of those services and modifications; and

- A statement of how the child's progress toward meeting the annual goals will be measured and how the child's parents will be regularly informed (at least as often as parents are informed of the progress of their children without disabilities) of their child's progress toward the annual goals and the extent to which that progress is sufficient to enable the child to achieve the goals by the end of the year.

functional use of his or her vision and progress in the areas described in the expanded core curriculum.

The following is an example of a statement of the present level of educational performance of Marie, a ninth-grade student with a visual impairment, that provides some of the information that is helpful to the IEP team when establishing a student's specific strengths and needs.

On the basis of observations, the parents' reports, and the teacher's checklist evaluations, it was noted that Marie visually locates familiar objects in her environment. Her mobility in familiar environments is sufficient to travel safely around her home and within the school setting. Marie is insecure when traveling in unfamiliar environments and does not plan her travel routes or use low vision aids to locate objects in her environment. Academically, Marie maintains average grades if accomodations are made so that she is allowed to obtain classroom notes from a peer and handouts from the teacher before they are distributed to the rest of the class. She often chooses to use her closed-circuit television (CCTV) for reading. Because of a progressive vision loss, Marie's reading speed has decreased in the past year so that when large amounts of material have to be read, she must use a reader or listen to the materials on audiotape. Marie has shown an interest in expanding her braille skills and further investigating the use of low vision aids. She recognizes the braille contractions in isolation with 90 percent accuracy, but reads material written at the third-grade level slowly, at approximately 10 words per minute with 70 percent word recognition accuracy and 100 percent comprehsion.

Annual Goals and Short-Term Objectives. The annual goals and short-term objectives, or benchmarks, reflect the priorities for the student on the basis of the student's present level of educational performance and the desired school or postschool outcomes. Annual goals are broad statements related to knowledge, skills, behavior, or attitudes that will enhance the student's performance. Each statement of an annual goal should reflect a reasonable and realistic expectation that is compatible with the student's age; cognitive, social-emotional, and physical abilities; rate of learning; and interests. Annual goals must be measurable so that the IEP team can determine, at the end of the year, if the student has mastered them.

Short-term objectives describe the major milestones that must be accomplished to achieve the annual goals. They do not necessarily reflect the complete scope and sequence of a curriculum. Instead, they are sequential and reflect substeps of an annual goal.

For students with visual impairments, annual goals and short-term objectives should reflect areas of need related to the student's progress in the core curriculum (academic subjects and general education curriculum) and in the expanded core curriculum (the areas of instruction that must be specifically designed for students with visual impairments). Given the complexity of the needs of many students with visual impairments, IEPs often contain many annual goals and associated short-term objectives. In the following example, annual goals and short-term objectives are presented in relation to the present level of educational performance for Marie:

Goal: Marie will read materials written at the beginning fourth-grade level prepared in contracted braille at 30 words per minute with 90 percent word-recognition accuracy and greater than 95 percent comprehension.

Short-term objective 1: Marie will read one page of material written in contracted braille at the third-grade level at 20 words per minute, with 90 percent accuracy.

Short-term objective 2: Marie will read two pages of material written in contracted braille at the third-grade level at 25 words per minute with 90 percent accuracy.

Special Education, Related Services, and Supplementary Aids. For a student with a visual impairment, the content of the IEP must indicate the student's involvement in the core curriculum with the appropriate accomodations. All components of the IEP should reflect the effect of the student's visual impairment on the curriculum, instruction, and assessment. Accomodations may include the provision of materials in the student's preferred reading and writing media (braille or large or regular print with appropriate accomodations), changes in the physical environment (such as lighting or nearness to the presentation of instruction), changes in instructional and assessment strategies, or instruction in areas of the expanded core curriculum. Decisions regarding appropriate accomodations must be based on a functional vision assessment, learning media assessment, and accomodations noted during other assessments that were conducted. For Marie, the required special education, related services, and modifications and accommodations were as follows:

- Special education: teacher of students with visual impairments;
- Related services: O&M
- Supplementary aids: closed-circuit television (CCTV), braille, a telescope, and a variety of handheld magnifiers.

Participation with Nondisabled Peers. The IEP must include a statement of the extent, if any, that a student will participate with nondisabled children in the general education classroom. This requirement reflects a preference for providing services in the general education classroom and for the student to participate in the activities of peers without disabilities. A description of the activities that remove students from the general education classroom for special education services is part of this requirement. Opportunities to participate with nondisabled peers may include off-campus activities, such as vocational work on a job site, after-school community activities, or other extracurricular activities in which the student participates after school or on weekends. The following is a description of this component of Marie's IEP:

> To maximize progress through one-to-one instruction in a quiet environment, Marie will be removed from activities in the general classroom for braille skill training and training in other skills related to the expanded core curriculum, as appropriate. O&M services, which will be community based, will also require her removal from the regular class.

Modifications Needed for State- or Districtwide Assessment of Students' Achievement. This requirement of IDEA is intended to describe the specific modifications and accommodations that students need to participate in state- and dis-trictwide assessment programs, as in the following statement for Marie:

> Marie will participate in regular state and districtwide assessments, using braille and print materials (with appropriate electronic and/or handheld magnification equipment) as necessary. She will be given extended time limits, tested either in small groups or individually, and provided an alternate way to record her answers, as appropriate for each test.

If it is determined that a student cannot participate in these programs, the IEP team must indicate why this decision was made and how the student's progress will be assessed through an alternate procedure. Decisions about modifications and accommodations in testing should be based on the consideration of several factors, including the allowable accommodations for the test in question and the accommodations that the student typically uses in classroom instruction and testing, such as the allowance of additional time and the use of alternate response sheets or braille formats.

Date of Beginning, Anticipated Frequency, Location, and Duration of Services and Modifications. Four specific elements of a student's program include the initiation date of services, the anticipated frequency (how often and for what length of time during the school week), the anticipated location (where the service will take place), and the expected duration (such as a nine-week grading period, the regular school year, or the extended school year) of the services and modifications. All these elements are determined on the basis of the educational needs, annual goals, and short-term objectives for the student. This information for Marie was as follows:

- The provisions of this IEP will become effective on May 28, 2000.
- Instruction in braille will be conducted throughout the regular school year for a period of 1 hour each day, 5 days a week, by a teacher of students with visual impairments in a resource room.

◆ Two one-hour sessions of O&M services will be provided each week throughout the regular school year by an O&M specialist.

Reporting Students' Progress. One basic change that was included in the reauthorization of IDEA in 1997 was an emphasis on accountability for the progress of all students. The intent of this requirement was that the IEPs must provide information to parents about the progress of their children on the specific goals listed in the IEPs, as well as the children's general academic progress, specifically whether the children are expected to achieve each goal and objective listed on their IEPs by the end of the year. Parents must receive these progress reports at least as often as do parents of children who are not receiving special education services. On the IEP, an evaluation plan statement includes a description of the assessment procedure, the criteria for determining if the student has met the annual goal and short-term objectives (usually a percentage or ratio of errors made), and a schedule of evaluations for each short-term objective related to the annual goal (for example, every six weeks or once a semester). This is an example of an evaluation plan statement for Marie:

> Progress on the annual goals will be evaluated by direct observation and biweekly reviews of her braille reading. Marie will master the objectives when she can complete them in four out of five consecutive observations. Her progress will be reported to her parent on the report card every nine weeks.

Transition IEP

Beginning at age 14, a student's Transition IEP must contain statements of the student's need for transition services, when applicable. These statements focus on the student's course of study and generally describe the desired postschool outcomes in relation to independent living, enrollment in a vocational program or postsecondary educational institution, involvement in the community, and other areas of preparation for post-school life, depend-

ing on the student's strengths and needs. For students age 16 (or younger if determined by the IEP team), the IEP must include statements of transition services that the student needs, including interagency responsibilities and linkages that are necessary for attaining post-school outcomes.

The Transition IEP team usually consists of the student, parents or guardians, special educators, general educators, and appropriate adult service providers from the student's community. The Transition IEP must include a statement of goals or outcomes in four areas: employment, education-training, leisure-recreation activities, and living arrangements. It details the proposed activities to achieve desired outcomes, lists time lines for performing these activities, and assigns responsibility for providing support for each activity to the agencies or individuals represented at the meeting or to collaborative arrangements among them. Later, if it is discovered that an agency has not followed through on its assignment, the school must identify another responsible party or devise alternate plans to achieve the desired outcome. The complete Transition IEP for Marie is presented in Appendix A at the end of this chapter.

It should be noted that IEPs for students at the preschool and early elementary levels should also contain annual goals and short-term objectives related to career and vocational education, one area of the expanded core curriculum. For students with visual impairments, who have difficulty acquiring information about work, it is essential to provide instruction about career alternatives; acceptable work habits; and the relationships among school, work, and economic independence throughout their entire school careers.

DETERMINING PLACEMENTS

After the IEP team has written goals and objectives, the members need to determine the appropriate environment in which the student will be educated. As with other activities of the IEP team, the parents' input is vital to this decision.

IDEA places a high priority on educating students with disabilities with peers without disabilities. Section 612 (5) (a) states:

> To the maximum extent appropriate, children with disabilities, including children in public or private institutions or other care facilities, are educated with children who are not disabled, and special classes, separate schooling, or other removal of children with disabilities from the regular educational environment occurs only when the nature or severity of the disability of a child is such that education in regular classes with the use of supplementary aids and services cannot be achieved satisfactorily.

This component of IDEA, referred to as the least-restrictive environment provision, has been the source of considerable debate. Because the phrase "to the maximum extent appropriate" is vague, state agencies and LEAs have been left to interpret the intent of the law and implement it accordingly. Some educators and parents and advocacy groups believe that the least-restrictive environment for all students is the general education classroom, despite the IDEA regulations that require that a continuum of alternative educational placements be made available. Even though services for the majority of students with visual impairments are provided in general education classrooms for most of the school day (U.S. Department of Education, 1995), experienced educators of these students have generally been opposed to this "one size fits all" approach to providing educational services. Many students with visual impairments have complex educational needs that may be difficult to address appropriately in only the general education classroom; other educational placements may be more appropriate and less restrictive at any time during the students' education.

In 1995, The Office of Special Education and Rehabilitative Services (OSERS) of the U.S. Department of Education issued a *Policy Guidance on Educating Blind and Visually Impaired Students* that clarified OSERS' position with regard to the placement of students with visual impairments:

> It is the special education and related services set out in the student's IEP that must constitute the basis for the placement decision. After the IEP of a blind or visually impaired student is developed, the placement determination must be made consistent with the special education and related services reflected in the student's IEP. In addition, the harmful effect of the placement on the visually impaired student or the quality of services he or she needs must be considered in determining the [least restrictive environment]. (Huemann & Hehir, 1995, pp. 11–12)

This document emphasizes the importance of determining placements on the basis of individual needs:

> The overriding rule in placement is that each student's placement must be determined on an individual basis. As in other situations, placements of blind and visually impaired students may not be based solely on factors such as category of disability, configuration of delivery system, availability of educational or related services, availability of space, or administrative convenience. . . .
>
> Determination of appropriate education and related services . . . must examine the development of skills necessary to address the effects of blindness or low vision on the student's ability to learn and to access the curriculum. (Huemann & Hehir, 1995, pp. 12–13)

When determining the appropriate educational placement and least-restrictive environment, the IEP team must consider in what environment or environments the goals and objectives that have been identified for the student can best be met. This environment becomes, by definition, the least-restrictive environment. One factor that should be considered in deliberations on the least-restrictive environment is the importance of being educated with peers who are not disabled and of having meaningful contact with peers with similar disabilities. The least-restrictive environment varies according to the intensity of the specialized instruction and services the student needs. Since placement must be reevaluated at least annually, it is likely that the placement for a particular student will change as the student's needs, abilities, and strengths are appropriately addressed.

The regulations of IDEA require public agencies to make available a continuum, or range, of placement options to meet the needs of students with disabilities in special education and related services. The options on this continuum include general education classes, special classes, separate schools, and instruction in hospitals and institutions. As was described in Chapter 1, certain kinds of services for students with visual impairments have evolved over time, and these services now include itinerant and resource room instruction, the consultant model, and residential placement.

Placement Options

The placement options identified in the discussion that follows are presented in order from the least intensive to the most intensive direct services. It is important that readers not ascribe any higher value to one placement over another. Students who receive itinerant services are not necessarily "better" or "more capable" than are students who receive services at a residential school. Placement in a particular setting or with a particular kind of service should reflect only a student's need for specialized instruction at a specific time in his or her development. The receipt of appropriate services from a qualified teacher of students with visual impairments is indicative that needs are being identified and addressed and, it is hoped, that students are mastering more complex skills in more complex environments.

The Consultant Model

Students who are served under the consultant model require minimal, or no, direct services from a teacher of students with visual impairments. These students function at the same level as do other students in their classes, and their general education teachers make the necessary modifications or adaptations in conjunction with the teacher of students with visual impairments.

Many students who are appropriately served under the consultant model are children whose multiple disabilities include visual impairment. These students are often given the most beneficial services when their teachers adopt a transdisciplinary approach to programming. In the transdisciplinary approach, one primary teacher uses assessment and instructional strategies that have been devised by a team that may include a parent, a physical therapist, a speech-language specialist, a teacher of students with visual impairments, an O&M specialist, and an occupational therapist. Together, the team members identify appropriate routines in which the student can engage that maximize the number of skills to be mastered in each categorical area. They note the language to be used, how the child is to be positioned, and appropriate modifications for each task. Generally, however, only one teacher implements these suggestions.

Consultation does not necessarily imply a limited commitment of time. The involvement of the teacher of students with visual impairments on the educational team requires considerable time. Time is needed to become acquainted with the student and family, understand the student's complex needs, learn about the student's educational environments, meet with other team members for planning, explain the unique learning experiences of children with visual impairments to other teachers, and evaluate the impact of interventions. Providing consultation services does, however, imply that the service is provided to another adult on behalf of the child with a visual impairment and that this service may be intermittent, based on the changing needs of the child or the changing environments in which the child spends time.

Some students without severe and multiple disabilities do not require direct special education services from a teacher of students with visual impairments. For example, a student with a progressive vision loss whose visual functioning is still within the normal range may not need direct services. In this situation, classroom teachers, parents, and others may need to consult with the specialist in visual impairments about potential changes in the student's vision and ways to prepare the youngster for the future. Similarly, a student who no longer qualifies as visually impaired because of a new prescription may require consultative services while he or she is adjusting to the new lenses and life conditions. Infrequently, a comprehensive assessment may reveal that a student is making adequate academic progress, is not lacking any disability-specific skills, and has appropriate natural supports that facilitate the ongoing development of skills related to functioning in all areas. The student may only need accommodations for testing, or the student's general education teachers and parents may benefit from consultation with the teacher of students with visual impairments. This student may be appropriately served through a consultant model.

Itinerant Services

Under the itinerant teaching model, students with visual impairments are assigned primarily to either the general classroom teacher they would have been assigned to if they did not have a visual impairment or to a special educator in a self-contained classroom for students with multiple disabilities. A teacher of students with visual impairments is assigned to each student to address the special educational needs described in the student's IEP. The time that the itinerant teacher spends with any student should be based only on the time required to meet the special education goals identified in the IEP and may vary from several hours a day to short weekly or biweekly instructional periods.

Generally, specialists in visual impairments who provide itinerant services do not have classrooms at each of the schools their students attend, although they may occasionally be assigned small work areas in which they can store equipment and materials and provide instruction. More often, they are based at a school district's office and spend their time traveling among their students' schools. Any special equipment or materials that

the students need, such as CCTVs, braille dictionaries, embossers, or Talking Book machines must be brought to the students by the specialist in visual impairments. While some special skills are best addressed in the general education classroom, others require privacy or a quiet environment. Itinerant teachers of students with visual impairments should work with school administration to find locations where they can provide appropriate instruction to students.

Students who are best suited for services under the itinerant teaching model are those with few special education needs related to their visual impairments and those whose needs can best be met by general education or other teachers. They must be able to function in the educational environment in which they are placed with intermittent and generally limited support from a teacher of students with visual impairments. Unlike students who are served under the consultant model, however, these students have some instructional needs that must be provided directly and regularly by a teacher of students with visual impairments and/or an O&M specialist.

In many communities in which few students with visual impairments are enrolled in the local school districts, service by itinerant teachers is the only option regularly available. Nonetheless, students' needs, as detailed in the goals and objectives listed on the IEPs, must drive the determination of the anticipated frequency and duration of services. It is unethical and illegal to write goals and objectives on the basis of the amount of time that an itinerant teacher has available or the number of times the teacher can drive to a particular location. In these circumstances, other professionals and parents both assume that all the students' needs have been identified and are being adequately addressed, when, in fact, the duration and number of hours of service are based on other factors. Determining services according to the convenience of administrators and teachers may limit the skills that students learn in school and ultimately, the vocational, independent living, and other life options of students after they leave the educational system.

The limited interaction of the itinerant teacher

of students with visual impairments with students is both the strength and the weakness of this model. Students who do not receive unnecessary special treatment by their teachers; who attend their neighborhood schools; and for whom educational, social, and community expectations are similar to those for the other students with whom they are educated can develop a strong sense of efficacy, interdependence, and competence. Students in itinerant placements must rely on their own resources to solve problems, locate necessary assistance, and manage their school activities. Often, their schoolmates are their siblings and other children from their neighborhoods, and school- and peer-related activities occur in locations that are geographically accessible.

On the other hand, it can be difficult for itinerant teachers of students with visual impairments to get to know these students, their instructional programs, and their needs well. As a result, some students may struggle unnecessarily with nonacademic issues related to their visual impairments of which they, their parents, or their teachers are not aware and, consequently, may experience distress and sometimes failure, both of which could have been prevented. To avoid such circumstances, specialists in visual impairments and other members of assessment teams must be certain that their assessments are comprehensive and address all the potential needs of students with visual impairments. It also is critical that those who are in contact with the students communicate effectively and regularly, so they can quickly recognize any difficulties the students are having.

Resource Room Model

The resource room model of providing services to students with visual impairments offers more intensive, ongoing support from teachers of students with visual impairments. It differs from the itinerant model in two basic respects:

1. Students may not attend the school to which they would be assigned if they did not have visual impairments; rather, they attend a school that has been designated as a "magnet" school for students of their age with visual impairments who need daily contact with a teacher of students with visual impairments.

2. The teacher of students with visual impairments is based at the school these students attend and does not travel among schools in the area.

Students who receive services in resource rooms, like those who receive itinerant services, are assigned to a general or special education classroom for most of the school day, and the teacher of students with visual impairments is generally not their primary teacher. Students attending resource rooms, however, have intensive instructional needs related to their visual impairments. Although the amount of time spent in the resource room varies among students, they usually spend part of each day receiving instruction in the areas of the core curriculum and support that facilitates their academic progress. It should be noted that the teacher of students with visual impairments is not an academic tutor, but he or she may spend some time in the resource room ensuring that the students understand concepts introduced in academic courses. Some students even receive instruction in basic academic subjects, such as reading or basic mathematics, in resource rooms to build a strong foundation upon which future learning can occur.

There are many advantages to the resource room model. First, teachers of students with visual impairments have more opportunities in this model to observe students in a variety of situations, including classrooms, bus lines, the cafeteria, and the playground, and are thus more likely to get to know the students well. Second, since they are available to students and general education teachers throughout the school day, they can provide immediate assistance to teachers who are uncertain how to include students with visual impairments in the curriculum by helping these teachers adapt materials or modify instruction or by teaching classroom activities that cannot be easily adapted in other ways in the resource room.

Third, as members of the school staff, specialists in visual impairments who teach in resource rooms have assigned classrooms where books, materials, and electronic equipment can be stored and made available to students as needed. They also attend faculty meetings; monitor halls; and supervise students in the cafeteria, on bus lines, or on the playground as other teachers at the school do. Being on site facilitates these specialists' familiarity with teachers, staff, and administrators, so that discussions of issues related to students' progress and the means to achieve students' goals are more relaxed. Teachers in resource rooms learn which general education teachers have high expectations for the performance of students with visual impairments and can develop ongoing in-service programs to increase the faculty's and staff's awareness of these students' needs. Finally, students in resource rooms meet and frequently interact with other students who have visual impairments. Through planned and unplanned activities, they can discover issues they may have in common and solutions to problems related to their visual impairments.

The primary disadvantage of the resource room model is that students may not attend their home schools and therefore may not attend school with their siblings and other children in their neighborhoods. Because of the geographic distances between their homes and the school, students may find it impossible to attend planned or impromptu after-school or evening activities, and parents may be challenged to feel part of the school community and to participate in parent-teacher activities or school advisory committees.

Settings Designed Specifically for Students with Visual Impairments

Settings that are designed specifically for students with visual impairments include special day classes (located in either regular or special schools) or classes at schools that have a residential option. Usually, only densely populated areas and those with a large number of students with similar, intensive special education needs offer special day classes. In a special day class, the teacher of students with visual impairments is responsible for the majority of the educational goals identified in the IEPs in both academic and nonacademic areas. Special day classes are typically established for preschoolers who are working on basic foundation skills or students whose multiple disabilities include visual impairments. In the latter case, the teacher is also skilled in working with children who have severe and multiple disabilities and devises programs that are based on the best practices of both specializations.

Originally based on the boarding-school model, residential schools served the majority of students with visual impairments without additional disabilities until the 1960s. Leaders at residential schools developed comprehensive programs that were based on the unique needs of students with visual impairments, addressing both the academic and nonacademic needs of this population as they were understood at the time. Today, there are 52 residential schools in 42 states (Council for Exceptional Children, 1998), serving approximately 9 percent of the students who have been identified as being visually impaired (U.S. Department of Education, 1995). (For additional information on the evolution of these and other educational services, see Chapter 1.)

Residential schools, along with the few day schools for students with visual impairments in the country, offer an environment in which all the adults who are involved in the students' education understand the unique learning style of the population. In theory at least, all the instructors are teachers of students with visual impairments and hence can identify the students' needs and adapt materials and modify the curriculum to meet those needs. Becuase instruction is specifically designed for students for whom visual activities are difficult, the students spend their entire days engaged in learning, not in waiting while the larger number of sighted students receive visually based instruction, as may happen in general education classrooms. At residential schools, students have opportunities to continue their education after the typical six-hour school day, with instruction in dormitories and community-based settings after school and on weekends, during which goals related to all areas of the expanded core curriculum are easily infused for all students.

No one description can characterize all residential or special day schools. Residential schools have evolved differently in each state or region, depending on the state's history and politics, and the services provided by LEAs. In some states, residential schools serve only students whose multiple disabilities include visual impairments. In other states, the residential schools primarily serve students with no other disability besides visual impairment. Some schools have identified as their mandate the provision of services to all students with visual impairments in their states and have established extensive outreach programs—technical assistance, assessment, and other services in addition to their on-campus activities.

Such comprehensive, long-term residential services are not only expensive to provide, but are associated with nonmonetary issues, the foremost being the psychosocial impact of being separated from one's parents and other family members for extended periods. Many residential schools for the blind attempt to alleviate the impact of this separation by providing transportation for students to return home frequently and regularly and by working with families to develop and maintain strong ties with their children.

Students who attend residential schools usually require special education and support services beyond those that can reasonably be provided in local school programs (Hazekamp & Huebner, 1989). Some families believe that their children will receive higher-quality educational services in residential schools or recognize that they cannot deal effectively with the extensive needs of their children at home (Corn, Bina, & DePriest, 1995). Indeed, for many children, residential schools provide the opportunity to develop compensatory and disability-specific skills naturally and to interact with other students and adults who have visual impairments, and through these interactions, come to terms with themselves as competent and capable individuals with visual impairments.

Most special day classes, special schools, and residential schools are not "segregated" environments in which students with visual impairments have no contact with individuals without disabilities in typical community settings. It is the policy of most of these schools to take full advantage of the benefits of community-based instruction, providing appropriate educational and vocational services in local community settings. Many residential schools enroll students, as appropriate and directed by the IEPs, in courses offered by local school programs, so that the students spend part of their instructional days in general education programs and part of their days in the special schools' programs.

The "Ideal" Placement

It is important to recognize that the ideal placement, in which all of a student's needs can be met, probably does not exist in most cases. Because students with visual impairments have many complex needs, it is challenging to find time in the school day or year to meet them all. Teachers and parents may need to establish priorities among the students' needs and be creative in discovering options for instruction that are not among the continuum of services described in the law. When setting priorities, members of an IEP team may choose to focus on a student's most pressing needs but must resolve not to lose sight of the less immediate goals. Sometimes, the work schedules of teachers of students with visual impairments and O&M specialists can be altered to take advantage of time before or after school or on weekends. Some specialists in visual impairments plan optional summer programs that focus on the acquisition of new independent living, recreational, or career skills. Many residential schools offer short-term placements for students who need intensive instruction in specific areas, such as the use of assistive technology or O&M. Interested and involved parents can also provide valuable assistance by giving their children opportunities to practice newly mastered skills at home and in the community, although some consultations with a teacher of students with visual impairments may be required to discuss adapted methods or techniques.

Once again, it is essential for educators to view different placement options as equally valuable. Any placement can be the most or least "restrictive," depending on a particular student's needs. If a placement enhances a student's understanding of the world and creates an environment in which intended learning occurs, then it should be considered appropriate for the student. If a placement restricts a particular student's ability to learn, then it is inappropriate for that student, regardless of its value to other students.

ADMINISTRATION OF EDUCATIONAL PROGRAMS

Involvement of Families

The success of any educational program for a child is largely dependent on the ongoing meaningful involvement of the child's parents and other family members. Teachers cannot—and should not—be the only individuals involved in a child's education. The level of involvement of parents and families, while mandated in the law, is often influenced by the attitudes and actions of teachers.

The passage of P.L. 94-142 in 1975 was in large measure the result of the work of parents whose children with disabilities had been denied appropriate educational programs and services. Since parents were instrumental in writing both the law and its regulations, it is not surprising that the law strongly supported the role of parents in designing programs for their children and guaranteed them certain rights in the educational planning process. Successive reauthorizations of P.L. 94-142, including the IDEA amendments of 1997, have reiterated the pivotal role of families and strengthened the importance of teaming with family members during all phases of educational programming.

Legal Rights of Parents

IDEA established certain rights of parents of children with disabilities, among which are protections in (1) evaluation procedures, (2) the development of IEPs and placement decisions, (3) impartial hearing procedures, and (4) the ensurance of confidentiality. Confidentiality is protected by guaranteeing that parents may review and make copies of their children's educational records and correct errors in these records. In addition, parents are guaranteed the rights to have reasonable requests for interpretations of records by knowledgeable school personnel honored in a timely way and to give their consent before identifiable personal information is disclosed.

Parents must give their consent for evaluations of their children to take place and have the right to review the procedures and instruments to be used in the evaluations. They must be informed of the results of the evaluation and have the right to review all records related to the identification, evaluation, and placement of their children. Furthermore, parents can obtain independent educational evaluations of their children, and those results must be considered in any decisions regarding the children. Upon the parents' request, school districts must provide the names of independent evaluators and, in some circumstances, pay for independent evaluations when the parents dispute the findings and conclusions of the educational teams.

With regard to the development of IEPs and placement of children, parents have the right to be notified in their primary language or system of communication before IEP meetings are held. Similarly, they must be notified of any changes in educational placement, including recommendations for assignment, reassignment, or denial of assignment in any special education program. In addition, parents must sign consent forms for the initial placement of children in a special education program, and they have the right to refuse services at that time. School personnel may not further assess students or change students' placements without the parents' consent.

When there are serious disputes or disagreements between parents and educators regarding the provision of the free, appropriate public education of their child, including the child's identification, evaluation, and educational placement, either party has the right to request a mediation or due process hearing. According to IDEA, a due process hearing must be held within a strictly defined period and is presided over by a hearing officer, an impartial third party who has no connections with either the parents or the school and no personal or professional interest in the outcome of the case. During a due process hearing, the parents and the school district have the right to be accompanied by and consult with counsel and educational experts, present evidence, compel witnesses to appear, cross examine witnesses, prohibit the introduction of evidence that has not been disclosed at least five days before the hearing, and obtain a verbatim record of the hearing. The child may be present during the hearing, which is open to the public. The decision of a due process hearing can be appealed.

To avoid costly due process hearings that are clearly litigious, the 1997 amendments to IDEA require states to establish a mediation process that can be used to solve differences. Participation in a mediation must be voluntary, cannot be used to delay the parents' right to due process, and must be conducted by a qualified and impartial mediator who is familiar with effective mediation techniques. As with a due process hearing, the school district must pay for the mediation. An agreement reached by the parties during the mediation must be written. Involvement in a mediation does not preclude either party from requesting a due process hearing, although information disclosed during the mediation is confidential and may not be used in other hearings.

Collaborating with Parents and Families

Although it is important for special educators to know and understand the legal protections af-

forded parents, it is even more critical that they respect the ethical rights of parents to be perceived as the most significant adults in their child's life and hence the people with the most to offer the educational team during all phases of educational programming. Effective teachers of students with visual impairments sincerely welcome the involvement of the parents and other family members of all their students and recognize that these are the people, besides the student, who have the most to gain from the student's optimal development. They are also the first to realize that their jobs are made much easier by the trust, support, and participation of such committed, involved family members.

In most cases, parents are not trained for the roles they must play in their children's lives and may be struggling to achieve control over unanticipated circumstances. Most new parents have never known people who are blind and have only limited knowledge of the abilities of people with visual impairments—often based on negative stereotypes—to guide them in developing expectations for their children. Furthermore, although effective techniques for communicating with and involving children with visual impairments may seem simple, they are actually difficult and not intuitive. Because of these various limitations, parents may approach the task of raising their children who are visually impaired with low expectations and self-confidence and a lack of understanding of how their children learn and of the specialized techniques that can lead to success.

Therefore, it is the role of teachers of students with visual impairments to help parents change these circumstances by helping them to understand their children's specific ways of experiencing the world, learn specialized techniques for introducing and reinforcing skills, develop self-confidence, and dream of their children's potential. Similarly, it is the parents' role to help teachers of students with visual impairments and other educators to understand the behavior, preferences, joys, dislikes, and other critical information about their children. By working together, parents and teachers discover each other to be valuable allies in determining appropriate outcomes and delivering meaningful instruction to children with visual impairments.

Working closely with parents requires teachers to gain the trust and respect of family members. Margolis and Brannigan (1986) identified eight strategies for developing trust and respect:

◆ Accept families as they are;

◆ Listen carefully and empathically for the cognitive and emotional content of the family's message;

◆ Help families feel comfortable by sharing information and resources with them when legally possible;

◆ Prepare for all meetings;

◆ Focus on the hopes, aspirations, concerns, and needs of family members, since attending to concerns communicates caring;

◆ Keep promises;

◆ Allow the family's expertise to shine; and

◆ Be there when needed.

Effective teaming occurs when teachers and family members view one another as competent, communicate effectively, and focus on a common goal. Parents do not want to be told what is best for their children; rather, they want to be given information and options and be empowered to make decisions that are based on their families' needs. Parent-professional partnerships thrive when a teacher makes these kinds of assumptions:

◆ That the relationship is important and worth the expenditure of time and effort to establish;

◆ That families of children with disabilities are more similar to other families than they are different;

◆ That adopting a longitudinal life-cycle perspective is valuable;

◆ That family members can provide valid and unique information that is not always available through other, formalized means;

◆ That all families have inherent strengths, but that families' strengths, resources, and needs are individual; and

◆ That interactions between families and community agencies are often intimidating and stressful for parents (Mallory, 1986).

Teaming can occur during every phase of educational programming. Teachers can help parents understand this process and encourage them to participate fully, by helping them if necessary, to acquire the skills they need to ensure success.

Involving Parents in Assessments. Parents should be invited to establish the emphases of assessments, describe their children's level of involvement in typical routines, provide information about their children's past and present levels of functioning, and share their hopes and expectations for their children. Those parents who watch formal and informal testing can confirm the results or be asked to indicate their children's typical performance. In addition, parents can be asked to demonstrate the techniques that work for them as they involve their children in everyday tasks, through either videotapes of these techniques or observations by the assessors in the children's natural environments. The extensive involvement of parents during assessments can help all the adults involved to gain a better understanding of the children, to trust one another, and to develop shared goals.

Involving Parents at IEP Meetings. Parents should be encouraged to come to IEP meetings with their own lists of proposed goals for their children, as well as any questions they would like answered about their children's educational programming. They should be encouraged to take time to review fully the documents that are written during the IEP meetings and to ask questions to clarify their understanding of the proposals. For parents who are new to the special education system, it may be helpful if the teacher of students with visual impairments spends time before the first IEP meeting explaining the process, predicting who will attend and making the parents comfortable about their important role in planning their child's education. Parents should be informed that they have the right to bring a friend or advocate to this meeting, for moral support or advice or to help them remember the decisions after the meeting.

Involving Parents in Placement Decisions. Placement should be discussed during every IEP meeting. No assumptions about a child's placement should be made until the goals and objectives have been determined. If, during the discussion of placement, the parents are unfamiliar with one or more of the options being recommended or considered, the IEP team should stop the meeting and resume it only after the parents have had a chance to observe the class or program in question and evaluate it in relation to their child's needs. Parents need to be informed of the entire continuum of placement options that are mandated by law, including the services offered by their state's residential school, and be given guidelines to help them determine a program's appropriateness for their child.

Involving Parents in Instruction. Although parents generally choose not to be involved in the day-to-day instruction of their children at school, they should be invited to observe their children in the school environment and welcomed when they feel the need to do so. Observation of their children may give parents valuable information about how the children function when they are away from home, the techniques that school personnel use to manage the children's behavior, and the demands of the environment on the children. It may be necessary to provide visiting parents with guidelines to ensure that instruction is not unnecessarily interrupted. Teachers may feel threatened when parents observe them working with students; instead, they should consider frequent visits from parents to be a signal that the parents want to improve their communication with the educational team about their educational programming.

Students with visual impairments, as well as their parents, benefit when instruction in some skills is provided at home by teachers of students with visual impairments. These youngsters, who often have difficulty generalizing skills, frequently are more successful in developing independent living skills when they learn to perform tasks at home, such as cleaning the bathtub, folding laundry, and preparing snacks. In the children's homes, the individual tasks are introduced as part of a process, of which the children are a part. The parents benefit from watching this instruction, since they do not always understand the techniques used by teachers of students with visual impairments, which may seem mysterious or complicated to them. By watching effective teaching strategies, listening to instructional prompts, and imitating words of praise, parents discover that the mystery of teachers' success often is in the expectation for performance, not necessarily some "magic" way to accomplish tasks.

If parents do not have the time to come to school or students cannot be instructed in their homes, the teacher of students with visual impairments needs to ensure that parents are informed of their children's progress, are familiar with the ways in which their children accomplish tasks, and feel comfortable reinforcing the skills their children are mastering. Frequent telephone conferences are one way to communicate with parents, although telephone conferences and written notes do not have the same impact as face-to-face conversations in which the parents and teacher can exchange information about the students' challenges and the solutions to overcoming them.

Involving Parents During the Transition. It is also essential for parents to be involved in decisions related to their children's postschool outcomes and the entire transition process. As was mentioned earlier, transition planning is a highly individualized process that is based on students' and families' preferences, strengths, weaknesses, and resources. It is during transition planning that all parents—some for the first time—come to terms with their children's continued dependence or need to exert autonomy and independence from them. Parents can experience severe stress when they contemplate issues related to insurance, medical care, income and benefits maintenance, and the like without the ongoing and continuing support of the school system, on which they have relied for the past 18 to 20 years. Transition planning and services help to ease parents' stress by providing a framework for joint action among students, parents, school personnel, and representatives of adult service agencies.

According to Crane, Cuthbertson, Ferrell, and Scherb (1998, p. 81), it is the parents' responsibility to do the following during the transition:

◆ Help the young adult develop self-determination and self-advocacy by creating opportunities for making choices and expressing preferences;

◆ Become knowledgeable about the laws governing transition and the criteria for high school graduation;

◆ Insist that these young adults participate in planning and IEP meetings;

◆ Provide guidance to the transition planning team in their development of goals that reflect the family's values and preferences;

◆ Advocate for the development of an IEP that integrates the young adult into the community and reduces his or her dependence on family and social systems;

◆ Request information on the potential supports that the young adult or the family think will be needed as the young adult moves to postschool educational, vocational, recreational, and living settings; and provide opportunities for the young adult to develop and practice independent living skills.

Non-Public School Placement

The provisions of IDEA guarantee a free, appropriate, public education to all eligible students with disabilities. Over the years, questions have been raised about the responsibilities of public school districts with regard to students who attend private, including parochial (i.e., religious), schools. As detailed in IDEA, public school districts are obligated to conduct child-find activities with students in private schools, evaluate students who are suspected of having disabilities in these schools, and develop IEPs for students who are found to be eligible for special education and related services. As part of the development of IEPs, special education and related services to achieve the goals and objectives must be identified and made available to the students. If an IEP team determines that the appropriate placement for a student is a private school, then it is the school district's responsibility to pay that school's fees. If the parents choose to place their child in a private school, however, and the school district has made an appropriate educational placement available to the student, then the school district is not obligated to pay the private school's fees.

The location in which special education and related services can be provided has been considered by policy-making bodies and the courts and has frequently been determined by the policies of local school districts. Generally, the courts have found that school districts are not required to provide services on the grounds of private schools, but such a practice is permitted. Some judicial decisions (*Fowler v. Unified School District*, 1996, and *Russman v. Sobel*, 1996) have supported the position that the responsibilities of school districts to students in private schools (including parochial schools) are comparable to their responsibilities to students in public schools.

It is important for teachers of students with visual impairments to be aware of a district's policy on the provision of services to students enrolled in parochial schools, particularly with regard to instruction in O&M and the provision of religious texts in alternate media. The use of public funds for religious purposes is prohibited (EDGAR, 34 C.F.R. § 76.532 [a]), but if the funds are provided in a "religiously neutral" manner, they may be acceptable. In *Zobrest v. Catalina Foothills School District*, 113 S. Ct. 2462 (1993), the Supreme Court ruled that services on a parochial school site are permissible if they "provide assistance to the student without regard to the religious nature of the school." Although the *Zobrest* case specifically addressed the provision of a sign-language interpreter, who was deemed to be making class material accessible to the student, not advancing a particular religious philosophy, its principle has been applied to the provision of books in alternate media that are used in parochial school classrooms.

The 1997 reauthorization of IDEA does not require school districts to provide special education and services on private school sites, but allows them to provide such services to the extent consistent with the law. Yell (1998, p. 376) reported that the standard that school districts must achieve is that students with disabilities are provided with a "genuine opportunity for meaningful participation."

Accountability

Accountability of all students has become a critical focus of the educational system. School personnel are mandated through IDEA and, often, state legislation to provide information about students' progress and the effectiveness of programs. The public's demand for accountability has forced the educational community to develop plans for determining students' progress, evaluating programs for efficiency and effectiveness, and reporting these accountability measures.

Students with visual impairments must be assessed periodically to determine their progress in the academic or core curriculum, as well as in unique skill areas (expanded core curriculum). (For additional information on the core curriculum and expanded core curriculum, see Chapters 1 and 10.) As was discussed earlier, appropriate assessments provide invaluable information to teachers and parents that can help guide effective learning strategies and teaching techniques. (For additional information on assessment, see Chapters 2, 3, and 4 in *Foundations of Education: Instructional Strategies for Teaching Children and Youths with Visual Impairments.)*

Students with visual impairments and no other disabilities can be easily included in regular state- and district-required testing programs if attention is given to appropriate testing accommodations. The results of these assessments help administrators and other school personnel understand the effectiveness of students' educational programming with regard to the general education curriculum. When appropriate testing accommodations have been provided, the students' academic progress can be compared to that of their grade-level peers. If the students are not making the same academic gains as their grade-level peers, then the effectiveness of the students' entire programs must be evaluated.

Program evaluation involves the examination of the procedures and principles that are used to obtain information for decision making in relation to the total program provided to students with visual impairments. Decisions may require the determination of the current status of a particular aspect of a program and then a specification of desired modifications of that program. Information must be gathered and analyzed systematically to ensure that the decisions are based on both valid and reliable data. Each school or program should develop a plan for using evaluative data to improve special programs. The types of data that are needed for program evaluation include students' progress in attaining academic goals, as well as unique skills; students' and staff's attendance rates; parents', students', and staff's satisfaction; graduation rates; and postschool outcomes. The expanded core curriculum provides a basis for general school outcomes for students with visual impairments (see Hatlen, 1996). Hazekamp and Huebner (1989) described standards and criteria for evaluating programs that serve students who are visually impaired.

Liability

Parents and administrators sometimes voice concerns about the safety of students with visual impairments that are grounded in the belief that these students are at a greater risk of injuring themselves because of their lack of (or limited) vision than are sighted students. Typical administrative concerns center on the use of private automobiles to transport students with visual impairments for O&M lessons and the provision of training in other skills in environments away from the school. Parents occasionally express their fears that students may be hurt in classrooms, cafeterias, and playgrounds, and some request that special treatment or personnel be provided to their children to prevent such accidents. Generally, school personnel are responsible for the safety of students with visual impairments in the same way that they are responsible for the safety of all other students. All school staff must perform their jobs safely and responsibly so that no student is unnecessarily put in danger.

It is wise to make parents aware of all aspects of the programs for students with visual impairments, including transportation in private vehicles, teaching environments away from the school, and what is involved in O&M training. Some administrators may insist that parents sign consent statements to ensure that they are informed. Any signed release of liability may not be honored by the legal system if school personnel are found to be negligent in performing duties that involve students. It is suggested that teachers of students with visual impairments and O&M specialists who transport students in their private automobiles obtain liability insurance through their personal automobile insurance plans or through insurance plans issued to their school districts. Professional liability insurance, available for members of the Association for Education and Rehabilitation of the Blind and Visually Impaired (see Chapter 10), is also recommended.

Caseloads and Class Sizes

The determination of caseloads and class sizes is often the responsibility of administrators of LEAs. Many factors must be considered in making these decisions, which may change frequently as students' needs change. Administrators must be aware of the roles of teachers of students with visual impairments, O&M specialists, and other

support personnel to make informed decisions in these areas. Although Hazekamp and Huebner (1989) recommended a general range of 8–12 students per teacher of students with visual impairments, decisions on caseload size need to be based on the following factors:

- The time required for instruction in unique skills;
- The time required for consultation with other personnel regarding teaching strategies;
- The time required for consultation with medical personnel, community agencies, and parents;
- The time required for travel;
- The time required to obtain or produce specialized and adapted materials;
- The time required to keep records, write reports, order textbooks, and perform other organizational tasks;
- The severity of visual impairments, presence of additional disabilities, and age of the students who are served; and
- The intensity of students' needs.

See Appendix B at the end of this chapter for an example of a formula for determining an appropriate caseload.

It is recommended that the administrator meet with the teachers of students with visual impairments, O&M specialists, and other support personnel to discuss the size of caseloads and classes and include these staff members in the decision-making process. Once the sizes of caseloads and classes are established, the administrator must continually monitor the caseloads, keeping the factors just listed in mind. Being aware of spur-of-the-moment and hidden time commitments (such as the evaluation of new students or students' immediate need for specialized instruction in particular areas) that affect specialists in visual impairments and other staff will allow the administrator to make sound decisions about the number of students each teacher serves and the need for paraeducators and other support personnel, such as braillists or clerical workers (Knowlton, Woo, & Voeks, 1990). Adjustments in the sizes of caseloads and classes will allow programs for students with visual impairments to meet the needs identified on students' IEPs.

Paraeducators

The presence of "overly helpful" paraeducators can impair students' acquisition of independent work and advocacy skills and can inadvertently foster dependence in children by solving all their problems for them. Students with these kinds of paraeducators rarely have to advocate for themselves because they rarely have problems to solve. Their classrooms are well organized, their materials are always available, and their needs are magically met by the paraeducators who have been assigned to them. However, some students with overly helpful paraeducators may begin to perceive themselves as incompetent. Without the daily challenges of encountering and solving problems, these students may not develop the organizational, social, and functional skills they need to be successful adults.

Paraeducators may also interfere with typical interactions among children in the classroom. Many teachers of students with visual impairments attempt to solve this problem by assigning paraeducators to general education teachers. In this case, although the primary duty of a paraeducator is to facilitate the successful involvement of a child with a visual impairment, the paraeducator helps all the children with a their work and is perceived by the children as just another adult in the class.

Decisions regarding assignment of paraeducators should be made by the IEP team only after thoughtful consideration. For some students, a readily available adult provides the support necessary to function successfully in a particular educational environment. This individual may support the student by transcribing classroom materials into accessible formats, describing videos, explaining visual events that are occurring in the classroom, and reinforcing newly introduced or emerging skills. In addition, a paraeducator can effectively facilitate the partial participation of a young student or a student with additional disabilities in the social, functional, and academic activities of the class.

Because paraeducators require training and supervision, administrators need to consider these two activities when they develop the schedules of teachers of children with visual impairments. In addition, administrators need to remember that good teachers are constantly assessing while they instruct their students, evaluating the rate at which the students are acquiring skills and the effectiveness of their teaching. Administrators should ensure that students who are assigned paraeducators who are reinforcing newly learned skills are also seen frequently by the specialist in visual impairment so that their progress is adequately assessed and the instructional approach is changed, if necessary.

Links to Rehabilitation

One primary purpose of the transition process is to provide a formal link between educational services and services provided to adults with and without disabilities. Before the passage of the IDEA amendments of 1990, many students completed school without discussing or planning for their postschool activities. Parents and students were left to discover on their own that the world of adult services was different from that of educational services. Today, when transition planning is successful, students are taught the skills they need to be advocates for themselves; are made aware of the vocational, independent living, and recreational options that are available to them; and are encouraged to establish links with adult service agencies that will enhance their functioning as adults.

Not all students with visual impairments will need or be eligible for services provided by state or private agencies after they graduate. Some students who are visually impaired who receive special education and related services through IDEA will not qualify for services, since most state and private agencies require that their clients be legally blind or demonstrate substantial limitations in activities of daily living. Others will find that they have the skills necessary to function successfully as adults without formal or continuing contacts with agencies serving individuals with visual impairments. Still others will need intensive and ongoing services to participate in vocational and adult living environments.

Most students with visual impairments should view participation in rehabilitation services as a means to an end, not the end itself, and hence should not think that they will always be clients of one system or another (Erin, 1988). Rather, they need to be provided with services that encourage them to strengthen their sense of autonomy and control over their lives. Educational programming from early elementary school through high school should include instructional goals and objectives in self-knowledge, career and work awareness, and job-seeking and maintenance skills. Teachers and parents need to convey their high expectations for students, provide realistic feedback, facilitate opportunities to work, and promote the development of socialization and compensatory skills—key skills for the successful transition to adult living (Wolffe, 1996).

Individuals who have developed these skills can use rehabilitation services to their best advantage. Most state vocational agencies provide young adults with financial support while they attend college or trade school, are searching for jobs, and are getting established in new jobs. These services are most effective when clients of rehabilitation services do not depend heavily on rehabilitation counselors but, rather, recognize their own personal responsibility for finding and keeping jobs and for honing their independent living skills.

Many young adults with visual impairments require direct instruction in, and frequent practice of, the skills necessary to get and maintain jobs or to live independently or with support. For them, ongoing contact with state vocational rehabilitation services or private agencies is necessary. Most state vocational agencies operate residential rehabilitation centers, in which skills related to vocational training and independent living are taught to adults. Some private agencies offer similar services, both in center-based settings and individually in clients' homes. Again, except in cases when additional disabilities limit the independent functioning of adults with visual impairments, these services should be viewed as necessary only in the short term, with occasional recontact occurring when adults need disability-specific instruction to master new skills.

While they are still in school, students with visual impairments benefit from close cooperation between providers of educational and rehabilitation services. Rehabilitation counselors can assist teachers in their efforts to help students understand the reality of the demands of adult life and can facilitate planning to meet those demands. Through such coordination and linkages, the transition to adult living is made smoother for students and their families.

Coordinated transition services are mandated by IDEA, and a commitment to the spirit of the law truly improves students' outcomes. Successful transition to rehabilitation services begins not at age 14, but with the development of attitudes of self-sufficiency, competence, and personal value that are achieved through careful educational planning, thoughtful involvement of parents and families, and high-quality instruction. Educators must always keep in mind the reality that their students will become adults some day and hence need to direct educational programming toward the needs of their students as adults.

CONCLUSION

Federal legislation in the form of IDEA defines the process of educational programming. It establishes the requirements that local education agencies must follow in their efforts to locate and appropriately serve children with disabilities, including students with visual impairments. Among these requirements are: (1) that local education agencies must actively search for students with disabilities, (2) that they assess each student referred for special education, (3) that they hold a meeting to determine the referred student's eligibility for services, (4) that they create a plan describing the special education and related services that they will provide that student, (5) that they place the student in the least-restrictive environment, and (6) that they provide appropriate services. IDEA also describes the responsibility of the school to work with families of children with disabilities, as well as setting forth a process that parents may follow if they are not satisfied with their child's education.

All teachers need to be familiar with the components of educational programming as identified in IDEA. In addition, they must realize that *quality* educational programming requires a positive attitude on the part of teachers who believe that their job is to work closely with parents to facilitate the development of young people into adults who can manage their own lives. Through such collaboration, students with visual impairments can make steady progress and achieve exciting results.

STUDY QUESTIONS

1. How are each of the following processes defined for educational programming for students with disabilities: referral and identification, assessment, determination of eligibility, development of IEPs, determination of placements, and administration of educational programming?

2. Why is it important to include parents of students with disabilities in every step of the educational process?

3. What is "child find"? Explore how child find occurs in your community and participate in child-find activities if possible.

4. Interview a teacher of students with visual impairments. What are the procedures he or she follows in planning the educational programs for his or her students (including the determination of appropriate assessment procedures, the development of IEPs, and meetings of the IEP team)? Write a summary of your findings.

5. Interview the parents of a student who is visually impaired about the same issues

just listed (assessment, development of IEPs, and team meetings). How did the interviews with the teacher and the parents differ? Write a summary of your findings.

6. What are the essential components of an IEP? List and describe them.

7. What is the difference between an overall educational goal and a short-term objective or benchmark? Practice writing samples of both.

8. How is *least-restrictive environment* defined in this chapter? Why is there controversy over the definition of this term? What are the implications of misunderstanding the term?

9. How are the following placement options defined, and what are the advantages and disadvantages of each: the consultant model, itinerant services, the resource room model, and settings designed specifically for students with visual impairments?

REFERENCES

Bishop, V. E. (1996). *Teaching visually impaired children* (2nd ed.). Springfield, IL: Charles C Thomas.

Corn, A. L., Bina, M. J., & DePriest, L. B. (1995). *The parent perspective on schools for students who are blind and visually impaired: A national study.* Alexandria, VA: Association for Education and Rehabilitation of the Blind and Visually Impaired.

Corn, A. L., Hatlen, P., Huebner, K. M., Ryan, F., & Siller, M. A. (1995). *The national agenda for the education of children and youths with visual impairments, including those with multiple disabilities.* New York: AFB Press.

Council for Exceptional Children, Division for the Visually Handicapped. (1991). *Family-focused services for infants and young children with visual handicaps.* Reston, VA: Author.

Council for Exceptional Children. (1998). *National plan for training personnel to serve children with blindness and low vision fact sheet: Schools for the blind.* Reston, VA: Author.

Crane, P., Cuthbertson, D., Ferrell, K. A., & Scherb, H. (1998). *Equals in partnership: Basic rights for families of children with blindness or visual impairment.* Watertown, MA: National Association for Parents of the Visually Impaired.

Education Department General Administrative Regulations (EDGAR), 34 C.F.R.§ 76.532 (a).

Erin, J. N. (1988). Better to give than to receive? *RE:view, 20*(1), 35–37.

Florida Department of Education (1992). *Meeting the needs of students: Section 504 of the Rehabilitation Act of 1973.* Tallahassee, FL: Author.

Florida Department of Education (1995). *Volume 1-C, Federal laws and regulations pertaining to the education of students with disabilities.* Tallahassee, FL: Author.

Hatlen, P. (1996). The core curriculum for blind and visually impaired students, including those with additional disabilities. *RE:view, 28*(1), 25–32.

Hazekamp, J., & Huebner, K. M. (Eds.). (1989). *Program planning and evaluation for blind and visually impaired students: National guidelines for educational excellence.* New York: American Foundation for the Blind.

Huemann, J., & Hehir, T. (1995). *Policy guidance on educating blind and visually impaired students.* Washington, D.C.: Office of Special Education and Rehabilitative Services.

Individuals with Disabilities Education Act, 20 U.S.C. §§ 1400 *et seq.* (1997).

Individuals with Disabilities Education Act Regulations, 34 C.F.R. § 300, 301. (1993).

Knowlton, M., Woo, I., & Voeks, J. (1990). Caseload management for itinerant personnel to provide instruction in compensatory skills to visually handicapped children. *DVH Quarterly, 35*(3), 5–23.

Mallory, B. L. (1986). Interaction between community agencies and families over the life cycle. In R. R. Fewell & P. F. Vandasy (Eds.), *Families of handicapped children: Needs and supports across the life span* (pp. 317–356). Austin, TX: PRO-ED.

Margolis, H., & Brannigan, G. (1986). Building trust with parents. *Academic Therapy, 22*(1), 71–75.

Martin, J. E., Marshall, L. H., Maxson, L., & Jerman, P. (1993). *Self-directed IEP.* Colorado Springs, CO: University of Colorado at Colorado Springs, Special Education Program.

U.S. Department of Education (1995). *Seventeenth annual report to Congress on the implementation of the Individuals with Disabilities Education Act.* Washington, D.C.: Author.

Wolffe, K. (1996). Career education for students with visual impairments. *RE:view, 28*(2), 89–93.

Yell, M. L. (1998). The law and special education. Upper Saddle River, NJ: Merrill.

Individualized Education Program

IEP Development Date ___4-23-00___ Student Name _Marie Rosado_____

Grade _9_ School _Century High School_ Birth date ___2-16-84___ ID# ___123-45-6789___

Exceptionality (ies) _Visual Impairment_____

Date of most recent evaluation ___4-1-00___ Date of last IEP ___4-21-99___

DESIRED SCHOOL OR POSTSCHOOL OUTCOMES
To be completed for all students. May include outcomes regarding involvement in the general curriculum, school programs and courses of study, extracurricular activities, post-secondary education, continuing and adult education, vocational training, employment, adult services, and community living.

The student desires to _grow up and raise a family. Marie talks of becoming either a biologist or a veterinarian. School is important to her, and she indicates a desire to attend a state college._

Indicate if this is a Transition IEP ___✓___ YES _____ NO

GENERAL FACTORS
Briefly describe each of the following factors.

Strengths of the child _Marie is persistent and determined to be "the best" at whatever she attempts._

Results of the most recent evaluation _Marie's visual impairment has progressed to the point where her mobility and reading speeds are affected._

Parent's concern for enhancing their child's education _Mrs. Rosado is worried that Marie's changing visual status will cause her to fall behind in her academic subjects._

SPECIAL FACTORS
Special factors have been considered for this student. CHECK (✓) ALL identified needs addressed in this IEP:

❏ Need for positive behavior intervention or strategies
☑ Braille needs of blind/visually impaired
❏ Language needs of Limited English Proficient
❏ Communication and language needs
☑ Need for assistive technology devices and services
☑ Need for extended school-year services
❏ Need for specially designed/adaptive physical education
❏ Need for special transportation services

(continued on next page)

Individualized Education Program *(Continued)*

CHECK (✓) the instructional structure (i.e., domains, transition services activity areas) you will use and the area within the structure in which present level of educational performance statements, measurable annual goals, and short-term objectives or benchmarks will be written. Transfer the domains or areas checked to the following page(s).

❑ DOMAINS

✓ Curriculum and Learning Environment

___ Social and Emotional Behavior

✓ Independent Functioning

✓ Communication

☑ TRANSITION SERVICES ACTIVITY AREAS

✓ Instruction   ✓ Daily Living Skills

✓ Community Experience   ___ Functional Vocational

✓ Employment Evaluation   Evaluation

✓ Postschool Adult Living

MEASURABLE ANNUAL GOALS AND SHORT-TERM OBJECTIVES OR BENCHMARKS
(additional pages as needed)

PRESENT LEVEL OF EDUCATIONAL PERFORMANCE for *Independent Functioning*
Specify area checked on previous page and include a description of the student's strengths; what the student is able to do; how the student's disability affects the student's involvement and progress in the general curriculum or, for prekindergarten children with disabilities, how the disability affects the child's participation in appropriate activities.

Based on *Informal observations, parent's reports, and teacher's checklist evaluations. Marie visually locates familiar objects in her environment. Her mobility in familiar environments is sufficient to travel safely at home and in school. Marie is insecure when traveling in unfamiliar environments and does not plan her routes or use vision aids efficiently.*

Priority educational need *Improve orientation and mobility in unfamiliar settings.*

MEASURABLE ANNUAL GOAL
Annual goals and short-term objectives or benchmarks must relate to meeting the student's needs resulting from the student's disability in ways that enable the student to be involved in and progress in the general curriculum and to meeting each of the student's other educational needs resulting from the student's disability.

When placed in an unfamiliar environment, Marie will use landmarks and environmental cues to travel safely and efficiently to a desired destination, based on the teacher's observations and evaluation.

(continued on next page)

Individualized Education Program *(Continued)*

Student Name *Marie Rosado* ID# *123-45-6789* Date *4-23-00* Page *3* of *9*

Assigned Instructional Duties for this Goal:
Responsibilities may include planning, implementing, documenting student's performance, consulting, etc.

Lead Teacher/Staff *Orientation and Mobility* Other *Teacher, Students with Visual*

Specialist *Impairments*

<table>
<tr><td>Title/Position of Person(s) Responsible</td><td>Title/Position of Person(s) Responsible</td></tr>
</table>

SHORT-TERM OBJECTIVES OR BENCHMARKS   RESULTS

1.1 Marie will use a monocular to spot designated objects while traveling in an

unfamiliar environment within 10 seconds of their being named by the orientation and

mobility specialist.

1.2 Marie will use her cane to identify and appropriately respond to 100 percent of

the drop-offs and curbs encountered while traveling for 30 minutes in an unfamiliar

environment, as judged by the Orientation and Mobility specialist.

1.3 Marie will use appropriate route planning and environmental cues to travel by bus and

to locate a building at an unfamiliar address, as judged by the orientation and mobility

specialist.

EVALUATION PLAN
The evaluation plan includes a description of the assessment procedures, criteria, and schedule of evaluation for each short-term objective or benchmark related to the annual goal.

Progress toward the annual goal will be measured through the observations of the Orienta-

tion and Mobility specialist at least once every six weeks and will be considered met

when Marie plans for and safely travels to three unfamiliar environments without requir-

ing intervention from the Orientation and Mobility specialist during a three-week period.

The student's progress toward annual goals and the extent to which progress is sufficient to enable the student to achieve the annual goal by the end of the year will be reported to the student's family:

____ with report cards every ____ weeks   ✓ through written reports every *6* weeks
____ through conferences every ____ weeks   ____ other (specify)

(continued on next page)

Individualized Education Program *(Continued)*

PRESENT LEVEL OF EDUCATIONAL PERFORMANCE for *Communication*
Specify area checked on previous page and include a description of the student's strengths; what the student is able to do; how the student's disability affects the student's involvement and progress in the general curriculum or, for prekindergarten children with disabilities, how the disability affects the child's participation in appropriate activities.

Based on *Results of the Burns and Roe Informal Reading Inventory, Marie's print-reading*

speed has declined to 43 words per minute, with grade-level comprehension. The results

of informal testing show that Marie recognizes braille contractions in isolation with

90 percent accuracy and reads third-grade materials in braille at 10 words per minute

with 70 percent accuracy and 100 percent comprehension.

Priority educational need *To improve braille reading skills*

MEASURABLE ANNUAL GOAL
Annual goals and short-term objectives or benchmarks must relate to meeting the student's needs resulting from the student's disability in ways that enable the student to be involved in and progress in the general curriculum and to meeting each of the student's other educational needs resulting from the student's disability.

Marie will read materials written at the beginning fourth-grade level prepared in

contracted braille at 30 words per minute, with 90 percent word recognition accuracy and

greater than 95 percent comprehension.

Assigned Instructional Duties for this Goal:
Responsibilities may include planning, implementing, documenting student's performance, consulting, etc.

Lead Teacher/Staff *Teacher, Students with*   Other _____

             Visual Impairments   _____
Title/Position of Person(s) Responsible   Title/Position of Person(s) Responsible

(continued on next page)

Individualized Education Program *(Continued)*

SHORT-TERM OBJECTIVES OR BENCHMARKS   **RESULTS**

2.1 Marie will read one page of written material in contracted braille at the third-grade level at 20 words per minute, with 90 percent accuracy.

2.2 Marie will read two pages of written material in contracted braille at the third-grade level at 25 words per minute, with 90 percent accuracy.

EVALUATION PLAN
The evaluation plan includes a description of the assessment procedures, criteria, and schedule of evaluation for each short-term objective or benchmark related to the annual goal.

Reading speed and accuracy will be measured daily as part of instruction. Benchmarks will be considered achieved if rate and accuracy levels are maintained for four out of five consecutive sessions.

The student's progress toward annual goals and the extent to which progress is sufficient to enable the student to achieve the annual goal by the end of the year will be reported to the student's family:

✓ with report cards every _9_ weeks   ____ through written reports every ____ weeks
____ through conferences every ____ weeks   ____ other (specify)

EXCEPTIONAL STUDENT EDUCATION
Services and modifications relate to assisting the student to advance appropriately toward attaining annual goals, to be involved in and progress in the general curriculum, and to be educated and participate with other students with disabilities and nondisabled students in activities.

SPECIAL EDUCATION	**Dates: Initiation**	**Duration**	**Frequency**	**Location**
Teacher, Students with				
Visual Impairments	*4/26/00*	*1 year*	*5 hours weekly*	*Resource Room*

(continued on next page)

Individualized Education Program *(Continued)*

Student Name _Marie Rosado_ ID# _123-45-6789_ Date _4-23-00_ Page _6_ of _9_

RELATED SERVICES	**Dates: Initiation**	**Duration**	**Frequency**	**Location**
Orientation and				
Mobility Specialist	*4/26/00*	*1 year*	*2 hours weekly*	*Community*

PROGRAM MODIFICATIONS/ SUPPORTS FOR SCHOOL PERSONNEL	**Dates: Initiation**	**Duration**	**Frequency**	**Location**
Classroom accommodations				
and supports	*4/26/00*	*1 year*	*Ongoing*	*High School*
Material preparation				
(braille, audiotape, CCTV)	*4/26/00*	*1 year*	*Ongoing*	*Classroom*
Collaborative planning by				
all teachers	*4/26/00*	*1 year*	*Ongoing*	*Classroom*

SUPPLEMENTARY AIDS AND SERVICES	**Dates: Initiation**	**Duration**	**Frequency**	**Location**
Braille, tape recorder, CCTV,				
adaptive computer	*4/26/00*	*1 year*	*Ongoing*	*Classroom*
Braille 'n Speak, braille				
handouts, audiotaped books				*home as needed*

STATE AND DISTRICTWIDE ASSESSMENT MODIFICATIONS

Participation in state and districtwide assessment program(s) __✓__ YES _____ NO _____ NA

If yes, describe needed accommodations for each _Use of CCTV, braille, and/or handheld_ _magnification devices, as necessary. Use of extended time, individual administration, word_ _processor for writing tests, and alternate way to record test answers in test_ _booklet._

(continued on next page)

Individualized Education Program *(Continued)*

If no, explain why each assessment is not appropriate and describe each alternative assessment

_____

_____

_____

PARTICIPATION IN REGULAR/ VOCATIONAL EDUCATION	Amount of Time	Purpose
General education class for academics	75 percent	Acquire grade-level skills
After-school activities for journalism club	2 days per week	Participate in extra-curricular activities

REMOVAL FROM PROGRAMS WITH NONDISABLED STUDENTS

Explain the extent, if any, to which the student will NOT participate with nondisabled students in the general education class and extracurricular and nonacademic activities _Marie requires specialized instruction in braille and orientation and mobility to meet IEP goals and objectives._

PLACEMENT (Based on the percentage of time with nondisabled students)

_____ General Education Class (more than 79 percent with non-ESE)

__✓__ Resource Room (more than 40 percent, but less than or equal to 79 percent with non-ESE)

_____ Separate Class (less than or equal to 40 percent with non-ESE)

_____ Hospital/Homebound

_____ Separate Day School

_____ Residential Facility

_____ Juvenile Justice Program

SPECIALIZED TRANSPORTATION SERVICES

CHECK (✓) the statement describing the condition of the student that qualifies for weighted funding for specialized transportation services.

_____ 1. Medical equipment required (e.g., wheelchair, crutches, walkers, cane, tracheotomy equipment, positioning or unique seating devices).

_____ 2. Medical condition requires a special transportation environment as per physician's prescription (e.g., tinted windows, dust controlled atmosphere, temperature control).

(continued on next page)

Individualized Education Program *(Continued)*

Student Name _Marie Rosado_ ID# _123-45-6789_ Date _4-23-00_ Page _8_ of _9_

_____ 3. Aide or monitor is required due to disability and specific need of student.
      Describe: _____

_____ 4. Shortened school day required due to disability and specific need of student.
      Describe: _____

__✓__ 5. School assigned is located in an out-of-district school system.
      Describe: _Resource room at high school_____

PARTICIPANTS

LEA Representative _____ General Education Teacher _____

Parent(s) _____ Student _____

ESE Teacher _____ Evaluation Specialist _____

Other IEP Members

_____   _____

_____   _____

TRANSITION

For students who will become age 14 and above during the current school year, transition service needs may be addressed through components of the IEP that focus on the student's course of study. Provide a general description of the student's course(s) of study.

Marie attends all general education classes for academic subjects and receives

instruction in braille, daily living skills, vocational education, and orientation

and mobility from a teacher of students with visual impairments and an orientation and

mobility specialist.

Diploma   __✓__ Standard   _____ Special   [❑ Option 1 ❑ Option 2]   _____ NA

For students, beginning at age 16 (or younger), a statement of needed transition services for the student and a statement of interagency responsibilities or any needed linkages must be included. If the indication is that no services are needed, the team must indicate the basis on which this decision was made in the space provided below.

Required

1. Instruction _Marie will take academic classes required for a standard diploma with_

    appropriate supports.

(continued on next page)

Individualized Education Program *(Continued)*

Student Name *Marie Rosado*   ID# *123-45-6789*   Date *4-23-00* Page *9* of *9*

2. Community Experience *Marie will develop travel skills in unfamiliar environments within the community.*

3. Employment *Marie will continue to explore career options, personal aptitude, and career development strategies.*

4. Postschool Adult Living *Marie will develop knowledge and skills related to setting up and maintaining an apartment.*

If appropriate

5. Daily Living Skills *Marie will develop alternative methods to perform tasks of daily living, including cooking, cleaning, and shopping.*

6. Functional Vocational Evaluation *No services needed at this time.*

Transfer of Rights

CHECK (✓) if the student has been informed of transfer of rights at least one year prior to reaching age of majority. Indicate the date when the student was informed.

___✓___ The student has been informed.   Date of notification _____*4-23-99*_____

Responsibilities and/or Linkages for Transition Services.

The person's signature below indicates willingness to provide support(s), service(s), or skill(s) that relate to the Transition Plan.

Division of Blind Services   Provide instruction in living skills

Agency Represented	Responsibilities	Agency Representative's Signature
Agency Represented	Responsibilities	Agency Representative's Signature
Parents	Responsibilities	Parent's Signature
Student	Responsibilities	Student's Signature

APPENDIX B: RESOURCE ALLOCATION COMMITTEE, COLORADO DEPARTMENT OF EDUCATION, SUMMARY REPORT

May 1995
This is a summary of the work of the Resource Allocation Committee. The purpose of the Resource Allocation Committee has been to determine reasonable guidelines for caseload management. This committee was one of three established as a result of Colorado state legislation (House bill 94-1148) that was passed in the Spring of 1994, which addressed achievement of literacy by children who are visually impaired. The task of developing guidelines for caseload management turned out to be much more challenging than was first anticipated. The result, however, is a good product that we feel will enhance services in Colorado for children who are visually impaired.

The Resource Allocation Committee members included vision service providers from various parts of the state and representatives of an advocacy organization, the National Federation of the Blind. The members put in many hours both in and outside of meetings. Throughout this process, the co-chairs met periodically to keep updated and to ensure that general direction for each committee's work was the same.

INTRODUCTION TO CASELOAD MANAGEMENT GUIDELINES*

The Resource Allocation Committee's intent is to have guidelines for vision teachers that are "user friendly" and are specifically targeted to the needs of each district or service unit. The caseload management guidelines should be reviewed annually by vision teachers in order to address changes that occur in programs. By completing the steps listed in the guidelines that follow, districts will be bet-

* This section is reprinted from Hicks, N. K., & Barron, J. (Eds). (1995). Caseload Management Formula. Denver, CO: Colorado Department of Education.

ter able to assess and document their staffing needs and plan for anticipated changes.

The recommended guidelines to determine caseload management for vision services in Colorado include three components:

1. Direct and indirect services to students
2. Related professional responsibilities
3. Travel time (for itinerant personnel)

Each student's needs would be evaluated and given a rating. The district or unit vision teacher would total the hours of service that all students require. Then, they would add the minutes of travel time between destinations. Finally, a percentage of the workweek to meet other duties involved in operating a program for vision services would be determined. Read the following steps listed in determining caseload management for further details.

The Resource Allocation Committee members feel confident that this information will "assist the Colorado Department of Education to implement guidelines that are clear, efficient, and useful in maintaining an appropriate level of services to all children with a visual impairment in this state."

CASELOAD MANAGEMENT FORMULA

Three components combined determine caseload management: direct and indirect services to students, related professional responsibilities, and travel time (see Appendix Figure 9.1). The following steps will help you:

1. Determine your present caseload
2. Check whether your caseload matches your designated contract hours

Step 1: Begin by determining the individual rating for each child who is identified with a visual impairment based on the severity of needs determiners (Severity Rating Scale, Appendix Figure 9.2).

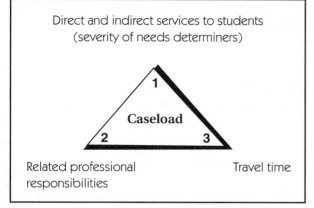

Direct and indirect services to students
(severity of needs determiners)

Caseload
1
2   3

Related professional   Travel time
responsibilities

Appendix Figure 9.1

Step 2: Total the number of hours of direct and indirect services to all students.

Step 3: Add to this number the total time for travel (minutes, *not* miles).

Step 4: Then consider the amount of time necessary to meet related professional responsibilities such as those listed below

◆ Parent contact

◆ Supervision of support staff

◆ In-services (preparation/presentations for staff, community, etc.)

◆ Community partnerships

◆ Consultation with staff and administrators

◆ Other district-assigned duties

◆ Referral assessments

◆ Writing reports

◆ Materials preparation

◆ Orders/materials inventory management

◆ Planning/management

◆ Meetings (general educational, team, vision—local, regional, state)

Note: This component (step 4) will vary to some extent based on individual programs. An average range for vision service providers is 25 percent to 40 percent of the week.

Step 5: A. Total the hours of the three components. This gives you your total hours per week.

B. Compare this with your contracted hours per week. These two numbers should match.
  • If they do not match, does a paraprofessional or other support staff account for the difference?
  • If they do not match and support staff does not account for the difference, the caseload should be re-evaluated.

Example

Component 1:	30.5 hrs.	(direct and indirect services)
Component 2:	5.0 hrs.	(related professional responsibilities)
+ Component 3:	7.5 hrs.	(travel time)
	43.0 hrs.	

43.0 hrs. is greater than 37.5 contracted hrs. An adjustment is necessary to meet guidelines.

Severity Rating Scale

Medical

0   Normal visual acuity with full visual field, no significant pathology

1   Possible progressive disease, but one eye still within normal limits; mild nystagmus, bilateral strabismus which cannot be corrected; pre/post eye surgery; other severe temporary eye treatment, such as patching; significant bilateral field loss

2   Student with most significant support needs related to cognitive disabilities; functionally visually impaired; delayed visual maturation

3   Acuity 20/70 to 20/200 in better eye after correction; a visual field of more than 20 degrees

4   Acuity of 20/200 to object perception in better eye after correction; a visual field of 20 degrees or less

5   Object perception to total blindness; a visual field of 10 degrees or less

Reading Medium

0   Regular print with no modification; multi-impaired nonreader; prereader

1   Regular print with magnification in addition to correction

2   Regular print with consistent use of magnification in addition to correction and/or large print

3   Technology for low vision; tapes

4   Braille or prebraille

5   Technology for braille

Compensatory Skill Needs/Adaptive or Developmental Training

0   Needs no compensatory skill instruction

1   Needs compensatory skill instruction in handwriting, fine and gross motor areas, and/or PE/recreational activities

2   Needs compensatory skill instruction in use of functional vision, sensory awareness, prevocational skills, use of low technology/adaptive equipment, and/or orientation to specific location

3   Needs compensatory skill instruction in concept development, use of basic low vision devices, computer/typing, map reading, geographical concepts and/or science concepts; career and vocational training; beginning Orientation and Mobility training

4   (In addition to 3) Needs compensatory skill instruction in tactual development, braille, abacus, slate and stylus, use of advanced low vision devices, daily living skills, advanced O&M training, vocational support

5   Needs advanced travel/cane skills; advanced math and science; transition between levels and placements; college preparation

(continued on next page)

Appendix Figure 9.2. Severity Rating Scale For Students with Visual Impairments

Severity Rating Scale *(Continued)*

Environmental and Instructional Adjustments

0   Needs no adaptations of instructional materials or presentations

1   Needs some adapted written materials; dark copies; special seating; some magnification; extra lighting; materials storage area, and/or work area for special equipment

2   Needs occasional use of tapes; some adaptation of maps/graphs; frequent magnification, and/or extra lighting; requires some production of braille materials

3   Needs individually developed multisensory materials and adaptation; adaptive equipment such as switches and communication boards

4   Needs tapes; enlargement or adaptation of all instructional materials

5   Needs major production of braille; tactual adaptation of instructional materials; requires modified assignments and/or curriculum

Affective and Independence

Note: Severe emotional/social/behavioral needs rely on partnerships with other professionals in conjunction with the vision service provider. The following reflects the responsibilities of the vision service provider.

0   Needs no assistance in completing all assignments; involved in age appropriate activities and adult/peer interactions; understands and positively accepts visual impairment; accesses own resources (role models, organizations, etc.); is self advocate; multi-impaired nonacademic; preacademic

1   Needs minimal assistance with completing assignments and ordering materials (other than CIMC); requires encouragement for self advocacy; support for developing friendships; needs help understanding and explaining vision

2   Needs monitoring to complete assignments and ordering materials; requires assistance coping with visual impairment; has difficulty initiating and maintaining friendships

3   Needs direct intervention for completing assignments and ordering materials; does not initiate or maintain friendships; denies visual impairment and/or its implications

Rating Scale Guidelines

0–4   No Service

5–9   Consult Service Only (1/2 hour per month—1/2 hour per week)

10–14   Light Service (1/2 hour per week—5 hours per week)

15–19   Moderate Service (5 hours per week—20 hours per week)

20–23   Heavy Service (more than 5 hours per week)

CHAPTER 10

Professional Practice

Alan J. Koenig and M. Cay Holbrook

KEY POINTS

- Teachers of students with visual impairments face complex ethical issues and need to use both personal and professional standards to address these issues.

- Specialized organizations provide professional development opportunities and literature for teachers.

- It is important that teachers of students with visual impairments participate in specialized training opportunities and receive certification in visual impairment.

- Teachers of students with visual impairments work with parents and a wide variety of professionals to provide educational services to students.

- Valuable support is available to teachers and parents through national organizations.

Those who are preparing for careers in educating students with visual impairments need to learn about and appreciate the richness of the professional practice that guides the provision of educational services for these students. Professionalism is nurtured by these factors:

- Adherence to the best professional practices and established ethics in the practice of the profession;

- Understanding of the roles that professionals play in the educational process;

- Knowledge about the preparation and continuing development of professionals;

- Familiarity with the professional literature; and

- Knowledge of and the ability to gain access to professional organizations, consumer organizations, and specialized agencies.

Teachers of students with visual impairments face many complex issues. They work in a variety of service delivery settings and may need to adjust their working practices to the demands of particular settings. They may also work with numerous professionals with whom they need to coordinate their efforts. Furthermore, those who work in itinerant settings need to work effectively with principals, general education teachers, and other personnel in many schools. In addition, specialists in visual impairment often have few resources available to them and must be creative in meeting pressures associated with time and money.

The students with whom these teachers work have a wide variety of needs, and their teachers serve them using a wide variety of methods. In many situations, teachers of students with visual impairments are independent professionals and have little contact with others who have expertise in visual impairment. Although the challenges are sometimes daunting, the rewards of teaching students with visual impairments are just as great as the challenges. Teachers of these students routinely describe their profession as "exciting," "interesting," and "fascinating." This chapter discusses the professional practices of teachers of students with visual impairments and provides information about addressing the challenges these teachers face.

BEST PROFESSIONAL PRACTICES

Much has been written about "best professional practices" in education, and the field of educating students with visual impairments is no different. However, there has not always been a clear delineation of the roles of educational specialists in visual impairment and the part these specialists play in developing and implementing programs for students. When students with visual impairments were first being integrated into regular classrooms, teachers believed that their role was to ensure that their students made progress in academic classes, and their practices involved modifying materials and making adaptations to allow this integration to occur (Hatlen & Curry, 1987). However, this approach ignored the development of other essential skills, such as daily living skills and vocational skills.

Like other professions, the field of visual impairment has grown from early practices. Many of these practices, while well intentioned, often failed to address holistically and comprehensively the special and unique needs of students with visual impairments. Today, there is a clearer differentiation of the focus of professional practice in educating students with visual impairments. In 1987, for example, Hatlen and Curry delineated the "disability-specific needs" or "unique needs" of students with visual impairment. This approach placed the focus of the curriculum on what was special or unique about these students' educational needs. However, when some practitioners in general education interpreted the concept of unique needs to mean that the fulfillment of these needs was something "extra," not necessary, the original conceptualization was refined.

Today, the curriculum for students with visual impairments has two parts: the core curriculum and the "expanded" core curriculum. The core curriculum consists of the general education curriculum that all students are expected to master, including language arts, science, mathematics, and social studies. The expanded core curriculum covers the unique, disability-specific skills that students with visual impairments need to live independently and productively (Corn, Hatlen, Huebner, Ryan, & Siller, 1995). Teachers of students with visual impairments generally use the expanded core curriculum as a guide in providing appropriate educational services for their students. In most situations, it is their role to address the skills in the expanded core curriculum, which include the following:

- ◆ Compensatory skills, including communication modes,
- ◆ Orientation and mobility (O&M) skills,
- ◆ Social interaction skills,
- ◆ Independent living skills,
- ◆ Recreation and leisure skills,
- ◆ Career education,
- ◆ Use of assistive technology, and
- ◆ Visual efficiency skills.

ETHICS

Codes of Ethics

The professional practice of specialists in visual impairment is governed by codes of ethics, both internal and external. One's internal "code" of ethics is a personally defined set of beliefs and standards that governs one's life in general, as well as one's professional practice. These beliefs and standards are molded from, and develop through, one's sense of personal responsibility and worth, parental influences, religious and moral convictions, schooling and professional preparation, and all other life experiences. How people respond to ethical dilemmas in life—whether to "tattle" on a friend, tell a store clerk when one is given back too much change, or engage in an unauthorized rally to promote a social cause—is governed by their individual internal belief systems and personal codes of ethics. Since teachers have a major influence on the lives of children and youths, it is essential that they have high standards of personal ethics.

External codes of ethics govern professional practice. The Council for Exceptional Children (CEC), the largest professional organization that addresses issues faced by special education teachers, has a widely recognized code of ethics, which is presented in Sidebar 10.1. The first principle states: "Special education professionals are committed to developing the highest educational and quality of life potential of individuals with exceptionalities" (CEC, 1998, p. 1). This principle and the actions that a professional would undertake to carry out this commitment reflect elements of best professional practices. Clearly, this commitment must emerge from one's internal code of ethics; a professional could not simply "practice" this commitment because he or she was told to or expected to do so. Following a carefully defined professional code of ethics and applying it throughout one's professional life helps to ensure that the education offered to children and youths with disabilities is of the highest quality and that improvements are continually sought.

The Association for Education and Rehabilitation of the Blind and Visually Impaired (AER), the largest professional organization in North America for teachers and other specialists in visual impairment, addresses issues that face professionals who serve individuals with visual impairments of all ages. AER has also established a code of ethics for teachers of students with visual impairments, O&M specialists, rehabilitation teachers, and low vision therapists (see Appendices B, C, D, and E at the back of this volume). Those who are certified to practice any of these professions must follow the specific code of ethics of their particular specialization. The certification guidelines for each profession contain a section on ethical practices, the professional's due-process rights, and the appropriate appeals procedure that must be followed if a professional is reported to have violated the established code of ethics. If the professional is found to be in violation, his or her certification could be revoked.

Ethical Dilemmas

Many professionals in visual impairment continually face ethical dilemmas in providing appropriate, high-quality educational services to students who are blind or visually impaired. Since there is a shortage of professionals in the field and caseloads tend to be high, the amount of time needed to meet a student's needs may be compromised by logistical or administrative factors. These factors instantly place a professional in an ethical dilemma, and questions arise, such as the following:

◆ Do I provide the amount of instructional service that fits into my schedule? Is providing some instructional time better than not providing any?

◆ Do I refuse to sign a student's Individualized Education Program (IEP) until an appropriate level of service is provided, even though I run the risk of angering my supervisor or losing my job?

◆ Do I advocate for the student and his or her parents, or do I fulfill the expressed or implied wishes of my supervisor?

◆ Do I allow a paraeducator to do some of my teaching, even though he or she is not qualified to do so?

Questions like these are asked more often than professionals and school administrators would like to admit, and there are no simple answers or solutions. The internal struggle between high-quality standards of practice and day-to-day reality is unsettling and uncomfortable for profes-

CEC Code of Ethics for Educators of Persons with Exceptionalities

We declare the following principles to be the Code of Ethics for educators of persons with exceptionalities. Members of the special education profession are responsible for upholding and advancing these principles. Members of The Council for Exceptional Children agree to judge and be judged by them in accordance with the spirit and provisions of this Code.

Special Education Professionals:

A. Are committed to developing the highest educational and quality of life potential of individuals with exceptionalities.

B. Promote and maintain a high level of competence and integrity in practicing their profession.

C. Engage in professional activities which benefit individuals with exceptionalities, their families, other colleagues, students, or research subjects.

D. Exercise objective professional judgment in the practice of their profession.

E. Strive to advance their knowledge and skills regarding the education of individuals with exceptionalities.

F. Work within the standards and policies of their profession.

G. Seek to uphold and improve where necessary the laws, regulations, and policies governing the delivery of special education and related services and the practice of their profession.

H. Do not condone or participate in unethical or illegal acts, nor violate professional standards adopted by the Delegate Assembly of CEC.

Excerpted, with permission, from The Council for Exceptional Children, *What Every Special Educator Must Know: The International Standards for the Preparation and Licensure of Special Educators,* 3rd ed. (Reston, VA: Author, 1998), p. 1.

---

sionals until they take appropriate action. To address this struggle, each professional must consider internal and external codes of ethics, the needs of students and their families, and other factors that are affected by any decision, and then decide on a course of action. In making such decisions, it is important for members of a student's educational team to take actions that will benefit the student and his or her family. To achieve this goal, the following guidelines may be used:

Do what is right for all students on the basis of their individual needs and focus on these needs in everything you do. Begin by clearly and convincingly establishing each student's needs through a high-quality, thorough assessment that presents clear and justified recommendations. Work within the IEP process to match the student's assessed needs with appropriate educational services. When the discussion shifts to logistical or administrative matters, immediately refocus on the student's needs. The IEP team meeting must focus on the student, not on the limitations of the school district or agency.

Serve as an advocate for the student and his or her family. Meeting students' educational needs is the teacher's primary goal. In determining how to do so and implementing this goal, teachers can avail themselves of many resources, such as experienced educators, trusted colleagues, and representatives of the many national organizations in the blindness field (for instance, the American Council of the Blind, the American Foundation for the Blind, and the National Federation of the Blind; see the section on organizations later in this chapter). Also, Advocacy, Inc., is a group that provides advocacy and legal services for people with any disability, including blindness, and their families.

Be a professional, not an employee. Professionals in visual impairment rarely have nine-to-five jobs. The role is demanding and complex, requiring the highest commitment to professional practice. In most situations, teachers of students with visual impairments are not supervised by other specialists in visual impairment. Therefore, they may need to educate their supervisors and co-workers about the needs of their students and the kinds of educational services that are required to address these unique needs. By educating administrators and co-workers, teachers are in a better position to advocate for an increased quality or quantity of specialized services.

Do not accept or condone the practice of allowing nonqualified persons or paraeducators to perform a teacher's duties. Having someone other than a teacher perform a teacher's duties violates both logic and laws, undermines the principle of adherence to the highest professional standards, and ultimately results in substandard educational programs for students with visual impairments. To help ensure appropriate staffing, develop written policies or guidelines on the role of paraeducators and have these documents approved by administrators. Also, use the IEP process to identify and document the amount of instructional time that a qualified professional needs to provide.

Advocate continually for high-quality and expanded services for students who are visually impaired. Work within the school district or agency to increase the available continuum of program options for students, so IEP teams can better match students' needs with the appropriate configuration of services.

Dealing with ethical dilemmas is extremely difficult. Although it may be uncomfortable to deal with these issues, addressing them directly will help solve them in the long run. When faced with an ethical dilemma, use a basic rule to guide the team's decision: Do what is right for the student.

REFLECTIVE PRACTICE

Reflective practice encompasses the "active, persistent, and careful consideration of any belief or supposed form of knowledge in light of the grounds that support it and the further conclusions to which it leads" (Dewey, 1933, p. 9). Using the principles of reflective practice to guide one's professional life is a proactive way to address the complexities and challenges of being a specialist in visual impairment (or any other field).

Given that empirical research in the field is sparse, many common professional practices are rooted in what is "commonly accepted" as good and effective. For example, some professionals "accept" that learning in an inclusive setting is preferable to learning in a segregated or specialized setting. However, no body of research provides convincing support for inclusive education. Through reflective practice, professionals weigh the advantages and limitations of a technique or method and gather information to support, reject, or modify their practice. The goal is to implement those practices that will be of maximum benefit to students. The following suggestions are offered to promote reflective practice.

- ◆ Do not jump on every bandwagon, or immediately seize on every professional fad. Like other fields, the field of visual impairment is prone to many swings of the pendulum, which may sometimes be disruptive to cohesive education. Professionals should take time to gather information and reflect on what is best for individual students.

- ◆ Seek advice and information from those who have experience dealing with pertinent issues. Because the field of visual impairment is small, it is not difficult to contact people who are leaders in the field for advice and guidance.

◆ Gain a variety of perspectives on an issue by talking with others and reading widely in the professional literature before making a decision. Use sound reasoning to consider the various perspectives and support from the professional literature.

◆ Take advantage of professional development opportunities and professional conferences to upgrade and expand instructional skills. It may be helpful to return to college to seek an advanced degree or to take needed graduate courses.

◆ Be open and flexible on professional issues, rather than closed to emerging ideas, issues, and practices. Make sure that changes in professional opinions and practices are made on a sound basis, not using the bandwagon approach just mentioned.

PROFESSIONALS IN VISUAL IMPAIRMENT

Several types of professionals, each of whom is important for a comprehensive educational program, provide services to students who are blind or visually impaired. The coordination of services among professionals and parents is critical in providing seamless services that build skills each year of students' school careers to prepare the students for adult life. The following section describes these professionals and the roles they play in the education of children with visual impairments. It should be noted, however, that some professionals receive training and are qualified to serve more than one role, so that one professional may provide services in a variety of ways.

Education Professionals

Teachers of Students with Visual Impairments. Teachers of students with visual impairments have specialized qualifications beyond those needed to teach in general or special education. Their contribution is thus essential. These teachers are trained at the undergraduate or graduate level to address the specialized needs of students who are blind or visually impaired and to teach the expanded core curriculum. They are also knowledgeable about and competent in making adaptations to the regular curriculum and in constructing adapted materials. A teacher of students with visual impairments, with input from other members of a student's educational team, is responsible for designing and implementing each student's IEP. (Chapter 9 presents detailed information on the requirements for and development of IEPs.)

Teachers of students with visual impairments generally are certified by the state in which they live. State certification is provided as part of teacher licensure procedures, and the certification is specialized in visual impairment. Most employment opportunities for teachers of students with visual impairments are advertised with all other job postings for individual school districts. However, to recruit specialists in visual impairment (who are not as readily available as other school professionals), school districts often send job announcements to universities with training programs in visual impairment and post notices in professional journals and newsletters or at professional conferences, and some use professional lists or Web pages to post these job openings.

Orientation and Mobility (O&M) Specialists. Students with visual impairments may also receive services from O&M specialists to learn how to maneuver safely, efficiently, and gracefully around their environment. O&M services, which were recognized in the 1997 amendments to the Individuals with Disabilities Education Act as a related service (that is, any service that will assist a student who has a disability to benefit from special education services), include, among other things, instruction in using the long cane. O&M specialists receive training at the graduate or undergraduate level and may or may not have a background in visual impairment before their O&M training. They typically receive national certification through the Academy for Certification of Vision Rehabilitation and Education Professionals (the Academy; for additional information, see the section on Certification Organization in this chapter). In some situations, those who work in public school settings with children who are blind or visually impaired are also required to have basic teacher certification; in other situations, they can work with school-age children with only national O&M certification.

O&M is typically a pull-out program since most skills must be taught in a community-based setting using real-life situations. Therefore, O&M specialists work with students on a one-to-one basis at various times of the day and in various school or community situations. When it is necessary for them to provide services to students at home, in the neighborhood, at a shopping center, or on public transportation, they need to coordinate their instruction with students' classroom teachers and other members of the students' educational teams.

Paraeducators.   Services for students who are visually impaired are often provided with the assistance of paraeducators, for whom there are no national standards for qualifications. The following are appropriate activities for paraeducators:

- ◆ Producing adapted materials,
- ◆ Assisting in the provision of classroom assistance to allow the classroom teacher to provide direct, individualized instruction to a student who is blind or visually impaired, and
- ◆ Helping a student with a visual impairment practice skills that have been taught by a qualified teacher of students who are blind or visually impaired.

Paraeducators are used in classrooms with students with visual impairments in many ways, and the method used by a particular school is based on the policy of its school district. In some cases, a classroom teacher is assigned a paraeducator when the class contains students with special needs; in these cases, the paraeducator receives work assignments and reports to the classroom teacher. In other cases, a paraeducator is under the direct supervision of a teacher of students with visual impairments. Caution must be exercised when assigning paraeducators duties related to working with students who are blind or visually impaired. These students need to be given opportunities to complete work independently and to socialize with peers without the intervention of adults, and they must be taught and encouraged to develop independent organizational skills. Thus, the temptation to provide one-to-one paraeducator assistance to students with visual impairments should be avoided so as not to compromise students' need to explore and learn independently.

Rehabilitation Specialists

Rehabilitation Teachers. Professionals who work primarily with adults on skills of daily living, such as cooking, sewing, ironing, and labeling, are called rehabilitation teachers. Often, rehabilitation teachers work for state agencies or private agencies for individuals who are visually impaired. They are not certified teachers of students with visual impairments unless they have fulfilled those qualifications in addition to the requirements for rehabilitation teaching and are certified in both fields. National professional certification for rehabilitation teachers of persons with visual impairments is available through the Academy (see the section on Certification Organization in this chapter). Some school districts use rehabilitation teachers to instruct students, especially those who are older and who are beginning the transition from school-based to adult services in daily living skills.

Rehabilitation Counselors.   Rehabilitation counselors are trained to work with children and adults on adjustment issues to acquired disabilities and may work with family members of these individuals. There is no national certification for rehabilitation counselors in visual impairment; rather, certification standards for rehabilitation counselors are used and supplemented with course work in visual impairment.

Vocational Rehabilitation Counselors.   Vocational rehabilitation counselors focus on the employment needs of individuals with disabilities. They, too, must have additional course work in visual impairment to be considered qualified to provide services to individuals with visual impairments, although they are not specially certified.

Clinical Specialists

Ophthalmologists. Ophthalmologists are physicians who specialize in treating diseases of the eyes. They are often involved with children who are blind or visually impaired because of the children's need for long-term, continuing treatment of eye conditions. For example, a child who has glaucoma (increased pressure in the eyes that leads to permanent damage of the nerve fibers in the light-sensitive layer of the eyes) requires ongoing treatment from an ophthalmologist, who monitors the pressure in the eyes and controls the pressure with medication. An ophthalmologist also monitors children for secondary eye conditions (that is, those that are caused by or associated with the primary eye condition). For example, a child with retinopathy of prematurity (a condition that affects premature infants in which blood vessels grow into and damage the retinas of the eyes) is more likely to experience glaucoma and detached retinas, so an ophthalmologist watches for and treats these conditions. Ophthalmologists are qualified to examine eyes, perform surgery, and prescribe eyeglasses and medications. They are sometimes involved in students' educational teams to provide information on the students' visual conditions and visual prognoses.

Optometrists. Optometrists are eye care specialists who receive training in graduate programs in optometry, but do not have medical degrees; the initials OD (doctor of optometry) follow their names. Optometrists are qualified to examine eyes; prescribe lenses; and, in some locations, prescribe selected medications. They are often involved in determining the best-possible visual correction for children through optical devices. Optometrists frequently work with teachers of students with visual impairments to determine the type of low vision device or devices that may

be appropriate for individual students with visual impairments. Ophthalmologists and optometrists may work together in a clinic to provide comprehensive medical and optical services.

Clinical Low Vision Specialists Clinical low vision specialists are either ophthalmologists or optometrists who have gained additional training and expertise in the area of low vision. They provide clinical low vision evaluations, prescribe optical nad nonoptical low vision devices, and offer follow-up services. These specialists may work in a specialized low vision clinic or may offer low vision services as part of their regular ophthalmological or optometric practice.

Low Vision Therapists. Some children have access to low vision clinics that address the needs of children with visual impairments. Low vision therapists who work in these facilities are often trained as teachers of students with visual impairments, O&M specialists, or rehabilitation teachers. They are responsible for participating in low vision evaluations of children to help determine appropriate optical or low vision devices given the children's specific needs and to provide training in using these devices. There is also national professional certification for low vision therapists through the Academy.

Opticians. Opticians grind and fit lenses into eyeglasses. They are often responsible for filling complicated prescriptions for eyeglasses and optical devices, such as spectacle-mounted telescopes.

GENERAL TEACHING APPROACHES

Roles and Responsibilities of Teachers of Students with Visual Impairments. For teachers to be effective, they must have a clearly defined role in the students' educational teams that must be clearly communicated to other members of these teams. Several attempts have been made to determine the role of teachers of students with visual impairments (Spungin, 1977, 1986, in press). In general, this role can be divided into three categories of responsibilities:

◆ Direct instruction in areas of the expanded core curriculum that the students need (for example, teaching braille reading and writing, use of optical devices, or daily living skills).

◆ Consultation and adaptation to make the regular classroom curriculum accessible to students (for instance, ordering braille textbooks or helping a general education teacher plan adaptations for a field trip).

◆ Provision of indirect services needed to inform and gather information from members of students' educational teams, including parents (for example, communicating with members of educational teams or conducting specialized assessments).

Defining One's Role.   Teachers of students with visual impairments are ultimately responsible for defining their role in relation to other members of children's educational teams. This role must be defined in the context of the needs of each student and should not be based on the availability of time, funding, or resources from the school district. For example, if a student needs direct, daily instruction in skills related to the expanded core curriculum, then the teacher must define his or her role as the provider of that direct instruction, even though it may be difficult to obtain the resources to do so. In some cases, the teacher's role may be more supportive and less direct. The teacher's role must be constantly evaluated and redefined to meet each student's current needs.

Communicating One's Role.   Since the role of the teacher of students with visual impairments is dynamic and cannot be defined in general, only in relation to a particular student, it becomes even more important to communicate that role clearly to the members of each student's educational team, who should also clearly define and commu-

nicate their roles to the team. Communication among team members helps to eliminate gaps and overlaps of service. (For additional information on working in teams, see Chapter 1 of *Foundations of Education: Instructional Strategies for Teaching Children and Youths with Visual Impairments*.)

Teachers of students with visual impairments have various communication styles and use a range of communication systems. The following are some of the most common ways in which teachers communicate with other members of the educational team, especially in relation to roles and responsibilities:

◆ *Written information.* Teachers often present written reports and memos that address roles and other issues to other members of the educational team. The use of written information is helpful because it provides documentation that can be referred to in the future and offers a starting point for discussions among team members.

◆ *Technology.* Teachers may communicate with members of the educational team using E-mail or the World Wide Web.

◆ *Conferences and meetings.* It may be effective for teachers of students with visual impairments to hold annual conferences during which the roles and responsibilities of team members are discussed and clearly delineated.

◆ *Informal discussions.* In many cases, informal discussions over time are the most effective in defining the role of teachers of students with visual impairments. Periodic contact in which specific situations are discussed may be helpful, especially when the roles of team members truly overlap (for example, in teaching the use of low vision devices for reading instruction).

Educational Settings.   Teachers of students with visual impairments work in a variety of settings (for a detailed discussion of these settings, see Chapter 9). Therefore, they must use sound professional judgment to determine the best way to encourage effective communication among members of an educational team. The service delivery model greatly influences the type of communication that the team members need to use.

PROFESSIONAL PREPARATION

University Preparation

Teachers of students with visual impairments and O&M specialists are prepared in recognized and accredited university programs throughout the United States and Canada. Most universities offer such preparation at the graduate level, although several include the option for undergraduate specializations. The course of study depends, to a great extent, on the requirements for certification of the state or province in which the teacher or O&M specialist is to practice.

Teachers of Students with Visual Impairments

The knowledge and skills that teachers of students with visual impairments must have as beginning teachers have been delineated by CEC. CEC's documents include a "common core" of knowledge and skills that all beginning special education teachers must have, as well as specific knowledge and skills for teachers of students with visual impairments. The knowledge and skills delineated as part of this common core are grouped into the following categories:

- Foundations of special education,
- Characteristics of learners,
- Assessment, diagnosis, and evaluation,
- Instructional content and practice,
- Planning and managing the teaching and learning environment,
- Managing student behavior and social interaction skills,

- Communication and collaborative partnerships,
- Professionalism and ethical practices.

(See Appendices F and G for additional information.) Those who are preparing to teach students with visual impairments generally take a sequence of courses in which these skills and knowledge are infused. Although the courses vary widely from university to university, the following courses are typical:

- Foundations of educating students with visual impairments;
- Braille reading and writing;
- Anatomy and physiology of the eye;
- Educational implications of low vision;
- Instructional strategies for teaching students with visual impairments, including those with multiple disabilities;
- Basic O&M skills; and
- Student teaching or a practicum in teaching children with visual impairments.

Students in undergraduate programs typically take four years to complete their bachelor's degrees. They generally take courses and complete student teaching in another field of education—elementary, secondary, or generic special education—along with preparation in visual impairment. This approach gives them a broad base of preparation for teaching that many in the profession believe is highly desirable. An understanding of the total educational context is essential for developing and implementing educational programs for students with visual impairments.

Most students in graduate programs are already certified in another area of education and have returned to a university to pursue specialization in visual impairment. A typical master's degree program takes at least one calendar year to complete if students are enrolled full time, but many students attend school part time to complete this specialization. In addition, many universities offer options for distance learning through off-campus courses, Internet-based courses, teleconference courses, or other arrangements that are designed for those who want to attend classes part time. To complete a master's degree, a university may require that a student spend one semester on campus to take courses and final examinations. Some universities have an option or requirement that students complete master's theses or final projects, either in place of, or in addition to, the comprehensive examination that students generally take at the end of the program.

Colleges of education have the option of obtaining accreditation from the National Council for Accreditation of Teacher Education (NCATE), a national organization that ensures that teacher education programs meet fundamental criteria for offering sound, professional preparation in education. As part of the NCATE accreditation process, teacher preparation programs in special education must meet the standards established by CEC. In searching for a university program, a student may want to inquire as to whether a university has NCATE accreditation.

O&M Specialists

O&M specialists are generally prepared to meet the rules and guidelines for national certification by the Academy for Certification of Vision Rehabilitation and Education Professionals (the Academy). Many states use national certification, rather than state-specific certification. National certification standards do not indicate the number or types of courses that must be taken, but require universities to show that their candidates master specific competencies. National certification is valid for five years, after which it must be renewed. The renewal process includes providing the Academy Certification Committee with proof of continuing education, work experience, and professional activities.

National program approval is available for universities that offer courses in O&M. Only graduates of programs approved by the national body are eligible for national certification. Program approval is granted by the Academy and is based on a comprehensive analysis of the program requirements, qualifications of faculty members, and requirements for practical experiences.

Doctoral Programs

About 11 universities in the United States and Canada offer doctoral programs in the area of visual impairment. Individuals with doctoral degrees generally work as faculty members in university programs that prepare specialists in visual impairment, as administrators or supervisors in agencies that serve persons who are blind or visually impaired, as private consultants, or in other similar leadership roles. Although a doctoral degree is sometimes required as a condition of employment, some leadership roles and positions, including some in university programs, do not require doctorates.

The requirements and programs of study for doctoral programs vary widely and are established by individual universities. These programs require their students to have bachelor's degrees at a minimum and generally master's degrees and several years of successful teaching experience. Full-time doctoral study takes about three years to complete, including two years for all or most of the formal courses and one year of an internship and dissertation research. Most doctoral programs require students to fulfill "residency" requirements, that is, students must be enrolled on campus in full-time studies for a specified period, usually one academic year. The purpose of residency is to allow students to immerse themselves fully in scholarly activities and pursuits without the demands of other daily work responsibilities.

Course requirements for doctoral degrees typically include a "research tool" requirement. This block of instruction, ranging from about 12 to 18 semester hours, focuses exclusively on research methodology and statistics. A student then uses the research tools to prepare a proposal for the dissertation research that must be approved by the student's dissertation advisory committee before the student can conduct the research and prepare a written doctoral dissertation. The student "defends" his or her dissertation in a final oral examination, during which members of the committee ask a variety of questions and assess the student's responses. Often, final revisions in the dissertation are agreed upon during the defense.

Alternative Approaches to Personnel Preparation

Some specialists in visual impairment are prepared in nonuniversity programs, although this is not usually the case. These alternative certification programs are generally sponsored by education agencies according to guidelines established by the states in which they are located. In Texas, for example, school districts or education service centers (regional collaborative programs comprising numerous school districts and counties) can develop a series of workshops or other learning experiences related to a certification area and submit a plan for carrying out the certification program to the state education agency. If approved, the alternative program is then free to prepare specialists in accordance with the plan. Participants who successfully complete the specified sequence and pass the state competency examination for teachers of students with visual impairments are then eligible for certification in this area.

In the field of O&M, a number of rehabilitation agencies that serve adults who are blind and visually impaired offer their own preparation programs. Generally, O&M specialists who are trained in such programs are employed only at the specific agencies that offered the training. There may not be reciprocity with other agencies or states. Agency-trained O&M specialists are not eligible for national professional certification through the Academy.

Ongoing Professional Development

Part of professional practice is engaging in ongoing professional development to update and expand one's professional knowledge and skills. This type of professional development is most often sponsored by school districts or other education agencies. In-service programs and workshops for teachers are offered throughout the school year and in the summer to provide more or new information on specific topics, which are generally identified as needed in a systematic needs assessment. For teachers of students with visual impairments, targeted in-service programs and workshops may be offered at residential schools for students with visual impairments, universities, or other specialized educational agencies.

Attending professional conferences also provides for continuing professional development. AER (discussed later in this chapter) hosts biennial international conferences at which the sessions relate specifically to teaching children or adults with visual impairments and specific areas of interest to professionals in visual impairment are highlighted. CEC hosts an annual international conference at which the CEC Division on Visual Impairment holds a number of sessions that target the needs of teachers of students with visual impairments. In addition to the national and international conferences, state or local chapters of professional organizations host conferences and workshops that provide for continuing professional development. Many teachers also belong to and participate in professional organizations with other emphases (for example, the International Reading Association).

Engaging in continuing professional development is an essential aspect of professionalism. All professionals must continue to expand their knowledge and skills to address the complex needs of students with visual impairments. Another aspect of professionalism is sharing one's professional expertise with others by presenting in-service programs or speaking at conferences. Teachers' presentations on effective practice and innovative, creative materials are important additions to state, regional, and national conferences. Some school districts provide financial support for teachers to attend conferences if the teachers are also presenting at them. Many states require a certain number of hours of continuing professional development each year for teachers of students with visual impairments, as AER requires for O&M specialists.

PROFESSIONAL PUBLICATIONS

A variety of written information is available to professionals in the field of educating students with visual impairment, including journals on visual impairment, journals on general special education, newsletters, and other sources of professional information. The following are among the primary sources of information for professionals:

- *Journal of Visual Impairment & Blindness (JVIB).* Considered the premier professional scholarly journal in the field of visual impairment, *JVIB* contains articles on research, practice, and other areas of interest to the field, as well as comments on timely issues.

- *RE:view. RE:view* is a practitioner-oriented journal that contains articles on practice and research, short notes and letters, and other features.

- *Journal of Vision Rehabilitation.* The *Journal of Vision Rehabilitation* has a more clinical emphasis, focusing on such topics as research studies of low vision rehabilitation, case studies of individuals with certain eye conditions, and new clinical assessment instruments and procedures.

- *AER Report.* The *AER Report* is a newsletter published by AER that includes information on legislative actions, new products and services, news items, and membership updates.

- *DVI Quarterly.* The newsletter of the Division on Visual Impairments of CEC, the *DVI Quarterly* contains articles, personal profiles, schedules of upcoming events, and announcements.

ORGANIZATIONS

Professional Organizations

Professionals in the field of visual impairment can become involved in organizations that are designed specifically to address issues related to services for the individuals they serve. The many benefits conferred by membership in professional organizations include these:

- A voice. Professional organizations advocate for issues that are important to the field. Although individuals may write letters and otherwise present issues of importance to the field, the efforts of membership organizations have a stronger impact because of the sheer number of the organizations' members.

- *Written materials.* Members of professional organizations receive journals, newsletters, updates on important issues, and announcements of job openings.

- *Professional development.* Many professional organizations regularly hold conferences that address relevant issues. These meetings are excellent opportunities for professionals to receive current information and to network with colleagues. As was mentioned earlier, AER holds biennial international conferences, and CEC holds annual international conferences.

Teachers can be involved in professional organizations at the national, state, or local levels by attending conferences, presenting at conferences, holding office, writing for professional journals and newsletters, and participating in advocacy activities.

AER. AER is the only professional organization for teachers, O&M specialists, and rehabilitation personnel that focuses on issues related to providing services to individuals with visual impairments at all ages and through all service delivery models. According to its bylaws, the purpose of AER is "to render all possible support and assistance to the professionals who work in all phases of education and rehabilitation of blind and visually impaired persons of all ages" (AER, 2000). Each of its 18 divisions (see Sidebar 10.2) addresses specific issues related to the field. AER's Web site (www.aerbvi.org) provides timely information and resources for its members.

Divisions of the Association for Education and Rehabilitation of the Blind and Visually Impaired

SIDEBAR 10.2

Division 1 :   Administration

Division 2 :   Vocational Rehabilitation Counseling and Employment Services

Division 3 :   Multiple Disabilities and Deaf-blind

Division 4 :   Psychosocial Services

Division 5 :   Information & Technology

Division 6 :   Business Enterprise Program

Division 7 :   Low Vision

Division 8 :   Infant and Preschool

Division 9 :   Orientation and Mobility

Division 10:   Elementary and Secondary Curriculum for Children

Division 11:   Rehabilitation Teaching and Independent Living Services

Division 15:   Division on Aging

Division 16:   Itinerant Personnel

Division 17:   Personnel Preparation

Division 18:   Veteran Services

CEC/DVI. CEC, the largest professional organization focusing on special education, has 17 divisions (see Sidebar 10.3). The division that most directly addresses the needs of professionals in the field of visual impairments is the Division on Visual Impairments (DVI). In addition to conducting annual international conferences, CEC publishes two journals—*Teaching Exceptional Children,* which contains practical articles on classroom methods, materials, and programs, and *Exceptional Children,* which includes major research reports in the field of special education—and a newsletter, *CEC Today,* which provides information on special education programs at the local, regional, national, and international levels. CEC also has a Web site (http://www.cec.sped.org/) that is continually updated for current issues and events in special education.

Certification Organization

Academy for Certification of Vision Rehabilitation and Education Professionals (the Academy). The Academy is a national certification organization that offers professional certificates for O&M specialists, rehabilitation teachers, and low vision therapists. The option of seeking national certification is important for these professionals, since many states and provinces do not provide such certificates or licenses. Each certification discipline has guidelines and standards for gaining initial certification, as well as national examination within the discipline. The responsibility for certifying O&M specialists, rehabilitation teachers, and low vision therapists was transferred to the Academy from AER in 2000. It is governed by a board of directors, which includes professionals, an individual who is blind or visually impaired, an employer, and a representative of AER.

Divisions of the Council for Exceptional Children

Division Name	Abbreviation
CEC Pioneers Division	CEC-PD
Council for Children with Behavioral Disorders	CCBD
Council for Educational Diagnostic Services	CEDS
Council of Administrators of Special Education	CASE
Division for Children's Communication Development	DCCD
Division for Culturally and Linguistically Diverse Exceptional Learners	DDEL
Division for Early Childhood	DEC
Division for Learning Disabilities	DLD
Division for Physical and Health Disabilities	DPHD
Division for Research	CEC-DR
Division of International Special Education and Services	DISES
Division on Career Development and Transition	DCDT
Division on Mental Retardation and Developmental Disabilities	MRDD
Division on Visual Impairments	DVI
Teacher Education Division	TED
Technology and Media Division	TAM
The Association for the Gifted	TAG

International Organizations

International Council for Education of People with Visual Impairments (ICEVI). ICEVI is a professional nongovernment organization that does not provide direct service but, rather, serves as a point of contact for individuals who need information about services to people who are visually impaired throughout the world. It publishes an international journal (*The Educator*) that is distributed worldwide and holds international conferences every five years. Their Web site (www.obs.org/icevi.htm) is another resource. The mission of ICEVI is "to promote educational opportunities for children and adults with visual impairment throughout the world. This means people who are totally blind or who have low vision, including those with additional disabilities" (ICEVI, 1999).

World Blind Union (WBU). WBU is an international organization that addresses the needs of people who are blind around the world and works actively to promote positive attitudes and a good quality of life for them. The organization has a Web site (www.once.es:82) and publishes a magazine, *The World Blind,* that updates activities related to people who are blind around the world. WBU provides a voice for over 50 million persons who are blind or visually impaired around the world.

Consumer Organizations

American Council of the Blind (ACB). ACB is a membership organization that addresses issues faced by individuals who are blind. It holds an annual conference, has a Web site (www.acb.org), publishes *The Braille Forum,* and, in addition to a range of other activities, produces a monthly half-hour radio information program for broadcast on local radio reading programs.

National Federation of the Blind (NFB). NFB is a membership organization of people who are blind. It provides help and support to individuals who are blind and their families through public education, publications, advocacy services, and other types of support and is dedicated to increasing the self-confidence and self-respect of individuals who are blind. NFB holds annual conferences, maintains a Web site (www.nfb.org), and publishes two major magazines (*Braille Monitor* and *Future Reflections*) that address a variety of issues that people who are blind and their families may face. In addition, it sponsors an annual contest, Braille Readers Are Leaders, which is open to braille readers from kindergarten through Grade 12, to encourage students to read braille and reinforce them for doing so.

Organizations of Parents

Parents of children with visual impairments have always played a vital role in advocating for appropriate services for their children. Many local parents' groups meet regularly and provide support for and advice to local school programs. Three national parents' organizations offer support for parents and families of children who are blind or visually impaired by providing written material, conferences, and links with other parents.

Council of Families with Visual Impairment. ACB has a council associated with the national organization that seeks to address the needs of families. The purpose of the Council of Families with Visual Impairment is to provide help when any member of a family is blind or visually impaired. The Council provides information, assists with advocacy efforts, and provides resources to families.

Division for Parents of Blind Children. This division of NFB is dedicated to the needs of parents of children who are blind. It publishes a quarterly publication, *Future Reflections,* that provides information that is relevant to parents and teachers of young children.

The National Association for Parents of Children with Visual Impairments (NAPVI). The purpose and mission of this organization is as follows: "NAPVI is a national organization that enables parents to find information and resources for their children who are blind or visually impaired, including those with multiple disabilities. NAPVI provides leadership, support, and training to assist parents in helping children reach their potential. NAPVI is dedicated to: giving emotional support, initiating outreach programs, networking, and advocating for educational needs and welfare of children who are blind or visually impaired" (NAPVI, 2000). NAPVI publishes a quarterly newsletter, *Awareness,* that is sent to its members and has a Web site (www.spedex.com/napvi).

SUMMARY

This chapter has presented many elements that encompass professional practice for specialists in visual impairment. Professionals in visual impairment should rely on professional and consumer organizations and specialized publications to gain information and advice on addressing the needs of students with visual impairments. In addition, their professional practices should be guided by their adherence to codes of ethics and by reflective analysis. Professionals' deepest commitment is to provide students with visual impairments with high-quality educational experiences and services that are based on sound instructional practices. Practicing in a manner that upholds this commitment ensures that each student will make maximum gains, given his or her individual abilities.

STUDY QUESTIONS

1. Teachers of students with visual impairments are encouraged to use "best professional practices" in providing educational services to their students. What do you believe these practices mean? Interview a teacher who is serving students with visual impairments and ask him or her what is meant by "best professional practices."

2. Teachers of students with visual impairments work in a variety of educational settings. How would professional practice be challenged in each of these service delivery options: itinerant services, resource room, consultation, residential services?

3. Write a justification to a school administrator (a special education administrator or school principal). Why is it important to provide instruction in the expanded core curriculum for a student who is visually impaired?

4. Why is reflective practice important? Provide three practical suggestions for teachers to encourage reflective practice.

5. Describe the importance of certification for teachers of students with visual impairments. Why is it important to advocate for qualified teachers?

6. What are the roles of the following professionals in the education of students with visual impairments: O&M specialists, rehabilitation teachers, ophthalmologists, optometrists, and clinical low vision specialists?

7. Why is it important to define clearly the role of the teacher of students with visual impairments?

8. What are three suggestions for communicating the teacher's role to other members of a student's educational team?

9. Why is it important for teachers of students with visual impairments to participate in ongoing professional development? What are some of the challenges that teachers may face in doing so? Provide three or four suggestions for overcoming these challenges.

10. Why is membership in professional organizations important?

REFERENCES

Association for Education and Rehabilitation of the Blind and Visually Impaired. (2000). AERBVI bylaws [On-line] Available: http://www.aerbvi.org/text_only/general/bylaws.htm

Corn, A. L., Hatlen, P., Huebner, K. M., Ryan, F., & Siller, M. A. (1995). *The national agenda for the education of children and youths with visual impairments, including those with disabilities.* New York: American Foundation for the Blind.

Council for Exceptional Children. (1998). *What every special educator should know: The international standard for the preparation and licensure of specialized educators* (3rd ed.). Reston, VA: Author.

Dewey J. (1933). *How we think. A restatement of the relation of reflective thinking to the educative process.* Boston: D.C. Heath and Company.

Hatlen, P. H., & Curry, S. A. (1987). In support of specialized programs for blind and visually impaired children: The impact of vision loss on learning. *Journal of Visual Impairment & Blindness, 81,* 1. 7–13.

International Council for the Education of the Visually Impaired. (1999). ICEVI's mission [On-line] Available: http://www.obs.org/icevi.htm#mission

National Association for Parents of the Visually Impaired. (2000). Mission statement [On-line] Available: http://www.spedex.com/napvi/

Spungin, S. J. (1977). *Competency-based curriculum for teachers of the visually handicapped: A national study.* New York: American Foundation for the Blind.

Spungin, S. J. (1986). DVH-CEC position paper: The role and function of the teacher of the visually handicapped. In G. T. Scholl (Ed.), *Foundations of education for blind and visually handicapped children and youth: Theory and practice* (pp. 471–473). New York: American Foundation for the Blind.

Spungin, S. J. (in press). The role of the teacher of students with visual impairments. In Division on Visual Impairment, *Position Papers of The Division on Visual Impairments 1990–2000.* Reston, VA: Council for Exceptional Children.

KEY READINGS

Barraga, N. C., & Erin, J. N. (1992). *Visual handicaps and learning*. Austin, TX: PRO-ED.

Bishop, V. E. (1996). *Teaching visually impaired children* (2nd ed.). Springfield, IL: Charles C Thomas.

Corn, A. L., & Huebner, K. M. (Eds.). (1998). *A report to the nation: The national agenda for the education of children and youths with visual impairments, including those with multiple disabilities*. New York: AFB Press.

Corn, A. L., & Koenig, A. J. (Eds.). (1996). *Foundations of low vision: Clinical and functional perspectives*. New York: AFB Press.

Crane, P., Cuthbertson, D., Ferrell, K. A., & Scherb, H. (1998). *Equals in partnership: Basic rights for families of children with blindness or visual impairment*. Watertown, MA: National Association for Parents of the Visually Impaired.

Dutsforth, T. D. (1951). *The blind in school and society: A psychological study*. New York: American Foundation for the Blind.

Erin, J. (Ed.). (1989). *Dimensions: Visually impaired persons with multiple disabilities*. New York: American Foundation for the Blind.

Fraiberg, S. (1977). *Insights from the blind*. New York: Basic.

Koestler, F. A. (1976). *The unseen minority: A social history of blindness in the United States*. New York: David McKay.

Lowenfeld, B. (1971). *Our blind children: Growing and learning with them* (3rd ed.). Springfield, IL: Charles C Thomas.

Lowenfeld, B. (1981). *On blindness and blind people: Selected readings*. New York: American Foundation for the Blind.

MacCuspie, P. A. (1996). *Promoting acceptance of children with disabilities: From tolerance to inclusion*. Halifax, NS: Atlantic Provinces Special Education Authority.

Monbeck, M. (1973). *The meaning of blindness: Attitudes toward blindness and blind people*. Bloomington, IN: Indiana University Press.

Sacks, S. Z., & Silberman, R. K. (Eds.). (1998). *Educating students who have visual impairments with other disabilities*. Baltimore: Paul H. Brookes.

Tuttle, D., & Tuttle, N. (1996). *Self-esteem and adjusting with blindness* (2nd ed.). Springfield, IL: Charles C Thomas.

Warren, D. H. (1994). *Blindness and children: An individual differences approach*. New York: Cambridge University Press.

Warren, D. H. (1984). *Blindness and early childhood development* (2nd ed. rev.). New York: American Foundation for the Blind.

Westling, D. L., & Fox, L. (1995). *Teaching students with severe disabilities*. Upper Saddle River, NJ: Prentice-Hall.

Wolffe, K. E. (Ed.). (1999). *Skills for success: A career education handbook for children and adolescents with visual impairments*. New York: AFB Press.

APPENDIX A
OSEP Policy Guidance on Educating Blind and Visually Impaired Students

November 3, 1995

To: Chief State School Officers

From: Judith E. Heumann
            Assistant Secretary
            Office of Special Education and
               Rehabilitative Services

            Thomas Hehir
            Director
            Officer of Special Education Programs

Subject: Policy Guidance on Educating Blind
            and Visually Impaired Students

INTRODUCTION

One of our highest priorities at the Office of Special Education and Rehabilitative Services (OSERS) is improving services for students with low incidence disabilities, particularly those with sensory deficits. On October 30, 1992, the Department published a Notice of Policy Guidance on Deaf Students Education Services[1] (Notice) to provide additional guidance to educators on the free appropriate public education (FAPE) requirements of Part B of the Individuals with Disabilities Education Act (Part B) and Section 504 of the Rehabilitation Act of 1973[2] as they relate to students who are deaf. In OSEP Memorandum 94-15, dated February 4, 1994, we clarified that the policy guidance in this Notice is equally applicable to all students with disabilities.

Nevertheless, it has come to our attention that services for some blind and visually impaired students are not appropriately addressing their unique educational and learning needs, particularly their needs for instruction in literacy, self-help skills, and orientation and mobility. We at OSERS are strongly committed to ensuring that our educational system takes the steps that are necessary to enable students who are blind or visually impaired to become productive and contributing citizens. Therefore, OSERS has determined that there is a need for additional guidance

---

[1] See 57 Fed. Reg. 49274 (Oct. 30, 1992).

[2] Section 504 of the Rehabilitation Act of 1973 (Section 504) prohibits discrimination on the basis of disability by recipients of Federal financial assistance. The

Department's regulations implementing Section 504, at 34 CFR Part 104, require recipients that operate public elementary and secondary education programs to provide appropriate educational services to disabled students. See 34 CFR §§104.33–104.36. Section 504 is enforced by the Department's Office for Civil Rights (OCR). The Americans with Disabilities Act of 1990 (ADA), Title II, prohibits discrimination on the basis of disability by State and local governments, whether or not they receive Federal funds; OCR enforces Title II of the ADA as it relates to public elementary and secondary educational institutions and public libraries, and interprets the requirements of Title II of the ADA as consistent with those of Section 504. OCR officials have reviewed this guidance and find it to be consistent with recipients' obligations to provide FAPE to blind and visually impaired students under Section 504 and Title II of the ADA.

on the FAPE requirements of Part B as they relate to blind and visually impaired students. This guidance will provide some background information on blind and visually impaired students and discussion of their unique needs, and will identify the steps that educators can take in meeting their responsibilities under Part B to blind and visually impaired students.

We hope that the attached guidance is helpful to you and educators in your State as you implement educational programs for blind and visually impaired students. If there are any questions, or if further information is needed, please contact the contact person listed above or Dr. JoLeta Reynolds in the Office of Special Education Programs at (202) 205-5507.

Attachment

cc: State Directors of Special Education
     RSA Regional Commissioners
     Regional Resource Centers
     Federal Resource Center
     Special Interest Groups
     Parent Training Centers
     Independent Living Centers
     Protection and Advocacy Agencies

BACKGROUND

The population of students who receive services under Part B because of blindness or visual impairment is extremely diverse. These students display both a wide range of vision difficulties and adaptations to vision loss. The diversity that characterizes the student population is true of the population of blind and visually impaired persons in general. So far as degree of vision loss is concerned, the student population includes persons who are totally blind or persons with minimal light perception, as well as persons with high levels of functional vision, though less than the norm. For some students, visual impairment is their only disability; while others have one or more additional disabilities that will affect, to varying degrees, their learning and growth.

Identifying other characteristics of this diverse population is far more complex. This is because adaptations to vision loss vary greatly and are shaped by individual differences in areas such as intellectual abilities and family supports. Degree of vision loss, therefore, does not give a full understanding of how that loss affects learning. Students with similar degrees of vision loss may function very differently. A significant visual deficit can pose formidable obstacles for some students and far less formidable obstacles for others. However, regardless of the degree of the student's vision loss or the student's ability to adapt to that loss, there is general agreement that blind and visually impaired students must acquire the skills necessary to function in settings in which the majority of people have vision sufficient to enable them to read and write by using regular print as well as to move about in their environment with ease.

To state the obvious, children begin at a very young age to imitate the actions of others, particularly by imitating what they see others doing. Typically, learning is based on this principle. The challenge for educators of blind and visually impaired students in schools is how to teach their students to learn skills that sighted children typically acquire through vision, including how to read, write, compose, and obtain access to information contained in printed materials. We recognize that blind and visually impaired students have used a variety of methods to learn to read and write. For example, for reading purposes, some students use braille exclusively; others use large print or regular print with or without low vision aids. Still others use a combination of methods, including braille, large print, and low vision aids while others have sufficient functional vision to use regular print, although with considerable difficulty. In order to receive an appropriate education under Part B, unless a student who is blind or visually impaired has other disabilities that would inhibit his or her ability to learn to read, we believe that instruction in reading must be provided for blind and visually impaired students in the medium that is appropriate for their individual abilities and needs to enable them to learn to read effectively.

One of the most serious concerns voiced by parents of blind children and their advocates, and by adults who are blind or visually impaired as well, is that the number of students receiving instruction in braille has decreased significantly over the past several decades. As a result, these individuals believe that braille instruction is not being provided to some students for whom it may be appropriate. Braille has been a very effective reading and writing medium for many blind and visually impaired persons. In fact, data from a recent study demonstrate that blind and visually impaired adults who know braille are more likely to be employed than those who do not, suggesting a strong correlation between knowledge of braille and a person's ability to obtain future employment. The American Foundation for the Blind's Careers and Technology Information Bank, which lists 1,000 different jobs held by blind and visually impaired people, indicates that 85 percent of those who use braille as their primary method of reading are employed.[3] Undoubtedly, there are numerous other benefits that individuals for whom braille instruction is appropriate would derive from knowledge of braille, particularly a heightened sense of self-esteem and self-worth that a student gains from the ability to read effectively.

Another significant concern voiced by parents of blind and visually impaired students and their advocates, as well as by many blind and visually impaired adults, is that these students are not receiving adequate instruction in orientation and mobility to address their individual needs. In some instances, it has been reported that these students do not even receive adequate evaluations of their needs for such instruction. The intent of Part B cannot be achieved fully if a blind or visually impaired student who needs instruction in orientation and mobility does not receive that instruction before completing his or her education.

I. Application of the Free Appropriate Public Education Requirements of Part B to Blind and Visually Impaired Students

Under Part B, each State and its public agencies must ensure that all children with specified disabilities have available to them a free appropriate public education (FAPE), and that the rights and protections of Part B are afforded to those students and their parents. FAPE includes, among other elements, special education and related services that are provided at no cost to parents under public supervision and direction, that meet State education standards and Part B requirements, that include preschool, elementary, or secondary school education in the State involved, and that are provided in conformity with an individualized education program (IEP).[4]

Before a student with a disability can receive special education and related services, a full and individual evaluation of the student's educational needs must be conducted in accordance with the requirements of 34 CFR §300.532.[5] Section 300.532 requires, among other factors, that the child be evaluated by a multidisciplinary team or group of persons, including at least one teacher or other specialist with knowledge in the area of suspected disability.[6] Thus, for blind or visually impaired students, an individual with knowledge of blindness and visual impairment would be an essential participant on this multidisciplinary team.

An assessment that meets the requirements of Part B must assess the child in all areas related to the suspected disability, including, if appropriate, "health, vision, hearing, social and emotional status, general intelligence, academic performance, communicative status, and motor abilities."[7] Assessments for blind and visually impaired students must evaluate the student in the areas listed above, as determined appropriate by the multidisciplinary team.

---

[3]Study of Issues and Strategies toward Improving Employment of Blind and Visually Impaired Persons in Illinois, American Foundation for the Blind (March 1991).

[4]20 U.S.C. §1412(2); 34 CFR §300.121; 20 U.S.C. §1401(a)(18) and 34 CFR §300.8.

[5]CFR §300.531.

[6]See 34 CFR §300.532(e).

[7]See 34 CFR §300.532(f).

For example, an assessment of academic performance would include an assessment of the student's ability to master the skills necessary for literacy, including reading, reading comprehension, composition, and computing. If appropriate, an assessment of vision would include the nature and extent of the student's visual impairment and its effect on the student's ability to learn to read, write, and the instructional method or methods that would be appropriate to enable the student to learn the above skills. For the teaching of reading and composition, these methods could include braille, large print or regular print with or without low vision optical devices, or a combination of braille and print. A range of devices that utilize computer-generated speech could be helpful tools in the instruction of children who are blind or visually impaired. Because of the importance for some blind and visually impaired students of mastering the skills necessary to acquire information, additional assessments may be necessary to determine whether the student should receive specific instruction in listening skills. Possible assessments that could be considered for this purpose could include assessments of hearing, general intelligence, or communicative status. The student's need for instruction in orientation and mobility and the appropriate method or methods for acquiring this skill could also be assessed. As with other educational decisions, the results of the student's assessments must be considered as the student's IEP[8] is developed, and the participants on the student's IEP team determine the specially designed instruction and related services to be provided to the student.

Under Part B, the public agency responsible for the student's education must initiate and conduct meetings to develop or review each student's IEP periodically, and if appropriate, revise its provisions. A meeting must be held for this purpose at least once a year.[9] Required participants at all IEP meetings include the child's teacher; an agency representative, who is qualified to provide or supervise the provision of special education; the parents, subject to certain limited exceptions; the child, if determined appropriate; and other individuals at the parent's or agency's discretion. If the IEP meeting occurs in connection with the child's initial placement in special education, the school district must ensure the participation of evaluation personnel, unless the child's teacher or public agency representative or some other person at the meeting is knowledgeable about the evaluation procedures used with the child and the results of those procedures.[10]

Each student's IEP must contain, among other components, a statement of annual goals including short-term objectives, the specific special education and related services to be provided to the student and the extent that the student will be able to participate in regular educational programs, and a statement of needed transition services under certain circumstances.[11] To ensure that blind and visually impaired students receive adequate instruction in the skills necessary to become literate, IEP teams must ensure that the instructional time that is allocated is appropriate for the required instruction or service.[12] For a student to become literate in braille, systematic and regular instruction from knowledgeable and trained personnel is essential. Likewise, for students with low vision, instruction in the utilization of remaining vision and in the effective use of low vision aids requires regular and intensive intervention from appropriately-trained personnel.

In all instances, IEP teams must consider how to address the needs of blind and visually impaired students for the skills necessary to achieve literacy. For students who are blind or for students with a minimal amount of residual vision, it is probable that braille will be the primary instructional method for teaching the student to learn to read. Therefore, for blind students and for students with a minimal amount of residual vision,

---

[8]The IEP is the written document that contains the statement for a disabled student of the program of specialized instruction and related services to be provided to a student. 34 CFR §§300.340–300.350.

[9]20 U.S.C. §1414(a)(5) and 34 CFR §300.343(d).

[10]34 CFR §300.344.

[11]34 CFR §300.346.

[12]Appendix C to 34 CFR Part 300 (question 51).

braille should be considered as the primary reading method, unless the student has a disability in addition to blindness that would make it difficult for the student to use his or her hands or would otherwise adversely affect the student's ability to learn to read. In developing IEPs for other students with low vision, IEP teams should not assume that instruction in braille would not be appropriate merely because the student has some useful vision. While IEP teams are not required to consider the need for braille instruction for every student with a visual impairment who is eligible for services under Part B, IEP teams may not fail to consider braille instruction for students for whom it may be appropriate. This consideration must occur despite factors such as shortages or unavailability of trained personnel to provide braille instruction, the ability of audiotapes and computers to provide blind and visually impaired persons with ready access to printed textbooks and materials, or the amount of time needed to provide a student with sufficient and regular instruction to attain proficiency in braille.

IEP teams also must select the method or methods for teaching blind and visually impaired students how to write and compose. Students whose appropriate reading medium is braille may benefit from using braille for these purposes. Alternatively, in addition to braille, they may benefit from using a personal computer with speech output for composition. Therefore, IEP teams must make individual determinations about the needs of blind and visually impaired students for instruction in writing and composition, and must include effective methods for teaching writing and composition in the IEPs of those students for whom instruction in this area is determined to be appropriate.

In addition to mastering the skills taught to all students, blind and visually impaired students must receive instruction in the skills necessary to acquire information, particularly because braille or large print documents frequently cannot be made accessible to them in a timely manner. The skills that could be taught to accomplish this include recordings that utilize compressed speech, personal computers with speech output, and optical scanners with speech output. As determined appropriate, use of these devices and methods would be considered on an individual basis. In appropriate situations, one or more of these devices could be used to supplement braille instruction for students for whom braille is the primary reading medium, or to supplement print or large print for students using print as their primary reading medium. In rare instances, methods for acquiring information could be used in place of braille or print for students who, by reason of other disabilities, cannot be taught to read.

To ensure that IEPs for blind and visually impaired students address their specific needs effectively, the following unique needs should be considered as IEPs for these students are developed:

- Skills necessary to attain literacy in reading and writing, including appropriate instructional methods;
- Skills for acquiring information, including appropriate use of technological devices and services;
- Orientation and Mobility Instruction;
- Social Interaction Skills;
- Transition Services Needs;
- Recreation; and
- Career Education.

This list is not intended to be exhaustive. Participants on IEP teams could determine that it would be appropriate to consider an individual student's need for other skills, in addition to the skills listed above. Therefore, in making decisions about the educational programs for blind and visually impaired students, IEP teams must consider the full range of skills necessary to enable these students to learn effectively.

II. Least Restrictive Environment and Placement Requirements

Part B requires States to have procedures for assuring that, to the maximum extent appropriate, students with disabilities are educated with students who are not disabled, and that special classes, separate schooling, or other removal of students with disabilities from the regular educational environment occurs only when the nature or severity of the disability is such that education in regular classes with the use of supplementary aids and services cannot be achieved satisfactorily.[13] This requirement is known as the least restrictive environment (LRE) requirement.

Recognizing that the regular classroom may not be the LRE placement for every disabled student, the Part B regulations require public agencies to make available a continuum of alternative placements, or a range of placement options, to meet the needs of students with disabilities for special education and related services. The options on this continuum, which include regular classes, special classes, separate schools, and instruction in hospitals and institutions, must be made available to the extent necessary to implement the IEP of each disabled student.[14]

Part B requires that each child's placement must be based on his or her IEP.[15] Thus, it is the special education and related services set out in each student's IEP that constitute the basis for the placement decision. That is why placement determinations cannot be made before a student's IEP is developed. Rather, it is the special education and related services set out in the student's IEP that must constitute the basis for the placement decision. After the IEP of a blind or visually impaired student is developed, the placement determination must be made consistent with the special education and related services reflected in the student's IEP. In addition, the potential harmful effect of the placement on the visually impaired student or the quality of services he or she needs must be considered in determining the LRE.[16] The overriding rule in placement is that each student's place-

ment must be determined on an individual basis.[17] As in other situations, placements of blind and visually impaired students may not be based solely on factors such as category of disability, severity of disability, configuration of delivery system, availability of educational or related services, availability of space, or administrative convenience.

In addition to the Part B requirements applicable to placement in the LRE, Part B requires that each student's placement decision be made by a "group of persons, including persons knowledgeable about the child, the meaning of evaluation data, and placement options."[18] While Part B does not explicitly require the participation of the child's parent on this placement team, many States include parents in the group of persons that makes placement decisions. It also is important to emphasize that parents of blind and visually impaired students, through their participation on the student's IEP team, can play a critical role in ensuring that the student's unique needs are appropriately addressed. Public agencies and parent information centers should take steps to ensure that parents are fully informed about the instructional media that are available to address the unique needs arising from the student's visual impairment.

In implementing Part B's LRE requirements, in some instances, placement decisions are inappropriately made before IEPs that address a child's unique needs are developed. Determinations of appropriate special education and related services for blind and visually impaired students must be made through the IEP process, and must examine the development of skills necessary to address the effects of blindness or low vision on the student's ability to learn and to access the curriculum. Since Part B requires that each child's placement be based on his or her IEP, making placement decisions before a student's IEP is developed is a practice that violates Part B and could result in the denial of FAPE in the LRE.

Still in other instances, some students have been inappropriately placed in the regular classroom although it has been determined that their IEPs cannot be appropriately implemented in the

---

[13]20 U.S.C. §1412(5)(B); 34 CFR §300.550(b).

[14]See 34 CFR §§300.551 and 300.552(b).

[15]See 34 CFR §300.552(a)(2). That regulation requires that each child's placement is determined at least annually, is based on his or her IEP, and is in the school or facility as close as possible to the child's home. 34 CFR §300.552(a)(1)–(3). Further, unless a disabled student's IEP requires another arrangement, the student must be educated in the school or facility that he or she would attend if not disabled. 34 CFR §300.552(c).

[16]34 CFR §300.552(d).

[17]34 CFR §300.552 and Note 1.

[18]34 CFR §300.533(a)(3).

regular classroom even with the necessary supplementary aids and supports. In these situations, the nature of the student's disability and individual needs could make it appropriate for the student to be placed in a setting outside of the regular educational environment in order to ensure that the student's IEP is satisfactorily implemented. By contrast, there are other instances where some blind and visually impaired students have been inappropriately placed in settings other than the regular educational environment, even though their IEPs could have been implemented satisfactorily in the regular classroom with the provision of supplementary aids and services. As is true for all educational decisions under Part B, the above concerns about the misapplication of the LRE requirements underscore the importance of making individual placement determinations based on each student's unique abilities and needs.

In making placement determinations, it is essential that placement teams consider the full range of placement options for blind and visually impaired students. The following are some examples of placement options that could be considered:

- Placement in a regular classroom with needed support services provided in that classroom by an itinerant teacher or by a special teacher assigned to that school;

- Placement in the regular classroom with services outside the classroom by an itinerant teacher or by a special teacher assigned to that school;

- Placement in a self-contained classroom in a regular school; and

- Placement in a special school with residential option.

III. Procedural Safeguards

Part B also requires that public agencies afford parents a range of procedural safeguards. These include giving parents written notice a reasonable time before a public agency proposes to initiate, or change, the identification, evaluation, educa-

tional placement of the child, or the provision of a free appropriate public education to the child. This notice to parents must include a description of the action proposed, or refused, by the agency, an explanation of why the agency proposes, or refuses, to take the action, and a description of any options the agency considered and the reasons why those options were rejected.[19] The requirement to provide a description of any option considered includes a description of the types of placements that were actually considered, e.g., regular class placement with needed support services, regular classroom with pull-out services; and the reasons why these placement options were rejected. Providing this kind of information to parents will enable them to play a more knowledgeable and informed role in the education of their children. Part B affords parents and public educational agencies the right to initiate an impartial due process hearing on any matter regarding the identification, evaluation, or educational placement of the child, or the provision of a free appropriate public education to the child.[20]

Disagreements between parents and public agencies over issues such as the extent that braille instruction should be included in a student's IEP and the educational setting in which the child's IEP should be implemented are examples of some of the matters that can be the subject of a Part B due process hearing. Since many States procedures call for mediation before resorting to formal due process procedures, issues that can be the subject of a Part B due process hearing also can be addressed through mediation if the State has such a process, or through other alternative dispute resolution mechanisms. We strongly encourage alternative dispute resolution without a need to resort to due process and informing parents about such procedures. Public agencies also need to inform parents of blind and visually impaired students of their right to initiate a Part B due process hearing when agreement cannot be reached on important educational decisions.

---

[19]See 34 CFR §300.504(a) and 300.505(a)(2)–(4).
[20]See 20 U.S.C. §1415(b)(1)(E) and 34 CFR §300.506(a).

Association for Education and Rehabilitation of the Blind and Visually Impaired Code of Ethics for Teachers of Students with Visual Impairments

PREAMBLE

The educator's primary commitment is to the students served. Educators are dedicated to help individuals attain maximum independence and to reach their fullest potential. The educator recognizes and protects the rights of students served. Educators pledge themselves to standards of acceptable behavior in relation to the following commitments:

1. Commitment to the persons served.
2. Commitment to the community.
3. Commitment to the profession.
4. Commitment to colleagues, other professionals, and to professional employment practices.

It is the duty of each certified educator to adhere to the spirit and the letter of the code of ethics and to encourage their colleagues to do the same. The following is a set of principles approved by the AER International Board of the conduct of teachers of students with visual impairments. These principles provide a guideline for ethical practice.

Source: Reprinted, with permission of the Association for Education and Rehabilitation of the Blind and Visually Impaired, Alexandria, VA.

1. COMMITMENT TO PERSONS SERVED

The Teacher of Students with Visual Impairments:

1.1 Believes in the dignity and uniqueness of each student served.

1.2 Provides high quality services and strives to become and remain proficient in professional practice.

1.3 Takes all reasonable precautions to insure the safety and health of the student served.

1.4 Protects the student served from conditions interfering with their personal growth, including physical or emotional harassment or abuse.

1.5 Respects the confidentiality of all information pertaining to the student and his or her family. The educator will not divulge confidential information about any student and family to any individual not authorized by the student or family to receive such information unless required to do so by law or unless withholding such information would endanger the safety of the student, the family or the public.

1.6 Before beginning services, obtains and evaluates relevant information about the student served at the minimum or a higher level than what is required by the right to education laws.

1.7 Respects the rights of the students and their families to participate actively in decision-making relating to services they receive and fosters involvement at the minimum or a higher level than what is required by the right to education laws.

1.8 Seeks the support and involvement of the family and/or guardian in promoting student's instructional goals and in advancing his or her continued success.

1.9 Prepares objective and timely reports of services provided at a minimum or higher level than is defined in the right to education laws.

1.10 Maintains responsibility for services to students referred to them and provides ongoing supervision when any portion of the service is assigned to interns or student teachers who are enrolled in supervised training programs.

1.11 Recognizes those services beyond the scope of their professional preparation and/or capabilities and refers to appropriate resources or services.

1.12 Maintains an awareness of, and abides by the right-to-education laws, policies, and other laws pertaining to their work with students and their families.

1.13 Strives, at all times, to maintain the highest level of instruction, including assessment, evaluation and instructional planning and to maintain an instructional environment that is conducive to learning.

1.14 Secures the consent of the student, the family/ guardian and/or the school before allowing others to observe lessons, photograph, or tape the student.

1.15 Endeavors to provide individuals involved with the student with sufficient knowledge, instruction and experiences in their area of expertise to facilitate realization of the student's educational goals.

1.16 Respects the worth, culture, and dignity of each individual, including exhibiting courtesy and temperance in situations of conflict and adheres to the principles of equal opportunity for all students with visual impairment or blindness regardless of sex, race, religion, or national origin.

1.17 Acts as an advocate for children served, and empowers the family and child with self-advocacy.

2. COMMITMENT TO COMMUNITY

The Teacher of Students with Visual Impairment:

2.1 Educates the public about the capabilities of persons with visual impairment or blindness, the benefit of appropriate services, and the causes, implication and prevention of blindness or visual impairment.

2.2 Takes appropriate action to insure that students and their families are not exploited by public education activities, fund raising activities, or any other manner.

2.3 Strives to develop a continuum of high quality comprehensive community services.

3. COMMITMENT TO THE PROFESSION

The Teacher of Students with Visual Impairments:

3.1 Strives to improve the quality of his or her services and the services of other practitioners.

3.2 Interprets and uses the writing and research of others with integrity.

3.3 Contributes to the growing body of knowledge, expertise and skills of the profession, including conducting and reporting research in an ethical and professional manner.

3.4 Supports and participates in staff development activities, training, and in state or provincial, regional and national conferences whenever feasible.

3.5 Maintains the necessary skills and certification of those skills.

3.6 Facilitates and enhances team efforts by sharing specialized knowledge, resources, experience, concepts and skills and by contributing relevant information and abiding by team decisions made on behalf of, and with students and their families.

3.7 Accepts no gratuities or gifts of significant value over/above the predetermined salary, reimbursed expenses, or fee for services.

3.8 Engages in no activity which results in an actual or implied conflict of interest.

3.9 Exposes incompetence and illegal or unethical behavior.

4. COMMITMENT TO COLLEAGUES, FELLOW PROFESSIONALS AND THE PROFESSIONAL EMPLOYER

The Teacher of Students with Visual Impairment:

4.1 Shares knowledge, concepts and skills with colleagues.

4.2 Offers professional services to a student receiving services from another practitioner of a similar discipline only by agreement with the other practitioner, after that practitioner has terminated services, or when quality services cannot be provided by the other practitioner.

4.3 Maintains professional relationships with colleagues, employers, the student and the family.

4.4 Assumes no responsibilities that are better provided by other practitioners who are available to the student served.

4.5 Conducts himself or herself with integrity in all professional actions in accordance with recognized standards for personnel practice.

4.6 Responds factually when complying with a request to provide references for a colleague.

4.7 Adheres to the policies and regulations of employers, except where these require violation of ethical principles such as those contained in this code.

4.8 Accepts no remuneration for a professional service from a person who is entitled to such service through an agency or school at a lesser cost, unless the student and family is fully informed of services available and chooses not to avail themselves of them.

4.9 Charges fees for services, if such fees are permissible, that are consistent with the reasonable and customary rate of the particular geographic region within which he or she is working.

4.10 Provides applicants seeking information about a position or a service with an honest description.

Adopted by Divisions 3, 8, 12 and 13, July 1992

Approved by AER International Board, October 1992

December 1997

Association for Education and Rehabilitation of the Blind and Visually Impaired Code of Ethics for Orientation and Mobility Specialists

PREAMBLE

Orientation and mobility specialists (peripatologists) recognize the significant role that independent movement plays in the overall growth and functioning of the individual and are dedicated to helping each individual attain the level of independence necessary to reach his or her full potential. Orientation and mobility specialists gather, develop, and utilize specialized knowledge in accomplishing this with all professions, the possession of specialist knowledge obligates the practitioner to protect the rights of the individuals who must avail themselves of the particular service. To assure the public of our awareness of this obligation, we commit ourselves to this Code of Ethics.

In order to fulfill this obligation, orientation and mobility specialists pledge themselves to standards of acceptable behavior in relation to the following five commitments:

Commitment to the Student;

Commitment to the Community;

Commitment to the Profession;

Commitment to Colleagues and Other Professionals; and

Commitment to Professional Employment Practices.

It is the responsibility of each orientation and mobility specialist to adhere to the principles in the Code and encourage colleagues to do the same.

1. COMMITMENT TO THE STUDENT

1.1 The orientation and mobility specialist will value the worth and dignity of each individual.

1.2 It is the responsibility of the orientation and mobility specialist to strive at all times to maintain the highest standards of instruction.

1.3 The orientation and mobility specialist will take all reasonable precautions to insure the safety of the student from conditions which interfere with learning.

1.4 The orientation and mobility specialist will respect the confidentiality of all information pertaining to the student. He or she will not divulge confidential information about any student to any indi-

Source: Reprinted, with permission of the Association for Education and Rehabilitation of the Blind and Visually Impaired, Alexandria, VA.

vidual not authorized by the student to receive such information unless required by law or unless withholding such information would endanger the safety of the student or the public.

1.5 Before beginning instruction with the student, the orientation and mobility specialist will make every attempt to obtain and evaluate information about the student which is relevant to the orientation and mobility instruction.

1.6 The orientation and mobility specialist will respect the rights of the student and/or parent/guardian to participate in decisions regarding the instructional program.

1.7 Decisions regarding continuing or discontinuing instruction will be made with the student and will be based upon evaluation of the student's needs, abilities, and skills. The decisions will be made in the student's best interest, independent of personal or agency convenience.

1.8 The orientation and mobility specialist will provide sufficient information regarding the various types of orientation and mobility guidance devices and will explore with the student which device will best meet specific needs.

1.9 The orientation and mobility specialist will seek the support and involvement of the family and/or guardian in promoting the student's instructional goals and in advancing his or her continued success. This will include sharing information with the family that will facilitate the student's welfare and independence, but not communicating information which violates the principles of confidentiality.

1.10 The orientation and mobility specialist will ask the consent of the student and/or guardian before inviting others to observe a lesson or before arranging to have the student photographed or tape recorded.

1.11 The orientation and mobility specialist will make all reports objective and will present only data relevant to the purposes of the evaluation and instruction. When appropriate, the orientation and mobility specialist will share this information with the student.

1.12 The orientation and mobility specialist will endeavor to provide individuals involved with the student sufficient knowledge, instruction and experiences relative to orientation and mobility so as to facilitate the goals of the student.

1.13 The orientation and mobility specialist will not dispense or supply orientation and mobility equipment unless it is in the best interest of the student.

1.14 The orientation and mobility specialist will not allow consideration of personal comfort or convenience to interfere with the design and implementation of necessary travel lessons.

1.15 The orientation and mobility specialist will be responsible for services to students who are referred and will provide adequate ongoing supervision when any portions of the service is assigned to interns or students teachers who are enrolled in orientation and mobility university programs, with the understanding that each individual will function under strict supervision.

2. COMMITMENT TO THE COMMUNITY

2.1 The student will not be refused service by the orientation and mobility specialist because of age, sex, race, religion, national origin or sexual orientation.

2.2 The student shall not be excluded from service because of the severity of his/her disabilities unless it is clearly evident that he cannot benefit from the service. The orientation and mobility specialist will attempt to influence decision making which establishes the rights of individuals to receive service.

2.3 The orientation and mobility specialist will contribute to community education by defining the role or orientation and mobility in the community, by describing the nature and delivery of service, and by indicating how the community can be involved in the education and rehabilitation process.

2.4 The orientation and mobility specialist will not engage in any public education activity that results in the exploitation of his/her students. Exaggeration, sensationalism, superficiality and other misleading activities are to be avoided.

3. COMMITMENT TO THE PROFESSION

3.1 The orientation and mobility specialist will seek full responsibility for the exercise of professional judgment related to orientation and mobility.

3.2 To the best of his or her ability, the orientation and mobility specialist will accept the responsibility, throughout the career duration, master and contribute to the growing body of specialized knowledge, concepts and skills which characterize orientation and mobility as a profession.

3.3 The orientation and mobility specialist will interpret and use the writing and research of others with integrity. In writing, making presentations, or conducting research, the orientation and mobility specialist will be familiar with and give recognition to previous work on the topic.

3.4 The orientation and mobility specialist will conduct investigations in a manner which takes into consideration the welfare of the subject, and report research in a way as to lessen the possibility that the findings will be misleading.

3.5 The orientation and mobility specialist will strive to improve the quality of provided service and promote conditions which attract suitable persons to careers in orientation and mobility.

3.6 The orientation and mobility specialist will, whenever possible, support and participate in local, state, and national professional organizations.

3.7 The orientation and mobility specialist will accept no gratuities or gifts of significance over and above the predetermined salary, fee, and/or expense for professional service.

3.8 The orientation and mobility specialist will not engage in commercial activities which result in a conflict of interest between these activities and professional objectives with the student.

3.9 The orientation and mobility specialist involved in development or promotion of orientation and mobility devices, books or other products, will present such products in a professional and factual way.

3.10 The orientation and mobility specialist will report suspected and/or known incompetence, illegal, or unethical behavior in the practice of the profession.

3.11 The orientation and mobility specialist will strive to provide fair treatment to all members of the profession and support them when unjustly accused or mistreated.

3.12 Each member of the profession has a personal and professional responsibility for supporting the orientation and mobility code of ethics and maintaining effectiveness.

4. COMMITMENT TO COLLEAGUES AND OTHER PROFESSIONALS

4.1 The orientation and mobility specialist will engage in professional relationships on a mature level and will not become involved in personal disparagement.

4.2 The orientation and mobility specialist will communicate fully and openly with colleagues in the sharing of specialized knowledge, concepts, and skills.

4.3 The orientation and mobility specialist will not offer professional services to a person receiving orientation and mobility instruction from another orientation and mobility specialist, except by agreement with the other specialist or after the other specialist has ended instruction with the student.

4.4 When transferring a student, the orientation and mobility specialist will not commit a receiving specialist to a prescribed course of action.

4.5 The orientation and mobility specialist will seek harmonious relations with members of other professions. This will include the discussion and free exchange of ideas regarding the overall welfare of the student and discussion with other professionals regarding the benefits to be obtained from orientation and mobility services.

4.6 The orientation and mobility specialist will not assume responsibilities which are better provided by other professionals who are available to the student.

4.7 The orientation and mobility specialist will seek to facilitate and enhance a team effort with other professionals. In such situations where team decisions are made, the orientation and mobility specialist will contribute information from his or her own particular perspective and will abide by the team decision unless the team decision requires that he or she act in violation of the code of ethics.

5. COMMITMENT TO PROFESSIONAL EMPLOYMENT PRACTICES

5.1 The orientation and mobility specialist will apply for, accept, or offer a position on the basis of professional qualification and will act with integrity in these situations.

5.2 The orientation and mobility specialist will give prompt notification of any change of availability to the agency or school where he has applied.

5.3 The orientation and mobility specialist will give prompt notification of any change of availability or nature of a position.

5.4 The orientation and mobility specialist will respond factually when requested to write a letter of recommendation for a colleague seeking a professional position.

5.5 The orientation and mobility specialist will provide applicants seeking information about a position with an honest description of the assignment, conditions of work, and related matters.

5.6 The orientation and mobility specialist will abide by the terms of a contract or agreement, whether verbal or written, unless the terms have been falsely represented or substantially changed by the other party.

5.7 The orientation and mobility specialist will not accept positions where proven principles of orientation and mobility practice are compromised or abandoned, unless the position is accepted with the intention of amending or modifying the questionable practices and providing that they do not participate in the behavior which violates the code of ethics.

5.8 The orientation and mobility specialist will adhere to the policies and regulations of the employer except where he or she is required to violate ethical principles indicated in this code. To avoid possible conflicts, the orientation and mobility specialist will acquaint the employer with the contents of this code.

5.9 The orientation and mobility specialist may provide additional professional service through private contracts, as long as these services remain of the highest quality and do not interfere with the specialist's regular job duties.

5.10 The orientation and mobility specialist will not accept remuneration for professional instruction from a student who is entitled to such instruction through an agency or school, unless the student, when fully informed of the services available, decided to contract privately with the specialist.

5.11 The orientation and mobility specialist will establish a fee for private contracting in cooperation with the contracting agency or school that is consistent with the reasonable and customary rate of that particular geographic region.

5.12 When providing additional service through private contracts, the orientation and mobility specialist will observe the agency or school's policies and procedures concerning outside employment including the use of facilities.

(Adopted by Interest Group #9 of the American Association of Workers for the Blind, July 1973 and by its successor, the Association for Education and Rehabilitation of the Blind and Visually Impaired.)

Revised by AER Division Nine, July 1990

Approved by AER International Board, April 1991

December 1997

Association for Education and Rehabilitation of the Blind and Visually Impaired Code of Ethics for Rehabilitation Teachers of Individuals with Visual Impairment

PREAMBLE

We, the Rehabilitation Teachers of Division XI of the Association for Education and Rehabilitation of the Blind and Visually Impaired (AER), recognize our commitment to provide the highest quality of services to those individuals whom we serve. The purpose of our profession is to instruct individuals with visual impairments in the use of those compensatory skills and aids that will enable them to live safely, productively, interdependent, and up to each persons maximum potential. Our primary obligation, as Rehabilitation Teachers, is to our clients. In all of our relationships, we will protect our clients welfare and will diligently seek to assist our clients toward achieving their goals. While fulfilling this commitment, we Rehabilitation Teachers become responsible to our clients and their families, to our employers and the community in which we work, to our profession and other professionals in the field of human services; and to ourselves. We recognize that both our actions and in-actions affect the lives of those whom we seek to serve and we accept the responsibility and consequences of our actions and/or

Source: Reprinted, with permission of the Association for Education and Rehabilitation of the Blind and Visually Impaired, Alexandria, VA.

in-action. Defined by this Code of Ethics a Rehabilitation Teacher is a professional practicing in the public or private sector who evaluates, instructs, and guides a person with a visual impairment through an individualized plan of rehabilitation instruction designed to help that person carry out daily activities. These competencies encompass specific, identifiable evaluation and teaching skills and knowledge to enable the person with the visual impairment to develop and/or enhance sensory and kinesthetic capabilities, personal management skills, communication skills, indoor orientation, low vision utilization, and home management skills. In addition to the instructional areas listed, the Rehabilitation Teacher will be involved with assisting the client to understand their vision loss, and to facilitate the development of appropriate coping mechanisms.

1. COMMITMENT TO THE CLIENT

1.1 The professional Rehabilitation Teacher shall respect the worth, culture, and dignity of each individual. This includes exhibiting courtesy and temperance in situations of conflict.

1.2 The role of the Rehabilitation Teacher as an advocate is to protect and promote the welfare of persons with visual impairments for the purpose of assisting them to achieve their desired levels of independence.

1.3 The purpose of confidentiality regarding client information, is to safeguard facts, data, and professional judgments that are obtained in the course of practice. Disclosures of information are restricted to what is necessary, relevant, and verifiable with respect to each client's right to privacy. Professional files, reports, and records shall be maintained under conditions of security.

1.4 The Rehabilitation Teacher shall obtain the informed consent of the client before inviting others to observe a lesson, having the client photographed or recorded, or involving the client in a research study in which personal identifying information would be gathered and disseminated.

1.5 The Rehabilitation Teacher shall take all reasonable precautions to ensure the safety of the client and will seek to provide an instructional environment that is conducive to learning.

1.6 Prior to the commencement of instruction, the Rehabilitation Teacher will seek to obtain and evaluate information that is relevant to the client's rehabilitation program.

1.7 Decisions regarding the continuation or discontinuation of instruction shall be made with each client, respecting the rights of the clients to participate in decisions regarding their instructional programs, and shall be based upon objective evaluation of the clients' needs and abilities to benefit from defined services.

1.8 The Rehabilitation Teacher shall seek, where appropriate, the support and involvement of the clients' support system in promoting an individual client's instructional objectives and in advancing continued success. This includes sharing information with the family, or others, that will facilitate the client's welfare and independence, but not communicating information which violates the principles of confidentiality.

1.9 The Rehabilitation Teacher will relate to all clients in a professional manner during the client's rehabilitation program and not engage in personal or private relationships that would jeopardize the rehabilitation process.

2. COMMITMENT TO THE COMMUNITY

2.1 The Rehabilitation Teacher, when using any specialized knowledge or abilities to contribute to community education, seeks to exhibit the highest standard of rehabilitation practices and client services, avoiding exaggeration, sensationalism, superficiality and other misleading activities; and to indicate how the community can become involved in the educational and/or rehabilitation process.

2.2 The Rehabilitation Teacher shall not engage in any public education activity that results in the exploitation of the client and/or the client's family.

3. COMMITMENT TO THE PROFESSION

3.1 The Rehabilitation Teacher should seek full responsibility for the exercise of professional judgment related to instruction.

3.2 The Rehabilitation Teacher has the responsibility to contribute to the growing body of knowledge, expertise, and skills of the profession.

3.3 The Rehabilitation Teacher is encouraged to support individual and public efforts to advance services to disabled persons through education, legislation, personal commitment, and improved agency practices and procedures. This includes promoting understanding and acceptance of current rehabilitation programs and past achievements in the fields; and participation in local, state, regional, and national organizations that are directly related to the profession of rehabilitation teaching.

3.4 The Rehabilitation Teacher should strive to provide fair treatment and support to all members of the profession.

3.5 The Rehabilitation Teacher shall make reasonable effort to oppose incompetent, illegal, or unethical behavior, and report such behavior to the proper regulatory bodies.

4. COMMITMENT TO COLLEAGUES AND OTHER PROFESSIONALS

4.1 The Rehabilitation Teacher is expected to facilitate and enhance team efforts, on a professional level, and to share specialized knowledge, resources, experience, concepts, and skills. In situations where team decisions are made the rehabilitation teacher is expected to contribute relevant information and abide by the team decision.

4.2 The Rehabilitation Teacher should avoid assuming responsibilities which are better provided by other professionals. Referrals to other professionals shall be done in agreement with the client and the client's service plan.

4.3 The Rehabilitation Teacher responds factually when requested to write a letter of recommendation for a colleague seeking a professional position.

5. COMMITMENT TO PROFESSIONAL EMPLOYMENT PRACTICES

5.1 The Rehabilitation Teacher should adhere to the policies and regulations of the employer and should abide by the terms of a contract or agreement, whether verbal or written, unless the job duties include behavior which violates the code of ethics. The Rehabilitation Teacher should not accept a position where proven principles of rehabilitation teaching practices are compromised or abandoned.

5.2 The Rehabilitation Teacher should demonstrate concern and appreciation of the heritage, values, and principles of the employing agency.

5.3 The Rehabilitation Teacher providing additional professional services through private contracts, shall avoid engaging in outside employment or other outside activity which is incompatible with the full and proper discharge of job duties and responsibilities, or which constitute a conflict of interest.

5.4 The Rehabilitation Teacher may not solicit or directly accept a gift, subscription, advance, rendering, or deposit of money, gratuity, favor, entertainment, loan, or anything of significant value from a person, business, or organization with whom they have official relationships. This does not preclude normal business practices which enable the rehabilitation teacher to maintain on-going services.

5.5 The Rehabilitation Teacher shall avoid distributing, or cause to be distributed, any advertisement, materials, or samples aimed at soliciting referrals for personal profit.

6. COMMITMENT TO PRIVATE BUSINESS PRACTICE

6.1 The Rehabilitation Teacher in private practice will adhere to all applicable federal, state, and local laws which establish and regulate business practices and shall refuse to participate in practices that are inconsistent with the rules or standards established by regulatory bodies regarding the delivery of rehabilitation teaching services to clients.

6.2 No person shall be refused service by the Rehabilitation Teacher on the basis of race, color, religion, national origin, gender, age, sexual orientation, or disability.

6.3 The Rehabilitation Teacher shall avoid causing misrepresentation of professional credentials or competencies.

6.4 The Rehabilitation Teacher in private contracting is encouraged to carry professional liability insurance protection.

6.5 No Rehabilitation Teacher shall effectuate or participate in the wrongful removal of professional rehabilitation files or other materials.

6.6 When asked to comment on cases being actively managed by another rehabilitation practitioner and/or agency, the reviewer shall make every reasonable effort to conduct an in-person evaluation before rendering a professional opinion.

6.7 Competitive advertising of services and products shall be factually accurate. The Rehabilitation Teacher shall promise or offer only those services or results which there is reason to believe can be provided.

6.8 The Rehabilitation Teacher shall establish a fee for private contracting in cooperation with the contracting agency that is consistent with the reasonable and customary rate of that particular geographic region.

6.9 The rehabilitation practitioner shall not enter into fee arrangements which would be likely to create a conflict of interest.

6.10 The individual Rehabilitation Teacher shall not behave in such a manner as to use the position to influence or cause the recipient of services to name them as a beneficiary of a will, insurance policy, or other assets as compensation for services of personal profit.

Accepted July 23, 1990 in Washington, D.C. by Division XI

Approved by AER International Board, April, 1991

December 1997

Association for Education and Rehabilitation of the Blind and Visually Impaired Code of Ethics for Low Vision Therapist

PREAMBLE

The preservation of the highest standards of integrity is vital to the successful discharge of the professional responsibilities of the Low Vision Therapist. This Code of Ethics has been established to safeguard the public health, safety, and welfare and to assure that low vision services of the highest possible quality are available to consumers. A violation of a provision of the Code of Ethics constitutes unprofessional conduct and makes the professional subject to disciplinary action. Accordingly, failure to specify a particular responsibility or practice in the code should not be construed as a deliberate omission.

I. A Low Vision Therapist shall be dedicated to providing competent vision rehabilitation with compassion and respect.

II. A Low Vision Therapist shall deal honestly with consumers and colleagues and strive to expose those Low Vision Therapists deficient in character or competence or who engage in fraud or deception.

Source: Reprinted, with permission of the Association for Education and Rehabilitation of the Blind and Visually Impaired, Alexandria, VA.

III. A Low Vision Therapist shall respect the law and also recognize a responsibility to seek changes in those requirements which are contrary to the best interests of the consumer.

IV. A Low Vision Therapist shall respect the rights of consumers, of colleagues, and of other professionals and shall safeguard confidences within the constraints of the law.

V. A Low Vision Therapist shall continue to study, apply and advance scientific knowledge, make relevant information available to consumers, colleagues, and the public, obtain consultations, and use the talents of other health professionals when indicated.

VI. A Low Vision Therapist shall, in the provision of appropriate care, except in emergencies, be free to choose with whom to associate, and the environment in which to provide services.

VII. A Low Vision Therapist shall recognize a responsibility to participate in activities contributing to an improved professional community.

VIII. A Low Vision Therapist shall practice in accordance with the body of knowledge related to low vision.

STANDARDS OF PROFESSIONAL BEHAVIOR

1. A Low Vision Therapist shall provide assessment, evaluation, and intervention in a collaborative low vision service; such service includes a medical examination by an eye care professional and a clinical examination by a low vision practitioner.

2. A Low Vision Therapist shall provide assessment, evaluation, and intervention for consumers with low vision disorders only within an interdisciplinary professional relationship. The Low Vision Therapist may not evaluate or intervene solely by correspondence. This does not preclude follow-up correspondence with a consumer previously seen or providing the consumer with general information on an educational nature.

3. A Low Vision Therapist shall participate in the evaluation of devices prescribed/dispensed to persons served to determine their effectiveness.

4. A Low Vision Therapist who performs assessments, evaluations, and interventions shall use instruments, techniques, and procedures commonly recognized by his/her profession and compatible with his/her education, expertise, and professional competence.

5. If, in the course of providing services, it is suspected that a consumer needs additional medical/clinical care, this will be addressed through appropriate referral.

6. A Low Vision Therapist shall use every resource available, including referral to other specialists as needed, to provide the best service possible.

7. A Low Vision Therapist shall fully inform a person served, a parent, or guardian, of the nature, costs, and possible effects of the services.

8. A Low Vision Therapist shall fully inform subjects participating in research or teaching activities of the nature and possible effects of these activities.

9. A Low Vision Therapist shall provide appropriate maintenance and access to the records of a consumer served professionally.

10. A Low Vision Therapist shall take all reasonable precautions to avoid injuring a consumer in the delivery of professional services.

11. A Low Vision Therapist shall evaluate services and products rendered to determine their effectiveness.

12. A Low Vision Therapist may not exploit a consumer in the delivery of or payment for professional services. Exploitation of services includes accepting persons for assessments or intervention or by continuing therapy when benefits to the consumer cannot reasonably be expected.

13. A Low Vision Therapist may not guarantee the results of a therapeutic procedure, directly or by implication. A reasonable statement of prognosis may be made, but caution shall be exercised not to mislead a consumer served professionally to expect results that cannot be predicted from sound evidence.

14. A Low Vision Therapist may not discriminate in the delivery of professional services on the basis of disability, race, sex, age, religion, sexual preference, health status, or any other basis that is unjustifiable or irrelevant to the need for and potential benefit from the services.

15. A Low Vision Therapist shall continue professional development through his/her professional career.

16. A Low Vision Therapist may not provide services or supervision which they are not qualified to perform, nor may they permit services to be provided by a staff person under their supervision who is not qualified.

17. A Low Vision Therapist may not offer pro-

fessional services by assistants, students, or trainees for whom appropriate supervision and responsibility is not provided.

18. A Low Vision Therapist may not require or suggest that anyone under his/her supervision engage in a practice that is a violation of the Code of Ethics.

19. A Low Vision Therapist will accurately represent his/her level of training, competence, and role in the interdisciplinary team.

20. A Low Vision Therapist's public statements providing information about professional services and products may not contain representations or claims that are false, deceptive, or misleading.

21. A Low Vision Therapist may not use professional or commercial affiliations in a way that would mislead consumers or limit the services available to them.

22. Consumers shall be provided with freedom of choices as to the source of services and products.

23. Devices associated with professional practice shall be dispensed to a consumer as a part of a program of comprehensive rehabilitative care.

24. Fees established for professional services shall be independent of whether a device is dispensed.

25. Price information about professional services rendered and devices dispensed shall be disclosed by providing to or posting a complete schedule of fees and charges in advance of rendering services. This schedule shall differentiate between fees for professional services and charges for devices dispensed.

26. A Low Vision Therapist may not participate in activities that constitute conflicts of professional interest.

27. A Low Vision Therapist is required to report a violation of the Code of Ethics.

28. A Low Vision Therapist may not engage in a violation of the Code of Ethics or attempt in any way to circumvent it.

29. A Low Vision Therapist may not engage in dishonesty, fraud, deceit, misrepresentation, or any other form of illegal conduct.

30. A Low Vision Therapist shall not practice while unable to do so with reasonable skill and safety (e.g., illness, drunkenness, nonprescriptive use of controlled substances, chemicals, or other types of materials).

31. A Low Vision Therapist shall not withdraw professional services after a professional relationship has been established without informing the consumer of where to obtain necessary and equivalent professional services in a timely manner.

32. Harassing, abusing, or intimidating a consumer is prohibited. In addition, sexual contact, or requests for sexual contact, with a consumer is prohibited.

33. Committing an act of dishonesty, corruption, or criminal behavior which directly or indirectly affects the health, welfare, or safety of others is prohibited.

December 1997

Council for Exceptional Children (CEC) International Standards for Entry into Professional Practice

I. To be qualified to enter into practice as a special education teacher, an individual must possess no less than a bachelor's degree that encompasses the knowledge and skills consistent with the entry level into special education practice.

II. To be qualified to enter into practice as a special education teacher, an individual must possess the knowledge and skills set forth in the CEC Common Core of Knowledge and Skills Essential for Beginning Special Education Teachers.

III. To be qualified to enter into practice as a special education teacher, an individual must possess the knowledge and skills set forth in at least one of the CEC Specialized Knowledge and Skills Essential for Beginning Special Education Teachers.

IV. Each new professional in special education should receive a minimum of a 1-year mentorship during the first year of his or her professional special education practice in a new role. The mentor should be an experienced professional in the same or a similar role, who can provide expertise and support on a continuing basis.

V. Approval of individuals for professional practice in the field of special education should be for a limited period of time with periodic renewal.

Source: Council for Exceptional Children,
www.cec.sped.org

VI. Each professional in the field of educating individuals with exceptionalities (e.g., teachers, supervisors, administrators, college/university faculty) should participate in a minimum of 25 clock hours each year of planned, preapproved, organized, and recognized professional development activities related to his or her field of professional practice. Such activities may include a combination of professional development units, continuing education units, college/university coursework, professional organization service (e.g., in CEC federations and chapters, divisions, subdivisions, and caucuses), professional workshops, special projects, or reading professional literature. Employing agencies should provide resources to enable each professional's continuing development.

CEC COMMON CORE OF KNOWLEDGE AND SKILLS ESSENTIAL FOR ALL BEGINNING SPECIAL EDUCATION TEACHERS

Preamble

The standards of the profession of special education are a formally codified set of beliefs. These belief statements represent the special educator's principles of appropriate ethical behavior and are based on several assumptions.

One assumption is that special education has within its heritage the perspectives of advocacy for persons with disabilities and of embracing individual differences. These differences include the traditional consideration of the nature and effect of exceptionalities. As the community of exceptional children, youth, and adults has become increasingly diverse, these perspectives have been broadened to include other characteristics that significantly influence their quality of life. To maintain their ability to successfully function as advocates for their multicultural clients, special educators must broaden their perspectives to ensure vigilant attention to the issues of diversity. Current demographic trends clearly indicate that:

◆ The numbers of children and youth from culturally and linguistically diverse backgrounds served in public schools are growing rapidly.

◆ Cultural and linguistic diversity is expected to continue as well as to increase.

◆ The number of professionals who are culturally and linguistically diverse entering the special education profession has been declining even as the numbers of students who are culturally and linguistically diverse are rising.

Given the pervasive nature of diversity, professional standards are needed that guide professional practice in ways that are relevant to the multicultural populations served in special education. Specifically, these standards reflect the premise that, to design effective interventions, special educators must understand the characteristics of their learners, including factors such as culture, language, gender, religion, and sexuality. This premise has been addressed in two ways. First, most statements are inclusive in nature; that is, they identify knowledge and skills essential to effectively serve all exceptional learners, including those from culturally and linguistically diverse backgrounds. Second, selected items address the most critical aspects of diversity and are infused throughout the model.

Another assumption is that the sustained involvement of families and the larger community is fundamental to delivering high-quality educational services to individuals with exceptional learning needs. The knowledge and skills contained in this document should be interpreted broadly to include learners of all ages, beginning with infants and preschoolers and extending to young adults who are exiting the school program. Similarly, the term families should be interpreted broadly to include, as appropriate to given situations, biological mothers and fathers, adoptive parents, legal guardians, foster parents or primary caregivers, siblings, and extended family members. Finally, while not specifically stated, it is assumed that special educators may provide learning opportunities in a variety of learning environments, including the home, preschool, school, and community settings, as well as in both specialized and integrated environments.

This document focuses on the unique set of knowledge and skills needed to practice in special education, not on specific areas of exceptionality or age groupings, general education methods, or subject matter content. Special educators who practice in a specific area (or areas) of exceptionality or age grouping must possess the exceptionality-specific knowledge and skills adopted by CEC in addition to the Common Core. Also, it is assumed that a special educator who is required to teach specific subjects or content areas (such as science, social studies, foreign languages, vocational education) has additional preparation, practicum experiences, and expertise in those areas.

An additional assumption is that this Common Core of Knowledge and Skills will change over time. As with the adoption of the CEC Code of Ethics, time should be provided for continuing examination, debate, and further articulation of the knowledge and skills for entry-level special educators.

A final assumption of this Common Core of Knowledge and Skills is that the professional conduct of entry-level special educators is governed foremost by the CEC Code of Ethics. Special education professionals

◆ Are committed to developing the highest educational and quality of life potential of exceptional individuals.

◆ Promote and maintain a high level of competence and integrity in practicing their profession.

◆ Engage in professional activities that benefit exceptional individuals, their families, other colleagues, students or research subjects.

◆ Exercise objective professional judgment in the practice of their profession.

◆ Strive to advance their knowledge and skills regarding the education of exceptional individuals.

◆ Work within the standards and policies of their profession.

◆ Seek to uphold and improve, where necessary, the laws, regulations, and policies governing the delivery of special education and related services and the practice of their profession.

◆ Do not condone or participate in unethical or illegal acts, nor violate professional standards adopted by the Delegate Assembly of CEC.

It was through significant professional and personal commitment that the members of CEC crafted this product. In the process we learned not only about knowledge and skills but also about each other and developed a deep mutual respect. May those who use this Common Core of Knowledge and Skills experience that same mutual respect from all who serve children and their families.

KNOWLEDGE AND SKILLS STATEMENTS

CC: Common Core
1. Philosophical, Historical, and Legal Foundations of Special Education

Knowledge

K1 Models, theories, and philosophies that provide the basis for special education.

K2 Variations in beliefs, traditions, and values across cultures within society and the effect of the relationship among child, family, and schooling.

K3 Issues in definition and identification procedures for individuals with exceptional learning needs including individuals from culturally and/or linguistically diverse backgrounds.

K4 Assurances and due process rights related to assessment, eligibility, and placement.

K5 Rights and responsibilities of parents, students, teachers and other professionals, and schools as they relate to individuals with learning needs.

Skills

S1 Articulate personal philosophy of special education including its relationship to/with regular education.

S2 Conduct instructional and other professional activities consistent with the requirements of law, rules and regulations, and local district policies and procedures.

CC: Common Core
2. Characteristics of Learners

Knowledge

K1 Similarities and differences among the cognitive, physical, cultural, social, and emotional needs of individuals with and without exceptional learning needs.

K2 Differential characteristics of individuals with exceptionalities, including levels of severity and multiple exceptionalities.

K3 Characteristics of normal, delayed, and disordered communication patterns of individuals with exceptional learning needs.

K4 Effects an exceptional condition(s) may have on an individual's life.

K5 Characteristics and effects of the cultural and environmental milieu of the child and the family including cultural and linguistic diversity, socioeconomic level, abuse/neglect, and substance abuse.

K6 Effects of various medications on the educational, cognitive, physical, social, and emotional behavior of individuals with exceptionalities.

K7 Educational implications of characteristics of various exceptionalities.

Skills

S1 Access information on various cognitive, communication, physical, cultural, social, and emotional conditions of individuals with exceptional learning needs.

CC: Common Core
3. Assessment, Diagnosis, and Evaluation

Knowledge

K1 Basic terminology used in assessment.

K2 Ethical concerns related to assessment.

K3 Legal provisions, regulations, and guidelines regarding assessment of individuals.

K4 Typical procedures used for screening, prereferral, referral, and classification.

K5 Appropriate application and interpretation of scores, including grade score versus standard score, percentile ranks, age/grade equivalents, and stanines.

K6 Appropriate use and limitations of each type of assessment instrument.

K7 Incorporation of strategies that consider the influence of diversity on assessment, eligibility, programming, and placement of individuals with exceptional learning needs.

K8 The relationship between assessment and placement decisions.

K9 Methods for monitoring progress of individuals with exceptional learning needs.

Skills

S1 Collaborate with families and other professionals involved in the assessment of individuals with exceptional learning needs.

S2 Create and maintain records.

S3 Gather background information regarding academic, medical, and family history.

S4 Use various types of assessment procedures appropriately.

S5 Interpret information from formal and informal assessment instruments and procedures.

S6 Report assessment results to individuals with exceptional learning needs, parents, administrators, and other professionals using appropriate communication skills.

S7 Use performance data and information from teachers, other professionals, individuals with exceptionalities, and parents to make or suggest appropriate modification in learning environments.

S8 Develop individualized assessment strategies for instruction.

S9 Use assessment information in making instructional decisions and planning individual programs that result in appropriate placement and intervention for all individuals with exceptional learning needs, including those from culturally and/or linguistically diverse backgrounds.

S10 Evaluate the results of instruction.

S11 Evaluate supports needed for integration into various program placements.

CC: Common Core
4. Instructional Content and Practice

Knowledge

K1 Differing learning styles of individuals with exceptional learning needs and how to adapt teaching to these styles.

K2 Demands of various learning environments such as individualized instruction in general education classes.

K3 Curricula for the development of motor, cognitive, academic, social language, affective, and functional life skills for individuals with exceptional learning needs.

K4 Instructional and remedial methods, techniques, and curriculum materials.

K5 Techniques for modifying instructional methods and materials.

K6 Life skills instruction relevant to independent, community, and personal living and employment.

K7 Cultural perspectives influencing the relationship among families, schools, and communities as related to effective instruction for individuals with exceptional learning needs.

Skills

S1 Interpret and use assessment data for instructional planning.

S2 Develop and/or select instructional content, materials, resources, and strategies that respond to cultural, linguistic, and gender differences.

S3 Develop comprehensive, longitudinal individualized programs.

S4 Choose and use appropriate technologies to accomplish instructional objectives and to integrate them appropriately into the instructional process.

S5 Prepare appropriate lesson plans.

S6 Involve the individual and family in setting instructional goals and charting progress.

S7 Conduct and use task analysis.

S8 Select, adapt, and use instructional strategies and materials according to characteristics of the learner.

S9 Sequence, implement, and evaluate individual learning objectives.

S10 Integrate affective, social, and career/vocational skills with academic curricula.

S11 Use strategies for facilitating maintenance and generalization of skills across learning environments.

S12 Use instructional time properly.

S13 Teach individuals with exceptional learning needs to use thinking, problem-solving, and other cognitive strategies to meet their individual needs.

S14 Choose and implement instructional techniques and strategies that promote successful transition for individuals with exceptional learning needs.

S15 Establish and maintain rapport with learners.

S16 Use verbal and nonverbal communication techniques.

S17 Conduct self-evaluation of instruction.

CC: Common Core
5. Planning and Managing the Teaching and Learning Environment

Knowledge

K1 Basic classroom management theories, methods, and techniques for individuals with exceptional learning needs.

K2 Research-based best practices for effective management of teaching and learning.

K3 Ways in which technology can assist with planning and managing the teaching and learning environment.

Skills

S1 Create a safe, positive, and supportive learning environment in which diversities are valued.

S2 Use strategies and techniques for facilitating the functional integration of individuals with exceptional learning needs in various settings.

S3 Prepare and organize materials to implement daily lesson plans.

S4 Incorporate evaluation, planning, and management procedures that match learner needs with the instructional environment.

S5 Design a learning environment that encourages active participation by learners in a variety of individual and group learning activities.

S6 Design, structure, and manage daily routines, effectively including transition time, for students, other staff, and the instructional setting.

S7 Direct the activities of a classroom paraprofessional, aide, volunteer, or peer tutor.

S8 Create an environment that encourages self-advocacy and increased independence.

CC: Common Core
6. Managing Student Behavior and Social Interaction Skills

Knowledge

K1 Applicable laws, rules and regulations, and procedural safeguards regarding the planning and implementation of management of behaviors of individuals with exceptional learning needs.

K2 Ethical considerations inherent in classroom behavior management.

K3 Teacher attitudes and behaviors that positively or negatively influence behavior of individuals with exceptional learning needs.

K4 Social skills needed for educational and functional living environments and effective instruction in the development of social skills.

K5 Strategies for crisis prevention/intervention.

K6 Strategies for preparing individuals to live harmoniously and productively in a multiclass, multiethnic, multicultural, and multinational world.

Skills

S1 Demonstrate a variety of effective behavior management techniques appropriate to the needs of individuals with exceptional learning needs.

S2 Implement the least intensive intervention consistent with the needs of the individuals with exceptionalities.

S3 Modify the learning environment (schedule and physical arrangement) to manage inappropriate behaviors.

S4 Identify realistic expectations for personal and social behavior in various settings.

S5 Integrate social skills into the curriculum.

S6 Use effective teaching procedures in social skills instruction.

S7 Demonstrate procedures to increase the individual's self-awareness, self-control, self-reliance, and self-esteem.

S8 Prepare individuals with exceptional learning needs to exhibit self-enhancing behavior in response to societal attitudes and actions.

CC: Common Core
7. Communication and Collaborative Partnerships

Knowledge

K1 Factors that promote effective communication and collaboration with individuals, parents, and school and community personnel in a culturally responsive program.

K2 Typical concerns of parents of individuals with exceptional learning needs and appropriate strategies to help parents deal with these concerns.

K3 Development of individual student programs working in collaboration with team members.

K4 Roles of individuals with exceptionalities, parents, teachers, and other school and community personnel in planning an individualized program.

K5 Ethical practices for confidential communication to others about individuals with exceptional learning needs.

Skills

S1 Use collaborative strategies in working with individuals with exceptional learning needs, parents, and school and community personnel in various learning environments.

S2 Communicate and consult with individuals, parents, teachers, and other school and community personnel.

S3 Foster respectful and beneficial relationships between families and professionals.

S4 Encourage and assist families to become active participants in the educational team.

S5 Plan and conduct collaborative conferences with families or primary caregivers.

S6 Collaborate with regular classroom teachers and other school and community personnel in integrating individuals with exceptional learning needs into various learning environments.

S7 Communicate with regular teachers, administrators, and other school personnel about characteristics and needs of individuals with specific exceptional learning needs.

CC: Common Core
8. Professionalism and Ethical Practices

Knowledge

K1 Personal cultural biases and differences that affect one's teaching.

K2 Importance of the teacher serving as a model for individuals with exceptional learning needs.

Skills

S1 Demonstrate commitment to developing the highest educational and quality-of-life potential of individuals with exceptional learning needs.

S2 Demonstrate positive regard for the culture, religion, gender, and sexual orientation of individual students.

S3 Promote and maintain a high level of competence and integrity in the practice of the profession.

S4 Exercise objective professional judgment in the practice of the profession.

S5 Demonstrate proficiency in oral and written communication.

S6 Engage in professional activities that may benefit individuals with exceptional learning needs, their families, and/or colleagues.

S7 Comply with local, state, provincial, and federal monitoring and evaluation requirements.

S8 Use copyrighted educational materials in an ethical manner.

S9 Practice within the CEC Code of Ethics and other standards and policies of the profession.

Council for Exceptional Children (CEC) Knowledge and Skills for All Beginning Special Education Teachers of Students with Visual Impairments

KNOWLEDGE AND SKILLS STATEMENTS

VI: Visual Impairment
1. Philosophical, Historical, and Legal Foundations of Special Education

Knowledge

K1 Federal entitlements (e.g., American Printing House for the Blind Quote Funds) that relate to the provision of specialized equipment and materials for learners with visual impairments.

K2 Historical foundations for education of children with visual impairments, including the array of service options.

K3 Current educational definitions of students with visual disabilities, including identification criteria, labeling issues, and current incidence and prevalence figures.

Source: Reprinted, with permission from What Every Special Educator Must Know: The International Standards for the Preparation and Licensure of Special Educators, 3rd ed. *(Reston, VA: The Council for Exceptional Children), pp. 75–80. ©1998 The Council for Exceptional Children.*

Skills

S1 Articulate the pros and cons of current issues and trends in special education visual impairment.

VI: Visual Impairment
2. Characteristics of Learners

Knowledge

K1 Normal development of the human visual system.

K2 Basic terminology related to the structure and function of the human visual system.

K3 Basic terminology related to diseases and disorders of the human visual system.

K4 Development of secondary senses (hearing, touch, taste, smell) when the primary sense is impaired.

K5 The effects of a visual impairment on early development (motor system, cognition, social/emotional interactions, self-help, language).

K6 The effects of a visual impairment on social behaviors and independence.

K7 The effects of a visual impairment on language and communication.

K8 The effects of a visual impairment on the individual's family and the reciprocal impact on the individual's self-esteem.

K9 Psychosocial aspects of a visual impairment.

K10 Effects of medications on the visual system.

K11 The impact of additional exceptionalities on students with visual impairments.

Skills

(None in addition to Common Core.)

VI: Visual Impairment
3. Assessment, Diagnosis, and Evaluation

Knowledge

K1 The impact of visual disorders on learning and experience.

K2 Specialized terminology used in assessing individuals with visual impairments, both as it relates to the visual system and in areas of importance.

K3 Ethical considerations and legal provisions, regulations, and guidelines (federal, state/provincial, and local) related to assessment of students with visual impairments (including the legal versus functional definitions of blindness and low vision).

K4 Specialized policies regarding referral and placement procedures for students with visual impairments.

K5 Procedures used for screening, prereferral, referral, and classifications of students with visual impairments, including vision screening methods, functional vision evaluation, and learning media assessment.

K6 Alternative assessment techniques for students who are blind or who have low vision.

K7 Appropriate interpretation and application of scores obtained as a result of assessing individuals with visual impairments.

K8 Relationships among assessment, IEP development, and placement as they affect vision-related services.

Skills

S1 Interpret eye reports and other vision-related diagnostic information.

S2 Use disability-specific assessment instruments appropriately (e.g., Blind Learning Aptitude Test, Tactile Test of Basic Concepts, Diagnostic Assessment Procedure).

S3 Adapt and use a variety of assessment procedures appropriately when evaluating individuals with visual impairments.

S4 Create and maintain disability-related records for students with visual impairments.

S5 Gather background information about academic, medical, and family history as it relates to the student's visual status for students with visual impairments.

S6 Develop individualized instructional strategies to enhance instruction for learners with visual impairments, including modifications of the environment, adaptations of materials, and disability-specific methodologies.

VI: Visual Impairment
4. Instructional Content and Practice

Knowledge

K1 Methods for the development of special auditory, tactual, and modified visual communication skills for students with visual impairments, including:

- ◆ Braille reading and writing.
- ◆ Handwriting for students with low vi-

sion and signature writing for students who are blind.

- ◆ Listening skills and compensatory auditory skills.
- ◆ Typing and keyboarding skills.
- ◆ The use of unique technology for individuals with visual impairments.
- ◆ The use of alternatives to nonverbal communication.

K2 Methods to acquire disability-unique academic skills, including:

- ◆ The use of an abacus.
- ◆ The use of a talking calculator.
- ◆ Tactile graphics (including maps, charts, tables, etc.).
- ◆ Adapted science equipment.

K3 Methods for the development of basic concepts needed by young students who do not learn visually.

K4 Methods for the development of visual efficiency, including instruction in the use of print adaptations, optical devices, and non-optical devices.

K5 Methods to develop alternative reasoning and decision-making skills in students with visual impairments.

K6 Methods to develop alternative organization and study skills for students with visual impairments.

K7 Methods to prepare students with visual impairments for structured precane orientation and mobility assessment and instruction.

K8 Methods to develop tactual perceptual skills for students who are or will be primarily tactual learners.

K9 Methods to teach human sexuality to students who have visual impairments, using tactual models that are anatomically accurate.

K10 Methods to develop adapted physical and recreation skills for individuals who have visual impairments.

K11 Methods to develop social and daily living skills that are normally learned or reinforced by visual means.

K12 Strategies for developing career awareness in and providing vocational counseling for students with visual impairments.

K13 Strategies for promoting self-advocacy in individuals with visual impairments.

K14 Functional life skills instruction relevant to independent, community, and personal living and employment for individuals with visual impairments including:

- ◆ Methods for accessing printed public information.
- ◆ Methods for accessing public transportation.
- ◆ Methods for accessing community resources.
- ◆ Methods for acquiring practical skills (e.g., keeping personal records, time management, personal banking, emergency procedures).

K15 Sources of specialized materials for students with visual impairments.

K16 Techniques for modifying instructional methods and materials for students with visual impairments, and assisting classroom teachers in implementing these modifications.

Skills

S1 Interpret and use unique assessment data for instructional planning with students with visual impairments.

S2 Choose and use appropriate technologies to accomplish instructional objectives for students with visual impairments, and integrate the technologies appropriately into the instructional process.

S3 Sequence, implement, and evaluate individual disability-related learning objectives for students with visual impairments.

S4 Use strategies for facilitating the maintenance and generalization of disability-related skills across learning environments for students with visual impairments.

S5 Teach students who have visual impairments to use thinking, problem-solving, and other cognitive strategies to meet their individual learning needs.

VI: Visual Impairment
5. Planning and Managing the Teaching and Learning Environment

Knowledge

K1 A variety of input and output enhancements to computer technology that address the specific access needs of students with visual impairments in a variety of environments.

K2 Model programs, including career-vocational and transition, that have been effective for students with visual impairments.

Skills

S1 Prepare modified special materials (e.g., in Braille, enlarged, outlined, highlighted) for students who have visual impairments.

S2 Obtain and organize special materials to implement instructional goals for learners with visual impairments.

S3 Design learning environments that are multisensory and that encourage active participation by learners with visual impairments in a variety of group and individual learning activities.

S4 Create a learning environment that encourages self-advocacy and independence for students with visual impairments.

S5 Transcribe, proofread, and interline grade

II Braille and Nemeth code Braille materials.

S6 Use Braillewriter, slate and stylus, and computer technology to produce Braille materials.

VI: Visual Impairment
6. Managing Student Behavior and Social Interaction Skills

Knowledge

K1 Teacher attitudes and behaviors that affect the behaviors of students with visual impairments.

Skills

S1 Prepare students with progressive eye conditions to achieve a positive transition to alternative skills.

S2 Prepare students who have visual impairments to access information and services from the community at large.

S3 Prepare students who have visual impairments to respond to societal attitudes and actions with positive behavior, self-advocacy, and a sense of humor.

VI: Visual Impairment
7. Communication and Collaborative Partnerships

Knowledge

K1 Strategies for assisting parents and other professionals in planning appropriate transitions for students who have visual impairments.

K2 Sources of unique services, networks, and organizations for students with visual impairments.

K3 Roles of paraprofessionals who work directly with students who have visual impairments (e.g., sighted readers, transcribers, aides) or who provide special materials to them.

K4 Need for role models who have visual impairments, and who are successful.

Skills

S1 Help parents and other professionals to understand the impact of a visual impairment on learning and experience.

S2 Report disability-related results of evaluations to students who have visual impairments, their parents and administrators and other professionals in clear, concise, "laymen's" terms.

S3 Manage and direct the activities of paraprofessionals or peer tutors who work with students who have visual impairments.

VI: Visual Impairment
8. Professionalism and Ethical Practices

Knowledge

K1 Consumer and professional organizations, publications, and journals relevant to the field of visual impairment.

Skills

S1 Belong to and participate in the activities of professional organizations in the field of visual impairment.

GLOSSARY

Accommodation The ability of the eye to adjust its focus for seeing at different distances by changing the shape of the lens through action of the ciliary muscle.

Achromatopsia A congenital defect or absence of cones, resulting in the inability to see color and reduce clear central vision.

Acquired Immune Deficiency Syndrome *See* AIDS

Acuity *See* Visual acuity

Adaptive technology *See* Assistive technology

Adventitious visual impairment Loss or impairment of vision that occurs after birth, usually as a result of an accident or disease. *See also* Congenital visual impairment

AIDS (Acquired Immune Deficiency Syndrome) A chronic disease of the immune system that is caused by infection with the human immune deficiency virus. As a result of a compromised immune system, individuals with AIDS may develop eye conditions leading to visual impairment, such as cytomegalovirus retinitis, the most frequent opportunistic intraocular infection among individuals with AIDS.

Albinism *See* Ocular albinism; Oculocutaneous albinism

Ambylopia Reduced vision without observable changes in the structure of the eye, caused by eyes that are not straight or by a difference in the refractive errors in the two eyes, sometimes formerly called "lazy eye"; not correctable with lenses because the brain's suppression is the cause.

Americans with Disabilities Act (ADA) of 1990 An act granting civil rights to individuals with disabilities. The ADA prohibits discrimination against individuals with disabilities in the areas of public accommodations, employment, transportation, state and local government services, and telecommunications. It is the most far-reaching civil rights legislation ever enacted in the history of disability policy in the United States.

Amsler grid A graphlike card used to determine central field losses, as in macular degeneration.

Anisometropia Different refractive errors of at least 1 diopter in the two eyes.

Aphakia The absence of the crystalline lens, usually resulting from the removal of a cataract.

Aqueous The clear fluid in the space between the front of the vitreous and the back of the cornea, produced by the ciliary processes, that bathes the lens and nourishes the iris and inner surface of the cornea. Also called Aqueous humor.

Assessment In education, the process through which present needs and skill levels of the student are determined.

Assistive technology Equipment used to help individuals compensate for the loss of vision or a visual impairment such as speech, braille, and large-print devices that enable a person who is visually impaired to use a personal computer and software programs.

Astigmatism A refractive error that is caused by an irregular curvature of the cornea and that prevents light rays from coming to a point or focus on the retina.

Autosome Any nonsex-determining chromosome, of which there are 22 pairs in a human.

Binocular vision Vision that uses both eyes to form a fused image in the brain and that results in three-dimensional perception.

Biomicroscopy The examination of the eyelids and anterior portion of the eyeballs with a slit lamp (biomicroscope) for magnification.

Blindness The inability to see; the absence or severe reduction of vision. *See also* Adventitious visual impairment; Congenital visual impairment

Blind spot *See* scotoma

Braille A system of raised dots based on a structure of cells that enables functionally blind persons to read and write.

Braille printer A computer printer that embosses braille by using software to convert from print to grade 2 braille.

Braillewriter A machine used for embossing braille.

Brain injury A physical injury or impairment that affects the brain resulting from such causes as anoxia, trauma, tumors, or stroke. The effects range from little to no visual impairment to a combination of poor visual acuity, visual field loss, diplopia, distortion, glare sensitivity, and such visual perceptual difficulties as visual agnosia (in which objects are seen but not recognized).

Cataract A clouding of the lens of the eye, which may be congenital, traumatic, secondary to another visual impairment, or age related. When a cataract is surgically removed, an intraocular lens implant, contact lens, or spectacle correction is necessary to provide the refractive function of the absent lens.

Certification A formalization indication or approval attesting to the fact that indicates that an individual is recognized as meeting all the criteria necessary for practice within a profession.

Choroid The vascular layer of the eye, between the sclera and the retina, that nourishes the retina; part of the uveal tract.

Ciliary body Tissue inside the eye, composed of the ciliary processes and ciliary muscle; the former secretes aqueous, and the latter controls the shape of the lens.

Code of ethics A standard, typically consisting of guidelines, intended to ensure that those who have entered a profession have the appropriate preparation and that they practice in accordance with acceptable and respected principles.

Coloboma A congenital cleft in some portion of the eye caused by the improper fusion of tissue during gestation; may affect the optic nerve, ciliary body, choroid, iris, lens, or eyelid.

Color perception The perception of color as a result of the stimulation of specialized cone receptors in the retina.

Concave lens A lens that spreads out light rays and is used to correct myopia. Also called minus lens. *See also* Spherical lens

Cone-rod dystrophy The hereditary degeneration of cones, resulting in decreased vision and the lack of color perception.

Cones Specialized photoreceptor cells in the retina, primarily concentrated in the macular area, that are responsible for sharp vision and color perception. *See also* Rods

Congenital visual impairment Loss or impairment of vision that is present at birth. *See also* Adventitious visual impairment

Conjunctiva The mucous membrane that lines the eyelids and part of the outer surface of the eyeball.

Conjunctivitis An inflammation of the conjunctiva that is viral, allergic, bacterial, or fungal in origin some varieties of which are contagious.

Contrast sensitivity The ability to detect differences in grayness and background.

Convergence The movement, as an object approaches, of both eyes toward each other in an effort to maintain fusion of separate images.

Convex lens A lens that bends light rays inward and is used to correct hyperopia. Also called plus lens. *See also* Spherical lens

Core curriculum The general education curriculum that all students are expected to master, including language arts, science, mathematics, and social studies.

Cornea The transparent tissue at the front of the eye that is curved and provides approximately 66 percent of the eye's refracting power.

Cortical visual impairment Vision loss that is the result of damage to any part of the visual pathways in the brain. Sometimes caused by injury to the optic chiasma (the point at which images are transmitted to the right or left brain), which may be injured and unable to transmit the visual impulses. Individuals who are cortically blind may exhibit a reduced visual field or a hemianopia (blindness in half of the visual field). Also called cortical blindness; cortical vision loss.

Deaf-blindness Concomitant hearing and visual impairments, the combination of which may present unique communication, learning, developmental, orientation and mobility, and social needs.

Deafness A loss of hearing that is so severe that the individual's sense of hearing it is nonfunctional for the ordinary activities of daily living.

Developmentally delayed Functioning at a level below one's chronological age.

Diabetes mellitus A metabolic disorder related to faulty pancreatic activity and an inability to oxidize carbohydrates, resulting in the inadequate production or utilization of insulin; it results in an elevated blood sugar level and presence of sugar in the urine.

Diabetic retinopathy A noninflammatory disease of the retinal blood vessels caused by diabetes; a leading cause of blindness in the United States.

Diagnostic teaching The analysis of learning difficulties during lessons, and targeted instruction to minimize or eliminate the difficulties identified.

Diplopia A vision disorder in which two images of a single object are seen because of unequal action of the muscles in the eyes. Also called double vision.

Disability A condition that exists when, in a particular setting, an individual cannot independently perform a specific set of functional activities.

Distance education Academic or other learning programs to accomodate students by offering instuction off campus, such as at satellite locations or over the Internet.

Dog guides A specially trained dog that assists a person who is blind or visually impaired in orientation and mobility. Dog guides can learn to respond to commands and to judge when doing so would endanger the owner.

Double vision *See* Diplopia

Education for All Handicapped Children Act (PL 94-142) Federal legislation enacted in 1975 that guarantees free appropriate public education in the least restrictive environment, with special education, related services, and Individualized Education Programs mandated for each child needing special services. Now known as the Individuals with Disabilities Education Act (IDEA), it is the most significant legislation on behalf of students with disabilities.

Enucleation A surgical procedure consisting of removal of the entire eyeball.

ESL English as a second language.

Esotropia A form of strabismus in which one or both eyes deviate inward.

Exotropia A form of strabismus in which one or both eyes deviate outward.

Expanded core curriculum A curriculum that covers the unique, disability-specific skills, such as independent living skill and orientation and mobility skills, that students with visual impairments need to live independently and productively.

Eyelids Structures that cover the front of the eyes to protect them, control the amount of light entering them, and distribute tears over the cornea.

Farsightedness *See* Hyperopia

Field of vision *See* Visual field

Focal distance The distance between a lens and the point at which parallel light rays are brought to a focus.

Fovea A depression in the center of the macula that contains only cones and lacks blood vessels.

Functional blindness Condition in which some useful vision may or may not be present but in which the individual uses tactile and auditory channels most effectively for learning.

Functional vision The ability to use vision in planning and performing a task.

Functional vision assessment An assessment of an individual's use of vision in a variety of tasks and settings, including measures of near and distance vision; visual fields; eye movements; and responses to specific environmental characteristics, such as light and color. The assessment report includes recommendations for instructional procedures, modifications or adaptations, and additional tests.

Glaucoma A disease in which increased intraocular pressure results in the degeneration of the optic disk and eventual defects in the visual field. If not treated, the outcome is total blindness.

Habilitation *See* Rehabilitation

HIV *See* AIDS

Hyperopia (farsightedness) A refractive error in which light rays converge behind the retina, resulting in vision that is better for distant than for near objects; corrected with a plus (convex) lens.

Hypertropia The upward deviation of one eye.

Hypotropia The downward deviation of one eye.

Inclusion A philosophy that promotes the placement of a student with a disability in a general education classroom for all or part of the school day; often used interchangeably with "mainstreaming."

Independent living skills Skills for performing daily tasks and managing personal needs, such as those for self-care, planning and cooking meals, maintaining a sanitary living environment, traveling independently, budgeting one's expenses, and functioning as independently as possible in the home and in the community.

Individualized Education Program (IEP) A written plan of instruction by a transdisciplinary educational term, which includes a student's present levels of educational performance, annual goals, short-term objectives, specific services needed, duration of services, evaluation, and related information. Under the Individuals with Disabilities Education Act (IDEA), each student receiving special services must have such a plan.

Individualized Family Service Plan (IFSP) A plan for the coordination of early intervention services for infants and toddlers with disabilities, similar to the Individualized Education Program (IEP) that is required for all school-age children with disabilities. A requirement of the Individuals with Disabilities Education Act (IDEA).

Individuals with Disabilites Education Act (P.L. 101.476) The 1990 amendments to the Education for All Handicapped Children Act (P.L. 94.142), the federal legislation that safeguards a free, appropriate public education for all eligible children with disabilities in the United States.

Integration The placement of children with impairments in regular classrooms with children who are not disabled.

Interdisciplinary team Professionals from various disciplines who conduct and share the results of assessments and jointly plan instructional programs. *See also* Multidisciplinary team; Transdisciplinary team

Iris The colored, circular membrane of the eye that is suspended between the cornea and the lens and that expands or contracts to control the amount of light entering the eye.

Iritis An inflammation of the iris that may cause blurred vision, a constricted pupil, pain, and tearing. Iritis must be treated medically.

Itinerant teacher An instructor who moves from place to place (e.g., from home to home, school to hospital, or school to school) to provide instruction and support to students with special needs.

Lawrence-Moon-Biedl-Bardet syndrome An autosomal recessive disorder that is characterized by a range of impairments or abnormalities, including mental retardation, pigmentary retinopathy, and spastic paraplegia.

Learning media Various supplementary aids that enhance the ability of a student who is visually impaired to learn, such as braille, closed-circuit television (CCTV), magnifiers, and tapes.

Least-restrictive environment (LRE) Placement of a child with a disability in a classroom environment that is adapted only to the extent necessary to maximize learning.

Legal blindness Visual acuity for distance vision of 20/200 or less in the better eye after best correction with conventional lenses, or a visual field of no greater than 20 degrees in the better eye.

Lens The transparent biconvex structure within the eye that allows it to refract light rays, enabling the rays to focus on the retina; also called the crystalline lens. Also, any transparent material that can refract light in a predictable manner.

Literacy The ability to read and write.

Long cane A mobility device in the shape of a cane.

Low vision A visual impairment after correction, but with the potential for use of available vision, with or without optical or nonoptical compensatory visual strategies, devices, and environmental modification, to plan and perform daily tasks.

Low vision device A type of optical or nonoptical device used to enhance the visual capability of persons with visual impairments. Low vision devices range from bold-line felt-tip markers to magnifiers and telescopes.

Macula A small portion of the retina, with a concentration of cones for sharp central vision, that surrounds the fovea.

Macular degeneration Deterioration of central vision caused by a degeneration of the central retina.

Mainstreaming The placement of a student with a disability in a genearl education classroom with children who are not disabled for all or part of the school day; often used interchangeable with "inclusion."

Marfan syndrome An inherited congenital disorder of the connective tissue, characterized by abnormal elongation of the extremities, partial dislocation of the lens, cardiovascular abnormalities, and other disorders.

Microphthalmia An abnormally small eyeball.

Minus lens *See* Concave lens

Mobility The act or ability to move from one's present position to one's desired position in another part of the environment. *See also* Orientation

Monocular vision Vision in one eye, typically caused by injury or enucleation.

Multidisciplinary team A team made up of professionals from different disciplines who work independently to conduct assessments of a student, write and implement separate plans, and evaluate the student's progress within the parameters of their own disciplines.

Myopia (nearsightedness) A refractive error resulting from an eyeball that is too long; corrected with a concave (minus) lens.

Multiple disabilities Two or more concomitant disabilities (physical, mental, or emotional) that have a direct effect on the ability to learn.

Nearsightedness *See* Myopia

Nemeth code A braille code system designed for use in science and mathematics.

Night blindness A condition in which visual acuity is diminished at night and in dim light.

Nystagmus An involuntary, rapid movement of the eyes, usually rhythmical and faster in one direction that may be side to side or up and down.

Ocular albinism A hereditary condition that results in pigmentation loss in the retinal pigment epithelium, iris, and choroid.

Oculocutaneous albinism The congential lack of pigment in the iris, choroid, hair, and skin that results in reduced acuity, light sensitivity, and nystagmus.

Ophthalmologist A physician who specializes in the medical and surgical care of the eyes and is qualified to prescribe ocular medications and to perform surgery on the eyes. May also perform refractive and low vision work, including eye examinations and other vision services.

Optical character recoginition (OCR) A system used to convert printed material into computer files so it can be produced in a form (such as braille or voice output) that is useful for people with sensory losses, using a scanner interfaced with a computer.

Optical device Any system of lenses that enhances visual function.

Optic atrophy An ocular condition characterized by degeneration of the optic nerve and resulting in loss of vision and construction of the visual fields.

Optic disk The point at which the nerve fibers from the inner layer of the retina becomes the optic nerve and exit the eye; the "blind spot" of the eye.

Optic nerve The sensory nerve of the eye that carries electrical impulses from the eye to the brain.

Optic nerve hypoplasia A congenitally small optic disk, usually surrounded by a light halo and representing a regression in growth during the prenatal period; may result in reduced visual acuity.

Optometrist A health care provider who specializes in refractive errors, prescribes eyeglasses or contact lenses, and diagnoses and manages conditions of the eye as regulated by state laws. May also perform low vision examinations.

Orbits Two pyramidal cavities in the front of the skull that contain the eyeballs, eye muscles, and fatty cushioning layers, as well as nerves and blood vessels.

Orientation The knowledge of one's distance and direction relative to things observed or remembered in one's surroundings and the ability to keep track of these spatial relationships as they change during locomotion. *See also* Mobility

Orientation and mobility (O&M) The field dealing with systematic techniques by which persons who are blind or visually impaired orient themselves to their environments and move about independently. *See also* Mobility; Orientation

Orientation and mobility (O&M) assistants Paraeducators who are trained and certified to practice specified skills under the direction of orientation and mobility instructors.

Orientation and mobility (O&M) instructor A professional who specializes in teaching travel skills to persons who are visual impaired, including the use of canes, dog guides, sophisticated electronic traveling aids, as well as the sighted guide technique.

Orthoptics The techniques of treating problems in eye movement and coordination, binocular vision, and functional amblyopia through nonsurgical means, using lenses, prisms, or exercises; the orthoptist usually works under the supervision of an ophthalmologist.

Paraeducators Also called Paraprofessional

Partial sight A term formerly often used to indicate visual acuity of 20/70 to 20/200 but also used to describe visual impairment in which usable vision is present.

Peripheral vision The perception of objects, motion, or color outside the direct line of vision or by other than the central retina.

Personnel preparation programs Federally supported programs that offer college and university courses to prepare specialized teachers to educate students with visual impairments.

Photocoagulation The use of a laser to burn or destroy selected intraocular structures, such as intraocular tumors or abnormal blood vessels, and to create chorioretinal adhesions in retinal detachment surgery.

Photophobia Light sensitivity to an uncomfortable degree; usually symptomatic of other ocular disorders or diseases.

Plus lens *See* Convex lens

Presbyopia A decrease in accommodative power (focusing at near) caused by the increasing inelasticity of the lens-ciliary muscle mechanism that occurs approximately anytime after the age of 40.

Prism lenses Special triangle-shaped lenses that are incorporated into regular eyeglasses, to redirect the rays of light enetering the eye, resulting in a realignment of the eyes or, in some cases, a shifting of image to permit binocular vision.

Radial keratotomy A surgical procedure in which a series of deep radical cuts are made in the cornea to shorten the eye optically to reduce myopia.

Refraction The bending of light rays as they pass through a substance. Also, the determination of the refractive errors of the eye and their correction with eyeglasses or contact lenses.

Refractive disorder Defects in the eye that cause visual acuity loss if uncorrected.

Refractive errors Conditions, such as myopia, hyperopia, and astigmatism, caused by corneal irregularities, in which parallel rays of light are not brought in focus on the retina because of a defect in the shape of the eyeball or the refractive media of the eye.

Rehabilitation The process of bringing or restoring an individual to a normal or optimum state of health or level of constructive activity means of medical treatment and physical or psychological therapy; specifically, the relearning of skills already acquired prior to the onset of a visual disability.

Rehabilitation counselor A rehabilitation professional who serves as a case manager, usually at a state agency, and may provide therapeutic counseling.

Rehabilitation teacher A professional whose primary goal is to instruct persons with visual impairments to utilize adaptive skills to help them to cope with the demands of everyday life, primarily in the areas of communication, personal management, home management, leisure time, and movement in familiar environments.

Resource room A sevice delivery option designed to support students with visual impairments who are enrolled in a general education classroom by providing specialized instruction and support from a qualified teacher who is housed on site.

Retina The innermost layer of the eye, which receives the image formed by the lens, containing light-sensitive nerve cells and fibers connecting with the brain through the optic nerve.

Retinal degeneration A classification of a number of conditions in which retinal cells break down such as retinitis pigmentosa.

Retinal detachment The separation of the retina from the underlying choroid, nearly always caused by a retinal tear, which allows fluid to accumulate between the retina and the retinal pigment epithelium. It usually requires surgical intervention to prevent loss of vision.

Retinitis pigmentosa (RP) A hereditary degeneration and atrophy of the retina, of unknown etiology; causes night blindness and results in optic atrophy and construction of the peripheral visual fields.

Retinoblastoma An intraocular malignant tumor of early childhood, often hereditary or caused by a mutated gene. Symptoms include redness, pain, inflammation, or a gray or white pupil. Treatment options include chemotherapy, cryotherapy, radiation, and enucleation (surgical removal of the eye).

Retinopathies Diseases of the retina as a result of various causes, including diabetes mellitus and hypertension.

Retinopathy of prematurity (ROP) A series of retinal changes (formerly called retrolental fibroplasia), from mild to total retinal detachment, seen primarily in premature infants, that may be arrested at any stage. Believed to be connected to immature blood vessels in the eye stimulated in reaction to oxygen, but may be primarily the result of prematurity with very low birthweight. Functional vision can range from near normal to total blindness.

Rods Specialized retinal photoreceptor cells that are located primarily in the peripheral retina, responsible for seeing form, shape, and movement and function best in low levels of illumination.

Rubella A common, mild, viral infection that, when contracted by women during the first trimester of pregnancy, has a likelihood of generating fetal abnormalities, such as mental retardation, heart disease, hearing defects, and eye disorders.

Scanner A device that uses a moving electronic beam to convert visual images, such as printed text or graphic images, into an electronic format that can be transmitted or converted into other formats.

Sclera The tough, white, opaque outer covering of the eye that protects the inner contents from most injuries.

Scotoma A gap or blind spot in the visual field that may be caused by damage to the retina or visual pathways. Each eye contains one normal scotoma, corresponding to the location of the optic nerve head, which contains no photoreceptors.

Seizure disorder A sudden, involuntary contraction that disrupts the functioning of the nervous system and may result in changes in awareness, motor activity, and general behavior that occur alone or in combinations. A partial seizure occurs in one area of the brain in one cerebral hemisphere; generalized seizures occur in both hemispheres or begin in one and travel to both.

Snellen Chart The traditional eye chart whose top line consists of the letter *E* and which is used in routine eye examinations.

Spherical lens A lens who shape is a segment of a sphere. A convex (plus) lens is thicker in the center and is used to correct hyperopia; a concave (minus) lens is used to correct myopia. Other types of spherical lenses are biconvex (when both surfaces curve outward), plano-convex (a single-sided curve), biconcave (both surfaces curing inward), and plano-concave (when only one surface curves inward).

Stargardt's dystrophy A condition transmitted in an autosomal recessive manner, in which the macular pigment epithelium slowly degenerates, leading to loss of central vision.

Strabismus An extrinsic muscle imbalance that causes misalignment of the eyes; includes exotropia, esotropia, hypertropia, and hypotropia.

Talking book program A free national library program administered by the National Library Service for the Blind and Physically Handicapped (NLS) of the Library of Congress for persons with visual and physical limitations, in which books and magazines are produced in braille and on recorded discs and cassettes and are distributed to a cooperative network of regional libraries that circulate them to eligible borrowers; the program also lends the devices on which the recordings are played.

Teacher of students with visual impairments A specially trained and certified teacher who is qualified to teach special skills to students with visual impairments.

Technology device *See* Assistive technology

Tonometry The measurement of intraocular pressure.

Transdisciplinary team A team made up of professionals from different disciplines who cooperate and collaborate during initial assessment and planning phases of designing a student's educational program and offer ongoing support and input. Implementation of the program is carried out by one or a few team members who are designated as primarily responsible for providing direct care or services.

Transition IEP A program, written for a student age 14 and older, that addresses the need for transition services in the areas of employment, education and training, leisure and recreation, and living arrangements and details the proposed activities to achieve desired outcomes, establishes time lines for reaching these goals, and assigns responsiblity for providing support to the agencies and individuals responsible for following through on each activity.

Traumatic brain injury *See* Brain injury

Usher syndrome The hereditary degeneration of the retinal pigment epithelium, accompanined by congenital nerve deafness.

Visual acuity The sharpness of vision with respect to the ability to distinguish detail, often measured as the eye's ability to distinguish the details and shapes of objects at a designated distance; involves central (macular) vision.

Visual acuity test An assessment of detailed central vision; infants are tested by ascertaining pupillary responses to light and, later, light fixation reflexes; subsequent assessments include the standard Snellen Chart and other charts.

Visual disability A disability that causes a real or perceived disadvantage in performing specific tasks.

Visual efficiency The degree to which specific visual tasks can be performed with ease, comfort, and minimum time, contingent on personal and environmental variables; the extent to which available vision is used effectively.

Visual field The area that can be seen when looking straight ahead, measured in degrees from the fixation point.

Visual impairment Any degree of vision loss that affects an individual's ability to perform the tasks of daily life, caused by a visual system that is not working properly or not formed correctly.

Visual memory The retention of mental imagery of environments or objects in one's environment gained through original visual input.

Vitreous The transparent physiological gel that fills the vitreous cavity, the back potion of the eye between the lens and the retina; it is 99 percent water and its surrounding cavity accounts for 75 percent of the weight and about 66 percent of the volume of the globe; it maintains the shape of the eyeball and any injury or insult that allows the vitreous gel to escape can result in the collapse of the eyeball. Also called vitreous humor.

Vitreous cavity The third chamber of the eye, located behind the lens and filled with vitreous gel.

Vocational rehabilitation A system of services that evaluates personal, work, and work-related traits, designed to result in optimal placement in employment.

Working distance The distance from the eye of the viewer to an object or surface being viewed, as with a low vision device.

RESOURCES

A wide variety of organizations and groups provide information, assistance, materials, and equipment to benefit students who are visually impaired, their families, and the professionals who work with them. The listings that follow attempt to provide a representative sampling of the resources that are available and relate to the education of students who are visually impaired; a more complete listing can be found in the AFB Directory of Services for Blind and Visually Impaired Persons in the United States and Canada, *published by the American Foundation for the Blind.*

The following section on national and governmental organizations presents sources of further information and referral. Readers should bear in mind that elements such as names and addresses, specific product and publication information, and information related to the Internet constantly change and may need later verification.

American Association of the Deaf-Blind
814 Thayer Avenue, Suite 302
Silver Spring, MD 20910
(301) 588-6545 (TTY/TDD)
Fax: (301) 588-8705
Promotes better opportunities and services for people who are deaf-blind and strives to ensure that a comprehensive, coordinated system of services is accessible to all deaf-blind people, enabling them to achieve their maximum potential through increased independence, productivity, and integration into the community.

American Council of the Blind
1155 15th Street, N.W., Suite 720
Washington, D.C. 20005
(202) 467-5081 or (800) 424-8666
Fax: (202) 467-5085
E-mail: ncrabb@access.digex.net
http://www.acb.org
Strives to improve the well-being of all blind and visually impaired people, through state, regional, and special-interest affiliates by: serving as a representative national organization of blind people; elevating the social, economic, and cultural levels of blind people; improving educational and rehabilitation facilities and opportunities; cooperating with the public and private institutions and organizations concerned with blind services; encouraging and assisting all blind persons to develop their abilities; and conducting a public education program to promote greater understanding of blindness and the capabilities of people who are blind. Provides information and referral on all aspects of blindness, scholarship assistance to blind and visually impaired post-secondary students, public education and awareness training, support to consumer advocates and legal assistance on matters relating to blindness, leadership and legislative training, consultation to

industry regarding employment of blind and visually impaired individuals, and governmental monitoring, consultation, and advocacy. Publishes *The Braille Forum.*

American Foundation for the Blind
11 Penn Plaza, Suite 300
New York, NY 10001
(212) 502-7600 or (800) 232-5463
Fax: (212) 502-7777
E-mail: afbinfo@afb.net
http://www.afb.org
Provides services to and acts as an information clearinghouse for people who are blind or visually impaired and their families, professionals, organizations, schools, and corporations through legislative advocacy, program initiatives, and publications. Conducts research and mounts program initiatives to promote the inclusion of and improve services to people who are blind or visually impaired, including the National Literacy Program and the National Technology Program; advocates for services and legislation; maintains the M. C. Migel Library and Information Center and the Helen Keller Archives and a toll-free information line; provides information and referral services; operates the National Technology Center and the Careers and Technology Information Bank; produces videos and publishes books, pamphlets, the *Directory of Services for Blind and Visually Impaired Persons in the United States and Canada,* the *Journal of Visual Impairment & Blindness,* and *AccessWorld.* Maintains the following offices throughout the country in addition to the headquarters' office:

AFB Midwest
401 N. Michigan Avenue, Suite 308
Chicago, IL 60611
(312) 245-9961
Fax: (312) 245-9965
E-mail: chicago@afb.net

AFB Southeast
National Literacy Program
100 Peachtree Street, Suite 620
Atlanta, GA 30303

(404) 525-2303
Fax: (404) 659-6957
E-mail: atlanta@afb.net

AFB Southwest
260 Treadway Plaza
Exchange Park
Dallas, TX 75235
(214) 352-7222
Fax: (214) 352-3214
E-mail: afbdallas@afb.net

AFB West
111 Pine Street, Suite 725
San Francisco, CA 94111
(415) 392-4845
Fax: (415) 392-0383
E-mail: sanfran@afb.net

Governmental Relations
820 First Street, N.E., Suite 400
Washington, D.C. 20000
(202) 408-0200
Fax: (202) 289-7880
E-mail: afbgov@afb.net

American Printing House for the Blind
P.O. Box 6085
Louisville, KY 40206-0085
(502) 895-2405 or (800) 223-1839
Fax: (502) 895-1509
E-mail: info@aph.org
http://www.aph.org
Produces a variety of books and learning materials in braille and other media; manufactures computer-access equipment, software, and special education and reading devices for persons who are visually impaired; maintains an educational research and development program and reference-catalog databases providing information about textbooks and other materials produced in accessible media.

Association for Education and Rehabilitation of the Blind and Visually Impaired
4600 Duke Street, Suite 430
Alexandria, VA 22304
(703) 823-9690
Fax: (703) 823-9695
E-mail: aer@aerbvi.org
http://www.aerbvi.org
Promotes all phases of education and work for people of all ages who are blind or visually impaired, strives to expand their opportunities to take a contributory place in society, and disseminates information. Serves as the primary professional organization for teachers, counselors, orientation and mobility specialists, and other professionals in the field of blindness and low vision and is organized into a variety of special divisions. Publishes *RE:view* and *AER Report.*

Council for Exceptional Children
Division on Visual Impairments
1920 Association Drive
Reston, VA 22091-1589
(703) 620-3660 or (800) 328-0272
TDD: (703) 620-3660
Fax: (703) 264-9494
http://www.cec.sped.org
Acts as a professional organization for educators and other individuals serving children with disabilities and children who are gifted and is organized into a variety of specialized divisions. Primary activities include: advocating for appropriate government policies; setting professional standards; providing continuing professional development; and helping professionals obtain conditions and resources necessary for effective professional practice. Publishes numerous related materials, journals, and newsletters.

DB-LINK
National Information Clearinghouse on Children Who Are Deaf-Blind
c/o Teaching Research Division of Western Oregon State College
345 North Monmouth Avenue
Monmouth, OR 97361
(800) 438-9376

TDD: (800) 854-7013
Fax: (503) 838-8776
E-mail: dblink@tr.wou.edu
http://www.tr.wou.edu/dblink/index.htm
Serves as an information clearinghouse that identifies, coordinates, and disseminates information concerning children and young adults who are deaf-blind. Maintains a resource database. A collaborative effort between Helen Keller National Center for Deaf-Blind Youths and Adults, Perkins School for the Blind, and Teaching Research.

Hadley School for the Blind
700 Elm Street
Winnetka, IL 60093-0299
(847) 446-8111 or (800) 323-4238
Fax: (847) 446-9916
E-mail: Info@Hadley-School.org
http://www.hadley-school.org
Provides accredited distance education programs that allows students to study at home with free correspondence course materials. Courses are offered to parents of blind children, professionals working with people who are blind or visually impaired, high school students preparing for college, and adults who have become blind.

Helen Keller National Center for Deaf-Blind Youths and Adults
111 Middle Neck Road
Sands Point, NY 11050
(516) 944-8900
TDD: (516) 944-8637
Fax: (516) 944-7302
Provides short-term rehabilitation services, comprehensive vocational and personal adjustment training, job preparation and placement, and diagnostic services to people who are deaf-blind through its national center and 10 regional offices. Provides technical assistance and training to those who work with deaf-blind people. Publishes *Nat-Cent News.* Sponsors the National Family Association for Deaf-Blind [(800) 255-0411, ext. 275].

**National Association for Parents
of Children with Visual Impairments (NAPVI)**
P.O. Box 317
Watertown, MA 02272-0317
(800) 562-6265 or (617) 972-7441
Fax: (617) 972-7444
http://www.spedex.com/NAPVI/index.htm
Provides leadership, support, and training to assist parents and families of children and young adults with visual impairments. Operates a national clearinghouse for information, education, and referral; initiates outreach programs and networking; and advocates for the educational needs and well-being of children who are blind or visually impaired. Publishes a newsletter, *Awareness.*

National Association for Visually Handicapped
22 West 21st Street, 6th Floor
New York, NY 10010
(212) 889-3141
Fax: (212) 727-2951
Provides information and services to people with low vision, their families, and professionals. Offers a catalog of low vision devices and large-print publications.

National Braille Association
3 Townline Circle
Rochester, NY 14623
(716) 427-8260
Fax: (716) 427-0263
Assists in the development of skills and techniques required for the production of reading materials for individuals who are print handicapped through seminars, workshops, consultation, and publications on the production of braille, tape recording, tactile graphics, and computer assisted transcription. Provides braille textbooks and materials at reduced cost to students and professionals. Publishes the **NBA Bulletin.**

National Federation of the Blind
1800 Johnson Street
Baltimore, MD 21230
(410) 659-9314
Fax: (410) 685-5653
http://www.nfb.org

Strives to improve social and economic conditions of blind persons and to integrate people who are blind or visually impaired as equal members of society. Evaluates and assists in establishing programs and provides public education and scholarships. Interest groups include the National Organization of Parents of Blind Children and the Committee on the Concerns of the Deaf-Blind. Publishes *The Braille Monitor* and *Future Reflections,* a magazine for parents.

**National Information Center for Children
and Youth with Disabilities**
P.O. Box 1492
Washington, D.C. 20013-1492
(202) 884-8200
TDD: (800) 695-0285
Fax: (202) 844-8441
Serves as a national clearinghouse for information about children and youngsters with disabilities. Provides information and referral to national, state, and local resources. Disseminates numerous free publications.

**National Library Service for the Blind
and Physically Handicapped**
Library of Congress
1291 Taylor Street, N.W.
Washington, D.C. 20542
(202) 707-5100 or (800) 424-8567
Fax: (202) 707-0712
Conducts a national program to distribute free reading materials of a general nature to individuals who are blind or who have physical disabilities. Provides reference information on all aspects of blindness and other physical disabilities that affect reading. Conducts national correspondence courses to train sighted persons as braille transcribers and blind persons as braille proofreaders.

**National Technical Assistance Consortium
for Children and Young Adults Who Are
Deaf-Blind (NTAC)**
c/o Teaching Research Division of Western Oregon State College
345 North Monmouth Avenue
Monmouth, OR 97361

(503) 838-8391
Fax: (503) 838-8150

and

Helen Keller National Center (see Helen Keller National Center for Deaf-Blind Youths and Adults)
Voice & TTY: (516) 944-8900, ext. 307
Fax: (516) 944-8751
E-mail: ntac@wou.edu
http://www.tr.wou.edu/ntac/ntac.htm
Provides technical assistance, including training, information, and support, to families and agencies serving children and young adults who are deaf-blind through state and multistate projects for children who are deaf-blind. NTAC assists in the development and maintenance of comprehensive services for families, early intervention programs, educational programs, and adult services to meet the unique needs of children and young adults who are deaf-blind. The primary mission of NTAC is to assist states in improving the quality of services for individuals (birth to age 28) who are deaf-blind, and to increase the numbers of children, young adults, their families, and their service providers who will benefit from these services. NTAC is a consortium of Teaching Research and the Helen Keller National Center for Deaf-Blind Youths and Adults.

Office of Special Education Programs
U.S. Department of Education
400 Maryland Avenue, S.W.
Washington, D.C. 20202
(202) 205-5507
http://www.ed.gov/offices/OSERS/OSEP/index.html
Administers the Individuals with Disabilities Education Act and related programs for the free appropriate public education of children and youth with disabilities from birth through age 21, including research and demonstration projects, support to states and local school districts for the education of disabled children, and special programs, such as centers and services for children who are deaf-blind.

Prevent Blindness America
500 East Remington Road
Schaumburg, IL 60173
(847) 843-2020 or (800) 221-3004
(800) 331-2020 PBA Center for Sight
Fax: (847) 843-8458
E-mail: preventblindness@compuserve.com
http://www.prevent-blindness.org
Conducts a program of public and professional education, research, and industrial and community services to prevent blindness. Services include public education concerning vision conservation, vision screenings in schools, promotion of industrial eye safety, and efforts to improve environmental conditions affecting eye health in schools and colleges. Collects data on the nature and extent of causes of blindness and defective vision. Maintains the PBA Fight for Sight research division and the PBA Center for Sight information line.

Recording for the Blind and Dyslexic
20 Roszel Road
Princeton, NJ 08540
(609) 452-0606 or (800) 221-4792
Fax: (609) 987-8116
E-mail: info@rfbd.org
www.rfbd.org
Provides recorded and computerized textbooks, library services, and other educational resources to people who cannot read standard print because of visual, physical, or specific learning disabilities. Maintains a lending library of recorded books and acts as a recording service for additional titles.

The Association for Persons with Severe Handicaps (TASH)
29 West Susquehanna Avenue
Suite 210
Baltimore, MD 21204
(410) 828-8274
Fax: (410) 828-6706
E-mail: nweiss@tash.org
http://www.tash.org
Promotes full inclusion and participation of persons with disabilities in all aspects of life through local chapters. Publishes a monthly newsletter, quarterly journal, and other publications.

INDEX